Linked in Friendship, Connected in Service

Transformational
LINKS

Linked in Friendship, Connected in Service

Transformational
LINKS

Empowering Purposeful Lives and Strong Communities

A History of The Links, Incorporated, 1946–2019

Earnestine Green McNealey, PhD
Editor and Principal Author

Raven L. Hill
Assistant Editor

THE LINKS, INCORPORATED
Washington, DC

Kimberly Jeffries Leonard, PhD, *National President*
Kristie Patton Foster, *Executive Director*
1200 Massachusetts Avenue, NW
Washington, DC 20005

Earnestine Green McNealey, PhD, Editor and Principal Author
Raven L. Hill, Assistant Editor

THE
DONNING COMPANY
PUBLISHERS

Editorial Services: Philip Briscoe
Design Services: Stephanie L. Danko

Library of Congress Cataloging-in-Publication Data

On file with the Library of Congress
ISBN 978-1-68184-250-9

**Printed in the United States of America by The Donning Company Publishers
and Walsworth**

Dedication

In Memory of Co-Founders
Margaret Rosell Hawkins and Sarah Strickland Scott

For Marjorie H. Parker, PhD, whose inaugural history
laid the foundation for future editions

and

With Gratitude to
National President Kimberly Jeffries Leonard
and
14th National President Gwendolyn Byrd Lee

For the Opportunity and Freedom
to Capture the History of
The Links

Contributors

Raven L. Hill
Assistant Editor
Raven L. Hill, a member of the Prince George's County (MD) Chapter, was previously appointed to the National Arts Committee. Since her 2014 induction into the Penn Towne (PA) Chapter, she has also served as chapter journalist. Raven works professionally in school public relations, currently as communications officer for Prince George's County Public Schools and previously as communications director for The School District of Philadelphia. A member of Alpha Kappa Alpha Sorority, Incorporated, she has received regional and international appointments to its Archives and Communications committees. Raven was a contributing writer/editor to three official Alpha Kappa Alpha history books.

Nancy Shade Anderson
Nancy Shade Anderson, the 15th Southern Area director, has been a member of the Greenville (SC) Chapter for more than 35 years. A past president of the Greenville Chapter, her area and national service includes Southern Area vice director, Southern Area Nominating Committee, National Chapter Establishment Committee chair, and an appointment to the National Services to Youth Committee. Nancy, a retired educator, is married to Robert W. Anderson and has three children and five grandchildren.

Alpha Coles Blackburn
Alpha Coles Blackburn, a former National Arts director, is a past president of the Indianapolis (IN) Chapter. She also served on the National Buildings and Property Committee for the total renovation of The Links' headquarters and at the Area level as chair of Services to Youth. Notably, Alpha conceived the idea of The Links Medal, the organization's highest honor, and worked with the sculptor on its design. An artist, national award-winning fashion designer, interior designer, and the retired president and CEO of Blackburn Architects, she serves as the chairperson of the Indiana Civil Rights Commission.

Mary P. Douglass
Mary P. Douglass is a former chief administrative officer and executive director of The Links, Incorporated and The Links Foundation, Incorporated. A 40-year charter member of the Prince George's County (MD) Chapter, she coordinated three Eastern Area Conferences. Mary was a senior program associate for the Association of Junior Leagues International and manager of the group's Washington, DC, office

and served as vice president of B&C Associates, a public relations and marketing firm. Her daughter, Tequel D. Hager, is also a member of The Links. In addition, Mary has a son, Thomas L. Douglass, and four grandchildren.

Delores Henderson, PhD

Delores Henderson, a 45-year member of the Minneapolis-St. Paul (MN) Chapter, is a former Central Area director and vice director. As Area director, she initiated Leadership Summits and organized clusters and the first three JoAhn Brown Nash Reading Rooms in Detroit, Chattanooga, and Cleveland, respectively. A past president of the Minneapolis-St. Paul (MN) Chapter, she has also served on various local and national boards and foundations and received numerous honors worldwide. Delores retired as the longest-sitting school administrator in Minnesota after more than 45 years with St. Paul Public Schools. She has one daughter, Mercedes Henderson Clark, who is also a member of The Links.

Sandra Dorsey Malone

Sandra Dorsey Malone, a member of the Dallas (TX) Chapter for more than 30 years, is a past Western Area director and vice director. She was National chair of the Commission on Ethics and Standards and Chapter Establishment Committee and a past vice president of the Dallas Chapter. A retired Dallas Independent School District assistant superintendent, Sandra later monitored the school district's compliance with a federal desegregation order as a court auditor of the District Court for the Northern District of Texas.

She is currently chief executive officer of Malone and Associates, Inc. Sandra is married to Joseph L. Malone and has one son, Terence Dorsey Malone.

Linda Simmons-Henry

Linda Simmons-Henry, a member of the Raleigh (NC) Chapter, is a certified senior archivist at the North Carolina African American Heritage Foundation, Inc. She also served for 35 years as dean of the Library and Archives at Saint Augustine's University in Raleigh, North Carolina. A historically Black colleges and universities (HBCU) archivist, oral history consultant, and records management expert, she was recently reappointed by the North Carolina Heritage Board of Certified Archivists to a four-year term as a consultant to the state's 11 HBCUs. Married to Dr. Philip N. Henry, she has one son, Philip M. Henry, and one grandson, Philip Nasier Henry.

Alethia Spraggins, PhD

Alethia Spraggins, a 37-year member of the Washington (DC) Chapter, is a former Eastern Area director and vice director. Alethia worked professionally as a research biologist at the National Institutes of Health and spent 32 years in the DC Public Schools system as a high school biology teacher, school administrator, and regional office administrator. A past president of the Washington (DC) Chapter, Alethia is also a two-term national president of The Society, Incorporated, supporting youth in the arts. Since her retirement, she has been engaged in educational consulting and teaching at the graduate school level. Alethia is the mother of three and grandmother of three.

Barbara Denson Trotter, EdD

Dr. Barbara Denson Trotter is a 22-year member of the Los Angeles (CA) Chapter, where she has served in several capacities, including second vice president. She is a former member of the National Constitution and Bylaws Committee. Barbara is a retired director of grants and development and the recipient of numerous civic and professional appointments, among them the California Commission on Teacher Credentialing/Bias Review Committee. Barbara is the 24th Far Western regional director for Alpha Kappa Alpha Sorority, Incorporated and published the 2013 official regional history during her term. She is married to Dr. Alvin Trotter and has two children, Allison and Alvin Jr.

Marcia Denise White

Marcia Denise White, a 24-year member of the Long Island (NY) Chapter, was 12th National director of The Arts. She was the first National Poster Art Contest chair, Eastern Area Arts chair, and a contributing writer to the third official history of The Links, Incorporated. Under her leadership, "Classics through the Ages" was approved as the first Signature Arts Program. She also served on the National Legacy Affairs Committee and as president of the Long Island Chapter. Professionally, she is the owner of Personalized Skin Care by Marcia and state examiner for cosmetology, esthetics, and nails. She is married to John C. White.

SPECIAL ESSAYISTS AND RESEARCHERS

Rozalynn S. Frazier, Metro-Manhattan (NY) Chapter
National Chair, Communications Committee

Mildred A. Edwards, PhD, Topeka (KS) Chapter
Dean, Scott Hawkins Leadership Institute

Pamela Freeman Fobbs, JD, Fresno (CA) Chapter
Director, National Programs

Crystal L. Kendrick, Queen City (OH) Chapter
National Recording Secretary

Alice Strong Simmons, Oklahoma City (OK) Chapter
Former Central Area Director and National Chair, Ethics and Standards Committee

Table of Contents

Acknowledgments

Producing an organizational history is necessarily a protracted and laborious process. Thank you, Raven L. Hill, Prince George's (MD) Chapter, assistant editor and Archives and History (A & H) Committee member, for your exceptional contributions. We are grateful to other members of the A & H Committee who lightened our load by penning exemplary entries and reviewing drafts. Thank you, also, to guest essayists Rozalynn Frazier and Mildred Edwards, PhD, for your fine work.

The 1981 and 1992 editions of the history of The Links, Incorporated were invaluable for content and organization, and we posthumously acknowledge the brilliance and fortitude of Marjorie H. Parker, PhD, in producing the two. We also built on *Linked for Friendship and Service* (McNealey), the third edition. Some entries were updated, and we continue to be grateful to those essayists.

This edition was also enriched by the 2010 unpublished history *Partners in the Progress of Black America — The Links Incorporated,* Sadie Winlock, DM, compiler, to whom we express our sincere thanks for your diligence and contributions. We also continued to rely on early accounts of the history, penned by Lillian Stanford, the first historian for both the founding group and National Links, and Dorothy Wright, treasurer for the founding group, as well as Assembly minutes and reports by the Co-Founders and other officials through the years. Further, we appreciate subsequent efforts by Alexia Hudson-Ward to update and expand The Links' history in *Answering The Clarion Call: A Social Justice History of The Links, Incorporated, 1946–2015,* an unfinished manuscript.

We also express our appreciation to a number of individuals who helped us to amass and retrieve materials. Thank you, Mrs. JoEllen Elbashir, director, Moorland-Spingarn Research Center, Howard University, for your never-ending cooperation; Crystal Kendrick, National secretary, for sharing your files; and Dr. Gwendolyn Boyd, Links interim executive director, and her staff, for facilitating our work. We would like to note particularly the assistance provided by Keisha Prue, executive assistant; LaKisha Harrison, vendor coordinator; Naia Wood, manager, membership services; Jennifer Hudnell, senior manager, communications/community programs; and Mehari Debas, director, finance.

Our Purpose and Our Mission

*L*inkdom is built on a pledge, a purpose, and a promise. Our rich, proud, and storied history was gifted to all of us by Margaret Rosell Hawkins, Sarah Strickland Scott, and the dynamic women who chartered chapters all over the world. Our legacy lives through the leaders whose vision shapes our program and philanthropy. Our future is determined by the work we do in our chapters and communities to transform the lives of the vulnerable, the marginalized, and the voiceless.

Over more than 70 years of progress, the purpose of The Links, Incorporated has remained steadfast. At our foundational core lies the belief that friendship, coupled with service, has a transformational impact on our communities and our own lives. When we expand access to educational opportunities to youth and enhance the cultural legacy of our people, we fulfill our purpose. When we fight for social justice and raise awareness of health disparities, we fulfill our purpose.

And when we link hands and hearts around the globe in friendship and service, we fulfill our purpose.

The history of The Links, Incorporated began with nine friends in Philadelphia. Their story and its continual evolution merit telling. We take pleasure in making this fourth edition a reality. As you become part of this 73-year-old journey, be ever-mindful of the path they laid for us, and of the transformational power of a pledge, a purpose, and a promise.

~ Kimberly Jeffries Leonard, PhD
National President

Introduction

The Power of Linkdom

The girls have done it, again! During The Links, Inc. national meeting in Nassau, the Bahamas, the group of national socialites agreed to a most ambitious project which will run over a three-year period … they promised to give $75,000 to the legal defense and educational Fund, begun many years ago, by the NAACP.
~ *PITTSBURGH COURIER*, AUGUST 8, 1964

Some of my most informed acquaintances called Sunday and Monday to ask if that $276,000 to the United Negro College Fund (UNCF) was a typographical error. Three individuals, including a veteran journalist—couldn't believe that any black volunteer group had ever made that kind of contribution to a black cause.
~ *CHICAGO TRIBUNE*, OCTOBER 5, 1975

The Links had done it before, The Links did it again and again, and The Links have vowed to do it perpetually. Their actions were purposeful, all designed to fulfill The Links' mission of empowering purposeful lives and strong communities. Such has been the Links' modus operandi since Margaret Rosell Hawkins and Sarah Strickland Scott created a club of friends committed to service. What began in 1946 as a Philadelphia, Pennsylvania Club of nine has burgeoned into a dedicated force of 15,870 women.

The NAACP was the first National project of The Links, Inc. It culminated with a 1954 check for life memberships that totaled $26,850, which the NACCP's official journal described as "the largest single gift to the NAACP by a Negro group." In 1988, the 26th Assembly named the NAACP Legal Defense and Educational Fund, a separate entity, as the second beneficiary of a million-dollar grant, payable over a 10-year span. Both grants added more power to the fight for first-class citizenship, equality, and social justice for all.

Championing education as the passport to progress, The Links gave its first million-dollar award to the United Negro College Fund in 1984 as a means of making a college education accessible to those who could least afford it. By joining forces with the NAACP and the United Negro College Fund, The

Links Co-founder and 2nd National President Margaret R. Hawkins presenting a check to NAACP executive Roy Wilkins.

National President Glenda Newell-Harris presents latest million-dollar award to St. Jude Children's Research Hospital.

Links became an even more potent force for progressive movement in communities of color. Other million-dollar grantees included the National Civil Rights Museum in Memphis, Tennessee (2006), the Smithsonian Museum of African-American History and Culture in Washington, DC (2014), and St. Jude Children's Research Hospital, Memphis (2018).

Million-dollar donations were just one of the vehicles The Links used to improve educational disparities, economic hardships, and social inequalities in communities. Other identifiable expressions included the donation of equipment valued at half a million dollars and an $11,000 check to a New Orleans health clinic still reeling from the devastation wreaked by Hurricane Katrina in 2006. Additionally, Links funding for Education across the Miles, its program that builds and renovates primary and secondary schools in South Africa, passed the $600,000 mark.

But ongoing stellar initiatives have been the bread and butter of Links programming in communities, executed through five facets that now include Health and Human Services. Links have annually logged more than one million programming hours that have strikingly changed lives. "HeartLinks" raised the defense against heart disease, the number one killer of African-American women, and the $938,000 "Project LEAD: High Expectations" program averted teenage substance abuse, adolescent pregnancy, and sexually transmitted diseases.

The million-dollar initiative "Links to Success: Children Achieving Excellence" offered an array of mentoring and nurturing services for children, with academic and social developmental needs and companion services for their parents. The Links became the first African-American women's organization to establish a STEM National Program Model, STEM-U-Lation Left Brain-Right Brain, and The Links sponsored performances that included a Black chamber group.

Reiterating The Links' *raison d'être* at the 29th (1994) Assembly, 10th National President Marion Sutherland (1990–1994) said, "Our major focus is empowering the African-American family for the 21st century through health, youth services, artistic linkages, and a concern for our brothers and sisters around the world." The Links circle of compassion was extended to Haiti, Liberia, Mozambique, Zimbabwe, and Jamaica, assisting pregnant mothers and children and offering survival kits, clothing, nutrition education, dental screenings, and more. Schools were also built in Liberia.

The Links has also maximized its impact and reach by partnering with agencies that espouse postures consistent with The Links' Program direction. From mentoring underserved youths with "Essence Cares" to reaching and teaching African Americans about proper breast health care through the Susan G. Komen for the Cure "Circle of Promise," the efforts enhance the Links' mission of improving the quality of life for African Americans and people of African descent. As this indomitable force approaches its 75th anniversary, The Links continues to fulfill its purpose of creating and delivering solutions that help people of African descent live more fully. Hawkins's ideal has germinated into a recognizable force of women of influence—transformational Links empowering purposeful lives and strong communities.

~ *Earnestine Green McNealey, PhD*

Part I

Power Ignition
Vintage Fuel

When I stop to think back for the reason why I wanted to start The Links, I believe it was simply that in the world of war and stress and strain as it was then, that I recognized a need to spread the warmth of real friendship among the fine women and to draw them together in groups in various cities.

~ MARGARET JOSEPHINE ROSELL HAWKINS, CO-FOUNDER

CHAPTER 1

THE VISION CONCEIVED:
The Power of One

This aim was, and is, three-fold: to do some good to help less fortunate citizens, to raise the cultural level of our race, and to enjoy the social company of our friends.

~ MARGARET JOSEPHINE ROSELL HAWKINS

Hawkins

Philadelphia, Pennsylvania, in 1946 was brimming with organizations—church auxiliaries, professional societies, social clubs, cultural guilds, political action networks, mutual aid societies, bridge clubs, and even a mothers' group. Like Jack and Jill of America—founded in Philadelphia eight years earlier—many had Philly roots. Margaret Josephine Rosell Hawkins, a Philadelphia native and resident for nearly four decades, not only was aware of the proliferation of associations but she belonged to more than a few of them.

Such was standard for women of her ilk. A descendant of David Henry Rosell and Anna Nicholson, Margaret and older sister Anna Teresa grew up as members of Philadelphia's Negro elite. Their roots were seeded in Philadelphia in 1872 with her father's birth, and further planted in 1903, when her "New Yorker" mother married her father. Rosell was president of the Board of Commissioners for Darby Township, Pennsylvania, and his membership in the Philadelphia Club, a respected Negro men's social club, was a testament to his eminence in the community.

Concomitantly, mother Anna Rosell became a settler in Philadelphia. She lovingly embraced the city of brotherly love, gave birth to two daughters on whom she doted, and immersed them in the rituals of life, beginning with baptism at Philadelphia's Crucifixion Episcopal Church, where David and Anna had exchanged vows in 1903.

Along with privilege and tradition, Margaret Rosell was a teacher cloaked in erudition, conviction, and beauty; and she married well. Rosell received a Philadelphia Board of Education four-year

Hawkins's Gravesite, William Penn Cemetery, Philadelphia

scholarship to attend the Philadelphia School of Design for Women (later known as Moore College of Art and Design), where she earned a bachelor's degree in fine arts from "the first and only visual arts college for women in the United States."

Hawkins was also a person of conviction. As a high school student at the Philadelphia High School for Girls, she had also exhibited a sense of courage. Her defiance of a whites-only prom led to the eventual cancellation of the annual event after school officials scoffed at the idea of an integrated social. She was also "stunning." Seventeen years after the couple exchanged vows in 1936, society pages still described Margaret as "pretty," a crown conferred on her during her debutante days.

By all standards, Margaret Rosell was a woman of distinction, and she deemed the debonair Frederick Campbell Hawkins equally endowed. A Philadelphian, too, Hawkins was a member of the prominent Hawkins family, and he was also gainfully employed. He parlayed his position as a mail handler into a signal honor as the first African American superintendent of the Mt. Airy (PA) Post Office.

During the second year of their union, Margaret and Frederick welcomed Frederick Jr., and by 1946, their second child, Bruce R. Hawkins, had made his entry. She excelled at home, as well. "What I remember most was she was an excellent homemaker, providing a loving home and an environment in which a young person could flourish," Frederick Jr. said, and Bruce remembered "the wonderful times we had as a family. Unlike families today, we had meals together, where we talked about our days, our lives."

Along with caring for two active boys and running a household, Margaret continued her teaching duties in the neighboring Camden, New Jersey, school district, and she maintained her organizational memberships. The sheer number of affiliations gave credence to historian Arthur Schlesinger's 1944 hallowed conclusion that America was "a nation of joiners." She was deeply involved in mothers' clubs, faith groups, professional associations, bridge clubs, hostess groups, civic advocacy organizations, and social clubs.

Yet, an inkling that one more association was needed kept gnawing at Hawkins. She had "thought about it extensively and planned for it for almost three years" before she had an epiphany of what she really craved: "A club that would spread the warmth of real friendship among fine women and draw them together in groups in various cities; it would be purely a social organization made up of friends with a cultural and civic aim."

~ *Earnestine Green McNealey, PhD*

THROUGH THEIR EYES

Excerpts from *The Links Oral History Collection*

Frederick Campbell Hawkins, Jr., MD
on His Mother
MARGARET ROSELL HAWKINS
2:00 p.m. • June 7, 2013

Margaret Hawkins as "Mother"

First and foremost, she was my mother

I was the only child in the Hawkins' household for eight years, so I got to have my mother to myself for a long time before my brother Bruce was born. I experienced and was able to visit every compartment of my mother's life during those years. What I remember most was she was an excellent homemaker, providing a loving home and an environment in which a young person could flourish. She helped me to dream what would be possible if ...

I remember how she loved to cook, and she taught me how to cook. Her favorite meal was usually a roast that was extremely delicious. My favorite to cook were and is breakfast foods.

Margaret Hawkins as a Phenomenal Woman

She was a teacher, an artist, and an activist; but her passion was painting. My brother Bruce and I have five or six of my mother's finest art pieces perfectly placed in our homes. I don't know how many people know that my mother made jewelry as a hobby. I watched her for hours as she took each piece and intricately put it together, matching and coordinating colors of stone. That took a lot of organizational skills, a lot of strategy; and my mother had this innate ability for those things, and she combined that with her education to become the person I remember.

Margaret Hawkins, Links' Visionary

It seems like yesterday as I watched my mother put her ideas on paper about an organization for educated women. The 1940s in Philadelphia was so prejudiced and nasty times for African Americans. There was little if anything for educated Black women to do. My mother wanted an organization where women like her could come together and socialize.

My mother wanted the club to have three functions: civic, cultural, and social. After getting her ideas down on paper, she contacted Sarah Strickland Scott. Sarah helped make connections with people like Roy Wilkins and Adam Clayton Powell in order to help make the plans for a women's club that would serve the community a reality.

Margaret Hawkins as a Link in the Friendship Chain

Mom was a good friend with Daisy Lampkin. Daisy's and my family had homes on Morris Beach, a beach located near the peninsula of the Jersey shores. It was the one place Blacks could go, have fun, and socialize. I don't remember seeing it mentioned in any of The Links' publications, but Daisy was the vice president of *The Pittsburgh Courier*. In those days, it was the paper of choice for news about Blacks. Daisy, who became a Link, used her position at the paper to publicize what The Links were doing. She brought life and breath to the organization by letting people know who The Links were and the contributions they were making.

Margaret Hawkins as a Links Legend

She loved what the organization did and dreamed of what it could do ... She gave it her all, like she did everything. I am amazed at what The Links have become. I had no idea there are 276 chapters across the United States. Unbelievable! When comparing yesterday to today, there is more emphasis on the civic and cultural aspects of the organization; there seems to be more of a balance of the three areas my mother wanted the organization to focus. I experienced and can see the impact the organization had and continues to have on opportunities for African Americans.

I am so proud of The Links, Incorporated; its growth and the impact it is having today and its plans for tomorrow. I am proud of the young women who are being brought into the organization who will continue the legacy my mother started. I am humbled to be an Heir-O-Link. I am most of all grateful to call Margaret Josephine Rosell Hawkins my mother. My family and I gladly shared her with the Philadelphia Club. We shared her with the many chapters and members across the country.

~ From *The Links Oral History Collection*, Marcia Denise White, Editor

CHAPTER 2

THE VISION FUELED:
The Co-Founders

*... it was not until then that I called Mrs. Sarah Scott and told her
my plans and asked her opinion. She thought it was a grand idea.*

~ MARGARET ROSELL HAWKINS

With clarity about what she wished to set in motion, Hawkins sought feedback. "It was not until then that I called Mrs. Sarah Scott and told her my plans and asked her opinion," Hawkins said in a 1954 interview with the news editor of the *Philadelphia Courier*. "This aim was, and is, three-fold: to do some good to help less fortunate citizens, to raise the cultural level of our race, and to enjoy the social company of our friends," Hawkins said.

Scott "thought it was a grand idea." Buoyed by the enthusiasm from her church member, fellowship commission comrade, bridge buddy, and Jack and Jill cohort; Hawkins moved to actualize her conception. The new group began to take shape immediately, helped in part by the equally engaged Scott, who accepted Hawkins's invitation to join her in organizing the group. Scott subsequently was branded as a Co-Founder, but sons Frederick Hawkins, Jr. and Bruce Hawkins begged to differ. In an October 4, 2013, tribute, they hailed their mother as the "sole founder of The Links, Inc."

Fred Hawkins, Jr. had expressed that belief earlier in a June 7, 2013, interview, where he noted, "After getting her ideas down on paper, she contacted Sarah Strickland Scott." He credited Scott for helping his mother to make connections with people like Roy Wilkins and Adam Clayton Powell," but still extolled his mother as the force behind the "plans for a women's club that would serve the community."

Several of the clubs that Hawkins and Scott shared were excellent in advocacy and citizenship, community assistance and outreach, and the fine arts and intellectual discourse. Some were even providing two of the services in an acceptable fashion, but none was a master in all three. It was the triumvirate

National President Kimberly Jeffries Leonard in front of the newly restored portraits of Co-Founders Hawkins (right) and Scott (left).

Hawkins and Scott (seated fourth and fifth from the left) with members of the Philadelphia Club.

of services that Hawkins believed a women's group could deliver in an exceptional manner, and Scott willingly came on board.

Hawkins had not turned to Scott haphazardly; she had seen Scott's work on behalf of youth as a member of the Fellowship Commission, she had supported efforts by the NAACP to break down barriers to progress, and she was a patron of the arts. Scott was also a wife, a mother, and a teacher who was willing to commiserate; and she had bested Hawkins in a few bridge duels. Through those interactions and more, each developed a respect and sense of appreciation, which gradually turned into friendship. Consequently, when Hawkins contemplated a club that could be a panacea for many of their interests and concerns, she called Scott.

Rather than duplicating the single-serve or dual-dip purposes behind other clubs and agencies, the new club would foster civic, charitable, and intercultural programs. All were needed in 1946 in Philadelphia, where World War II and segregation continued to take their toll on Negroes: in their homes, where father-less households had become more common because of deployments; in the workplace, where Negroes were denied jobs and training in private industry and the government; and in public spaces that included schools, hotels, and restaurants that served as constant reminders of the inequality in America.

Hawkins had seen the injustices, the poverty, and other vestiges of slavery, but she was confident that the paradigm for the new club would be "a balm in Gilead" for youth and the community at large. What would make the difference was the fuel at its core: a few highly regarded women who enjoyed the company of friends and who also had the economic resources and *noblesse oblige* to impact their communities.

~ Earnestine Green McNealey, PhD

CHAPTER 3

THE VISION ACTUALIZED:
The Philadelphia Chapter

And then we called nine ladies together …
and so The Links were born.

~ MARGARET ROSELL HAWKINS

From their wide circles of friends, Hawkins and Scott vetted seven of Philadelphia's finest for inclusion. "We called nine ladies together … and so The Links were born." The group was composed of Frances Vashon Atkinson, Katie Murphy Greene, Myrtle Manigault, Marian Minton, Lillian Stanford, Lillian Hudson Wall, and Dorothy Bell Wright. Atkinson, Manigault, Minton, and Stanford lived outside the city limits; but the label fit, as all were members of Philadelphia's Negro elite—standing ascribed in relation to their husbands' professions, the standard affluence gauge in Philadelphia and the nation in 1946.

All were married and lived within a 25-mile radius of each other, with five—Greene, Hawkins, Scott, Wall, and Wright—residing in Philadelphia, three—Atkinson, Minton, Stanford—in neighboring towns in Pennsylvania, and one—Manigault—in New Jersey. Like Hawkins's husband, Frederick, the men held venerable positions: five were medical professionals and one was heir apparent to a bank presidency. Scott, Atkinson, Minton, Stanford, and Wall were wives of doctors, Greene's husband was a dentist, and Wright's husband was a bank executive.

Even in the 21st century, the positions suggest prosperity, but against the backdrop of the first half of the 20th century, The Links' first members were clearly upper crust. While the war-driven expansion of industry, the armed forces, and government services had improved economic conditions for Negroes, Frederick Hawkins's managerial appointment at the post office was still novel—not just in Philadelphia, but throughout the country, where Negroes were relegated to mail handlers and only a handful had been appointed as clerks, even in Negro communities.

Complaints that Negroes were not being promoted in keeping with their abilities resulted in a 1944 investigation by legendary civil rights attorney Clarence Mitchell, who had led the implementation of President Franklin Roosevelt's 1941 policy barring racial discrimination in employment in the national defense and war industry programs. Mitchell confirmed, "Upon checking our regional office, I have learned that the Negroes were appointed as mail handlers, and not as clerks."

Census reports and statistical abstracts reflected the rarity of Negro professionals. While Negroes made up 10 percent of the nation's population, Negro physicians constituted only 1.9 percent of practicing physicians. The 3,753 black physicians translated into one physician for every 3,681 Negroes, as compared to one Caucasian physician for every 755 whites. A Negro bank president was even more uncommon. Of the 134 Negro banks established in the country between 1888 and 1934, Southern Bank in

Philadelphia was one of only 12 that did not fold by 1938 in the aftermath of the Great Depression. By 1947, Wright's husband, Emanuel, had become president of Southern Bank, succeeding his father R. R. Wright upon his death.

Their husbands were also social connectors. Greene's husband, Harry, served more than 10 terms as president of the Philadelphia NAACP prior to his 1960 appointment as national treasurer. Scott's husband, Horace, was a favored Republican, and his political appointments included a stint as deputy health secretary for the Commonwealth of Pennsylvania in 1944.

Spouses Nolan Atkinson, Sr., Russell Minton, Stephen R. Stanford, and Horace C. Scott were "Archons" of Philadelphia's Alpha Boule of Sigma Pi Phi Fraternity, the first and oldest African American Greek-letter fraternal organization, and their "Archousa" wives had participation privileges in civic, educational, social, and inspirational events.

The women also shared affiliations in other organizations. A link for six of them—Hawkins, Scott, Atkinson, Minton, Stratton, and Wright—was Jack and Jill of America, a mothers group created in Philadelphia in 1938 "to provide social, cultural and educational opportunities for youth between the ages of 2 and 19." Greene and Minton were members of the Fellowship Commission, while Wall and Scott were affiliated with the Fellowship House. Hawkins, Scott, and Atkinson attended St. Thomas Protestant Episcopal Church, Greene and Wright were members of the NAACP and Philadelphia Council of Negro Women, Scott and Minton were members of Delta Sigma Theta, and Greene was a member of Alpha Kappa Alpha. Hawkins and Greene were also members of the Young Women's Christian Association.

A love for bridge was another common bond for five. With their husbands, Atkinson, Minton, Scott, and Wall formed CHO (Center-Hand-Opponent) bridge club, and Hawkins, Atkinson, and Manigault were members of Dealers. Other affiliations included the Urban League, the Philadelphia Grand Opera Company, Heritage House, and the Visiting Nurses Association.

They were also members of the Montgomery Hospital Nurses Auxiliary; Mount Pisgah AME, St. Colman Roman Catholic, Union AME, and Reeve Memorial United Presbyterian churches; the National Freedom Day Association; Friends of Fellowship; the New Jersey and National Teachers Association; the Eastern Arts Association; Friends Select School; Women's Auxiliary to the National Dental Association; and the Chestnut Hill Community Association.

Although gender norms and male-dominancy ideologies automatically tied the charter members to the privileged class, they needed no such buttressing. The women were distinguished in their own rights: educated, professionally established, socially connected, and civic minded. The US population on July 1, 1946, was 141,388,566. The corresponding educational attainment data (1950) showed only 3.8 percent of all women and 1.3 percent of Negroes nationwide held a bachelor's degree. All had college experiences.

Minton, Scott, and Wright held bachelor's degrees from the University of Pennsylvania, Philadelphia, while Greene, Hawkins, Stanford, and Stratton attained honors from Temple University in Philadelphia, the Philadelphia School of Design for Women (now Moore College of Art and Design), Glassboro State Teachers College (now Rowan University) in New Jersey, and West Virginia State College (now University), Institute. Scott also held a master's degree from Columbia University in New York.

Both Wall and Atkinson moved to Philadelphia with their physician husbands. Lil Wall and her husband Lonnie Cole Wall graduated from Haines Normal and Industrial Institute in Augusta, Georgia. Founded by legendary educator Lucy Craft Laney, the school included a kindergarten to junior college curriculum, the Lamar School of Nursing, and offered a fifth year of college preparatory high school in which Laney taught Latin. Haines graduates matriculated at Howard, where Lonnie Wall attended medical school, and Fisk, which has been associated with Lil Wall.

Atkinson had higher education roots that emanated from her grandparents, George and Susan Vashon. He was the first Negro graduate of Oberlin College in Ohio and the first practicing African American lawyer in the state of New York. Along with Frederick Douglass, Vashon was also one of the

The Philadelphia Club charter members and inductees: (standing, left to right) Sarah S. Scott, Lillian C. Stanford, Myrtle Manigault Stratton, Frances Atkinson, Margaret Hawkins, (seated, left to right) Katie Greene, Marion Minton, Courtney Duckrey (inductee), Lillian Wall, and Barbara Wilkins (inductee). Not pictured: Dorothy Wright.

five abolitionists who authored "The Claims of Our Common Cause," an address to the 1853 National African American Convention in Rochester, New York. Susan Vashon was founder and president of the Missouri State Federation of the National Association of Colored Women's Clubs in 1902.

Degrees were the passports into one of two professions (the other was preaching) readily open to Negroes, and credentials further ensured that they could continue in their profession, even when

certification became the norm in the 1950s and forced many Negro teachers out of the classroom. Hawkins, Scott, Greene, Manigault, and Stanford were among the more than 50 percent of Negro professionals who were teachers.

Wright's career stood out even more because she journeyed into basically unchartered waters. Of the 58.9 million people employed in 1950, only 1.9 million worked in the combined category of finance, insurance, and real estate, as opposed to the 18.5 million who worked in goods-producing industries. A stamp of approval in business and economics from the vaunted University of Pennsylvania enabled her to win a position at the Internal Revenue Service, where she worked for 27 years.

The women's prominent husbands, highly preferred professions, and lineage had served as gateways to meeting others in the upper social and civic echelon and subsequently forming the most select group. Reminding the 25th (1986) Assembly of the exclusivity of The Links' founding group, 5th National President Helen Edmonds called the group's makeup natural. "People of the same cultural training and milieu tended to organize around their own," Edmonds said.

It was this power group that gathered for the initial meeting on November 9, 1946. Lillian Hudson Wall, who was known as one of the outstanding hostesses along the Eastern seaboard, opened her home at 2101 South 46th Street for the historical gathering. "They had dinner, then cake and coffee." In many of the social organizations where the women held memberships, dessert would have been the last course. But the invitation from Hawkins and Scott made it clear that dinner was just the prelude to the order of the day: the creation of an organization that would have a dual mission of friendship and service.

With the purpose defined, the group turned its attention to organizational rudiments that included the leadership, structure, and policies. The top officer slots, naturally, went to Co-Founders Hawkins and Scott, and Manigault, Atkinson, and Wright were elected as recording secretary, corresponding secretary, and treasurer. Committees were also formed, with Wright selected to chair Constitution and Bylaws, the defining committee.

Along with the purpose, the resulting document, adopted in 1947, enumerated officers, corresponding duties, and tenure, mandated ten monthly meetings hosted by individual members on a rotational schedule, and set out conditions for active membership and the selection of new members. A commitment to duties, residency within a 25-mile radius, expulsion for three meetings missed consecutively, and dues of 50 cents were required to maintain active status.

Restrictions imposed for the intake of new members included a chapter cap of 14, unanimous selection by secret ballot, and no affiliation with another national intercity social club, excluding sororities. Induction guidelines could have forced reconsideration in the first year, as there was little room for growth. The Links "almost immediately" added Courtney Duckrey, a teacher and the wife of Tanner Duckrey, the first Negro in Philadelphia to become a district superintendent, and Barbara Wilkins to the roster before its November 9 anniversary date.

The Links reached capacity with the induction of Doris Reynolds, wife of Philadelphia mortician and national ELKS leader Lee Roy Reynolds; Kitty Stratton, a Philadelphia teacher and wife of Dr. Henry Stratton; and Helen Reid Sullivan, a Philadelphia public school teacher and wife of Dr. William H. Sullivan. However, the clause functioned just as the group had intended—it cemented the exclusivity that was inherent and perpetual.

At the January 1947 meeting, the club embraced "Links" as its name. Suggested by Wall, "Links was heartedly accepted by all of us as carrying out the purpose of friends linking for friendship." The club also adopted additional identifiers: a bracelet designed by Hawkins, a song written by Atkinson, and a pledge authored by Scott. The pledge left no doubt about the group's work: "It spelled out our purpose," said Dorothy Wright, who dutifully collected memorabilia that captured the early history.

"We worked hard from the start," Wright noted, as she described how she and her cohorts labored to create an organization that fulfilled Margaret Rosell Hawkins's and Sarah Strickland Scott's ideal: "Their [Hawkins's and Scott's] hope was for a meaningful, enjoyable relationship with friends whose interests extended to service in their communities," she said.

The Links' work turned on its heels a 1940 assertion that when middle-class Negroes with "relatively secure positions, homes, cars, and a glittering social life" got involved in civic activities, it was they who benefitted most from fights for justice and equality that should have been raising the masses. In stark contrast to the characterization by a young Ralph

Bunche, the Philadelphia Links engendered progress in their community, particularly for those in need.

In 1946, Negroes in Philadelphia, like those throughout the United States, were still seeking the freedom and equality promised in wartime rhetoric. The Links pushed social action initiatives and made donations to agencies working to empower communities. One of the first projects was a Vigilance Committee that monitored publicity about Negroes as a means of identifying favorable and unfavorable publicity. "We picked up things that were derogatory as far as blacks were concerned, and we'd write in about it," charter member Dorothy Wright said in a 1986 interview."

Merchants in Philadelphia removed toys, books, and clothing from windows and shelves after the committee voiced objections about the portrayal of the images. By contrast, the group praised celebrities and employers who promoted equity and justice. They lauded Josephine Baker for refusing to accept an engagement at the Earle Theatre in Philadelphia without an assurance that Negro musicians and stagehands would be employed for their performance. Philadelphia employers and agencies that exhibited fairness toward all youth, regardless of race, creed, or color, also received congratulatory missives.

The monitoring was not limited to Philadelphia. When the group learned that Bing Crosby refused to let Negro golfer Teddy Rhodes play in his California golf tournament, "We sent Mr. Crosby a telegram condemning him for his actions. We reminded him that men of Mr. Rhodes' racial group were fighting and dying in Korea for democracy, the principle of which he was denying Mr. Rhodes," Lillian Stanford wrote in a 1950 history of the Philadelphia Chapter.

The Bureau of Colored Children gets $1,000, representing proceeds from the Philadelphia Club's first Queen of Love and Beauty contest.

The Philadelphia Inquirer (PA), Sunday, December 28, 1986, page 121

Another major focus was the well-being of children. Wright, the first treasurer, recalled the early activities that included the Bureau of Colored Children (BCC), a child placement agency, which had some 1,000 Negro children on the roll. The first program was a picnic in Fairmount Park for the residents of a Germantown children's home in 1947. The Links sponsored the food and transported the children to the park. In December, the children were also treated to a Christmas party at BCC's headquarters.

However, the most substantial support, a $1,000 check, was awarded in 1948. The proceeds came from the group's 1948 fundraiser, the Coronation of the Queen of Love and Beauty, and Wright produced a "yellowed newspaper clipping" to prove it. She quickly noted that the photo of "pretty women with well-coiffed hair and stiff, white dresses was not a typical event. Most of the Links' projects did not have such a high society tone" because it was difficult to raise that kind of money within the community, Wright explained.

However, the carnival became the pinnacle. Calling it the "annual event of beautiful pageantry," charter member Lillian Stanford said it yielded $1,300 the next year. Rummage sales provided an additional source for revenue. "For those, we have been able to make as high as $125 per sale."

The Links also worked to facilitate the upward mobility of Negroes, giving both time and dollars to the NAACP, the National Urban League, and the United Negro College Fund. Donations were backed by a series of workshops for high school seniors who were not college bound," enabling them to begin employment "at almost twice the salary that they would have received if they had not had this opportunity."

For those going to college, the group made contributions to the American Friends' Scholarship Fund, subsequently established its own, and became a clearinghouse for matching scholarships for students. Among the cultural offerings were an African art exhibition, an international tea, and piano recitals.

As individuals, the members were also leaders in the cultural, civic, and social life of the community. Wright not only served as president of the Philadelphia Chapter of Jack and Jill, which was founded in Philadelphia in 1938 to increase enrichment opportunities for children, but she also served as Jack and Jill's first national president. Wall won the Blue Star Brigade Award for war bonds sales, Scott served as a national program director for Jack and Jill, Stanford was on the board of the American Red Cross, and Greene served as president of the Philadelphia Chapter of Alpha Kappa Alpha and "worked side by side with her husband." Dr. Harry J. Greene served as president of the Philadelphia branch of the NAACP for 10 terms.

The nine who gathered created something beyond their families, professions, and their endless organizations with disparate social and civic activities. The new club was a transformational connection to new beginnings. It linked nine women as friends and ambassadors of service, giving rise to a powerful force for the betterment of communities. Hawkins had the idea, she and Scott formulated a design, and with seven friends, they fueled the launch.

~ Earnestine Green McNealey, PhD

THE FIRST OFFICERS	
President	Margaret Rosell Hawkins
Vice President	Sarah Strickland Scott
Recording Secretary	Myrtle Manigault
Corresponding Secretary	Frances Atkinson
Treasurer	Dorothy B. Wright

FIRST CONSTITUTION (1947)
UP-CLOSE

- Commitment to duty required.
- Ten monthly meetings mandated.
- Expulsion for three meetings missed consecutively.
- One-year tenure for officers.
- Dues: 50 cents
- Membership cap of 14.
- Unanimous vote required for new members.
- No affiliation with another national intercity social club, excluding sororities.
- Residency within a 25-mile radius of Philadelphia.

THE PHILADELPHIA CHAPTER GEOGRAPHICAL MAKEUP

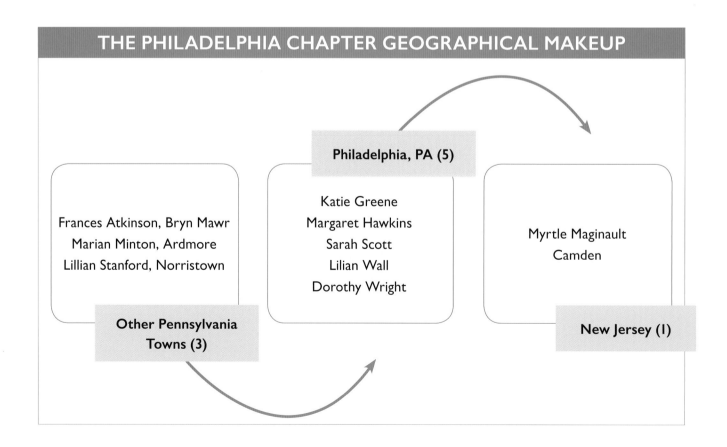

Philadelphia, PA (5)

Katie Greene
Margaret Hawkins
Sarah Scott
Lilian Wall
Dorothy Wright

Frances Atkinson, Bryn Mawr
Marian Minton, Ardmore
Lillian Stanford, Norristown

Other Pennsylvania Towns (3)

Myrtle Maginault
Camden

New Jersey (1)

MEMBER CONNECTIONS

Wives of Medical Professionals
Atkinson
Greene
Minton
Scott
Stanford
Wall

Jack and Jill
Atkinson
Hawkins
Manigault
Minton
Scott
Wright

CHO (Bridge) Club
Atkinson
Minton
Scott
Wall

St. Thomas Protestant Episcopal Church
Atkinson
Hawkins
Scott

VITALS: CHARTER MEMBERS

There was a 13-year difference in the charter members' ages, which ranged from 34 (Atkinson) to 47 (Greene), with a mean of 40. Co-Founders Hawkins and Scott were 38 and 45, respectively.

Atkinson, the youngest member of the group, also lived longer and was the last survivor, expiring in 2009 at age 97. Hawkins, the first to expire, was just 55 when she died in 1963, but the remainder reached their three scores and ten.

Key Sources: Files accessed through on-line data bases of Ancestry.com, Find-a-Grave, Newspapers.com and RootsWeb.com

Margaret Josephine Rosell Hawkins

Artist, Educator

Hawkins was the visionary behind The Links. She shared "founder" honors with Sarah Strickland Scott and served as the first president of the Philadelphia Club.

Birth:	January 12, 1908 Philadelphia, Philadelphia County, Pennsylvania, USA
Death:	October 4, 1963 (age 55) Philadelphia, Philadelphia County, Pennsylvania, USA
Burial:	Eden Cemetery Collingdale, Delaware County, Pennsylvania, USA Harriet Tubman Lot 2, ID: 170939284
Education & Profession:	Received Philadelphia Board of Education scholarship to attend the Philadelphia School of Design for Women (later known as Moore College of Art and Design); received bachelor's degree in fine arts in 1931 and became an art teacher and superintendent in the Camden, New Jersey, schools.
Father:	David Rosell
Mother:	Anna Nicholson
Siblings:	Anna Rosell
Spouse:	Frederick C. Hawkins, first African American superintendent of the Mt. Airy (PA) post office.
Children:	Frederick C. Hawkins, Jr., MD Bruce R. Hawkins
Other Affiliations:	St. Thomas Protestant Episcopal Church, Jack and Jill, Mothers' Study Club, Sunday Niters, CHO bridge club, Dealers, Eastern Arts Association, National Arts Association, New Jersey Teachers Association, and the Young Women's Christian Association.
Sources:	Find-A-Grave, Memorial ID: 170939284; Pennsylvania Death Certificates, 1906–1965; Historic Pennsylvania Church and Town Records, Philadelphia, Pennsylvania; 1920 United States Federal Census [database on-line]

Sarah J. Strickland Scott
Educator, Guidance Counselor, Principal

Scott was the Co-Founder of The Links and served as vice president. When The Links was nationalized, Scott was elected as the first National President.

Birth:	January 17, 1901 Philadelphia, Philadelphia County, Pennsylvania, USA
Death:	July 4, 1988 (age 87) Philadelphia, Pennsylvania, USA
Burial:	
Education & Profession:	Received bachelor's degree in English from the University of Pennsylvania and a master's degree in vocational guidance from Columbia University, New York, 1931. Taught in the Philadelphia school district and later worked as a guidance counselor and then principal in the Wilmington, Delaware, school system. After retiring, Scott volunteered as a teacher at Philadelphia's Berrien Institute, where she contributed 75 books on Black history and life.
Father:	George G. Strickland, MD
Mother:	Minnie L. Strickland
Siblings:	Younger brother, Wilbur H. Strickland, MD
Spouse:	Horace C. Scott, MD; received appointment as Pennsylvania State Deputy Health Secretary (1944).
Children:	Marjorie Ann Scott Upshur (preceded her mother in death in 1981)
Other Affiliations:	St. Thomas Protestant Episcopal Church, Jack and Jill (national program director), Friends Select School (executive council), Mothers Child Study Club, CHO bridge club, Fellowship Commission, and Delta Sigma Theta (charter member of college chapter); was a registrar for the 1940 Republican National Convention in Philadelphia

Frances Vashon Atkinson

Law Office Stenographer, Community Volunteer

Birth: March 18, 1912
St. Louis, Missouri, USA

Death: September 29, 2009 (age 97)
Philadelphia, Philadelphia County, Pennsylvania, USA

Burial: Rolling Green Memorial Park
Westchester, Pennsylvania

Education & Profession: Attended public school in St. Louis, Missouri, and worked as a stenographer for a law firm before marrying Dr. Nolan N. Atkinson and moving to Philadelphia, Pennsylvania, where she became a community volunteer.

Father: Frank C. Vashon

Mother: E. Prestina Story Vashon

Siblings: She and her older sister Blanche Vashon grew up in her uncle's home in St. Louis, Missouri.

Spouse: Nolan Atkinson, MD

Children: Nolan N. Atkinson, Jr.
Carolyn Thornell

Other Affiliations: West Chester State Teachers College (trustee), St. Thomas Protestant Episcopal Church, Jack and Jill of America, Mothers Child Study Club, Bryn Mawr School & Home Group, CHO bridge club, Hostesses, and Matinee Ensemble

Katharine "Katie" Belle Murphy Greene
Educator, Civic Leader

Birth:
November 23, 1899*
Eufaula, Alabama, USA

Death:
March 18, 1973 (age 73)
Philadelphia, Philadelphia County, Pennsylvania, USA

Burial:
Rolling Green Memorial Park
Westchester, Pennsylvania

Education & Profession:
Bachelor of science, education degree, Temple University; taught kindergarten in the Philadelphia school system for 35 years.

Father:
Sidney M. Murphy

Mother:
Belle M. Glascow Murphy

Siblings:
The first girl and fifth of six children (three girls, three boys): Sidney, Cipis, John L., Teresa, and Connie L.

Spouse:
Harry Julian Greene, DDS; served as president of the Philadelphia NAACP for 10 consecutive terms before his 1960 appointment as national treasurer.

Other Affiliations:
Philadelphia Grand Opera company (board member), Union African Methodist Episcopal Church (trustee and Sunday School teacher), NAACP (life member), Philadelphia Council for Negro Women (vice president), YWCA Committee on Management, Philadelphia Piano Ensemble (manager), Fellowship Commission, Heritage House, Alpha Kappa Alpha (Philadelphia Chapter president), and Hostesses; Gold Seal Award, Philadelphia Tribune charities

Age in obituary is at variance with year, but birth, census, social security, and death records reflect 1899.

Myrtle Calvary Manigault (Stratton)

Educator, Society Page Contributor

Birth:	February 2, 1908 Philadelphia, Pennsylvania, USA
Death:	October 7, 1995 (age 87) Brighton, Pennsylvania, USA
Burial:	
Education & Profession:	Bachelor's degree, New Jersey State Teachers College at Glassboro (now Rowan University); taught elementary school for 43 years in the Camden, New Jersey, system, and freelanced as a society page writer for the Pittsburgh Courier, one of the top-selling Negro newspapers in the country, for 25 years.
Father:	Cyrus Calvary
Mother:	Margaret D Sayles, waitress
Spouses:	William L. Manigault (1931), florist Howard H. Stratton, DDS (1973)
Children:	Meryl Ann Manigault, MD
Other Affiliations:	St. Augustine Protestant Episcopal Church, Jack and Jill, Mothers Child Study Club, Philadelphia women's auxiliary to the National Dental Association, Sunday Niters, Dealers, Hostesses, Friends of Fellowship, Book and Theater

Marian Elizabeth Roland Minton

Volunteer

Birth: April 8, 1901
Philadelphia, Pennsylvania, USA

Death: November 29, 1979 (age 78)
Philadelphia, Philadelphia County, Pennsylvania, USA

Burial: Old Cathedral Cemetery
Philadelphia, Pennsylvania

Education & Profession: Bachelor of science degree in education, University of Pennsylvania. Taught in the Philadelphia city schools for 32 years, with assignments at Arthur, Harrison, and Stanton schools.

Father:

Mother:

Siblings:

Spouse: Russell F. Minton, MD

Children: Russell Minton, Jr.
Raymonde Minton Stevens

Other Affiliations: NAACP (auxiliary vice chairman), Fellowship Commission, Urban League, St. Colman's Roman Catholic Church, Jack and Jill, League of Women Voters, Mainline Charity League, Mothers Child Study Club, CHO bridge club, women's auxiliary of the Philadelphia County and National Medical (first secretary) societies, International Service Club, and the Chestnut Hill Community Association

Lillian Virginia Cobbs Stanford
Educator

Birth:	January 18, 1909 Pulaski, Beaver, Pennsylvania, USA
Death:	Circa 2000 Norristown, Pennsylvania, USA
Burial:	Rolling Green Memorial Park West Chester, Pennsylvania
Education & Profession:	Bachelor's degree, West Virginia State College
Father:	John H. Cobbs
Mother:	Anna E. Rose Cobbs
Siblings:	Second of three children, older brother, Robert, and younger sister Marian
Spouse:	Stephen R. Stanford, MD, first Negro doctor on staff at Norristown Hospital
Children:	Daughter, Stephanie
Other Affiliations:	AUMP Methodist Church, Visiting Nurses Association, Montgomery Hospital

Lilian Hudson Wall

Community Stalwart

Birth:	14 August 14, 1900
	Waynesboro, Georgia, USA
Death:	September 12, 1975 (age 75)
	Philadelphia, Pennsylvania, USA
Burial:	
Education & Profession:	Haines Normal and Industrial Institute, Augusta, Georgia; awards included the Blue Star Brigade Award for war bonds sales.
	Volunteer "Hostess with the Mostest"
Father:	
Mother:	
Siblings:	
Spouse:	Lonnie Cole Wall, MD
Other Affiliations:	Fellowship House (frequent fundraiser), Reeve Memorial United Presbyterian Church, Hostess Club (president), Sponsors Club (treasurer), Friends of Fellowship (president), Women's Army Corps

Dorothy Bell Wright

Senior Reviewer and Instructor, IRS

Birth:
March 22, 1910
Philadelphia, Pennsylvania, USA

Death:
September 6, 1996 (age 86)
Philadelphia, Pennsylvania, USA

Burial:
Mt. Lawn Cemetery
Sharon Hill, Delaware County, Pennsylvania, USA
ID: 199072878

Education & Profession:
University of Pennsylvania
IRS reviewer, instructor

Father:
George R. Bell

Mother:
Fannie Griffin Bell

Spouse:
Emanuel C. Wright, president, Citizens and Southern Bank

Children:
Gwendolyn Wright

Other Affiliations:
Mt. Pisgah African Methodist Episcopal Church, St. Matthews AME church, Women's Missionary Society of the Philadelphia Conference (archivist), Jack and Jill (first national president), West Side Day Care (trustee), National Council of Negro Women, National Freedom Day Association, founding member, Heritage House

PART II

Power Connections

Purposeful Mapping

In Philadelphia on June 4, 1949, when the organization The National Links was born, we adopted as our purpose "to bring together outstanding women in various sections of our country for a three-fold purpose, namely civic, intercultural, and social."

~ SARAH STRICKLAND SCOTT, CO-FOUNDER

CHAPTER 4

CONNECTIONS:
Club Linkages

We were busy, following thru with assistance, personal
contacts, letters, long distance calls, and installing chapters.
~ DOROTHY WRIGHT, FOUNDING GROUP MEMBER

Margaret Rosell Hawkins's vision for an intercity club of friends that would become a force for good took shape in 1946 as The Links. Their work was hailed locally, and members eagerly extolled the virtues of their new organization to friends and relatives outside Philadelphia. As a result, "there were many friends in other cities who were anxious to start chapters," Philadelphia charter member Dorothy Wright said.

Less than three years after the Philadelphia Links emerged, 13 other groups of friends had formed along the Eastern seaboard. Seven clubs were established in 1948, and six were added in 1949. "We were busy, following thru with assistance, personal contacts, letters, long distance calls, and installing chapters," Wright wrote in a 1969 memoir.

Admiration for the group's members and activities was buzzing. Thrilled by the success of their fledgling gem, members took delight in helping others experience the dual joys of friendship and service. When friends, relatives, and acquaintances expressed interest in starting a club of their own, the Philadelphia Club was more than happy to oblige. The support engendered Links roots in eight states and a territory—New Jersey, Missouri, North Carolina, Maryland, Delaware, New York, Virginia, Ohio, and the District of Columbia.

National Vice President Kimberly Jeffries Leonard (seated third from the left) attending 2016 gala, "A Platinum Celebration: 70 Years of Friendship and Service," hosted by The Atlantic City (NJ) Chapter, the second chapter in the chain.

The Wilson-Rocky Mount-Tarboro (NC) Chapter, the first Southern Area chapter, attending the biennial White Rose scholarship luncheon.

Co-Founders Margaret Hawkins and Sarah Scott were among the Philadelphia Links who installed and welcomed the new clubs. Original members Katie Greene, Myrtle Manigault Stratton, and Frances Vashon Atkinson also served as officiants, as did Doris Reynolds, a member of the first group of inductees. Atlantic City, New Jersey, earned bragging rights as the first club established beyond Philadelphia. Like the Philadelphia Links, the charter members were movers and shakers, but close friendships fortified on the bridge circuit might have resulted in Atlantic City's anointing over the Delaware Chapter, which was c hartered six weeks later.

Card connoisseurs Lillian Wall—a.k.a. "social-ite Mrs. Lil Wall"—and her husband, Dr. Lonnie C. Wall, were card regulars on the Atlantic City circuit; and their Atlantic City friends often visited them in their Philadelphia home, which was entertainment central for many high-society affairs (and interactions), as well as bridge challenges and disputes. However, the honor of installing the first linkage on February 28, 1948, went to Myrtle Manigault. She was also a card player, and she taught in the New Jersey schools, and she was a freelance society page journalist.

Philadelphia members were also closely bonded to the third and fourth clubs in the Links chain: Sarah Strickland Scott, with Wilmington, Delaware, established April 10, 1948; and Frances Vashon Atkinson, with St. Louis, Missouri, installed on April 15. Each had lived in the respective city and was a sister of one of the members. For Scott, it was her Delta line sister and friend Pauline L. Young, and the

nexus was even closer for Frances Vashon Atkinson and her blood sister Blanche Vashon Sinkler, the group's organizer. "St. Louis was the first group to have an installation service."

Two additional clubs—#6, Washington, DC, and #7, Wilson-Rocky Mount-Tarboro, North Carolina—were also established in April. The installations on April 15 and April 17, respectively, increased the number to four, a record one-month high. The Baltimore, Maryland, and the Pittsburgh, Pennsylvania, clubs, the eighth and ninth, were the last clubs established in 1948—Baltimore on September 24, and Pittsburgh on December 5. The Pittsburgh organizers—Jesse Vann, publisher and owner of the *Pittsburgh Courier*, and Daisy Lampkin, the *Courier*'s vice president and a member of the national NAACP board of directors—were power brokers who later played key roles in public relations and programming in The National Links.

Activity resumed in 1949 with the establishment of #10, Raleigh, North Carolina, on April 18. Three clubs were added in May: #11, Greater New York on May 12, #12, Central New Jersey on May 28, and #13, Dayton, Ohio, also on May 28. At-will instal-lations culminated on June 1 with the installation of #14, the North Jersey Club. The connected 14 groups, with 161 charter members, were destined to become the foundational linkages in a lengthening chain of friendship and service.

~ *Earnestine Green McNealey, PhD*

THROUGH THEIR EYES

Excerpts from *The Links Oral History Collection*

Thelma Hardiman* on Her Friend
SARAH STRICKLAND SCOTT

5:00 p.m. • July 25, 2013 • Tacoma, Washington

How She Met Sarah Strickland Scott

On or around the year 1950, Link Alice Hayes from Niagara Falls, New York, contacted me and four other women in Buffalo, New York, and discussed the possibility of forming a club in our area called The Links. I had heard about The Links, but at the time didn't know that much about them. I accepted the invitation. Sarah was at our chartering and that is how we first met.

How She and Sarah Strickland Scott Became Friends

I became active right away in The Links and participated in several phone calls to learn about the organization. Once becoming an officer, I communicated with Sarah on a regular basis. We would discuss what the chapters were doing and how the organization was growing, and what was needed in my position of leadership. So, our friendship really began over the phone. I was president of my chapter for eight years, so I would also see her at every conference or meeting, and we would chat and share experiences at that time.

How Her Friendship with Sarah Strickland Scott Grew

Our friendship was one that was as close as one could be when living in different cities and doing most of our work by phone and or correspondence.

I don't remember exactly what happened (I am 93 years old and don't remember so good anymore), but Sarah had some type of accident. I told her I wanted to help her in any way I could. You see, Sarah was in a wheelchair, and I would push her wheelchair anywhere she wanted or needed to go. When she traveled, I traveled with her.

Sarah to me was such a kind, gentle, and caring person. This is one of the reasons we got together. I would do anything for her.

How Sarah Strickland Scott Embodied Linkdom

If I had to describe her as a Link, it would be with one word: Proud. She was proud of being one of the organizers and proud of what she watched the organization become.

She always wanted to get up early so she could get into The Links meeting room first. She would have me push her wheelchair down front, as close to the dais as possible. She wanted to be able to look out at all the beautiful women who had come together to be a part of the organization she helped to found. No matter how long the meeting, she would sit, attentive, never getting tired or sleepy. She loved The Links and wanted to show her commitment and dedication to the organization. She could not do much at that time, but her presence to me, was evidence of her love.

She knew how to be a friend, make a friend and serve others. She was the Link in Friendship's Chain.

My friend, Sarah Scott, was a beautiful, pleasant, outstanding, friendly women who wanted to give to the world the best that she had – and I feel that she did do that – she made so many women happy – she was such a gentle person.

How Sarah Strickland Scott Should Be Remembered

I want young people all across the country to know who Sarah Strickland Scott was and how she touched so many women across the world and in Linkdom. I am so honored to be a part of sharing my friendship in writing about her so people will know.

~ From *The Links Oral History Collection*, Marcia Denise White, Editor

*Hardiman was a charter member of the Buffalo (NY) Chapter (1950).

CHAPTER 5

FREQUENCIES:
A National Force

*A June 4, 1949, date was set, and via formal invitations,
every chapter was invited to come to Philadelphia for a confab
that would pave the way for a transformation of the first order.*

With 14 clubs populated by 161 charter members in 10 states, the Philadelphia Links concluded that the groups should be linked through a formal structure. A June 4, 1949, date was set, and via formal invitations, every chapter was summoned to Philadelphia for a confab that would pave the way for a transformation of the first order. The move had been anticipated. Seven of the nine Philadelphia Club members were also members of Jack and Jill of America. Three years earlier on June 1, 1946, they had witnessed Jack and Jill form a national body.

For the Philadelphia Links, the move toward nationalization was also deliberate. As the number of clubs increased, the women realized that aside from enabling clubs to colonize, it had little control or authority over member selection, governance, or programming. In order to protect the destiny of Margaret Hawkins's ideal of spreading friendship and service through interconnected groups, a framework for systems, structures, operations, and programs was essential. It was time to pull the 14 loosely scattered clubs into a cohesive unit.

All 13 clubs accepted the invitation to be a part of the organizational meeting. Each club was limited to a single delegate, but any Link could register. As a result, 53 women participated in the first convention. Delegations ranged from one representative for five

A 2016 display by the Greater New York (NY) Chapter commemorates the 70th anniversary of The Links' founding.

Charter members, Indianapolis (IN) Chapter, 1951

clubs to a high of 14 for the host Philadelphia Club, which named Frances Atkinson as its vice president. Philadelphia Links Co-Founder and President Sarah Strickland Scott, who had succeeded Margaret Hawkins, Co-Founder and founding president, was serving as temporary chair.

The first order of business was to nationalize the group, and the vote was unanimous. The new structure also required a governance board, and the group subsequently elected Scott as the first National President. Three other Philadelphia Links were also chosen to serve on the first Executive Council. Myrtle Manigault, Lillian Stanford, and Katie Greene were named corresponding secretary, historian, and chair of the Handbook Committee, respectively.

The remaining seats went to eight other clubs, with Letitia Rose of Dayton, Ohio, taking the nod as vice president. Honors for recording secretary, treasurer, parliamentarian, and Area coordinator went to Beatrice Butler, Baltimore, Maryland; Dorothy Reed, Greater New York; Julia Delany, Raleigh, North Carolina; and Blanche Sinkler, St. Louis, Missouri. Public Relations chair Jessie M. Vann and Membership chair Lillian Brown were both from the Pittsburgh, Pennsylvania

Club; and Publications and Journalism chair Claudine Lewis hailed from Central New Jersey.

Delegates also voted to retain elements that defined the Philadelphia Club and entreated them to emulate it. The name "Links" was even more reflective of the new organization, a union of 14 clubs, but they added "National" to distinguish it from local groups that had formed. They were also true to the mission enumerated in the Philadelphia Club's constitution, with one exception: "civic" replaced "charitable" in the purpose statement. The National Links also retained the founding group's pledge, song, and bracelet and pledged to operate under the constitution during the first year (as the national document was developed).

Prior to the January 4, 1949, confab, The Philadelphia Links had duly registered the name Links in the Commonwealth of Pennsylvania, but registration equated to a listing in the official directory of nonprofits in Pennsylvania. Registration was not a form of corporation; nor did it offer protection for organizational or member assets. Whether incorporation was necessary surfaced following the consummation of the Philadelphia Club in 1947, but it became thornier once the group nationalized in 1949.

OFFICE OF RECORDER OF DEEDS. D. C. 80**2964**

Corporation Division
Sixth and D Streets, N. W.
Washington, D. C. 20001

CERTIFICATE

THIS IS TO CERTIFY that all provisions of the District of Columbia

Non-profit Corporation Act have been complied with and ACCORD-

INGLY this Certificate of ___Incorporation___

_____

is hereby issued to the ___LINKS, INC.___

_____

as of the date hereinafter mentioned.

Date May 14, 1980

Recorder of Deeds. D.C.
MARGUERITE C. STOKES
Acting Recorder Of Deeds, D.C.

John M. Duty
Assistant Superintendent of Corporations

Government of the District of Columbia
Form RD-C 55
Oct. 1962

DC Charter, 1980

State of New Jersey

Department of State.

I, the Secretary of State of the State
of New Jersey Do hereby Certify that the foregoing is a true
copy of the Certificate of ___Incorporation,___

of ___THE LINKS,___

_____

_____ and the endorsements thereon,
as the same is taken from and compared with the original filed
in my office on the ___Twenty-ninth___ day of ___March,___ A D
1951 and now remaining on file and of record therein.

In Testimony Whereof, I have hereunto
set my hand and affixed my Official
Seal at Trenton, this ___Twenty-ninth___
day of ___March,___ A.D. 19_51._

Secretary of State.

NJ Charter, 1951

National President Sarah Strickland Scott placed the discussion on the January 20, 1951, agenda of the Executive Council. Based on legal advice from Adler and Mezey of New Brunswick, New Jersey, corporate status would "provide better legal status, thereby eliminating any questions of personal responsibility of its members," the opinion read. The Executive Council heeded the opinion, and Scott began the process by naming an Incorporation Committee, chaired by Christine Moore Howell of the Central New Jersey Chapter.

In less than two months (March 28, 1951), incorporation status was granted; however, not by the Commonwealth of Pennsylvania, but by the State of New Jersey, which the group deemed the best fit for satisfying residency requirements, as well as other conditions. Two of the chapters were housed in New Jersey; Philadelphia charter member Myrtle Manigault and Chairman Howell were also New Jersey residents, and New Brunswick, the granting office, was a short drive from Philadelphia.

The nine trustees of the corporation included Scott and Co-Founder Margaret Hawkins, along with Letitia Rose (Dayton, Ohio), Manigault (Camden, New Jersey), Bernice Butler (Baltimore, Maryland), Ethel Lowry, Dorothy Reed (Long Island, New York), Claudine Lewis (New Brunswick, New Jersey), and Julia Delany (Raleigh, North Carolina).

The signatories were Scott, Howell, Broadus, and three other members of the Central New Jersey Chapter: Lillian H. Alexander, Sadie P. Dickerson, and Claudine Lewis. With glee, Scott proudly reported the action to the 3rd National Links Convention on June 23, 1951. "We have become an incorporated body with charters for each chapter. This was due to the fine work of Christine Howell and her committee," Scott said.

In 1980, The Links received notification that the organization was no longer in compliance with corporation requirements for the state of New Jersey. National President Julia Brogdon Purnell brought the matter to members' attention in the May 1980 *Link to Link*, informing the membership that the National Links' corporate status in New Jersey had expired. The state required each corporate entity to have a New

Jersey resident on its Executive Council or to engage a Registered Agent. The Links had met neither criterion over the past years.

Purnell further informed members that The Links, headquartered in the District of Columbia, had also failed to file as a foreign corporation, a mandatory requirement for organizations doing business in the District, though incorporated in another state. On the basis of advice from Hogan and Hartson, "a highly reputable Washington, DC, law firm," Purnell outlined three options the Executive Council had considered: Take steps to become compliant in New Jersey only, satisfy requirements in New Jersey and the District, or incorporate in the District only.

Based on the Executive Council's vote to incorporate in the District, The Links filed the required documents, and on May 14, 1980, the District issued a certificate, which read, in part: "This is to certify that all provisions of the District of Columbia Nonprofit Corporation Act have been complied with and ACCORDINGLY this Certificate of Incorporation is hereby issued to The Links, Inc."

Over the years, incorporation was one of many steps The Links took to strengthen and protect the organization and its mission. Under the National Links banner, as things changed, they remained the same: The exponential increase in frequencies created by a National force also came with a broader ban for service; yet, the mission is still powered by the original ideal—linking friends for service.

~ *Earnestine Green McNealey, PhD*

THE FIRST 14 CLUBS

Clubs	Charter Members	Organizers/Officiants
1946 #1 Philadelphia, PA November 9	9 Margaret Rosell Hawkins (president), Sarah Strickland Scott, Frances Vashon Atkinson, Katie Murphy Greene, Myrtle Manigault (Stratton), Marian Elizabeth Roland Minton, Lillian C. Stanford, Lillian Hudson Wall, Dorothy Bell Wright.	Margaret Rosell Hawkins Sarah Strickland Scott
1948 #2 Atlantic City, NJ February 28	11 Leonora S. Garland (president), Carrie Esters, Emily Fowler, Anna Freeman, Josephine Hayes, Helen C. Hoxter, Edythe P. Marshall, Louise F. Martin, Viola Murray, Isabelle Scott, Myrtle Usry.	Edythe P. Marshall Myrtle Usury *Officiant:* Myrtle Manigault Stratton
#3 Wilmington, DE April 10	12 Alice Brown (president), Beulah Anderson, Edith Barton, Grace Goens, K. Lorraine Hamilton, Ann Harris, Marjorie Hopkins, Marjorie Jackson, Sarajane Hunt, Rozelia O'Neal, Elizabeth Parker, Sara Taylor.	Alice Brown
#4 St. Louis, MO April 15	8 Blanche Vashon Sinkler (president), Joy Blanche, Orlie Carpenter, Mary Evans, Charlotte Ford, Alice Harding, Anna Lee Scott, Melba Sweets.	Blanche Vashon Sinkler *Officiant:* Frances Vashon Atkinson
#5 Washington, DC April 17	6 Bernice Thomas (president), Ruth Young, Vasti Cook, Kaye Harris, Anne Cooke-Reid, Eula Trigg.	Bernice Thomas Ruth Young *Officiant:* Philadelphia Chapter
#6 Wilson-Rocky Mount-Tarboro, NC April 18	13 Nan Delany Hines Johnson (president), Ann Armstrong, Marguerite Armstrong, Sallie Armstrong, Grace Artis, Addie Butterfield, Norma Darden, Vera Shade Green, Vera Esmeralda Hawkins, Ethel Hines, Jessie Pash, Helen Quigless, Jennie Taylor.	Julia Delany *Officiant:* Doris Reynolds

Clubs	Charter Members	Organizers/Officiants
#7 Petersburg, VA May 7	14 Eunice Brown-Robbins, Cleopatra Armstrong, Ruth Baker, Gladys Bland, Alma Brown, Marietta Cephas, Gladys Green, Evelyn Jenkins, Josephine Jones, Uarda Parnell, Susie Verdell, Adelaide White, Helen Williams, Virginia Williams.	Eunice Brown-Robbins *Officiant:* Doris Reynolds
# 8 Baltimore, MD September 24	12 Audrey Butler Norris (president), Catherine Adams, Mae Adams, Lillian Berry, Helen Burwell, Beatrice Butler, Florence Gloster, Marie Bourne Hicks, Pauline Watts, Xavieria McDonald, Pearl Pennington, Etta Phifer, Theresa Weaver.	Audrey Butler Norris Etta Phifer Theresa Weaver *Officiants:* Margaret Rosell Hawkins Sarah Strickland Scott
#9 Pittsburgh, PA December 5	15 Jessie M. Vann (president), Jewel Blow, Lillian Brown, Betty Butler, Wilhelmina Butler, Lucille Cuthbert, Kathleen Douglas, Gertrude Holmes, Daisy Lampkin, Harriet Lewis, Rachael Lewis, Corinne Lindsay, Winifred Moss, Carolyn Stevenson, Esther Summers.	Daisy Lampkin Jessie Vann *Officiants:* Margaret Rosell Hawkins Sarah Strickland Scott
1949 # 10 Raleigh, NC April 18	14 Julia Delany (president), Blanche Daniel, Ruby Fisher, Amelia Hamlin, Ernestine Hamlin, Gertrude Harris, Nannie Imboden, Willie Kay, Mamie McCauley, Louise McClennan, Louise Perrin, Mildred Taylor, Geraldine Trigg, Marguerite White.	Julia B. Delany
#11 Greater New York Harlem, NY May 12	8 Dorothy Reed (president), Bernie Austin, Myrtle Howard, Estelle Jarratt, Ethel Lowery, Emilie Pickens, Mable Trent, Marie Vidal.	*Officiant:* Sarah Strickland Scott

Clubs	Charter Members	Organizers/Officiants
#12 Central New Jersey Princeton, NJ May 28	7 Madeline Broaddus (president), Sadie Dickerson, Louise Granger, Christine Moore Howell, Claudine Lewis, Eddye Maye Shivery, Augusta Smith.	Madeline Broadus *Officiants:* Sarah Strickland Scott, Katie Greene, Lillian Stanford, Lillian Wall, Marion Minton, Frances Atkinson, Courtney Duckrey
#13 Dayton, OH May 28	14 Letitia D. Rose, Lillian Taylor, Melissa Bess, Beatrice Darnell, Viola Finley, Remitha Ford, Bessie Jones, Ruth Lewis, Cora Peters, Hortense Poindexter, Margaret Robinson, Ruth Smith, Lucy Taylor, Louise Wesley.	Letitia D. Rose *Officiant:* Katie Greene
#14 North Jersey, NJ June 1	15 Lillian Alexander, Fannie Holland Curtis, Mamie Jean Darden, Elizabeth Ghee, Marjorie Granger, Marguerite Gross, Bessie Hill, Bessie Marsh, Alvan Martin, Ella McLean, Gertrude Norris, Bertha Randolph, Galdys Shirley, Virginia Savoy, Mildred Morris Williams.	Fanny Holland Curtis *Officiant:* Katie Greene

Data compiled from National files and individual chapter accounts in the Chartering Date Index, The Journal.

THE FIRST CONVENTION
Key Actions

- Changed name to The National Links.
- Replaced "club" terminology with chapter.
- Retained Philadelphia Club's pledge, song, and bracelet as brands.
- Approved Philadelphia Club's constitution as governing document for first year.
- Elected Philadelphia Links president Sarah Strickland Scott as the first National President.

THE FIRST CONVENTION

Club		Delegate
Atlantic City	4	Mrs. Lenore Morgan
Baltimore	8	Mrs. W. Berkeley Butler
Central New Jersey	4	Mrs. Claudine Lewis
Dayton	2	Mrs. Letitia Rose
New York	3	Mrs. Dorothy Reed
North Jersey	1	Mrs. Fannie Curtis
Petersburg	1	Mrs. Eunice Robbins
Philadelphia	14	Mrs. Frances Atkinson
Pittsburgh	2	Mrs. Lillian Brown
Raleigh	1	Mrs. Julia Delany
St. Louis	1	Mrs. Blanche Sinkler
Washington	3	Mrs. Bernice Thomas
Wilmington	8	Mrs. Alice Brown
Wilson & Rocky Mount	1	Mrs. Nan Hines
Total # of Links	53	

Compiled from The Links Business Conference Proceedings, June 4, 1949.

THE FIRST OFFICERS

President	Sarah S. Scott, Philadelphia
Vice President	Letitia Rose, Dayton
Recording Secretary	Beatrice Butler, Baltimore
Corresponding Secretary	Myrtle Manigault, Philadelphia
Treasurer	Dorothy Reed, New York
Parliamentarian	Julia Delany, Raleigh
Historian	Lillian Stanford, Philadelphia
Area Coordinator	Blanche Sinkler, St. Louis
Public Relations Chair	Jessie M. Vann, Pittsburgh
Membership Chair	Lillian Brown, Pittsburgh
Chair, Publications & Journalism	Claudine Lewis, Princeton
Handbook Chair	Katie M. Greene, Philadelphia

CHAPTER 6
TURBO CHARGES:
Expansion

*The Links will continue to study and explore potential sites for new chapters in
towns and cities where substantial populations exist which could support an active
Links program, provide services to a primarily localized community, and offer the
opportunity of its programs and services to the people of these potential communities.*

~ ANNA JOHNSON JULIAN, FIRST CHAIR, CHAPTER ESTABLISHMENT

At its 1950 convention, the one-year-old National Links voted to turbo charge the organization through expansion. More chapters and members not only would increase the strength and vitality of the 14, but they would also power remarkable outputs. Providing a fanfare for the common woman, however, was never the intent. A closed society was a characteristic of the founding group in 1946; and the constitution—crafted by the nine women in 1947 and adopted as a model by the national body in 1949— required both a cap on the number of members and a unanimous vote for future admits. Such chartered a course strewn with exclusion in precept and practice.

Cognizant that expansion and growth were essential to move the organization forward, however, The Links, over the years, dropped zip codes as gatekeepers, raised the membership cap, replaced unanimous with a two-thirds affirmative vote, adopted provisions for reinstatement, and removed other barriers to build a diverse group of "women … who have identifiable abilities and interests in educational, civic, and intercultural activities."

How rapidly the 14 original chapters should expand was a thorny issue from the outset, and the subject became pricklier as the links in the chain grew.

The major artery for growth was chapters, and the quandary centered not only on the number conducive to the organization's mission, but also on how and where to colonize. On January 20, 1951, 1st National President Sarah Strickland Scott admonished her Executive Council to end the "hit and miss establishment of chapters" that had made certain states and sections of the country "top heavy, while … there was not sufficient representation or none at all, where there is a large Negro population and fine Links material."

Scott's remarks came in response to Membership Chair Lillian Brown's report that placed at 11 the number of chapters added since April 8, 1950. Rather than the number, which increased the number of Links chapters to 29, Scott was dismayed that the breadth of Linkdom had not kept pace; only three new states—Illinois, California, and Nebraska—were in the mix.

Awaiting installation, however, were groups in four additional states: Texas, Massachusetts, West Virginia, and Indiana; and combined with applications that had been approved from Georgia, South Carolina, and Michigan, the Links map became more acceptable to Scott by the June 23, 1951, Convention. "We have now 42 chapters, instead of our original 14.

CONSTITUTIONAL AND BYLAW PROVISIONS

	Then (1949–1950)	Now (2019)
Name	National Links	The Links, Incorporated
Purpose	To bring together outstanding women in various sections of our country for a three-fold purpose, namely civic, intercultural, and social.	To promote and engage in educational, civic, and intercultural activities in order to enrich the lives of members and the larger community; and to work together towards achieving common goals.
Members	All members shall be active and conscientious about club duties.	Members shall be women, duly inducted into any Chapter, and women elected to honorary status, who have identifiable abilities and interests in educational, civic, and intercultural activities.
Member Requirements	Residency within 25-mile radius, attendance at chapter meetings, commitment to service, financial obligations.	Members shall reside within the locality the Chapter is established to serve; meet minimum attendance requirements for Chapter, Area, and Assembly meetings; meet minimum 48-hour service requirement; and participate in Chapter activities and programs designed to implement the National programs of The Links, Incorporated.
Membership Cap	14	60 non-DOL members.
Meetings Required	10	8
Financial Requirements	Chapter dues, assessments, joining fees, chapter tax.	All Chapter and National financial obligations.
New Member Threshold	Membership by nomination and unanimous vote.	Membership by nomination and two-thirds ($^2/_3$) affirmative vote of the active Chapter members who are present and voting. For DOLs: majority vote.
Areas	1	4
National Officers	President, Vice President, Recording Secretary, Corresponding Secretary, Treasurer, Historian, Parliamentarian.	President, Vice President, Secretary, Treasurer, Recording Secretary, and Parliamentarian (non-voting).
Philanthropic Arm	Aid incorporated in budget	The Links Foundation
National Meeting Terminology	Convention	Assembly
National Meeting Frequency	Annually the first weekend after the 17th of June	Annually. In even-numbered years, the National Assembly shall constitute the Annual Meeting. In odd-numbered years, the meeting of the Executive Council shall constitute the Annual Meeting.
Requirement for Amendments	Two-thirds ($^2/_3$) in the affirmative	*Constitution:* Three-quarters ($^3/_4$) affirmative vote of the voting delegates at the National Assembly. *Bylaws:* Two-thirds ($^2/_3$) affirmative vote of the voting delegates at the National Assembly.

Source: Constitution and Bylaws 2018–2020 and Assembly Minutes

We are exactly three times as large, and Lillian Brown and her committee have done an excellent job in bringing us so many fine women from various parts of the country," Scott reported.

Commenting on the 1951 and 1952 growth spurts, the *Pittsburgh Courier* called The Links "the fastest growing, most interesting group of Black women in the country."

Membership had also grown to 700. Combined with the nine states and the territories represented, the Links chain extended across 19 states and the District of Columbia. More progress followed in the 1950s, with inroads in nine other states: Florida, Kentucky, Arizona, Tennessee, Colorado, Iowa, Oklahoma, Mississippi, and Kansas, bringing the total number of states and territories to 29. The 42 chapters had also multiplied. By 1959, a decade after nationalization, The Links had colonies in more than half of the country, growing from 161 members in 14 chapters to more than 1,800 in 84 chapters.

But not everyone was pleased by the proliferation of chapters and the parallel growth in membership. Existing chapters complained about charter members falling short of Links quality, boundaries being crossed, and fundraising sources being compromised. Contending that the organization was amassing too many chapters, growing too rapidly, and simply getting too large, members appealed for more stringent guidelines.

The 12th (1960) Assembly responded by mandating chapter reviews by the Area director of the proposed locale, granting review power to existing chapters within a 25-mile radius, and requiring a three-fourths affirmative vote of the Assembly for approval; additionally, a two-year moratorium was imposed. The process was a sharp contrast from the

President Edmonds appointed the first Chapter Establishment officer

laissez-faire atmosphere charm of earlier years. Coupled with a defiance by some chapters to forgo initiations, the revised practice resulted in a precipitous drop in membership. Seventy chapters had been chartered in the 1950s, but the yield for the 1960s was 30, less than one-half. There was a parallel drop in the number of initiates; in 1962, membership registered 700, but hovered under 2,500 for the next decade, registering less than a 50 percent increase when the 18th (1972) Assembly convened.

Links officials declared the system was off course, and 5th National President Helen Gray Edmonds pleaded for an overhaul as she addressed the 18th (1972) Assembly. "I would like to think that my tenure democratized the organization a little," but, she lamented, "We had chapters that had 12 members in the 1950s, 12 members in the 1960s and 12 in the 1970s. The old directory will show that often all of them came from the same streets, boulevards, or lanes in their cities."

Social exclusion as a factor was further illuminated in newspaper articles. *The Oregonian* concluded the elitism was natural: "Women without careers of their own, married to doctors, lawyers, judges … like most upper-class groups, tend to be exclusive." Some chapters justified being under the limit as remaining true to the purpose of Linkdom. "We only want to take in just those who work" was a common ruse.

Another manifestation of the snobbery was the "Links quality" shield. Casting aspersions on its authenticity, Edmonds retorted: "I look across this Nation and see large cities with populations of over 100,000 and further note that there is no Links chapter there. I am forced to say, 'I cannot believe that in 100,000 women, we cannot find twenty women of

Links quality. But as long as we have to establish chapters under the restrictive circumstances that now engulf us, we shall be continuously hamstrung in our projection of this organization.'"

Another key barrier was obstruction. Existing chapters tied sponsorship to being able to choose members for the new group. Edmonds's plea to the 18th (1972) Assembly was for a new approach, and delegates "accepted a mechanism, termed the Chapter Establishment program, which was largely responsible for sharing the membership of Links with more than 500 new Links," she noted. At the heart of the system was a Chapter Establishment Committee that would receive and screen applications for chapters, and subsequently submit those approved to the president for referral to the Executive Council.

Cognizant that chapter establishment and membership were interrelated, The Links conducted a demographics survey, which targeted the 50 cities with the largest Negro populations, as well as cities with Negro populations that could support more than one chapter. Edmonds named former National Vice President (1964–1968) Anna Johnson Julian as chair. Characterizing resistance to chapter establishment as "a fear of loss of identity and of confusion as well as competition," Julian accentuated the positives.

New chapters "can be a source of strength," she proposed. "In unity there is strength should be the goal of the Links ... growth can be achieved harmoniously, or indeed it must, if the organization is to survive," Julian said. Her sentiments were echoed by Co-Founder Sarah Strickland Scott, who declared, "If Linkdom is to march steadily forward in its service to humanity, we must multiply the avenues for service."

In her report to the 19th (1974) Assembly, Julian outlined the progress of the Chapter Establishment Committee and allayed concerns about the new policy. Sixteen chapters had been established—eight under the old provision and eight with the new process, wherein the Chapter Establishment Committee received and screened applications, and subsequently submitted those recommended to the president for referral to the Executive Council.

Addressing one of the problems with the old process, Julian noted, "The chairman is cognizant of the fact that there are some among us who feel that they should have the right to designate those persons comprising new chapters," and she emphasized that the Chapter Establishment Committee had taken a hands-off approach. The policy of the Chapter Establishment Committee had been to let the new group, itself, choose its constituents since the chapter had to assume responsibility for working harmoniously with the potential members, Julian emphasized. Even in those few instances where suggestions of persons interested had been requested, the final decision had been left to the group, she noted.

"Whether the quality of membership would be maintained under a more liberalized constitutional procedure of organizing new chapters by the Chapter Establishment Committee" had been a continuing query, she affirmed, but she quickly dismissed the misconception with the results of a study of the 130 members of the eight chapters established under the committee. "Ninety percent of the members comprising these eight chapters are holders of the bachelor's degree, 47 percent or 60 of these have attained the master's degree, and seven or 5.4 percent have earned the doctor's degree," Julian noted.

Julian, first Chapter Establishment officer

Further illuminating how the Chapter Establishment Committee groups meshed with chapters processed under the regular provisions, Julian listed their professions, revealing that most were teachers, four owned and operated their own or family business, and one each was president of her own business college, a bank manager, personnel manager for a large corporation, and financial director of a college. Julian also emphasized that the selections bode well for the perpetuity of The Links, as the emphasis on taking in younger members appeared to be bearing fruit. "Almost two-thirds of the new members range in age from 31 to 50 years," she said.

Expressing concern that only 95 members had been added from the 134 chapters in 1975, National Vice President and Membership Chair Vera A. Codwell warned, "I sadly predict a slow demise for Linkdom unless we become serious concerning membership growth." But the forecast was never tested. New chapter growth increased in the second half of the seventies. Eleven chapters were established in 1976 and 13 in 1979.

The Links also became more strategic, targeting nationalization and balance. Chapter growth was geared toward building a strong organization across the spectrum, rather than amassing a large, powerful group, sectionalized in some parts of the country. The 20th (1976) Assembly limited chapter establishment to the Western Area to enable it "to catch up." Despite efforts to colonize Salt Lake City, Utah, Wichita Falls, Kansas, Albuquerque, New Mexico, and other targeted locales, only four Western chapters had been established by the 1978 Assembly.

However, the effort pinpointed the necessity for population studies to determine whether "enough women who can afford the Links experience can be found and … risks that professional men perceive they take when their wives join an elitist group like the Links," Julian noted. As The Links continued to calibrate its efficiency model, other measures were instituted: individual members or chapters could no longer sponsor chapters, and another chapter could be established when a chapter in a large metropolitan area had reached the maximum membership of 30.

With the institution of the Chapter Establishment Committee and subsequent policies that opened more territories, there was a surge in chapter growth and membership. In 1982, 10 years after the Chapter Establishment Committee was instituted, membership numbered 5,482.

A decade later, 10th National President Marion Schultz Sutherland conceded that there were still problems, but she told the 28th (1992) Assembly, "Well, I think we have made progress." Acknowledging that chapter establishment had been "a very tender process as long as I can remember," Sutherland attributed the discomfort to territorial, membership, and fundraising concerns. Yet, she cautiously proclaimed, "We think we've got most of the bugs out of the thorny process."

The fine-tuning included defining commuting distance and setting boundaries for all chapters. The Links also lifted a required ratio of inductees to transferees. "Chapter establishment was under control," she concluded, but "vigilance and respect" were required to keep it in check. She encouraged chapters, "Exercise your right to vote, but also defer to the judgment of the Executive Council."

By 1998, The Links had 10,000 members. While the diligence for expansion continued, equal attention was devoted to ensuring that the growth was conducive to the mission and the members. Chapters with fewer than 10 members were banned from attending the National Assembly. The Executive Council placed a three-year moratorium (January 1, 1999–December 31, 2001) on groups interested in membership to address concerns about multiple chapters, and newly established chapters were forced to operate for two years before inducting members. Further, Chapter Establishment Officer JoAnn Brown reminded chapters, "strict rules also govern transfers."

The philosophy of enabling growth while simultaneously protecting the integrity of membership continued to guide expansion. Both the 32nd (2000) and 35th (2006) Assemblies enacted measures to protect the value of membership, mandating a "one in five" attendance policy to ensure that members understood the workings of the organization and a 48-hour service requirement to validate their commitment to

SNAPSHOTS OF MEMBERSHIP 1949–2019

Year	Membership	States/Territories
1949	161	7
2019	15,870	42

Source: National Headquarters, Assembly Minutes

CHAPTER STRENGTH BY AREA, DECADE BY DECADE

	Eastern	Central	Southern	Western	National
1950	16	8	3	3	30
1960	26	23	23	15	87
1970	32	30	31	22	115
1980	49	45	40	35	169
1990	68	63	63	48	242
2000	72	69	68	50	259
2010	72	72	76	54	274
2018	78	70	80	60	288
2019	78	71	80	60	289

NEW MEMBERS 2014–2018

	Total Membership Intake	New Members 40 and under	Percentage of Inductions
2014	740	246	33
2015	894	226	25
2016	806	234	29
2017	747	206	27.58
2018	867	238	27.45
Total	4,054	1,150	28.36

Data extracted from the National Membership Committee Report to the 41st (2018) Assembly

service. A Code of Ethics further sensitized members to the responsibilities inherent in being a Link.

Likewise, initiatives to propel tactical growth were instituted. Recommendations from the Strategic Planning Committee at the 35th (2006) Assembly resulted in increases in the overall membership cap of 12,000 to 15,000 and the Area chapter cap of 75 to 80 chapters. The provisions also enabled members with dual residencies to complete their service hours in two chapters. The 36th (2008) Assembly further addressed retention by waiving the service requirement for Links deployed to a high-risk or military zone and reducing the fee for reinstatements by 25 percent.

Helping small chapters to avoid falling below the "30" minimum member requirement was another avenue opened by The Links. As a result, the number of chapters with memberships below 30 was reduced by 61 percent in 2014. While two charters were pulled for the infraction after 2014, only 36 chapters had fewer than 26 members.

A continuing concern was the low percentage of younger members. Bringing "new birth" to the organization by targeting members between the ages of 21 and 40 was one of the reasons behind the establishment of the Scott-Hawkins Leadership Institute (SHLI) in 2004, said SHLI creator 13th National President Gladys Gary Vaughn. "I noticed that the young members of the organization were coming in, and after a very short time they were leaving; and that troubled me," she said.

Vaughn's intent was to immerse younger Links in the history of the roles Black women's organizations had played in maintaining the Black community and the nation, thereby awakening their passion and commitment to the work that The Links were doing. Embracing a "Membership Is our Priority" resolve, The Links also instituted a Chapter Development Committee to help chapters "create an environment of fairness and consistency, while respecting, supporting, and honoring one another."

The Links also encouraged chapters to reach out to potential candidates under 40. "We talked about bringing in our daughters, our nieces, and our granddaughters, and we made a real push to say they belonged; you don't have to be 55," said 16th National President Glenda Newell-Harris, vice president and chair of Membership when the renewed effort began during the administration of 15th National President Margot James Copland.

Targets included increasing membership in the under-40 demographic by 2 percent in Program Year 2015, by 3 percent in Program Year 2016, and by 4 percent in Program Year 2017. Sharing the results with the 41st (2018) Assembly, Vice President and Membership Chair (2014–2018) Kimberly Jeffries Leonard noted that the individual percentage goals had not been met, but progress had been made on the overall goal of increasing the induction of members under 40. Of the 4,054 members inducted from 2014 to 2018, the percentage of inductees under 40 was 28 percent.

Along with a more diverse membership, growth initiatives through the years have resulted in an optimal membership and a more proportionate distribution of chapters and members. For the year ending April 30, 2019, membership was 15,870 members. There were 289 chapters, with 78 in Eastern, 80 in Southern, 71 in Central, and 60 in Western. The membership number slightly pierced the 15,000 National cap (daughters of Links are not counted in caps), and the number of chapters in the Southern Area reached the limit of 80.

Outlining the direction for chapter establishment and member selection as part of her State of the Organization address to the Southern Area, President Kimberly Jeffries Leonard told members the mapping had been done "with our eyes fixed on The Links' purpose: What change is necessary to get us to where we have pledged to go?" Data-driven modifications in size, reach, and process were all deliberate actions that helped The Links "to build a membership base that values diversity, embraces member talents, and develops leaders," and Leonard promised that The Links would continue to institute strategic measures that ensured deployment of a force that was proficient in perpetually turbo powering The Links' twin engines—friendship and service.

~ Earnestine Green McNealey, PhD
~ Barbara Trotter, EdD

PART III

Power Grids

The Transformers

The National Assembly shall be the delegate body of The Links,
Incorporated with jurisdiction over all members, Chapters, and Areas.

~ CONSTITUTION, ARTICLE IV, SECTION 3

CHAPTER 7

PARAMOUNT FORCE:
The National Assembly

Voting delegates from a majority of the active Chapters and three (3) elected National Officers are necessary for the convening of the National Assembly.

~ BYLAWS, ARTICLE IV, SECTION 3

*W*hen the 14 unfettered Links clubs assembled in Philadelphia on June 4, 1949, the primary purpose was to form a National body. Following the unanimous vote to merge, the National Links agreed to be governed by doctrines and practices set out in the constitution of the Philadelphia Links, the original club, until the next meeting of the convention. The conference constituted the first business meeting, which was subsequently called the General Assembly, and eventually coined as the National Assembly.

Ten months later, on April 8, 1950, the group reconvened in Atlantic City, New Jersey. During the interim, a National constitution was developed, and delegates approved the document at the 1950 Business Conference. The governance authority set out in 1950 has remained unchanged. "The National Assembly shall be the delegate body with jurisdiction over all members, Chapters, and Areas."

The Assembly has been the paramount force in Linkdom. It is the power grid from which policy has been determined and influence has been endowed. The Assembly has had the final word on: establishing and configuring Areas; launching programs; operating a headquarters; receiving contributions, legacies, and donations; setting fees; appropriating funds; conducting elections; and more.

Governance authority is grounded in Areas and Chapters, which have the responsibility to determine when shifts are necessary, as well as the direction, emphasis, or focus required, and to act accordingly. But from time to time, National Presidents have had to ensure that the cogs were aligned and activated within the framework. "Our structure is that we have a national body, which is the core; and part of the core is four areas and all of the chapters," said 13th National President Gladys Gary Vaughn. Consequently, understanding the system and working within it, as opposed to creating a separate entity, was necessary. Policies and procedures must be "established to govern the organization in its entirety," Vaughn said. "You can't have everybody doing their own thing; that's no way to run a railroad."

The Assembly is the forum for conversation, debate, and adjudication in keeping with the decorum of The Links. In her Call to the 39th (2014) Assembly, 15th National President Margot James Copeland included a reminder of "the essential role delegates played in facilitating the proper conduct of the business of The Links." That spirit was also inherent in the Call by 14th National President Gwendolyn B. Lee, who also urged members to come to the 37th (2010) meeting with a serious agenda: "Be here … to deliberate and transact the business of this great organization," Lee told members.

National Presidents over time have heralded the unparalleled import of the Assembly and beckoned chapters to come with purpose-filled intentions. Fourth National President Vivian J. Beamon outlined the exigencies and urged engagement. "The rapidly changing issues of our times, the crises and dilemmas of the New Age, and the increased responsibility of group organizations require designed action. Let's come to our National Assembly as Link women fully dedicated to our civic duty to move ahead with strength, determination, and wisdom to the fulfillment of our commitments."

Crediting The Links' elevated discourse at the Assembly, 3rd National President Pauline Weeden (Maloney) characterized the Assembly as "the ultimate vessel that had given rise to vision in thinking, calmness in deliberation, boldness in approach, excellence in our performance, and integrity in all we do and say."

Because of the paramount nature of the National Assembly, requirements for the composition and summoning are set out in the *Bylaws*, Article IV. While the (now biennial) meeting is open to all active members—including a delegate and alternate from each chapter and elected National officers—the opening requires verification of delegates and officers. "Voting delegates from a majority of the active Chapters and three (3) elected National Officers are necessary for the convening of the National Assembly." Attendance by individual members, once voluntary, became a requirement at the 32nd (2000) Assembly, which imposed a one-in-five rule.

Margaret Hawkins (with flowers) arriving in Denver (CO) for the 8th (1956) National Assembly

Top: Official photo, 7th (1955) National Assembly, Columbus (OH)

The Executive Council executes the business of The Links when the Assembly is not in session. For pressing matters, an Executive Committee of the Executive Council meets at the call of the National President. The first Executive Board was comprised of the elected and appointed officers and committee chairs—president, vice president, recording secretary, corresponding secretary, Area coordinator, treasurer, historian, and parliamentarian, along with committee chairmen: Public Relations, Membership, Publications and Journalism, and Handbook.

As the number of chapters and members grew, corollaries in programming and operations necessitated modifications in the administrative body and the eventual creation of an Executive Committee. Through the years, the number of officers had decreased, but the overall size of the Executive Council had multiplied exponentially based on membership, community engagement, and operations. The flexible and unwieldy nature of the Executive Council was a byproduct of program and committee assignments by the National President.

The composition of the Executive Council, outlined in the 2018–2020 *Bylaws*, includes all Nationally elected officers, the parliamentarian, the immediate past president, the four Area directors, the five program directors, director of The Links Foundation, and an unspecified number of designated and selected committee chairs. By contrast, the composition of the Executive Committee is fixed.

RIGHT: National President Kimberly Jeffries Leonard (center), with National officers: (right) Ethel Isaacs Williams, vice president; (left) Crystal L. Kendrick, secretary; (far left) Ethelyn S. Bowers, treasurer; and (far right) Tyna D. Davis, parliamentarian.

BELOW: National President Kimberly Jeffries Leonard (fifth from the left) and members of the 2018–2020 Executive Council at November 2018 meeting.

As structured for more than a decade, the Executive Committee was composed of elected National officers and the parliamentarian. Despite the key roles they played in the governance structure as the liaison between the Areas and National, Area directors were excluded. They were not part of the Executive Committee, which met "at the call of the National President to transact business." Realizing the need to have Area directors included in all decision making, the 35th (2006) Assembly approved the addition of Area directors to the Executive Committee, returning a representative voice for Areas and chapters.

Day of Service at the 41st (2018) Assembly, Indianapolis (IN)

The Assembly met annually through 1960, but a vote by the 12th Assembly changed the frequency to biennial confabs. The key channel for defining, refining, and revising policies has been constitutional changes that addressed one or more times all elements of The Links, Incorporated—purpose, members, organization, officers, meetings, attendance, brands, and revisions, themselves, that included the following actions.

- Enabled Nationally sponsored Assemblies.
- Raised the floor and cap for chapters.
- Vested authority and responsibility for establishing chapters with National.
- Enumerated requirements and limited tenure for officers.
- Expanded program foci.
- Upgraded requirements for active membership.
- Established a philanthropic arm with corollary funding in membership fees.

Some changes received little reaction, while the reach of others precipitated counter amendments at subsequent Assemblies. Elevating committees from ad hoc to standing over the years barely drew a yawn, but passage of a 48-hour service requirement by the 35th (2006) Assembly revved reaction to the degree that delegates at subsequent meetings proposed amendments to eliminate the requirement. The propensity for modifications forced curtailments. The 17th (1970) Assembly suspended submissions, pending a four-year

comprehensive review, and the 29th (1994) Assembly also imposed a four-year moratorium.

National Assemblies have also engendered and provided showcases for new programs, processes, operational systems, awards, fund development, and financial security.

- The 2nd (1950) – Approved fees of $25 (national tax), $2 (per capita), and $8 (joining).
- The 4th (1952) – Approved the institution of National projects, naming the NAACP as the first beneficiary.
- The 6th (1954) – Decentralized The Links into four Areas.
- The 10th (1958) – Approved Links' first facet—Services to Youth—and implemented "The Search for the Talented Youth."
- The 12th (1960) – Changed meeting frequency for the National Assembly from annual to biennial, beginning in 1962.
- The 14th (1972) – Established memorials, setting up a trust fund in honor of Co-Founder Margaret Hawkins.
- The 23rd (1982) – Approved the purchase of a headquarters with all deliberate speed.
- The 25th (1986) – Changed two-thirds affirmative vote for induction to majority for daughters of Links (DOL).

Formal wear, 5th (1953) Assembly, Buffalo (NY)

Mass gathering, 25th (1986) Assembly, Nashville (TN)

- The 28th (1992) – Limited induction of honorary members to one per Assembly, with four-year intervals.
- The 30th (1996) – Culminated first major fundraiser for The Links Foundation with $770,000 cache.
- The 36th (2008) – Endorsed funding package for the expansion and renovation of the National Headquarters.
- The 37th (2010) – Approved Health and Human Services as the fifth facet.

Assemblies also provided opportunities for members to view, review, and evaluate the services they had delivered on the Chapter, Area, and National levels. Chapter exhibits, model demonstrations, advocacy for hot button issues, and scrapbooks have all taken center stage. Another feature has been exemplary chapter program awards, which received an extra spark with the addition of monetary grants of $1,000 to $5,000 for excellence in programming at the 37th (2012) Assembly.

While business was at the forefront, Assemblies also fostered bonding. Communal experiences engendered new friendships, renewed relationships, and deepened the commitment to Linkdom. From the opening Friendship Ceremony to the closing White Rose Banquet, the rites have not only increased members' pride, but they have also reminded each Link of the power and impact of the circle, thereby strengthening the resolve to perpetuate Linkdom.

Meeting sites, by policy, have rotated from Area to Area. Attendance has ranged from the 53 members and guests who attended the first Assembly in 1949

to the 3,214 members, Connecting Links, Heir-O-Links, and guests in attendance at the 60th anniversary celebration in Philadelphia in 2006. The record number of Links registrants was 2,882, at the 39th (2014) Assembly in National Harbor, Maryland, as compared to the 2,815 Links at the 35th (2006).

The thousand mark was first topped at the 21st (1978) Assembly with 1,005. The highest attendance for an Assembly in the Western Area, the smallest and most remote Area, was recorded at the 40th (2018) in Las Vegas, with a 2,946 total and 1,672 Links; but the 36th (2008) in Seattle, Washington, took honors for the highest number of Links attendees at a conference in the Western Area, with a 2,729 total, and 1,769 Links.

Registration fees increased over the years. The rate at the third Assembly was $2 for delegates, excluding hostess chapter members who paid $1. While the fee is contingent on the location, the rates for the last five meetings have topped $500.

The National Assembly has remained the center for actions that guide The Links, Incorporated. Between sessions, the Executive Council and the Executive Committee have served as entrusted levers for decisions, but the ground controls for continual planning, assessment, and reshaping have been steered by Areas, chapters, and members. Through this organizational structure, The Links has amended policies, fortified its membership, revolutionized programming, and strengthened its operational framework as a means of continually honoring its mission of friendship and service.

~ *Earnestine Green McNealey, PhD*

LINKS ASSEMBLIES ATTENDANCE MARKS			
Year	Location	Attendance	Distinction
1949	Philadelphia, Pennsylvania	61	The first and smallest.
1964	Nassau, Bahamas	393	The first to be held outside the continental United States.
1974	Washington, DC	746	Set attendance mark for event attendance. International Affairs luncheon featuring the president of the United States and drew 2,500.
1978	Chicago, Illinois	1,005	The first to top the 1,000 mark in attendance.
2006	Philadelphia, Pennsylvania	(Total) 3,269 (# of Links) 2,815	Highest number of attendees.
2008	Seattle, Washington	(Total) 2,729 (# of Links) 1,769	Highest number of Links attendees for a conference in the Western Area.
2014	National Harbor, Maryland	(Total) 3,167 (# of Links) 2,882	Highest number of Links attendees.
2016	Las Vegas, Nevada	(Total) 2,946 (# of Links) 1,672	Highest attendance for a conference in the Western Area.

Source: Assembly Minutes

Attending the 40th (2016), held in Las Vegas

Promoting the 43rd (2020), set for New Orleans (LA), June 17–21

INSIDE THE LINKS NATIONAL ASSEMBLY

Assembly	Features	Major Actions
1st – 1949 June 4–5 Pyramid Club Atlantic City, NJ Philadelphia Club **Sarah Strickland Scott** *President, Philadelphia Club, Temporary Chair* Attendance: 53 Links, their husbands, 6 visiting spouses, and 1 child.	Organizational policy and procedures, constitution, open house at home of Doris Reynolds, Philadelphia Club, and "outing" at Rosalie Farms in Chalfont, PA. Guest: James M. Fleming, Secretary for Race Relations, American Friends Service Committee.	Merged from 14 independent clubs into a national chain of chapters. Approved operating under the Philadelphia Club constitution during the first year (as the national document was developed). Established meeting frequency as once per year for National Assembly and bi-annually for Executive Board. Elected Co-Founder and Philadelphia Club President Sarah Strickland Scott as 1st National President.
2nd – 1950 April 8–9 Indiana Ave. High School Atlantic City, NJ Atlantic City Chapter **Sarah Strickland Scott** *National President*	Business sessions, program idea swap, banquet at home of Aquilla Matthews, Atlantic City Chapter.	Approved $25 national tax, $2 per capita, and joining fee of $8. Ratified "National" constitution. Adopted song written by Sallie Armstrong, Wilson-Rocky Mount-Tarboro Chapter as The Links National song.
3rd – 1951 Jun 23–24 East Liberty YWCA Pittsburgh, PA Pittsburgh Chapter **Sarah Strickland Scott** *National President* Attendance: 150+	Business sessions, program idea swap, constitutional revisions, Saturday luncheon, and closing brunch at Oakmont Estate of Jessie Vann, Pittsburgh Chapter. *Of Note:* 300 gardenia corsages from the San Francisco Chamber of Commerce sealed the city's selection as the next site.	Approved Executive Council's recommendation for two-year terms for officers with succession option. Reelected Sarah Strickland Scott as National President and retained all other officers, save the VP; named Lottie Lee Dinkins, Central New Jersey Chapter, to succeed Letitia Rose, Dayton Chapter.

4th – 1952 July 25–27 Mark Hopkins Hotel on Nob Hill San Francisco, CA San Francisco Chapter **Sarah Strickland Scott** *National President*	Business sessions; program idea swap; collective project proposal by the chair, Daisy Lampkin, Pittsburgh Chapter; appeal for support of Area Chairmen by Lorraine Richmond, Western Area Chair, and dinner dance at Fairmont Hotel. *Of Note:* First conference at a hotel.	Approved NAACP life memberships as the first National project. Appointed Area Coordinators and approved $10 allotment for operating expenses for each.
5th – 1953 June 19–21 Pyramid Club Lafayette Hotel Buffalo, NY Niagara-Buffalo Chapter **Sarah Strickland Scott** *National President*	*Our Responsibilities in Creating* *Better Human Relationships* Meetings, panel discussion on Links' finances, Niagara Falls luncheon, musical showcase featuring Links, banquet, open house at the Statler Hotel, activities for husbands (then Missing Links).	In a realignment move, shifted Denver from the Southern Area to the Western Area. Elected Co-Founder and first president of the Philadelphia Club Margaret Rosell Hawkins as National President.
6th – 1954 Bluefield State College Bluefield, WV Southern West Virginia Chapter **Margaret Rosell Hawkins** *National President*	First collective publication highlighting chapter programs, call for projects engendering recreational and cultural facilities and job placement for youth, notice of Link marker recognizing chapters that purchased life memberships to be placed at NAACP Headquarters.	Decentralized into four Areas. Presented first grant—a $28,000 payment for life memberships—to NAACP officials Roy Wilkins, executive director, and Thurgood Marshall, special counsel to the NAACP.
7th – 1955 Jun 24–26 Columbus, OH Columbus Chapter **Margaret Rosell Hawkins** *National President*	*What Can Links Do Today for the* *Youth of Tomorrow* Chapter establishment procedures, The Link' heritage, Area alignment, and a call for projects engendering integration at the local level.	Added a fifth (geographical) Area for a one-year period to foster proportionate distribution. Designated the first week in November as National Links Week. Presented a one-year study proposal to support the NAACP Legal Defense Fund through a $100 per-member assessment.

8th – 1956 June 28–July 1 Denver, CO Denver Chapter **Margaret Rosell Hawkins** *National President*	*What Can Links Do Today* *for the Youth of Tomorrow* Symposium on theme and discussion on Area alignment. Thurgood Marshall, Esq., director-counsel, NAACP Legal Defense Fund, banquet speaker.	Approved proposal to support NAACP Legal Defense Fund through $100 per-member tax. Appointed an ad hoc committee to study Area realignment with Pauline Weeden Maloney, Lynchburg Chapter, as chair.
9th – 1957 June 27–30 Atlanta University Center Atlanta, GA Atlanta Chapter **Margaret Rosell Hawkins** *National President* *Of Note:* First Assembly in the deep South.	*Links Responsibility* *in Establishing Better* *Inter-Cultural Relations* Workshops on theme, first National Program booklet, report on Area realignment by Chair Pauline Weeden Maloney.	Elected Pauline Weeden Maloney as chair, Area Redistricting; Lynchburg Chapter, 3rd National President, placing at the helm the first member outside the Philadelphia Club.
10th – 1958 Jun 26–29 Belmont-Plaza Hotel New York Brooklyn, Greater New York, and West Chester County Chapters **Pauline Weeden Maloney, LHD** *National President*	Common programming; salute to Marian Anderson; luncheon honoring women of achievement in education, business, politics, theater, and medicine; and United Nations (UN) Day with Ralph J. Bunche, UN undersecretary as the speaker.	Endorsed a common National theme for programming—Educating for Democracy. Approved Links' first facet—Services to Youth—and implemented "The Search for the Talented Youth."

11th – 1959
July 25–28
Palmer House
Chicago, IL
Chicago Chapter

**Pauline Weeden Maloney,
LHD**
National President

Educating for Democracy

Seminars on theme, friendship, and international luncheons.

12th – 1960
June 30–July 2
Beverly Hills Hilton
Beverly Hills, CA
Los Angeles Chapter

**Pauline Weeden Maloney,
LHD**
National President

Of Note: Last Assembly on annual meeting schedule.

The Emerging Link Image

Meetings, Civic Breakfast, cotillion, and trip to Disneyland.

Dr. Paul Laurence, superintendent of schools, Willowbrook School District, Los Angeles County.

Required that applications/recommendations for new chapters be reviewed by the Area Chairman.

Changed meeting frequency for the National Assembly from annual to biennial, beginning in 1962.

13th – 1962
July 5–8
French Lick Resort
French Lick, IN
Indiana Chapter

**Pauline Weeden Maloney,
LHD**
National President

Of Note: First biennial meeting

Appropriate Directions for Links in a Challenging Era

Panel of experts addressing civil liberties, among the group US Civil Rights Commissioner Clarence Ferguson, Jr.

Of Note: First meeting held at a resort and promoted as a family vacation.

Introduced National Trends and Services to the National Program.

Changed focus for talent search to the academically gifted child.

Elected Vice President Vivian Beamon, Cincinnati Chapter, as 4th National President.

14th – 1964
Jun 25–28
Nassau Beach Hotel
Nassau, Bahamas
British West Indies
Greater Miami (FL) Chapter

Vivian J. Beamon
National President

Attendance: 260 Links, 64 Connecting Links, 28 Bob-O-Links, 40 Friends

Links in an Era of Dynamic Dimensions

Memorial tribute to Co-Founder Margaret Rosell Hawkins, progress report on Woman Power Study profiling Link members by VP and Membership Chair Anna Julian, and ritual for Assembly opening.

Of Note: First meeting on foreign soil.

Approved Central Office on experimental basis. Increased National dues to $10 per capita.

Expanded National Trends and Services facet to include International Trends, and officially adopted second facet.

Established Margaret Hawkins Memorial Trust Fund (to be capitalized with $100 from each chapter by the next Assembly).

Barred Area Meetings after May 1, during Assembly years.

Approved $25 per-person, per-year Grants-in-Aid assessments.

Approved member-initiated transfers.

Approved $75,000 grant for NAACP Education & Legal Defense Fund payable over three years.

Approved continuation of Woman Power study.

15th – 1966
June 29–July 2
Sheraton Boston Hotel
Boston, MA

Vivian J. Beamon
National President

Links Projecting in an Era of Dynamic Dimensions

Constitutional session, review of the impact of the civil rights movement, report on NAACP Legal Defense Fund, panel discussions on leadership and the problems of birth defects, exhibit on Freedom and the Fine Arts, and results of Woman Power Study presented by VP Anna Julian.

Increased $75,000 commitment to the NAACP by $25,000, to be financed through a self-tax of $3.50 a year per member.

Ratified the *Constitution*, setting forth a bevy of changes, including:

Staggered election of officers, and phased out four-year terms, beginning after 1968.

Limited succession to one two-year term for all officers beginning in 1970.

Reelected Vivian Beamon as National President for a second four-year term.

16th – 1968 Jun 25–30 Claremont Hotel Oakland-Berkeley, CA **Vivian J. Beamon** *National President*	*Links' Innovations in an Era of Dynamic Dimensions* Appeal by Whitney M. Young from the Urban League for "Forward Thrust," a program to develop Black leadership; bound velvet journal of contributors to NAACP Legal Defense Fund, exhibit of works by Black artists, and memorial to Martin Luther King, Jr.	Approved Freedom and the Arts, previously a section of Services to Youth, as a facet. Presented $85,000 to NAACP and increased commitment to $100,000. Pledged $100,000 to the Urban League's Forward Thrust program. Approved National Links' Policy Position on Public Affairs.
17th – 1970 June 22–27 Netherland Hilton Hotel Cincinnati, OH Host: Cincinnati Chapter **Vivian J. Beamon** *National President*	*Links Commitments in an Era of Dynamic Dimensions* Presented Discovery 70, an art show featuring works of promising Black artists throughout the United States; recognized Bernice Munce, first Services to Youth director. Guest Speakers: Mayor Maynard Jackson (Atlanta)	Completed $100,000 pledges to the National Urban League and the NAACP Legal Defense Fund. Identified UNCF and sickle cell as next Grants-in-Aid recipients. Elected National and International Trends Director Helen Gray Edmonds, Durham Chapter, as 5th National President, for a two-year term. Added term limits. Approved Chapter Establishment officer.
18th – 1972 June 27–July 1 Royal Sonesta Hotel New Orleans, LA Host: Baton-Rouge, LA, Chapter **Helen Gray Edmonds, PhD** *National President*	*The Priorities of the 1970s: Effective Involvement Now* Charter Day marking 25th anniversary celebration, proposals for major amendments and operational changes, and a salute to historically Black colleges and universities.	Added Archives and History as standing committee. Established National Advisory Committee composed of all former National officers. Vested authority and responsibility for establishing chapters with National. Endorsed Nationally sponsored Assembly. Dispersed $68,000 to UNCF and $46,000 for sickle cell research. Approved UNCF as the single recipient for grants during the 1972–74 biennium. Approved establishing a National Headquarters on a trial basis.

19th – 1974
Jun 25–29
Washington Hilton
Washington, DC
Hosts: Washington, DC,
Arlington, VA, and Silver
Springs, MD, Chapters
Attendance: 746

Helen Gray Edmonds, PhD
National President

Of Note: Cluster hosting
begins.

The Priorities of the 1970s:
Effective Involvement Now

Memorial tribute to Philadelphia
Chapter charter member Katie
Greene for perfect Assembly
attendance over a 26-year
period.

International Trends luncheon
featuring President Gerald Ford
and 20 women ambassadors.

Approved revised *Constitution.*

Presented $132,000 to UNCF, the largest
single contribution by a Black organization.

Approved establishing a National
Headquarters on a permanent basis.

Completed four-year comprehensive
revision of the *Constitution.*

Set floor for chapters at 20 and a ceiling
of 50, with 35 slots set aside for members
initiated in said chapter and 15 for
transfers.

Ratified Area Meetings as biennial
gatherings to be held in non-Assembly
years.

Elected Services to Youth Director Pauline
Ellison, Arlington (VA) Chapter, as
6th National President.

20th – 1976
July 10–18
Washington Plaza
Seattle, WA
Host: Seattle Chapter

Pauline Allen Ellison,
LHD
National President

Of Note: Heir-O-Links
included in Services to
Youth luncheon

Improving the Quality of
Life by Linking Leadership
and Services to Meet the
Challenges of Community and
National Needs

First program booklet
containing program activities
and reports presented,
program resources and
consultation on career
development and minority
women's development, "fists"
in Linkdom saluted, update
on first two years of Links'
headquarters.

Approved establishment of a second
chapter in large metropolitan areas when
chapters reach their max of 30.

Approved Transition and Personnel
Committees to develop blueprint for a
volunteer-staff operation.

Presented $150,000 installment to
complete half-million-dollar pledge to the
United Negro College Fund to UNCF
Executive Director Christopher Edley.

Inducted honorary members Patricia
Roberts Harris, Marian Anderson, and
Mattiwilda Dobbs.

Limited chapter establishment to
Western Area for two-year period.

21st – 1978
July 5–8
Conrad Hilton Hotel
Chicago, IL
Hosts: Chicago, North
Shore, South Suburban,
West Towns, and
Northern Indiana
Chapters.
Attendance: 1,005
(753 Links)

**Pauline Allen Ellison,
LHD**
National President

*Links Innovations in an Era of
Dynamic Dimensions*

Presentation of portrait of
Co-Founder Margaret
Hawkins to grace the
National Headquarters.

Guest speakers: Martha
Mitchell, special assistant to
President James Earl Carter,
actor Ossie Davis.

Elevated International Trends to
independent status, making it the fourth
prong of the Program facets.

Added Personnel Committee as a
standing committee.

Increased National dues to $25 and
Grants-in-Aid to $35.

Presented $150,000 to UNCF, completing
half-million-dollar pledge.

Inducted HUD secretary Patricia Roberts
Harris as honorary member.

Elected Southern Area Director Julia
Brogdon Purnell, Baton Rouge Chapter,
as 7th National President.

22nd – 1980
June 27–July 3
Hyatt Regency Atlanta
Atlanta, GA
Host: Atlanta Chapter
Attendance: 1,408 (1,033
Links, 240 Connecting
Links, 84 Heir-O-Links,
and 54 guests.

**Julia Brogdon Purnell,
LHD**
National President

*Improving the Quality of Life
by Linking Leadership and
Service to Meet the Challenge
of Community and National
Needs*

Sessions on constitutional
interpretation and
incorporation basics, revised
documents.

Special Guests: Mayor Maynard
Jackson and Ambassador
Andrew Young, the US
ambassador to the United
Nations.

Presented first awards of National
Achievement Scholarship Program.

Dispersed $208,000 in grants, including
$160,000 to UNCF.

Ratified Links incorporation in the
District of Columbia.

23rd – 1982
July 5–10
Las Vegas Hilton
Las Vegas, NV

Julia Brogdon Purnell, LHD
National President

Attendance: 1,266
(903 Links)

Linking Friendship, Leadership, and Service to Meet the Challenge of Community Needs

National Headquarters status; 501(c)(3) bylaws; first history of The Links, Marjorie H. Parker, PhD, author.

Approved purchasing a headquarters with all deliberate speed.

Unveiled The Links first printed history.

Ratified *Bylaws* of The Links Foundation, completing the final step for 501(c)(3) status.

Elected International Trends and Services Director Dolly Desselle Adams, Arlington (VA) Chapter, as 8th National President

24th – 1984
July 5–9
Franklin Plaza Hotel
Philadelphia, PA
Hosts: Philadelphia Chapter, Bucks County, Delaware Valley, Montgomery County, Penn Town

Dolly Desselle Adams, PhD
National President

Attendance: 1,799
(1,322 Links)

Making History: Providing Hope

Tributes to charter members of the original Philadelphia Club; funding for National Headquarters; induction of Elizabeth Duncan Koontz, former president of the National Education Association, as an honorary member; and recognition of widows of the civil rights movement: Mesdames Martin Luther King, Jr., Whitney Young, Jr., and Medgar Evers (Betty Shabazz).

Dispersed $229,300 in grants, including $100,000 to complete $1 million pledge to United Negro College Fund.

Funded National Headquarters purchase and upkeep through a Capital Improvement Fund to be established with a $100 per-member assessment; a set aside of $100,000 from the unrestricted fund balance as of 04/30/84, and an allocation of $50,000 per year for a period of three years, beginning 1984–85.

Reelected Dolly Adams as National President.

25th – 1986
June 28–July 4
Opryland Hotel
Nashville, TN

Dolly Desselle Adams, PhD
National President

Attendance: 1,750 (1,283 Links, 322 Connecting Links, 80 Heir-O-Links, 65 guests)

Making History: Providing Hope

Progress reports on Links National Headquarters, The Links Foundation, and The Links' designation as a United Nations non-governmental organization; recognition of Illinois Poet Laureate Gwendolyn Brooks.

Guests: TransAfrica's Randall Robinson and the Katherine Dunham Youth Dancers.

Raised chapter size to 55.

Modified membership rules, including a majority vote (from two-thirds) for induction of a daughter of a Link (DOL), and restriction of alumnae members' privileges to attendance only.

Approved resolutions to continue support for Project LEAD as a National Umbrella Program and to establish a Black Family Institute.

Elected Vice President Regina Jollivette Frazier, Greater Miami Chapter, as 8th National President.

26th – 1988
June 25–July 2
Fontainebleau Hilton Hotel
Miami Beach, FL
Hosts: Greater Miami,
Dade County, Fort
Lauderdale, and West
Palm Beach

Regina Jollivette Frazier
National President

Attendance: 1,585

Enhancing the Legacy—
Fulfilling the Dream

Model Umbrella Programming
on Services to youth; panel
discussions on Project
LEAD: High Expectations;
international expansion; and
commercial exhibitors.

Instituted Project LEAD: High
Expectations, a $938,000 replicable
demonstration project to prevent
substance abuse, adolescent pregnancy,
and sexually transmitted diseases among
high-risk Black youth.

Adopted first reinstatement measures,
removed ban on transfers during first two
years, and raised membership cap to 55.

Approved NAACP Legal Defense and
Educational Fund as million-dollar grant
recipient, to be paid in installments of
not less than $100,000.

27th – 1990
June 27–July 3
Washington Hilton Hotel
Washington, DC
Hosts: Washington-
Virginia-Maryland
Links Cluster

Regina Jollivette Frazier
National President

Enhancing the Legacy—
Fulfilling the Dream

Organizational makeup; Project
LEAD: High Expectations;
Hawkins-Scott Memorial
Manor; public issues forum;
model Umbrella Programming;
and debut of a Links Choir at
an Assembly.

Limited appointed officers' service on the
Executive Council to two terms in the
same office.

Dispersed $250,000 in grants, including
$100,000 to the NAACP Legal Defense
and Education Fund and $10,000 to
Zambian women to support cottage
industries.

Added $43,000 profit accrued through
Frazier's modified closing banquet to
Hawkins-Scott Memorial Manor.

Elected Vice President Marion Schultz
Sutherland, Seattle (WA) Chapter, as
10th National President.

28th – 1992
June 29–July 3
Loews Anatole Hotel
Dallas, TX
Hosts: Dallas, Fort Worth,
Plano, North Metroplex,
and Mid Cities Chapters

**Marion Schultz
Sutherland**
National President

Attendance: 2,658 (2,063
Links, 404 Connecting
Links, 95 Heir-O-Links,
90 guests, 6 staff)

*Cherishing the Past—
Cultivating the Present—
Creating the Future*

International programming
focus, strategic planning
workshops, performance by
the first all-Black symphony in
America, first Links Boutique

Guest: Mayor Norm Rice
(Connecting Link), Seattle, WA

Limited induction of honorary members
to one per Assembly and intervals of
four years.

Approved the Links flag.

Established Presidential Legacy Award.
Approved $30 fee over two years to build
the base for a Program endowment.

Approved *Bylaws* change that fused Links
Foundation dues into the membership fee
structure of The Links.

Approved up to $75,000 to continue
Project LEAD: High Expectations as a
major Program focus.

Adopted "African Americans and persons
of African descent" lingo to acknowledge
members outside the boundaries of the
United States.

Established "majority vote" as the
requirement for the induction of
daughters of Links.

Approved mandatory purchase of the
official history book by new members.

29th – 1994
June 27–July 2
Galt House
Louisville, KY

**Marion Schultz
Sutherland**
National President

*Cherishing the Past, Cultivating
the Present, Creating the
Future*

Major *Bylaw* amendments,
public issues forum,
community service jamboree,
leadership enhancement.

Imposed four-year moratorium on *Bylaws*
amendments.

Eliminated member-at-large position.

Imposed largest increase in dues—
$60 to $100.

Adopted Strategic Plan.

Elected Vice President Patricia Russell-
McCloud, Esq., Dogwood City (GA)
Chapter, as 11th National President.

30th – 1996 July 7–14 New Orleans Hilton New Orleans, LA Hosts: New Orleans, Crescent City, and Pontchartrain Chapters **Patricia Russell-McCloud, Esq.** *National President*	*Linkages … Toward the Possible (Going for the Gold)* 50th anniversary celebration, including custom creation by Elizabeth Catlett, public forum on affirmative action, daily Linkspiration, community service day, Links Foundation Night at the Opera fundraiser, and salute to Corporate Links.	Culminated first major fundraiser for The Links Foundation, earning $770,000 plus. Awarded more than $200,000 in Grants-in-Aid, including $100,000 payment to the NAACP Legal Defense and Education Fund, and $30,000 to local Cordozo High School Concert Choir; also gave $35,000 to UNICEF in support of Rwanda children and pregnant mothers; and revived purchase of Links chapter NAACP life memberships with $25,000 contribution from chapters.
31st – 1998 June 29–July 4 Boston Copley Plaza Boston, MA **Patricia Russell-McCloud, Esq.** *National President* Attendance: 2,063 (1,568 Links, 340 Connecting Links, 111 Heir-O-Links, and 44 guests)	*Linkages … Toward the Possible (Freedom Train … Boston Bound … Get on Board)* Business sessions, program and operational workshops, daily breakfast series on wellness, Links Boutique, night at the Boston Pops.	Received $1 million grant to implement Links to Success: Children Achieving Excellence. Adopted Links to Success: Children Achieving Excellence and Education across the Miles as Signature Programs. Approved $25 technology fee. Endorsed expense-paid Assembly attendance by original members of the Philadelphia Chapter. Approved "pants restriction" for rituals. Endorsed support for Kemba Smith in her fight for fair sentencing. Elected Barbara Dixon Simpkins, EdD, Arlington (VA) Chapter, as 12th National President.
32nd – 2000 July 4–9 San Francisco Hilton & Towers San Francisco, CA **Barbara Dixon Simpkins, EdD** *National President*	*Yesterday's Courage, Today's Vision, Tomorrow's Hope (Meeting Challenges of the 21st Century)* Premier, Links University, technology training, and "Youths Talk: Links Listen," service project; Habitat for Humanity partnership; Justice for Kemba Smith; and schools in Africa.	Endorsed Linkages to Life, a bone marrow organ/tissue donor-education initiative, as a Signature Program. Approved one-in-five attendance requirement.

33rd – 2002
July 2–7
Chicago Hilton & Towers
Chicago, IL
Hosts: Chicago, Harbor
Lites, Hoffman Estates,
Lake Shore, North Shore,
South Suburban, West
Towns, and Windy City
Chapters

**Barbara Dixon Simpkins,
EdD**
National President

*Yesterday's Courage, Today's
Vision, Tomorrow's Hope*

Presented $100,000 installment of million-
dollar grant to NAACP Legal Defense and
Education Fund, and awarded more than
$250,000 more, including $230,000 to the
International Foundation for Self-Help.

Elected Vice President Gladys Gary
Vaughn, Potomac (VA) Chapter, as
13th National President.

34th – 2004
July 27–August 1
Hyatt Regency & Marriott
Marquis Hotels
Atlanta, GA
Hosts: Atlanta, Dogwood,
Magnolia, Azalea, and Buck-
head/Cascade Chapters

Gladys Gary Vaughn, PhD
National President

*Touching Tomorrow Today
(Bridges to the Future—
Conversations for Change)*

Debut of Scott-Hawkins
Leadership Institute and
Literary Links, public forum
on critical issues, and inclusion
of Connecting Links in the
Assembly Choir.

Approved 48-hour service requirement.

Added Platinum Member (highest honor
accorded a member) for members at least
80 with 30 years of service.

Set membership cap at 60 and floor at 20.

Approved alumna status for members in
good standing, active for 10 years and 70
years old; or those with 30 years of service.

Completed final payment on million-dollar
pledge to NAACP Legal Defense and
Education Fund.

Introduced Scott-Hawkins Leadership Institute.

35th – 2006
June 28–July 2
Philadelphia Marriott
Downtown
Pennsylvania Convention
Center
Philadelphia, PA
Hosts: Philadelphia Chapter

Gladys Gary Vaughn, PhD
National President

Attendance: 3,269
(2,815 Links)

Touching Tomorrow Today

Crossing Points: 60 Years—
Proud Past, Promising Future

Simultaneous voting with
electronic keypads, courtesies
to Links in chapters impacted
by Hurricane Katrina, first
Assembly fundraiser, and first
Platinum Members.

Added Area Directors to Executive Committee.

Approved Code of Ethics.

Established formula for allocation of
surplus from Assemblies.

Presented first installment of million-dollar grant
to the National Civil Rights Museum of Memphis.

Approved the Ritz Chamber Players, a
Black chamber group, as the Signature
Arts Program for the biennium.

Elected Vice President Gwendolyn Byrd
Lee as 14th National President.

36th – 2008 June 29–July 4 Washington Convention Center Seattle, WA **Gwendolyn Byrd Lee, PhD** *National President* Attendance: 2,729 (1,769 Links,18 Platinum)	*Seizing the Opportunity to Provide World Class Leadership, Friendship, and Service* Like a Phoenix Rising, Links Soar	Endorsed funding package for expansion and renovation of National Headquarters. Added Ethics & Standards Committee as standing entity. Approved HeartLinks and Classics through the Ages as signature projects. Exempted daughters of Links from head count in calculating maximum size of chapter. Reduced reinstatement fees from $2,000 to $500 for members who resigned in good standing. Presented second installment ($225,000) of million-dollar commitment to the National Civil Rights Museum and $155,000 in Grants-in-Aid to other recipients, with $25,000 going to the Northwest African American Museum in Seattle.
37th – 2010 June 30–July 4 The COBO Center Detroit, MI **Gwendolyn Byrd Lee, PhD** *National President* Attendance: 2,323 (2,161 Links)		Institutionalized Service Delivery Model. Monetary grants. Presented half ($500,000) of million-dollar grant to Susan G. Komen for the Cure. Added Health and Human Services as the fifth Program facet. Memorialized 12th National President Barbara Simpkins and Philadelphia charter member Frances Atkins. Elected Vice President Margot James Copeland as 15th National President.
38th – 2012 June 27–July 1 Orlando, FL **Margot James Copeland** *National President*	*Leading with Excellence ~ Serving with Grace*	Held inaugural Links Leadership Academy for members 40 and older. Completed payment of $1 million Legacy Grant to the National Civil Rights Museum, Memphis.

39th – 2014
July 3–5
Gaylord National
National Harbor, MD
(Washington, DC, Area)

Hosts: Washington, DC,
metropolitan chapters:
Arlington (VA), Capital
City (DC), Metropolitan
(DC), Old Dominion
(VA), Potomac (VA),
Prince George's County
(MD), Reston (VA), Silver
Spring (MD), Southern
Maryland Chain (MD), and
Washington (DC)

Margot James Copeland
National President

Attendance: 3,167
(2,882 Links)

Leading with Excellence ~
Serving with Grace:

Vision • Voice • Impact

Presentation of The Links
Medal to the National
Urban League.

Presentation of Co-Founders
Award for Leadership, Service,
Excellence, and Grace.

Fourth of July Celebration
commemorating the nation's
birthday.

Spotlight on partner
contributions.

Increased dues by $25, beginning fiscal
year 2015–2016.

Revoked the charter of the Southern West
Virginia Chapter.

Approved resolutions supporting the
Judicial Nominations of Alison Renee Lee
and Jennifer May-Parker.

Pledged $1 million to the National Museum
of African American History and Culture.

Adopted Oral Health as National initiative.

Elected Vice President Glenda Newell-
Harris as 16th National President.

40th – 2016
June 30–July 2
Mandalay Bay Hotel
Las Vegas, NV

**Glenda Newell-Harris,
MD** *National President*

Attendance: 2,946
(1,672 Links)

Building a Healthy Legacy:
Our Prescription for the Future

Introduced signature initiatives for HIV &
Hepatitis C, Mental Health, Black Lives
Matter, Human Trafficking, and new
program on voter education.

Completed payment of $1 million gift
to the Smithsonian National Museum of
African American History and Culture.

Retired the mortgage on National
Headquarters.

Voter Education Month.

Shifted international focus to Jamaica.

Approved provision for a granddaughter to
be sponsored by her grandmother who is
a Links member.

41st – 2018
June 28–June 30
JW Marriott Hotel
Indianapolis, IN

Glenda Newell-Harris, MD

Attendance: 1,812 Links

Building a Healthy Legacy:
Our Prescription for the Future

Awarded $1 million Legacy Grant to St. Jude Children's Research Hospital to help advance three sickle cell disease programs.

Offered health and safety education fair that included free dental screenings for children as part of Day of Service community activities.

Elected Vice President Kimberly Jeffries Leonard as 17th National President.

42nd – 2020
June 17–21
New Orleans, LA

Kimberly Jeffries Leonard, PhD

Transforming Communities ~
Fulfilling our Purpose

EXECUTIVE COUNCIL 2018–2020

Kimberly Jeffries Leonard, PhD Arlington (VA) Chapter	National President
Ethel Isaacs Williams, JD West Palm Beach (FL) Chapter	National Vice President Chair, Membership Committee
Crystal L. Kendrick Queen City (OH) Chapter	National Recording Secretary Chair, Committee of Secretaries
Ethelyn S. Bowers Essex County (NJ) Chapter	National Treasurer Chair, Finance Committee
Tyna D. Davis, EdD Montgomery (AL) Chapter	National Parliamentarian Chair, Constitution & Bylaws Committee
Shuana Tucker-Sims, PhD Fairfield County (CT) Chapter	Eastern Area Director
Sylvia Perry Bold City (FL) Chapter	Southern Area Director
Monica Boone Allen Windy City (IL) Chapter	Central Area Director
Lorna C. Hankins Gulf Coast Apollo (TX) Chapter	Western Area Director

Glenda Newell-Harris, MD Alameda Contra Costa (CA) Chapter	Immediate Past National President
Evelyn Rose Coker Las Vegas (NV) Chapter	National Financial Secretary
Kristie Patton Foster Affiliate – Eastern Area	Interim Executive Director
Margaret Elaine Flake, DMin Greater New York (NY) Chapter	Interim Chaplain Chair, Spiritual Enrichment & Wholeness Committee
Earnestine Green McNealey, PhD Columbia (SC) Chapter	Chair, Archives and History Committee
F. Denise Gibson Bailey Arlington (VA) Chapter	Chair, Awards/Recognition Committee
Michele V. Hagans, DMin Capital City (DC) Chapter	Chair, Building Operations Committee
Anne T. Herriott Greater Miami (FL) Chapter	Chair, Chapter Establishment
Rozalynn S. Frazier Metro-Manhattan (NY) Chapter	Chair, Communications Committee
Vivian R. Pickard Renaissance (MI) Chapter	Chair, Corporate Relations Committee
Gwendolyn B. Lee, PhD South Suburban Chicago (IL) Chapter	Chair, Council of Presidents 14th National President
Bridget W. Chisholm Greensboro (NC) Chapter	Chair, Economic Empowerment Committee
Jarnell Burks-Craig Indianapolis (IN) Chapter	Chair, Elections Committee
Stephanie Wilson, Esq. Morris County (NJ) Chapter	Chair, Ethics and Standards Committee
Caroline R. Lang, PhD Prince George's County (MD) Chapter	Chair, Evaluations Committee
Valerie Wardlaw, PsyD Southern Area Affiliate	Chair, Events, Conferences and Assembly Planning Committee
Rosalind L. Hudnell Sacramento (CA) Chapter	Director of Philanthropy/ Chair, Fund Development Committee
Marnese Barksdale Elder Mid-Cities (TX) Chapter	Chair, Human Resources Committee
Karen Jefferson Morrison, JD Columbus (OH) Chapter	Chair, Legislative Issues, Public Affairs, and Resolutions Committee
Carol H. Williams Oakland Bay Area (CA) Chapter	Chair, Marketing and Brand Management Committee

Raynetta C. Waters Asheville (NC) Chapter	Chair, National Nominating Committee
Larnell Burks-Bagley Indianapolis (IN) Chapter	Chair, Protocol Committee
Cynthia Hightower-Jenkins Shreveport (LA) Chapter	Chair, Rituals Committee
Stephanie Mays Boyd Philadelphia (PA) Chapter	Chair, Strategic Partnerships Committee
Patricia Bush Washington (DC) Chapter	Chair, Strategic Planning Committee
Sharon Dixon Gentry Music City (TN) Chapter	Chair, Technology Committee
Karen M. Dyer, EdD Greensboro (NC) Chapter	Co-Chair, Organizational Effectiveness/ Leadership Development
Jan T. Collins-Eaglin, PhD Claremont Area (CA) Chapter	Co-Chair, Organizational Effectiveness/ Leadership Development
Mildred A. Edwards, PhD Topeka (KS) Chapter	Dean, Scott-Hawkins Leadership Institute
Pamela Freeman Fobbs, JD Fresno (CA) Chapter	Director, National Programs
Tammy King Bergen County (NJ) Chapter	Director, Services to Youth Facet
Joyce M. Jackson, Ph.D. Baton Rouge (LA) Chapter	Director, The Arts Facet
Sonya Simril Alameda Contra Costa (CA) Chapter	Director, National Trends and Services Facet
Barbara Nance McKee Patuxent River (MD) Chapter	Director, International Trends and Services Facet
Nicholette M. Martin, MD Arlington (VA) Chapter	Director, Health and Human Services Facet

PART IV

Masterworks

Transformational Orchestrations

We believe that every effective leader must have these essential qualities: passion, authenticity, credibility, vision, accountability, courage, and integrity. Link Kimberly Jeffries Leonard possesses all of these.

~ FORMER NATIONAL PRESIDENTS:
PAULINE ELLISON, DOLLY DESSELLE ADAMS,
REGINA JOLLIVETTE FRAZIER, GLADYS GARY
VAUGHN, GWENDOLYN B. LEE

CHAPTER 8
THE NATIONAL
Presidents

Being president was an opportunity and a chance of a lifetime. I wouldn't take—as Maya Angelou would say—"I'd take nothing for my journey now." … It has been an honor and a privilege to serve.

~ GLENDA NEWELL-HARRIS, 16TH NATIONAL PRESIDENT

National President Kim Jeffries Leonard (seated, center) with former National Presidents at the 2019 unveiling of Co-Founders portraits.

The intense sentiment of gratefulness and graciousness expressed by 16th National President Glenda Newell-Harris mirrored the emotions of her 15 predecessors; and nine months into her presidency, her successor, 17th National President Kimberly Jeffries Leonard, exuded gratitude for the bestowal of the ultimate eminence in Linkdom. "Thank you for the honor of serving as your National President." Passing the mantle to 4th National President Vivian J. Beamon at the 13th (1962) Assembly, 3rd National President Pauline Weeden Maloney also praised the crown and the privilege: "I am most grateful for having had such an honored position."

"I must tell you how much I enjoyed my job; you have made … my days as your president some of the most satisfying of my life," 10th National President Marion Elizabeth Schultz gratefully acknowledged to the 28th (1992) Assembly. Two years later, the spirit had endured: "I've had a wonderful time serving as your President … these past four years have been as sweet as honey, as fulfilling as a good marriage, and as loving as I dreamed."

Members, too, have held the presidency and the presidents in high esteem and accorded absolute respect to the office and its elected holder. Consequently, delegates have entrusted the title to individuals deemed worthy—17 women who strikingly embodied both the rich heritage and infinite aspirations of Linkdom. They also met standards set out in The Links' *Bylaws*.

But the larger-than-life personalities were much more. The National Presidents embodied "essential qualities—passion, authenticity, credibility, vision, accountability, courage, and integrity." They also possessed the skills and fortitude required of a great leader: identification of needs, a vision of the possible, an enthusiasm for the cause, and to take the organization beyond. Through the years, 17 women have demonstrated their prowess in transforming The Links into a formidable force for friendship and service. Each

#3 Maloney with #5 Edmonds

came, knowing she was expected "to ascend the ladder of that high-calling" committed to wielding the power of Linkdom to realize unparalleled outcomes in achieving the three-fold aim set out by Margaret Rosell Hawkins: to do some good to help less fortunate citizens, to raise the cultural level of our race, and to enjoy the social company of friends.

There is no automatic succession in Linkdom, but the vice presidency as a lever to the presidency has been unfailing for the last ten aspirants. Delegates at the 21st (1978) Assembly rejected a proposal to have a president elect, noting that "the term of office of the President-Elect, running concurrently with that of the President, would have that person in office for a total of eight years." Yet, beginning with Regina Jollivette Frazier in 1982, one vice president after another has ascended to the presidency.

The efficacy can be traced to the duties prescribed for the office. While the vice president can stand in for the president and may occasionally do so on varied fronts, the rise in the stature of the vice president comes with her role as chair of The Links lifeline

National Presidents at 70th anniversary celebration. Left to right: #8 Adams, #9 Frazier, #11 Russell-McCloud, #13 Vaughn, #14 Lee, #15 Copeland, and #16 Newell-Harris.

National Presidents (left to right) #8 Adams, #5 Edmonds, and #9 Frazier

"doctor" of philosophy, law, or medicine. Edmonds, Adams, Russell-McCloud, Simpkins, Vaughn, Lee, Harris, and Leonard earned terminal degrees. All worked as professionals, with the majority (9, or 52 percent)—Scott, Hawkins, Weeden, Beamon, Edmonds, Purnell, Adams, Simpkins, and Lee— excelling in the educational arena as teachers and administrators. A history scholar, Edmonds lectured at more than 87 colleges and universities throughout the United States, Liberia, Sweden, and Germany; and as superintendent, Lee was named Illinois' administrator of the year.

Career choices represented by the remainder represent nontraditional, but growing paths for Black women. Newell-Harris was the first physician, and Frazier was a pharmacy chief. Ellison, Russell-McCloud, and Vaughn were federal officials with the US Department of Housing and Urban Development, the US Federal Communications Commission, US Department of Agriculture, and the US Department of Health and Human Services, respectively. James was the CEO of a multimillion-dollar bank foundation, and Sutherland was a nursing home administrator and newspaper editor.

Like members of the founding group, the National Presidents also chose equally successful men as their mates, with a predilection toward physicians, dentists, and corporate executives. Scott, Ellison, and Vaughn had physician husbands, Weeden and Beamon were married to dentists, and Newell-Harris exchanged vows with the vice president for a publicly traded utility with a customer base of 16 million. The Connecting Links of other National Presidents were successful clergy heads, civic administrators, and business men: church bishops (Adams and McCloud), Philadelphia's first Negro postal supervisor (Hawkins), a legendary high school athletic director (Purnell), a metallurgical engineer (Sutherland), an architect (Frazier), an accountant (Lee), and a fire battalion chief (Leonard).

Twelve (70 percent) of the National Presidents have earned the title of mother, nurturing and guiding the Bob-O-Links of early years and the Heir-O-Links of today, and exposing them to Linkdom

and gatekeeper—the Membership Committee. Of the eight National Presidents who preceded Frazier during the first 37 years, only 4th National President Vivian J. Beamon ascended from the vice presidency. Also elected were an Area director, an Operations Committee chair, three program directors, and the two Co-Founders. Of the eight who followed Frazier, 100 percent served as National vice president.

Their preparation and training have other common links. Four (Frazier, Copeland, Harris, and Leonard) got head starts, as they learned from their mothers. Six also saw their embrace of Linkdom validated by their daughters who also pledged allegiance to The Links: DOLs Paula and Karla (Ellison), Gaye, Jann, and Madelyn (Adams), Rozalynn (Frazier), Michelle (Lee), Kimberly (Copeland), and Brittany (Newell-Harris).

Like the founding group, Links leaders were professionals in their own right. All embraced intellectual vigor: fifteen (88 percent) earned a master's degree, and eight (52 percent) can answer to

through structured and informal activities for them and programming them for community service. Newell-Harris has the highest number of children with four, while Scott and Lee each have one. Adams, Frazier, and Copeland each have three, and Hawkins, Ellison, Schultz, Simpkins, Vaughn, and Leonard are each parent to two.

Always highly engaged in community affairs, National Presidents were tapped for leadership roles in other settings. Scott was national president of Jack and Jill of America; Purnell and Russell-McCloud served as national president and national parliamentarian, respectively, of Alpha Kappa Alpha; Copeland served as president of the Junior League of Cleveland (OH); Adams and Leonard were national president and national vice president, respectively, of Black Women's Agenda, Inc.; Maloney was Eastern Area director of Delta Sigma Theta; and Frazier was national parliamentarian of the Association of Black Hospital Pharmacists. Their work also dovetailed initiatives by other groups that included Jack and Jill, The Links, and Alpha Kappa Alpha/Delta Sigma

Attending the 41st (2018) Assembly in Indianapolis. Left to right: #16 Newell-Harris, #15 Copeland, #14 Lee, #13 Vaughn, #11 Russell-McCloud, and #9 Frazier.

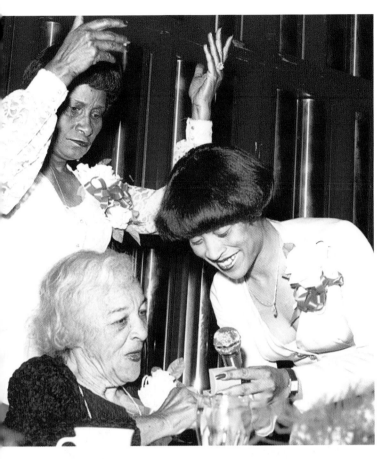

#1 Scott (seated) receiving gift from #9 Frazier, as #7 Purnell gives thanks.

Theta. Membership in the trilogy led to induction into the Society of "Our Kind of People," as popularized by author Lawrence Otis Graham.

Additionally, National Presidents have been trailblazers. Edmonds was the first Negro woman to second the nomination for a candidate for president of the United States of America (Eisenhower, 1956); Maloney was the first woman rector of the Norfolk State University Board of Visitors; Ellison was the first Black woman to serve as director of personnel for a federal agency; and McCloud was the first African American female to serve as chief of the Complaints Branch of the Federal Communications Commission.

Linkdom and its first two presidents (Scott and Hawkins) were born in Pennsylvania, but two other states dominate as the birthplaces of National Presidents, with three apiece born in Virginia (Edmonds, Ellison, and Copeland) and Florida (Simpkins, Vaughn, and Frazier). Two apiece hailed from Indiana (McCloud and Lee) and North Carolina (Newell-Harris, Leonard), while the remaining five were born in Maryland (Fletcher), Kentucky (Beamon), South Carolina (Purnell), Louisiana (Adams), and Illinois (Schultz).

There was a 22-year differential between the ages of the youngest and the eldest when elected. At 42, Frazier was the youngest, and Schultz was 64. Scott, Hawkins, and Russell-McCloud were also in their 40s; Maloney, Edmonds, Ellison, Adams, Lee, Copeland, and Leonard were in their 50s; and Beamon, Purnell, Simpkins, Vaughn, and Newell-Harris were in their 60s. Of the eight deceased National Presidents, Purnell (93) lived the longest, and Hawkins (55) had the shortest life span. Beamon and Simpkins died in their 70s, while Scott, Maloney, and Schultz scaled four score.

Seventeen women have been elected to the exclusive National Presidents Club of Linkdom. Their backgrounds are impressive; their presence, life-sized; and their personal achievements, outstanding; but members revere them most for the masterful orchestrations they have engineered to transform Linkdom into masterpieces of friendship and service, deeply entrenched in The Links' heritage and ensured by its deeds.

~ *Earnestine Green McNealey, PhD*

THE NATIONAL PRESIDENTS

President & Chapter (at Time of Election)	Vitals	Ascension Office	Profession / Degree(s)
#1 – 1949–1953 Sarah Strickland Scott Philadelphia (PA) Chapter (Co-founder, 1946) *Parents:* George G. Strickland, MD, and Minnie L. Strickland *Spouse:* Horace Scott, MD *Children:* (Link) Marjorie Ann (Upshur)	*Birth* January 17, 1901 Philadelphia, PA *Death* July 4, 1988 Philadelphia, PA	President, Philadelphia Club	English Teacher, Philadelphia high schools Guidance Counselor, Wilmington, DE BA, English, Columbia University, NY MA, University of Pennsylvania MA, Vocational Guidance, Columbia University, NY
#2 – 1953–1957 Margaret Rosell Hawkins Philadelphia (PA) Chapter (Co-founder, 1946) *Parents:* David Rosell and Anna Nicholson Rosell *Spouse:* Frederick C. Hawkins, first African American Superintendent, Mt. Airy (PA) Post Office *Children:* Frederick C., Jr., MD; Bruce	*Birth* January12, 1908 Philadelphia, PA *Death* October 4, 1963 Philadelphia, PA	President, Philadelphia Chapter	Artist High School Art Teacher and Supervisor Bachelor's degree, Philadelphia School of Design for Women (now Moore College of Art and Design)
#3 – 1957–1962 Margaret Pauline Fletcher Weeden (Maloney) (Ralston), Lynchburg (VA) Chapter, 1950 *Parents:* William and Eliza Fletcher *Spouse:* Henry P. Weeden, DDS	*Birth* November 11, 1904 Annapolis, MD *Death* June 22, 1987 Lynchburg (VA)	Chair, Area Realignment Committee	Speech and English Teacher, Winston-Salem, NC Teacher, Guidance Counselor, and Administrative Principal, Dunbar High School, Lynchburg, VA BA, Howard University, Washington, DC MA, Columbia University, NY

#4 – 1962–1970 Vivian Jones Beamon Cincinnati (OH) Chapter, 1950 (Charter Member) *Spouse:* Reginald Beamon, DDS	*Birth* March 15, 1902 Paris, KY *Death* August 27, 1974 Cincinnati, OH	National Vice President	Instructor, University of Cincinnati Teacher, Assistant Principal, and Principal, Cincinnati schools Bachelor's degree, University of Cincinnati, OH Master's degree, New York University.
#5 – 1970–1974 Helen Gray Edmonds, PhD Durham (NC) Chapter *Parents:* John Edmonds and Ann Williams Edmonds	*Birth* December 3, 1911 Lawrenceville, VA *Death* May 9, 1995 Durham, NC	National Director, National Trends and International Trends and Services	Dean of the Graduate School, Chair, Department of History, and Distinguished Professor, North Carolina College (now North Carolina Central University), Durham Dean of Women, Saint Paul's College, Lawrenceville, VA Teacher (History, Latin, and Greek), Virginia Theological Seminary Bachelor's degree, History, Morgan State University, Baltimore, MD Master's degree and PhD, The Ohio State University (the first African American woman to earn a doctoral degree)
#6 – 1974–1978 Pauline Allen Ellison, LHD Arlington (VA) Chapter, 1966 (Charter member) *Parents:* William and Rosa Allen *Spouse:* Oscar Ellison, Jr., MD *Children:* Oscar III, (Link) Paula Michelle, and (Link) Karla	*Birth* February 25, 1924 Iron Gate, VA	National Director, Services to Youth	Employee Relations Officer, Housing and Urban Development (first Black woman to serve as Director of Personnel for a federal agency) Personnel Placement Officer, Freedman's (now Howard University) Hospital Bachelor's, Chemistry, Howard University, Washington, DC MPA, American University School of Government and Public Administration, Washington, DC

#7 – 1978–1982 Julia Brogdon Purnell, LHD Baton Rouge (LA) Chapter *Parents:* Rev. Richard Brogdon and Sarah L. Christie Brogdon *Spouse:* Clifton Purnell, High School Athletic Director *Children:* Clifton Purnell, Jr.	**Birth** March 19, 1916 Belton, SC **Death** October 21, 2013 Baton Rouge, LA	Southern Area Director	Professor of Education, Southern University, Baton Rouge, LA Teacher, Avery Institute Charleston, SC; South Carolina State College, Orangeburg, SC; and Morris College, Sumter, SC Bachelor's degree, Allen University, Columbia, SC MA, Educational Psychology, Atlanta University, GA
#8 – 1982–1986 Dolly Desselle Adams, PhD Elected: Arlington (VA) Chapter Inducted: Seattle (WA) Chapter Current: Atlanta (GA) Chapter *Parents:* Moses J. and Thelma Tucker Desselle *Spouse:* Bishop John Hurst Adams, Senior Bishop, AME Church (Deceased) *Children:* Gaye Adams Massey, Esq., Dr. Jann Adams, and Madelyn R. Adams (all Links)	**Birth** August 13, 1931 Marksville, LA	National Director, International Trends and Services	Educator Elementary school teacher College dean and professor, University of Michigan, Ann Arbor; Wilberforce University, OH; Albany State College, GA; Paul Quinn College, Waco (now Dallas), TX; Howard University School of Law, Washington, DC BS, Southern University, Baton Rouge, LA MA, University of Michigan, Ann Arbor PhD, Education, Baylor University, Waco, TX
#9 – 1986–1990 Regina Jollivette Frazier Greater Miami (FL) Chapter, 1970 *Parents:* Cyrus Martin Jollivette and (Link) Frances Reeves Jollivette Chambers *Spouse:* Ronald Eugene Frazier, Architect and Urban Planner *Children:* Ronald Eugene II, Rozalynn Suzanne, and Robert Christophe	**Birth** September 30, 1943 Miami, FL	National Vice President Miami (FL)	Pharmacist Director of Pharmacy, University Hospitals and Clinics, Miami, FL Chief Pharmacist, National Association of Retired Teachers; American Association of Retired Persons Drug Service BS, Howard University, Washington, DC MBA, University of Miami, FL

#10 – 1990–1994
Marion Elizabeth Schultz
Sutherland

Parents: Rev. Clyde Mitchell
Schultz and Vella Cloyd

Spouse: Col. Earl Christian
Sutherland;
Colie Raymond Merriwether

Children: Chrystal Raynette M.
Weinberg and Clyde
Merriwether

Birth
July 3, 1926
Danville, IL

Death
June 24, 2015
Bothell, WA

National
Vice President
Seattle (WA)

State Licensed Nursing Home
Administrator

Editor, *Pacific Leader*, a
community newspaper in Seattle

BS, Speech and Sociology,
Portland State University,
Oregon

#11 – 1994–1998
Patricia A. Russell-McCloud,
Esq.
Elected: Dogwood City (GA)
Inducted: Arlington (VA)
Chapter, 1976

Parents: Willie and Janiel Russell

Spouse: Bishop Earl McCloud, Jr.

Birth
Sep 14, 1946
Indianapolis, IN

National
Vice President

Attorney

Professional Orator

Chief, Complaints Branch,
Federal Communications
Commission, Broadcast Bureau,
Washington, DC

BA, Kentucky State University,
Frankfort

JD, Howard University School of
Law, Washington, DC

#12 – 1998–2002
Barbara Jean Dixon Simpkins,
EdD
Prince George's County (MD)
Chapter

Parents: Rev. Joshua and
Celestine F. Dixon

Children: Monti LeMans
Simpkins and LuBara (Dickey)
Simpkins

Birth
September 24, 1934
Pensacola, FL

Death
December 9, 2009
Fort Washington,
MD

National
Vice President

Educator

Bachelor's degree, Florida A & M
University, Tallahassee

Master's degree, Temple
University, Philadelphia

EdD, Educational Leadership,
Nova Southeastern University

#13 – 2002–2006	Birth	National	Outreach Director, US
Gladys Gary Vaughn, PhD	July 23,1941	Vice President	Department of Agriculture
Potomac (VA) Chapter	Ocala, FL		
			BS, Home Economics, Florida
Parents: Homer and Ollie			A&M University, Tallahassee
Gary			
			MS, Clothing and Textiles,
Spouse: Joseph B. Vaughn, Jr.,			Iowa State University
MD (Deceased)			
			PhD, Home Economics
Children: Homer Vaughn and			Education and Administration,
Ollie Vaughn			University of Maryland-College
			Park

#14 – 2006–2010	Birth	National	Associate Superintendent of
Gwendolyn Byrd Lee, PhD	February 3, 1950	Vice President	Schools, Thornton High School
South Suburban Chicago (IL)	Gary, IN		District, Illinois
Chapter			
			BS, History and Political Science,
Parents: Willie and Emma			Ball State University, Muncie, IN
Byrd			
			MS, Education, Purdue
Spouse: Ronald W. Lee,			University, West Lafayette, IN
Accountant			
			PhD, Education, Leadership and
			Policy Development, Loyola
Children: (Link) Michelle			University, Chicago, IL
Victoria Lee-Murrah			

#15 – 2010–2014	Birth	National	Corporate Executive
Margot James Copeland	December 12, 1951	Vice President	
Cleveland (OH) Chapter	Richmond, VA		CEO, KeyBank Foundation;
			also, KeyCorp, Xerox, Polaroid,
Parents: Rev. William Lloyd			Picker International, Leadership
Garrison James, a Baptist min-			Cleveland, and Greater
ister, and (Link) Thelma Taylor			Cleveland Roundtable
James, a math teacher			
			BS, Physics, Hampton University, VA
Children: (Link) Rev. Kimberly,			
Dr. Garrison, and Michael			MA, Educational Research
			and Statistics, The Ohio State
			University, Columbus

#16 – 2014–2018	Birth	National	Regional Medical Director,
Glenda Newell-Harris, MD	February 7, 1953	Vice President	Corizon Health
Alameda Contra-Costa (CA)	Raleigh, NC		
Chapter			BS, Biology, Tufts University,
			Medford, MA
Parents:			
(Link) Virginia Newell			MD, University of Cincinnati
			(Ohio) School of Medicine
Spouse: Robert L. Harris, Esq.,			
retired VP, Pacific Gas and			
Electric Company			
Children: (Link) Brittany Harris			

#17 – 2018–	Birth	National	Health Executive
Kimberly Jeffries Leonard,	November 1, 1962	Vice President	
PhD	Fayetteville, NC		President and CEO, Envision
Arlington (VA) Chapter, 1996			Consulting, LLC, Washington, DC
Parents: (Link) Marye Jeffries,			Deputy director, US Department
EdD			of Health and Human Services
			Center for Substance Abuse
Spouse: Stephen V. Leonard,			Treatment
retired Battalion Fire Chief			
			Chief Operating Officer, District
Children: Victor and			of Columbia Department of Health
Alexander			
			Bachelor's degree, Fayetteville
			State University, NC
			MS, North Carolina Central
			University, Durham
			PhD, Psychology, Howard University

Sarah Strickland Scott
First National President (1949–1953)

My greatest wish as we ascend the ladder of that high-calling set for us is that we shall never forget those less fortunate, and that when duty calls, we answer.

THE IDEA FOR LINKDOM did not originate with Sarah Strickland Scott, but she, more than anyone, left her indelible imprint on The Links. As a Co-Founder, she was there from the beginning, and for 50 years, as president of the Philadelphia Chapter, first president of the National Links, and Services to Youth chair, she was a larger-than-life influence.

Scott's elevation above Co-Founder Margaret Rosell Hawkins, the visionary behind The Links, was a matter of timing. Having succeeded Hawkins as president of the Philadelphia Chapter, Scott was in office when the colonization meeting was held on June 4, 1949, in Philadelphia. Although the delegates paid homage to Hawkins as a founder, Scott's position as the presiding officer gave her the advantage; and with her poise, warmth, gentility, vision, and parliamentary prowess, Scott continued to soar, winning the coveted title as the first National President.

Her feat came as no surprise to Hawkins. She wanted someone who possessed similar values, intellect, talents, breeding, and a sense of civic responsibility as she; so, she invited Scott to unite with her in designing a different kind of women's organization. Scott, thrilled at the prospect of offering more aid in her community, gleefully accepted the offer, and together, two exceptional women gave wings to the dream. The extent to which Scott subsequently emerged as "the embodiment" of The Links was reflected in a *Journal* editorial comparing her to the founder of Christianity.

The name of Sarah Scott is used with the same degree of frequency, reverence, and honor as a devout New Testament preacher will refer to the name of Apostle Paul in preaching a sermon. It is assumed that all good Christians know of Paul and his good works. It is assumed that all Links know of Sarah Scott and her good works.

Scott's deep sense of responsibility to her fellow man, present from the beginning, was encapsulated in the last lines of The Links' pledge she penned: "I shall earnestly endeavor to uphold these standards and do my share toward serving my community and my chapter to the best of my ability. And this I promise." When Scott took office in 1949, the nation was still healing from a World War that had ended four years earlier. Americans were also watching the slow unfolding of President Harry S. Truman's 1948 executive order integrating the US Armed Forces and creating a Fair Employment Board to eliminate racial discrimination in federal employment.

It took a few years to plant the seeds for a national response, but at the 4th (1952) Assembly, Scott's plan for a unified program took root. The committee Scott charged to come up with a service project had considered many, but given the prevalence of injustices and discrimination, a human rights initiative was a natural choice. Impacting policy and shaping reforms would also be consistent with The Links' civic and intercultural mission. Rather than launch a solo venture, however, Scott embraced the committee's recommendation to support the NAACP Life Membership campaign.

Because the NAACP had already demonstrated prowess in effecting social progress, Scott was prepared to push her members, but little persuasion was necessary. The delegates understood the corollary between a strong NAACP and The Links' commitment to improve their communities. The $500 per-chapter assessment was approved by the delegates and subsequently ratified by the membership. The move successfully launched The Links' first National project, instituted Grants-in-Aid, and demonstrated the power of partnerships.

The NAACP endorsement was also a preview of the potential this new women's coalition could power. When Scott took office, there were only 14 clubs, but with the growth rate, she believed the number could easily reach 50 by the end of the two-year period when the funds were due, resulting in a minimum boost of $25,000. She smiled as she anticipated the National metamorphosis of the aspirations that she and Margaret Hawkins had set in motion with the Philadelphia Chapter.

Scott thanked and congratulated the Assembly for authorizing the move, but also earnestly pleaded that the National donation not come at the expense of chapter projects. At the heart of Linkdom, she often said, were members working together to identify needs in their communities and then offering programs that achieved the effect desired. She did not want them to cut back on chapter projects such as contributions to charities, vigilance, scholarships, career counseling for youth, and human relations workshops.

A teacher by profession, Scott also made youth a focal point. Her work in schools and membership on boards that served as advocates for youth gave her an up close and personal view of their plight and their potential. Chapters were encouraged to support their development by making recreational and cultural facilities available and providing job counseling and placement assistance.

As she did in programming, The Links' first National leader also set standards for membership and operations. Aware that continued chapter and membership growth would require clearer guidelines, more structure, and other modifications, she encouraged conversations on policies and direction. Among the changes was the reorganization of Area divisions, and further restrictions in membership were proposed. In all matters, Scott emphasized the need to ensure that the action taken facilitated The Links' mission. Addressing the 1951 Assembly, she reiterated that the order of the day was "to make the heritage large and more available," thereby increasing the ability to offer more services.

Through precept and example, Scott worked tirelessly to define and exhibit the dream of friendship and service. The only respite came during a period when she deemed that she could advance Linkdom more effectively from afar than in the circle. In addition to working diligently, women, she said, had to work harmoniously; so, she bowed out during the terms of Hawkins (1953–1957) and Hawkins's good friend, 3rd National President Pauline Weeden Maloney (1957–1962).

Scott continued her self-imposed exile until 1964, when 4th National President Vivian J. Beamon convinced her that she was still a vital link in the chain. Her participation in the 14th (1964) Assembly in Nassau enabled Scott to become part of another great moment in Linkdom. She had joined Margaret Rosell Hawkins in issuing the call to form the original chapter, she had presided at the first National Assembly when the 14 chapters united, she had initiated the first National project, and, now, she was christening the first Assembly to be held on foreign soil.

Totally renewed by the experience, Scott once again became a fixture, not only at Assemblies, but also at Executive Council and committee meetings, even chairing the Services to Youth facet. Taken aback by a school report on reading scores during the 1975 Executive Council meeting, she said, "Links must rededicate themselves so that our youth can get the kind of education and training they need." She was a thermostat, an inspiration, a prized authority, and an adviser through the 23rd Assembly, held July 5–10, 1982, in Las Vegas, Nevada, where, from her wheelchair, she exuded love and called on Links to continue to further Black progress.

For most, it would be the last face-to-face and heart-to-heart interaction with The Links icon, but over the next six years, she maintained contact by

#1 Scott (seated) with #3 Maloney

telephone. Links sisters also visited her in the nursing home, where she reveled in the joy that she had experienced in Linkdom—joy that took on a greater significance after her bout with illness in 1975. "I have become more appreciative of things we take for granted," she said. The next year, Scott used a *Journal* article to express her delight with the sisterhood. "Your fulfillment of the dream that Margaret Rosell Hawkins and I cherished in 1946 has more than satisfied our highest expectations. Thousands have found a better life because of our collective efforts," she said.

At the 24th (1984) Assembly in Philadelphia, founding chapter member Dorothy Bell Wright paid tribute to the ailing Scott on behalf of the four surviving charter members. Promising "to keep The Links' chain of friendship ever flourishing and expanding," Bell expressed the group's gratitude. "We thank you for your vision, wisdom, guidance, and abundant talents unselfishly shared with all Linkdom. We love you, Sarah Scott. We are sorry that you are not able to be with us today," she lamented.

On July 4, 1988, two days after the 26th Assembly closed, Scott was called to eternal rest. In a tribute, 9th National President Regina Jollivette Frazier honored the person and her record of service, extolling, "During more than 40 years of service, Link Sarah's contributions reflected her philosophy of loving each other and working for the common causes of American life, with emphasis upon the needs of Black Americans."

Memorials established in Scott's honor range from a statue the Eastern Area commissioned in the Great Blacks in Wax Museum in Baltimore, Maryland, to her name etched on The Links leadership academy, the Scott-Hawkins Leadership Institute. But the ultimate tribute to Scott has been the continual execution of the dream. "My greatest wish as we ascend the ladder of that high-calling set for us," she said, "is that we shall never forget those less fortunate, and that when duty calls, we answer."

As attested to by Frazier in that 1988 farewell tribute, "The dream lives and grows … we are enhancing the legacy and fulfilling the dream."

~ *Earnestine Green McNealey, PhD*

~ *Yvonne Horton, PhD*

Sarah Strickland Scott

Links Service

Co-Founder, Vice President, and President, Philadelphia Links

Chair, Services to Youth

Vice President, Philadelphia Links

Impact During Tenure

- Developed first constitution.
- Guided expansion efforts.
- Established Areas.
- Launched first National project, NAACP life memberships.
- Instituted Links brands, including insignia, music for hymn, and a new, smaller bracelet.

Selected National Honors

- National President and Program Director, Jack and Jill of America
- Wax figure in Great Blacks in Wax Museum, Baltimore, MD
- Lead moniker on Scott-Hawkins Leadership Institute

Margaret Rosell Hawkins
Second National President (1953–1957)

What Can Links Do Today for the Youth of Tomorrow?

I am filled with gratitude to the many friends who have contributed to the success of my administration, and filled too, with a sense of what I hope is pardonable pride ... $28,550 has been fully paid to the NAACP ... for the first time in its history, National Links has lived and capably operated within its yearly budget, [and] ... we have "fairly and impartially" enforced the rules.

MARGARET ROSELL HAWKINS'S installation as the second National President at the 5th Assembly in Buffalo, New York, in 1953 was both fitting and proper. It was Hawkins who had conceived the idea of a new women's club. It was Hawkins who had envisioned the club as a vehicle that provided "service for the less fortunate, inter-cultural relationships, and pleasurable times together." It was Hawkins who had been the incubator. It was Hawkins who had brought the idea to fruition in 1946. And it was Hawkins who had served as the first president of the Philadelphia Links, the chartering group.

When the 14 existing clubs convened in Philadelphia in 1949 to form a national organization, however, the nod for president went to Sarah Scott, who, by invitation, had assisted Hawkins in plotting the club's direction and selecting the core group of members. As president of the host club, Scott convened the opening session on June 4, 1949, and the 1st Assembly subsequently elected her. Four years later, however, the reins were extended to Hawkins, and she heartily grabbed them, grateful for another opportunity to steer the organization she had conceived.

When Hawkins took the oath in 1953, segregation and injustices plagued the nation. At the vanguard of the fight to excise the many atrocities Negroes faced was the National Association for the Advancement of Colored People (NAACP), but it needed funds to continue its impact. The 4th Assembly, one year earlier, had pledged to purchase

NAACP life memberships as its first National project. Hawkins had supported the initial move, and as National President, she made NAACP memberships her great calling.

Although Hawkins lived in Philadelphia (called the first "free" city above the Mason-Dixon Line), Hawkins not only witnessed discrimination, but she had also experienced it. Reminiscing, she imagined what could have happened had the NAACP or some other organization stepped in when she led the effort to integrate her high school prom, which school officials cancelled, rather than yield to the pressure of an integrated event. Hawkins, better than anyone, understood that the NAACP—its hands (still) full of desegregation battles and its coffers virtually empty—deserved The Links' support, and she energized the thrust.

By the 6th Assembly in June 1954, all 58 chapters had united, and Hawkins and Daisy Lampkin, chair of the committee that proposed the idea and an officer in the NAACP, presented a $28,000 donation to Roy Wilkins, executive secretary of the NAACP, and Thurgood Marshall, founder of the NAACP Legal Defense Fund (LDF). The contribution set The Links apart as one of the first women's groups to take out life memberships.

While Hawkins was pleased by the honor, she was more joyful that the National Links had become stakeholders in the march for progress, and she experienced sheer jubilation four months later on October 27, 1954, when the NAACP won a landmark decision, with the Supreme Court ruling that racial segregation in public schools was unconstitutional. With the fight for justice and dignity being played out in the courts, the NAACP LDF took center stage and subsequently launched a campaign for direct support.

At the 7th (1955) Assembly, Hawkins asked delegates to study a plan to provide support, and the following year, they endorsed it. Meeting from June 28 to July 1, 1956, the 8th Assembly approved a $100 per-chapter assessment. It was welcome news to LDF head and destined Supreme Court justice Thurgood Marshall, who was on hand to deliver the banquet address. Funds from the Links and other organizations fortified and enabled LDF to continue to provide legal assistance. Among the cases on the LDF docket was Rosa Parks, a Negro seamstress whose December 1, 1955, arrest for refusing to give up her seat in the first row of a "Colored" section of a Montgomery, Alabama, city bus forever linked her to the civil rights movement. Along with monetary support, Hawkins urged The Links to sponsor other human rights initiatives, and she encouraged educational forums geared toward integration.

Hawkins also pushed programs for youth, challenging chapters to provide cultural and recreational outlets for them. As a result of President Harry S. Truman's 1948 executive order creating a Fair Employment Board, new career options such as banking and insurance had opened up to Negroes, and Hawkins challenged The Links to help youth understand and traverse the landscape. In the tradition of the programs of the Philadelphia Links, career counseling, employment workshops, and other experiences were responses to The Links' self-posed question, "What can Links do today for the youth of tomorrow?"

Because National Links was still in its formative years, Hawkins focused on organizational policy and procedures, devoting much time to membership, which, by 1956, numbered 68 chapters. Hawkins regularly used committees to ferret proposals on concerns from selecting members to balancing chapters in Areas, including redistribution. Still, when the proposals went to the body, floor debates sometimes lasted for hours as delegates voiced their opinions.

Hawkins also championed formal recognition, documentation, and celebration of Linkdom. Service was highlighted in a booklet of chapter programs at the 1954 Assembly, and National Links Week was instituted in November 1955 to honor The Links' heritage. The week was also promoted as the ideal time to launch educational programs, thereby communicating the true spirit of Linkdom.

The 9th Assembly, held in Atlanta in 1957, marked the end of Hawkins's four-year tenure, and, as she prepared to pass the gavel, she did so with gratefulness and pride. "I am filled with gratitude to the many friends who have contributed to the success of my administration, and filled too, with a sense of

#2 Hawkins receives corsage at 7th (1955) Assembly.

what I hope is pardonable pride," she said. She pointed to her achievements in programs, noting that "$28,550 has been fully paid to the NAACP." She also expressed delight with operations, proclaiming, "For the first time in its history, National Links has lived and capably operated within its yearly budget, [and] … we have fairly and impartially enforced the rules." Assessing the success of her performance, Hawkins said, "The Links has now taken its place at the top of the organization among Negro women in this country," and she voiced confidence that The Links would "continue to maintain that level throughout the years."

It was the beginning of a new era. Control of the organization, for the first time since the founding, would be in the hands of someone outside the founding group. Some might have felt apprehensive about the change, but Hawkins did not hesitate as she entrusted the jewel to Pauline Weeden Maloney, 3rd National President. She had tapped Maloney for many duties, including chairing the committee on the geographical make up of Areas. Hawkins knew The Links would be in good hands, and entrusting the gavel to her "very good friend" removed some of the sentimentality of letting go.

Six years later, Hawkins's death on October 4, 1963, caught the Philadelphia community and The Links by surprise. Numerous newspapers reported the loss of one of the city's "very prominent citizens" and lamented her death in the fullness of her life. "The death of Margaret Hawkins stunned her friends everywhere. Margaret was such a vital, attractive, live

woman, with much to contribute," was the sentiment. For the memorial service, Frederick Hawkins, her husband for 30 years, surrounded her with the beauty Hawkins, the artist, would have painted, creating a gallery of flowers for the "lover of all things beautiful." The grand collection symbolized both the magnificence she had created in his life and their sons' lives (Fred, Jr. and Bruce) and the splendor her work had wrought for The Links and other organizations that were in her blood—from Jack and Jill of America to Saint Thomas Episcopal Church, home to 12 works of art she had donated for a new structure constructed after a fire.

The perennial testimony to her legacy, however, was what her vision had become, described in the 1962 *Journal* tribute as "the greatest movement of Negro women with the greatest potential to help advance social change and governmental reform in our nation today." Other marks of respect, accorded through the years, bear testimony to her impact. The 14th (1964) Assembly, the first after her death, bemoaned her absence: "National Links, Incorporated has witnessed deep tragedy … we are deeply grieved. We meet at this time without her physical presence, and she is sorely missed." The Assembly also approved the establishment of a charitable and educational trust in her honor.

Additional honors have been bestowed through the years. In 1978, The Links added her portrait as a permanent fixture that would grace the National Headquarters, and in 2003, the Eastern Area commissioned her image for the Great Blacks in Wax Museum in Baltimore, Maryland. The founders' award is a staple for Assemblies, the Margaret Rosell Hawkins/Sarah Strickland Scott School was among the first in the Education across the Miles program, and in 2004, The Links' new leadership initiative was christened the Scott-Hawkins Leadership Institute— markers that will keep the visionary forever Linked.

~ *Earnestine Green McNealey, PhD*
~ *Yvonne Roulhac Horton, PhD*

Margaret Josephine Rosell Hawkins

Links Service
Visionary, Co-Founder, and first President, Philadelphia Links

Designer, Links bracelet

Member, Executive Council (1951)

Impact During Tenure
- Presented Links National grant ($28,000) to NAACP.
- Launched project to support NAACP Legal Defense Fund.
- Championed formal recognition, documentation, and celebration of Linkdom that included the institution of Links Week and program booklets chronicling community service by chapters.
- Reviewed organizational policy and procedures, devoting much time to membership.
- Encouraged educational forums on integration and pushed career education and guidance for youth.
- Appointed an ad hoc committee to study realignment; fifth Area added for a one-year period.

Selected National Honors
- Co-Founder, The Links
- Establishment of a charitable and educational trust in Hawkins's honor
- Statue in Great Blacks in Wax Museum, Baltimore, MD
- Name on Scott-Hawkins Leadership Institute

Margaret Pauline Fletcher Weeden (Maloney) (Ralston)
Third National President (1957–1962)

Educating for Democracy

*The rapidly changing issues of our times and the crises and dilemmas
of the New Age require Links to accept the opportunity for service
that is uniquely ours … to strengthen and deepen (our) commitment
to the great cause which we faithfully and courageously serve.*

THE YEAR 1957 WAS REPLETE with events that changed the American landscape, as well as the history of African Americans in the United States. In politics, the United States was deeply entangled in the Cold War. In science and technology, Sputnik I and II were launched, and an intense race to dominate space began between the United States and the Soviet Union. IBM introduced the digital computer language FORTRAN, and Congress funded the National Cancer Institute. It was also an age when 20 percent of Americans were living below the poverty line, and the "Beatnik" counterculture movement was emerging.

Civil Rights issues also dominated the consciousness of many Americans. The landmark case *Brown v. Board of Education of Topeka* was decided by the Supreme Court in 1954. Mrs. Rosa Parks refused to relinquish her seat on a city bus in 1955, and the Montgomery bus boycott ended in 1956. No less historic was 1957, for despite the record-setting filibuster by Strom Thurmond, Congress approved the first significant civil rights legislation since 1875, and President Dwight D. Eisenhower ordered federal troops to enforce the integration of schools in Little Rock, Arkansas. The Southern Christian Leadership Conference, the brainchild of ministers active in the Montgomery bus boycott, was established in Atlanta, with Dr. Martin Luther King, Jr. as its first president. Business and sports contributed to African American history as well: Barry Gordy founded Motown Records, and Althea Gibson became the first Black American to win women's singles tennis matches at Wimbledon and Forest Hills (US Open).

Margaret Pauline Fletcher Weeden (Maloney) (Ralston), affectionately known as "Polly," was also elected National President of The Links, Incorporated in 1957. Co-Founders Margaret Rosell Hawkins and Sarah Strickland Scott set the framework for the organization and served as its first and second presidents. A vision of the organization beyond that of the founders unfolded with Ralston. As the third National President, she was the bridge that carried the organization from youth to maturity.

Weeden took pride in the contributions The Links had made, but she felt the times dictated that the organization become a more potent and focused force, and she saw programming as the key. Her love for youngsters also made the target obvious. As a member of the Lynchburg (VA) Chapter from the beginning, she was a diligent worker, who helped to shape her chapter through its programming for youth, including the famous "Keyboard" and "Steps with Links" programs. Under her guidance, the chapter had also worked with the Teen-Age Soul Cellar recreation center, transported young children to the public library, tested and identified talented children for support and guidance, and provided art scholarships.

So, when Weeden was elected, she saw an opportunity for The Links to serve community needs no other organization addressed at that time. "The rapidly changing issues of our times and the crises and dilemmas of the New Age" require Links "to accept the opportunity for service that is uniquely ours … to strengthen and deepen (our) commitment to the great cause which we faithfully and courageously serve," she proclaimed.

Therefore, she decided to focus on the identification and support of talented youth, an extension of the Services to Youth facet. This determination led to the current structure of individual Links and Links chapters providing service to the community based on the stated programming goals of the National organization. Acknowledging the transforming nature of the contribution, 5th National President Helen Gray Edmonds said that Link Polly "structured us more formally along the path of a program direction and made it emphatically clear that all of our activities were geared toward Educating for Democracy."

The theme became even more prophetic when The Links began to include issues on the international horizon, such as the concerns of emerging African countries. She created the template for service, and at the end of her term as president, the organization grasped its present course of action. "With a heart full of thanks and gratitude," she credited her Executive Board for "the successful growth of the organization," noting that "each of you has worked hard and efficiently." The last official letter also detailed the contributions of each and expressed her indebtedness for "having had such an honored position … My five years as your National President was one of my richest experiences, hard work, and rewarding," she longingly opined.

"Link Polly" loved The Links and attended most of its Area Conferences and National Assemblies after the conclusion of her tenure as National President. Service to her community and state sustained and guided her retirement journey. She enjoyed work as a consultant for Lyn-Cay Headstart, served on the Central Planning District Commission and the Virginia Cultural Laureate Center. Further, she served on boards that included the Red Cross, The United Way, the Polio Committee, the YWCA, The Lynchburg Community Action Group, Friends of the Library, the City Restoration Committee, the Fine Arts Center, Bethune Child Care Center, Meals-on-Wheels, and the NAACP.

Born in historic Annapolis, Maryland, Ralston was the daughter of William and Eliza Fletcher. She attended elementary school in Annapolis and Washington, DC, and high school in Baltimore, Maryland (the Morgan Academy). Her post-secondary education was received at Howard University (BA) and Columbia University in New York (MA). Her professional career began in Winston-Salem, North Carolina, where she taught English and speech to eager students she pushed, disciplined, and loved them to success. She also met Dr. Henry P. Weeden, known to his friends as "Dick." The happy couple married and moved to Lynchburg, Virginia, where Dr. Weeden opened his dental practice, and Weeden taught in the school system.

Weeden was very successful and her career blossomed. She served successively as teacher, guidance counselor, and administrative principal at the city's dynamic Dunbar High School. For 40 years, she touched the lives of countless students who still remember her counsel, encouragement, and support. She worked tirelessly to find financial support for deserving young people to follow their dreams and attend college, deeds that led to her designation as "Lynchburg's first lady of education."

Three Virginia governors were counted among her friends, and she received appointments from two of them. She maintained her relationship with Delta Sigma Theta Sorority, Inc., begun at Howard University with Alpha Chapter, and served as the sorority's Eastern regional director, an area that spanned nine states. An active member of Jackson Street United Methodist Church, Weeden was elected corresponding secretary for the Washington Conference of the Methodist Church.

One of the many testaments to Maloney's service and lasting impact

A consummate friend, Weeden filled her life with activities that promoted friendship. She played poker with a select group of friends from Richmond, Durham, Raleigh, Petersburg, Danville, and Washington, DC. In the 1950s, when African Americans specialized in entertaining in their homes because of the restricted social environment, the "Poker Group" visited for the weekend and played the game. Their children enjoyed these events as well. It became a family affair, and lifelong friendships developed among the children.

Weeden also enjoyed playing bridge and lavishly entertained her other fun clubs, especially "The Grannies," named in honor of the late Link Etta Moten Barnett. Similar to the poker group (but established three decades later), they also met in members' homes, but instead of cards, they shared a weekend of fun, shopping, and "girl talk." No statement about Weeden would be complete without mention of her love for beautiful clothes and shoes. She was an elegant lady from head to toe!

An educator, wife, mother, community leader, friend, and great American woman, Weeden died on June 22, 1987. Funeralized in Lynchburg, she was buried near her childhood home in Annapolis, Maryland. Ninth National President Regina Jollivette Frazier conducted her memorial service, and the November 1987 *Link to Link* was devoted to her service. In addition, during the 1987 Executive Council and Foundation meetings, a memorial in her honor was displayed at the National Headquarters building.

"Link Polly" inherited the gauntlet from founders Hawkins and Scott, crystallized their vision, and then added her own interpretation of The Links' culture and Program structure. The Links, Incorporated is a better organization because of her leadership.

~ *Bishetta D. Merritt, PhD*

Margaret Pauline Fletcher Weeden (Maloney) (Ralston)

Links Service

Charter member, Lynchburg Chapter

Principal, Keyboard Project, Lynchburg Chapter

Impact During Tenure

- Established a common National theme for programming—Educating for Democracy.
- Instituted The Links' first facet—Services to Youth—and implemented "The Search for the Talented Youth."
- Established National Trends and Services as a second facet.
- Added Area directors to review the process for new chapters.
- Widened the scope of international services by directing attention to emerging African nations.

Selected National Honors

- State historical marker erected in her honor (2015)
- "First Lady of Education" Endearment title
- First Black elected president of the Southern Regional Association of School Boards
- First Black elected to Lynchburg School Board
- First woman rector of the Norfolk State University Board of Visitors
- Director, Eastern Region, Delta Sigma Theta Sorority
- Honorary Doctor of Humane Letters, Saint Paul's College, Lawrenceville, VA

Vivian Jones Beamon
Fourth National President (1962–1970)

Dynamic Dimensions

In the defense of liberty and freedom, National Links,
Incorporated saw its duty boldly, made its decision wisely,
pursued its goals vigorously, and achieved its success completely.

WHEN VIVIAN JONES BEAMON was elected as National President, the landscape of America was defined by change that irrevocably transformed the social, cultural, political, and educational backdrop of the nation. Marked by watershed events, it was a time in which much was gained, and the nation was filled with unbounded aspirations and hope. Yet, it was also a period of confusion, deep despair, and shock.

John F. Kennedy's inauguration as America's 35th president in 1961 heralded a "New Frontier," and the peoples of the world were exhorted to fight the "common enemies of man—tyranny, poverty, disease and war itself." But two years later, Kennedy was assassinated. His successor, Lyndon Baines Johnson, introduced one of the most far-reaching domestic programs designed to eradicate poverty and racial injustice, and he ushered through two legislative milestones: the Civil Rights Act of 1964 and the Voting Rights Act of 1965. But Johnson also presided over the escalation of the Vietnam War. Dr. Martin Luther King, Jr. became the youngest recipient of the Nobel Peace Prize, and the women's rights movement took flight; but increased disharmony between the races, genders, classes, and generations led to continual violence.

Born March 15, 1902, in the Bluegrass countryside of Paris, Kentucky, Beamon experienced many atrocities of wars, the Great Depression, and racial discrimination. Surveying the landscape, she concluded, "Perhaps the major crisis in American domestic life is the stark reality of the fast-growing segments of our society; those of affluence and those who are poor and disadvantaged." Beamon realized that Negroes, locked "at the bottom of the heap, (used) riots, looting, arson, and acts of violence (to) articulate their frustrations, anxieties, and lack of hope," and she warned, "Unless some constructive dialogue is begun between the two elements in our own racial pot, the nation stands to suffer more violence."

Under the "Dynamic Dimensions" banner, Beamon offered multiple venues for the conversations, and for nearly all of the 1960s, her sure, purposeful, and visionary leadership guided The Links' contributions to the dialogue. In the words of 5th National President Helen Gray Edmonds, "Vivian Beamon structured the aspects of Links' programming: ... emphasis on The Arts, the National services we bear, the International services we should bear, and the continued Services to Youth."

Throughout her administration, Beamon challenged Links to "move ahead with strength, determination, and wisdom to the fulfillment of commitments. We must take inventory of the services we have rendered in our adult capacity as citizens in a democracy which is still becoming," she said; and she delineated the crux of each facet.

- Who shall fill the gap for the culturally deprived? Who (will) try to motivate and inspire the educationally disadvantaged?"
- The floodtide of human equality, dignity and equal rights engulfs us all. We as Links are concerned with national trends and will continue to seek and render national service.
- We live in an era of keen international trade competition, foreign aid, and foreign policy administration, a threatened world economy because of the uneasiness of the world money market. We cannot afford to be indifferent to the great world changes. We as Links rededicate ourselves toward helping to foster programs for peace, better international relations and racial understanding.

Beamon expected members to help chart the course. "We will determine together the most urgent work we must do, the most pressing needs we must meet, and the direction we must take if we are to respond courageously and creatively," she said.

The Assembly endorsed support for agencies working on behalf of those at the bottom. Delegates at the 14th (1964) Assembly pledged $75,000 to the NAACP Legal Defense Fund over a three-year period, but within two years, chapters had met the goal. As a result, the 15th (1966) Assembly raised the bar to $100,000, which would be collected through a $3.50 per-member assessment. By 1967, the pledge had been met.

In a proclamation to the 1968 Assembly, Beamon recorded the effort for posterity:

> The NAACP Legal Defense Fund, standing in front of legal battles for the oppressed, has moved mankind nearer to a society in which all shall be free. In the defense of liberty and freedom, National Links, Incorporated, saw its duty boldly, made its decision wisely, pursued its goals vigorously, and achieved its success completely.

Guided by Beamon's leadership, The Links also presented the first $50,000 of a $100,000 pledge to the Urban League, supporting "established organizations which were engaged in the task of making American democracy more meaningful and more functional for the humblest Negro citizens from our village hamlets to the ghettos of our inner cities."

Sisterhood also received attention during Beamon's eight-year term, the longest in The Links' history. A year after taking office, she led the 14th (1964) Assembly in memorializing the October 1963 passing of Co-Founder Margaret Hawkins with a trust fund. She also continuously urged involvement by all chapters. For the 17th Assembly in 1970, her last, she asked chapters to help her "bask in the one success I should like to consider my zenith—116 delegates seated at roll call."

In operations, Beamon engineered the centralization of administrative services on a trial basis. Outlining the administrative problems posed by nomadic conditions, she said:

> At present our headquarters reside in the residence of the president. The administrative assistant to the president has been elsewhere, principally on college campuses where materials are at a low cost and equipment available without cost to the organization. The quality of performance

of each officer is to a large extent due to the use of a paid office not under Links employment or the skills and expertise of friends of the office holder used as gratis.

A tribute carried in the June 1970 issue of *The Journal* was representative of the high marks she received for her sterling performance as National President:

> *We dedicate this issue of The Journal to our illustrious National President, Vivian J. Beamon, who has been the tremendous dynamo moving us on to greater responsibilities, areas of concern, commitments and accomplishments in an "Era of Dynamic Dimensions" during her eight years of outstanding, progressive, and dedicated leadership.*

The Cincinnati Enquirer, August 29, 1974, page 54

Dies Tuesday

Mrs. Vivian Beamon, Active In Civic Affairs

Services for Mrs. Vivian J. Beamon, widely known for her educational and civic contributions to the city, will be held at 10 a.m. Saturday at St. Andrews Episcopal Church, 1809 Rutland Ave., with burial in the Spring Grove Mausoleum. Visitation will be from 6 to 9 p.m. Friday at the Renfro Funeral Home, 647 Forest Ave.

Mrs. Beamon died Tuesday at her residence in the Regency Apartments, 2444 Madison Rd., Hyde Park. In the educational field, she was perhaps best known as principal of the Hays School, where she was the guiding light for at least eight assistant principals who became Cincinnati elementary school principals. Among many activities in the civic field, she gained distinction particularly as the first woman president of the Urban League, serving three one-year terms.

In 1969, she was one of The Enquirer's 10 Women of the Year.

Known in various other parts of the country as well as in Cincinnati for her work in producing more positive educational programs for the innercity child, Mrs. Beamon entered the Cincinnati Public School System in 1931. This was after graduation from Kentucky College and Industrial Institution in Frankfort. She earned a bachelors degree from the University of Cincinnati and a masters degree at New York University, where she was a Rosenwald Fellow, studying how to design educational programs that would motivate innercity children to stay in school and seek higher education. She also did advanced study at the University of Chicago, Columbia University and the University of Michigan.

While at Hays, during summer recesses Mrs. Beamon served as workshop consultant at Syracuse University, North Carolina College and the University of North Carolina

Vivian Beamon
. . . force in education

at Chapel Hill. On retirement in 1969 from the Cincinnati school system, she became an assistant professor in the UC School of Education.

Mrs. Beamon served on the boards of the National Urban League, Child Guidance Home, Children's Theater and the Community Chest of Greater Cincinnati. She was a past president of Links, Inc., a national association of black women interested in community service and youth. She was the second president of the Women's Auxiliary of the National Dental Association. Her husband, the late Dr. Reginald E. Beamon, a dentist, was the first black to run on the Charter ticket for Cincinnati City Council.

Mrs. Beamon was a member also of Delta Kappa Gamma, scholastic honorary. Her only survivor is a cousin, Mrs. Roberta Thompson, New York City.

Beamon's self-assessment of The Links' engagement in social action provided an even better barometer of The Links' impact during her tenure.

> *The search for first-class citizenship, social justice and the right to participate in the American mainstream burgeoned into the greatest Civil Rights Crusade in the Twentieth Century. We supported the strongest legal arm of our time in the defense of minority people.*
>
> *The past decade revealed wide-spread unemployment for Americans who had no saleable skills, and their concentration in our metropolitan centers created disillusionment and despair. We aided the strongest organization in the land in seeking to understand the problems of the inner cities, the National Urban League.*
>
> *The fields of Government, Education, and Industry turned their collective attention to the educationally disadvantaged and culturally deprived youth. In order to accommodate young men and women at both ends of the spectrum, the disadvantaged and the talented, Links restructured its emphasis to Services to Youth.*
>
> *When the talents of youth found little outlet for their creative expression, and when every testing device in the American educational system revealed that our youth were deficient in the creative and performing arts, Links moved to the program emphasis of Freedom and the Fine Arts.*

Beamon's administration defined The Links' programming and the course, creating additional facets and moving the boundaries "beyond local environs to the state and nation." The Links' engagement and results continue to be fueled by the "Dynamic Dimensions" Beamon instituted.

~ *Leila Gaston Rhodes, PhD*
~ *Earnestine Green McNealey, PhD*

Vivian Jones Beamon

Links Service

Charter member, Cincinnati (OH) Chapter

Central Area Director

National Vice President

Impact During Tenure

- Approved Central Office on experimental basis.
- Expanded National Trends and Services facet to include International Trends.
- Established Margaret Hawkins Memorial Trust Fund (to be funded by $100 from each chapter by the next Assembly).
- Barred Area meetings after May 1, during Assembly years.
- Approved $75,000 grant for NAACP Education and Legal Defense Fund payable over three years.
- Staggered election of officers and phased out four-year terms.
- Approved Freedom and the Arts, previously a section of Services to Youth, as a facet.
- Pledged $100,000 to the National Urban League's Forward Thrust program.

Selected Honors

- Longest-serving National President
- Rosenwald Fellow, New York University
- First National President from the Central Area
- First woman president of the Cincinnati Urban League
- Second president, Women's Auxiliary of the National Dental Association
- One of Cincinnati's ten most outstanding women

Helen Gray Edmonds, PhD
Fifth National President (1970–1974))

The Priorities of the 1970s—Effective Involvement Now

The essential requirement to be a Link continues to hold sway. What does this potential person have that will confer distinction upon The Links, Inc? Once inducted, the obligation continues, and the only legal tender is service.

HELEN GRAY EDMONDS was no shrinking violet. In writings, speeches, and deeds, she was "forthright in expressing her conservative philosophy, particularly in economics; and she remained both solidly in and detached from the black community to speak candidly of its shortcomings." She recognized the legal gains from the Black revolution of the 1960s, but she scoffed at the idea promulgated by the new leadership that the government was indebted to them. "What the government owes every able-bodied American are equal opportunity and equal justice," the veteran college dean and politician said.

It was this no-holds-barred approach that Edmonds brought to the presidency, and her stance was undergirded by a portfolio filled with experience as a National, Area, and chapter leader, as recapped by Edmonds in her address to the 1974 Assembly.

The heritage bequeathed to me and the long hours of experience in program effectiveness gave me a thorough acquaintanceship with this organization and its membership. Having consistently written the names of Link members over a span of years and having met you in Area Conferences and National

Assemblies, I could truthfully say that I know 2,000 of you by name. This was my heritage as I moved into the office of National President.

Throughout her tenure and beyond, Edmonds spoke with a sense of authority, and Links listened. Calling the notion that The Links bestows stature on members "backward," she held that members must bring honor to The Links. "The essential requirement to be a Link continues to hold sway. What does this potential person have that will confer distinction upon The Links, Inc?" Once inducted, the obligation continues, and the only legal tender is service.

Historians characterized the 1970s in America as a period of revolution, and with Edmonds at the helm, The Links' transformation was of epic proportions. A two-time Program director (1962–1967; 1969–1970), Edmonds targeted programming first, noting that it defined The Links. "It is what this organization has become, what it has done, that keeps it in the forefront of American life," she said. Accordingly, Edmonds demanded that chapters perform exemplary service.

Never before had the call for excellence in programming been so insistent. Reiterating that service was obligatory for anyone who wore the Links label, Edmonds also raised the bar on the kinds and levels of service, declaring, "In this day of pressing needs on so many fronts, we cannot give less." Sporadic events masquerading as programming particularly distressed her, and she gave notice of a higher standard. "The Links era of the one-shot involvement is over," she said. "No chapter can pay for a bus to take 25 children to a museum and write beautifully in its report that Chapter X has fulfilled its chapter responsibility to Services to Youth; or purchase $10 worth of paints, oils, or an easel for some young person in need, and write beautifully that Chapter Y has fulfilled its responsibility to Freedom and the Arts. Nor can chapters carry soup to some Senior Citizen who is ill or take her for a ride and write beautifully that Chapter Z has fulfilled its responsibility to National Trends and Services. We become involved in long-range programs, and we make our impact upon the community, or we are dead."

Edmonds said The Links needed "chapter presidents who energetically inspired their local flocks to latch on to the national programs" and members who "were not only foot soldiers in program fulfillment, but also the initiators of equating Links' programs with their communities' needs." Edmonds was just as adamant about chapters paying the $25 per-person, per-year Grants-in-Aid assessments. Noting that delegates had voted on the assessments in 1964, 1968, and 1970, she reiterated that "the decisions of the General Assembly are binding on each chapter." Calling out chapters

that had sent token funds or no funds, she warned that "this cannot be allowed to continue."

Chapters heeded the call on the local level and also responded nationally, sending in a record $100,000-plus for Grants-in-Aid. Edmonds maximized the impact and imprint by setting a record half-million-dollar goal for the United Negro College Fund (UNCF). The 19th (1974) Assembly voted to continue the effort, and by 1984, the effort had blossomed into the first of The Links' Million-Dollar campaigns. Presenting a check for $132,000 at the 18th (1972) Assembly in New Orleans to UNCF, Edmonds said the award was being made to UNCF "in recognition of the absolute importance of higher education to Black people at this time in history." UNCF said the amount was the highest donation presented by a Black organization.

Because Edmonds was a stickler for order, she insisted that a comprehensive document be developed, and then left intact. Making changes at every Assembly was unnecessary and a waste of time, she said. Consequently, her administration developed "the first full comprehensive constitution." Approved by the 1974 Assembly, the vote on the document followed Edmonds's institution of Assembly Workbooks that chapters received three months prior to each Assembly, thereby enabling full chapter discussions before the Assembly attendance and discouraging modifications after the Assembly.

Edmonds's penchant for regulations led to stricter formulation of statements on public policy, which she termed "most paramount" for a national organization. While the 16th (1968) National Assembly had adopted a "National Links' Policy Position on Public Affairs," Edmonds felt that "one clear voice" was still needed.

Every Link throughout the country where a microphone was placed before her was saying what Links were doing and what they were not doing, criticizing the US government on every issue and especially about emerging Africa and how our government should support all Black nations, and anything else they chose. To recognize that we were a non-profit and had no right to go political was difficult to get over to them.

As a result, Edmonds "was afraid to create a social action committee," but she was heartened by the response from chapters. "When chapters realized that IRS could demand an internal audit of the National and each of the chapters, they were willing to curb in a little," she said. Subsequently, each Assembly, in the interest of the new National approach, adopted a policy that not only reflected a unified voice, but one that was also apolitical.

Another sea change was wrought from Edmonds's love for history. The history professor, first Black woman to receive a PhD from The Ohio State University, and Ford Foundation post-doc European history scholar made numerous contributions to the study of history. She capitalized on her knowledge and experience to lay a foundation for historical preservation in The Links. Prior to her administration, little attention was assigned to preserving The Links' heritage. By the time she left office, Archives & History had been established as a standing committee, a call for materials had been issued, and initial steps had been taken to place The Links' collections within a repository.

Edmonds also took up the gauntlet that 4th National President Beamon had advanced for a National Headquarters. Like Beamon and 3rd National President Pauline Weeden Maloney, Edmonds believed that a central office with staff was critical for efficient operations and program delivery. She reminded the 18th (1972) Assembly that Links did not have one. "Though I use the term 'National Office,' we have no National Office. We have no secretary. We have not one file, nor one typewriter," she said.

Such was the state of things, despite the 14th (1964) Assembly's approval of a central office on a trial basis. To devise a strategy, Edmonds turned to her newly appointed National Advisory Council— former National officers and organizers of the Philadelphia Chapter. The committee endorsed the concept, and the 18th (1972) Assembly authorized another trial. At the 19th (1974) Washington Assembly, delegates approved the committee's recommendation for a permanent headquarters.

In a summary of her administration, Edmonds characterized her achievements as lengthy and laborious. "It was the long, hard task to move The Links' work from the dining room tables … to a central office," she said. But she took great pride that the establishment of the central office "belongs to my administration." Expressing "praise" to Ursula Murrell of Los Angeles, chairman of the National Advisory Council, Edmonds said the "superb job" by Murrell, including signing the lease, per the Assembly's authorization, which enabled her successor to walk in and set up operations. In her report to the 20th (1976) Assembly, 6th National President Pauline Ellison acknowledged Edmonds's feat. "Helen had put forth tremendous efforts to achieve a National Headquarters, and the establishment of the National Headquarters was only one of her many achievements," Ellison said.

Aware of the onerous responsibility placed on host chapters as a result of Links business and entertainment for Assemblies, Edmonds also pushed for Nationally sponsored Assemblies. Local chapters should not be "saddled with the providing of entertainment for three sets of guests— Links, Connecting Links, and Heir-O-Links," she told the 18th (1972) Assembly. The Assembly affirmed her view, and in 1974, Edmonds presided over the first Nationally sponsored Assembly, using local chapters as liaison resources.

She also improved operations, introducing standard materials and forms. Advising the Executive Council in May 1972 that "no Link chapters have charters," Edmonds not only presented two designs to facilitate selection, but she also scheduled a "Charter Day" ceremony as part of the upcoming Assembly in Baton Rouge. She further tweaked Assembly features through the institution of recognition awards for "persons who have achieved in national life in the three areas of our program facets," and she incorporated an Assembly Workbook to facilitate delegates' readiness to conduct business.

Links Journal editor Will Florence Robbins characterized Edmonds's leadership as "vigorous, capable, and strategic. She brings new organizational methods, techniques, and administrative expertise, enthusiasm, new expectations, and the added dimension of international experience to Linkdom," Robbins said.

In a keynote address to the 1986 Assembly, Edmonds pensively acknowledged her impact and explained her style.

Whatever contributions I have made to Links, as well as to other facets of this nation's existence, were made at the high noon of my life. I am now going down the other side of the mountain, reaching 75 years in December. I bear only good wishes to all. If I have said some things which made you displeased, I can only say that I spoke truth as I see it. If I have said some things which opened your eyes to new vistas for our organization, I am pleased.

The college history professor, graduate school dean, politician, alternate delegate to the General Assembly of the United Nations in 1970, and citizen extraordinaire audaciously and unapologetically channeled her talents and experiences to shake up Linkdom, and the seismic changes she engineered moved The Links to a higher peak.

~ Earnestine Green McNealey, PhD
~ Jessie M. Jones

Helen Gray Edmonds, PhD

Links Service
National Director of National and International Trends and Services

Impact During Tenure
- Structured the National Chapter Establishment Program.
- Established Grants-in-Aid as an integral part of Linkdom.
- Made archives a priority, elevating committee to standing status, and fostered establishment of the National Archives.
- Vested authority and responsibility for establishing chapters with National.
- Pushed Nationally sponsored Assembly.
- Revised the *Constitution*.
- Completed $100,000 Urban League payment.
- Initiated $1 million donation to UNCF to be paid over four-year period.
- Secured approval to establish National Headquarters.
- Issued first chapter charters and held Charter Day celebration.

Selected National Honors
- First African American woman to second the nomination for a candidate for president of the United States of America (Eisenhower in 1956)

- First Black woman to receive a PhD in history from The Ohio State University.
- First Black woman to become Dean of a Graduate School of Arts and Sciences in the United States
- Grant recipient, General Education Board – Rockefeller Foundation, The Ford Foundation Fund for the Advancement of Education, Southern Fellowship Fund, and the National Foundation of the Humanities
- US Department of State Appointment as Leader-Specialist in the International Education Exchange to Germany, Austria, Denmark, Sweden, and France
- O. Max Gardner Award from the North Carolina Consolidated System of Higher Education for the "greatest contribution to the welfare of the human race"
- Alternate-Delegate, General Assembly of the United Nations
- Name on Young Scholars research conference: Helen G. Edmonds Graduate Colloquium of History at North Carolina Central University.

Pauline Allen Ellison, LHD
Sixth National President (1974–1978)

Improving the Quality of Life by Linking Leadership and Services to Meet the Challenges of Community and National Needs

We have lifted our conscious-awareness above the level of self-centered, 'let's have a good time' policies and programs to the level of social consciousness that involves us in the social change process. Members of The Links, Incorporated can be proud of the fact that our standards are high—our goals lofty—and our plans were for excellence in performance and outstanding achievement in community service.

I N 1966, PAULINE ELLISON was invited to join her friend Mignon Johnson in establishing what would eventually become the Arlington (VA) Chapter of The Links, Incorporated. Ellison served as the group's first vice president, and in that capacity, designed a "Monte Carlo" event as a fundraiser. The affair debuted in 1970, and 38 years later, it remains the group's major fundraiser, increasing available resources to educate students and meet critical needs in the community.

When she took The Links' helm at the 20th National Assembly in 1974, Ellison brought the same desire to maximize program support with her. Her vision was to focus on local, state, and national resources and networks to help execute programs and increase national visibility. Recognizing Links' strength, Ellison introduced new ways to propel programming under the theme "Improving the Quality of Life by Linking Leadership and Service to Meet the Challenge of Community and National Needs."

Maximizing programs through connections was Ellison's chief goal when she assumed the presidency, as recapped in her closing address.

I came into service as your President with a vision of sharpening the focus on the opportunities available at the local, state, and national levels, which Links could utilize to better carry out their programs, and hopefully to expand existing programs to a point of national visibility as Links programs which were relevant, viable, and readily accessible and identifiable in local communities.

Ellison saw Links as a human resource to the nation, and she focused on developing leaders who served communities locally by combining their talents and assets to influence decision makers and policymakers at all levels. She subsequently demonstrated her prowess by calling on connections all the way up to the Office of the President of the United States. But the first order of business was to operationalize a national headquarters, as mandated by the 1974 Assembly.

Efforts to centralize operations began in 1964, with a two-year trial, but ten years passed before the Assembly issued the go ahead for leased space and staff. And now, as the new president, Ellison had been given the keys to the building and charged to transform it into a headquarters, including procuring the services of an experienced and efficient office employee, contacting Xerox and IBM to determine if equipment could be obtained under a demonstration loan or grant basis, and enabling the flow of all standard forms.

Coupled with the requisite launching of her program, she found the challenge more than daunting: "This was an assignment, which taxed not only my ingenuity and public management and administration background, but every ounce of my stamina…. A service organization of 4,000 members cannot survive and serve its members efficiently while implementing its programs effectively without a permanent headquarters," she said.

In accordance with the Assembly mandate, Ellison hired two part-time staffers. She also established two committees to map a strategy for the next steps: a Transition Committee to develop a blueprint for bringing the functions and duties into the central location and a Personnel Committee to staff headquarters with qualified individuals. By the end of Ellison's administration in 1978, a milestone had been achieved, and she praised the transformation.

"We have removed records from parlors, dining rooms, and bedrooms into a true business office—from an operation which was disparate to one which is centrifugal," she said.

Calling the National Headquarters at 1424 Sixteenth Street NW in Washington, DC, "more than an address," Ellison said it represented "the steps from amateurism to professionalism—a whole new plateau in organization management. The scale of its planning and operation must now be commensurate with the challenge." The Assembly subsequently approved the addition of a Personnel Committee as a standing committee.

Devoting attention to National Headquarters matters and programs required meticulous planning and execution, but there were even more demands on Ellison's time. She always believed that Links should become social change agents, as well as community and national leaders. In this spirit, she accepted an appointment as one of eight civil rights leaders who met regularly with President Gerald R. Ford and members of his cabinet and sought out high profile personalities for honorary membership. Ellison also participated in various White House briefings and conferences while serving on congressional- and cabinet-level task forces, including serving as a member of President James Earl Carter's transition team.

Ellison positioned the Links not only with the executive branch of government and personalities, but she also linked with government officials and the private sector, bringing in a team of experts who shared concepts on structuring programs and obtaining funding and other resources. These individuals understood the state of the nation, knew where to go for funding, and how to write winning proposals. Their presentations complemented the traditional Best of Show in chapter programs.

Ellison's experience as a government official was a key ally in building linkages. She had served as the first African American employee relations specialist for the Department of Housing and Urban Development (HUD), and later, she became HUD's White House Liaison to the president's Youth Opportunity Programs and a key member of Vice President Hubert Humphrey's committee on the Back-to-School program.

Concern for the Black family, with major emphasis on children, was another initiative Ellison pushed. She made career and family life education a central focus of Services to Youth. She also believed that Links had a responsibility to ensure that children were not culturally deprived, challenging chapters to "put a new light in someone's deprived eyes and new spirit in someone's hungry spirit." Holding that there was a link between education and culture, Ellison wanted chapters to use their great talent and varied experiences to provide outlets for cultural enrichment. "If our children are suffering educationally because of the lack of exposure to all that is culturally good, knowing what those needed exposures are, then that is our unmistakable challenge," she said.

Ellison also demonstrated the power of Linkdom, presenting a $150,000 check to the United Negro College Fund to complete an eight-year commitment to donate a half-million dollars to fund scholarships at historically Black colleges and universities. Expressing her pride during the 20th National Assembly in 1976 on making "the largest financial contribution to the United Negro College Fund, of any organization of our type," Ellison joyfully proclaimed:

> *We have lifted our conscious-awareness above the level of self-centered, 'let's have a good time' policies and programs to the level of social consciousness that involves us in the social change process. Members of The Links, Incorporated can be proud of the fact that our standards are high—our goals lofty—and our plans were for excellence in performance and outstanding achievement in community service.*

Another internal matter that Ellison addressed was organizational growth. From 1946 to 1976, the biggest challenge of The Links, Incorporated was survival, she said. The addition of a Chapter Establishment officer at the 1972 Assembly resulted in the addition of 16 new chapters after the 1972 Assembly; but at the 1976 Assembly, delegates put the brakes on new chapters, limiting establishment to groups in the Western Area. As a result, only four chapters were established between 1976 and 1978.

#1 Scott and #6 Ellison (third and fourth from the left) with Etta Moten Barnett, Eugenia Long, Hazel Boulware, and Jewel Thompson.

Yet, the number of chapters and the overall membership had increased to a level that pleased Ellison.

Ellison also gave attention to The Links' heritage. An ardent proponent of preserving history, Ellison "worked to present The Links' first national historical and statistical book" at the 21st Assembly in 1976. Because only 80 percent of chapters responded, the project was strapped. Ellison's endorsement of a history, however, remained strong. Addressing the 1976 Assembly, she declared, "Although this is a time of looking back in reverence, of looking ahead in faith, confidence and hope, this is also the time of recording our acts of service so that all may know the broad scope of service and dedication which was rendered by the Links, Inc. for generations to come."

That belief was further reflected in the commissioning of a portrait of Co-Founder and 2nd National President Margaret Hawkins to hang in the National Headquarters. The heritage recognition was a continuation of the 1976 Assembly, where Links firsts were featured. It was also Ellison who suggested "Journal" as the moniker for The Links' official organ. Also of concern was the way other writers and historians would treat The Links' record. Many still considered the organization to be an elitist group that placed more emphasis on class and good times than on service, but Ellison changed the perspective:

> *We have risen above the public criticism in publications which accused us of being middle-class bourgeois and out of step with the times by our practical day-to-day demonstration that social responsibility is our theme and service to humanity is our watchword.*

Ellison noted that The Links' self-sufficiency and philanthropy had also distinguished the organization. "We have been able to avoid the stereotype of just another service organization seeking handouts—by paying our own way," she said.

Ellison served the Links with uncommon grace and dignity. She used her enormous talents, keen intellect, and tireless energy to pave the way for others. As a leader, she inspired, mentored, and

challenged the membership to make a difference. Impacting the lives of others was the challenge she continuously issued, as she encouraged members to pick up the baton of service:

> *In the recesses of our minds and hearts, think seriously on the ways we can improve the quality of life for others as well as for ourselves, as we go forward in friendship. The harvest cries out for reapers. Will you take up the challenges? Will you break new ground in your community?*

And Ellison was confident that they would. She declared, "A challenge always carries with it the element of risk, the element of courage and impulse to do," and that "this term has never and will never frighten Links women, for we are well experienced in facing challenges." The simple eloquence to her life was grounded in faith, decency, and commitment to service that spanned many decades and touched many lives.

Her rich tradition of community service can be traced to the strong spiritual, family, and social values instilled in her by her parents, William and Rosa Allen, and further strengthened by her husband, Oscar, Jr., and their three children, Oscar III, Paula Michele, and Karla. Envisioning the future of The Links into the 21st century and on to higher ground, Ellison sees a bold sisterhood that has been triumphant, and she is confident that it will grow even stronger as it continues to respond to the challenges of the day.

~ *Tracey Tolbert Jones*
~ *Earnestine Green McNealey, PhD*

Pauline Allen Ellison, LHD

Links Service

National Director, Services to Youth

Charter Member, Vice President, and President, Arlington Chapter

Impact During Tenure

- Operationalized first National Headquarters.
- Fostered establishment of a second chapter in large metropolitan areas when chapters reached their maximum of 30.
- Pushed International Trends' elevation to independent status, making it the fourth prong of the program facets.
- Advanced Personnel Committee as a standing committee.
- Presented $150,000 to UNCF, increasing amount to $500,000 of $1 million pledge.
- Inducted honorary members Patricia Roberts Harris, Marian Anderson, and Mattiwilda Dobbs.

Selected National Honors

- First Black female Employee Relations Officer, Department of Housing and Urban Development
- First Black woman to become a member of the Board of Directors of Central Fidelity Banks, Inc.
- Board of Directors, Arlington (VA) Hospital
- Board of Directors, Federal Executives Institute
- LHD, Wilberforce University (OH); Livingstone College (NC)

Julia Brogdon Purnell, LHD
Seventh National President (1978–1982)

Linking Friendship, Leadership and Service
to Meet the Challenge of Community Needs

*My community is the place ... where my vote is cast, where my children
are educated, where my neighbors dwell, and where my life is chiefly lived
... My community has the right to my civic loyalty ... I should seek to
make better the best things, the worst things I should help to suppress ...
It is my community, and it is entitled to the best there is in me.*

JULIA BROGDON PURNELL "knew a
little about running a national organization"
when she took control of The Links at the close
of the 21st (1978) Assembly in Chicago, and that
knowledge served her well. From putting necessary documents at members' fingertips to securing
federal grants, Purnell drew on her experiences as
16th National President (1962–1966) of Alpha Kappa
Alpha Sorority, Incorporated. What positioned and
subsequently propelled her into The Links' top position, however, was her performance as The Links'
Southern Area director.

What a push she got! Nominated from the floor,
Purnell won a landslide victory, besting the total
votes garnered by two other contenders—the slated
candidate and the sitting vice president, who was also
a floor nominee. Purnell wasted no time in vali-
dating the confidence that had been vested in her.
During her first term, her administration moved the
National Headquarters into a larger space, housed

the archives in partnership with the United Negro
College Fund, partnered with a community col-
lege to sponsor the first National African-American
Crafts Conference and Jubilee.

Purnell urged members to perform their duties
with gladness. "'I serve'" is the motto ... as we
improve the quality of life," Purnell reiterated in

a May 1980 *Link to Link*. A staunch believer in casting down your nets where you are, Purnell championed community programming as the foremost responsibility. Links, she said were the trustees of public good, and her goal was to have each Link claim ownership for the progress of her community:

> *My community is the place ... where my vote is cast, where my children are educated, where my neighbors dwell, and where my life is chiefly lived ... my community has the right to my civic loyalty ... I should seek to make better the best things, the worst things I should help to suppress ... It is my community, and it is entitled to the best there is in me.*

Known for her frankness and openness, Purnell employed a "There are no victims here" approach toward Links members, telling them that despite being placed in an age of peril by destiny, rather than choice, they had inherited power, and their heritage compelled them to use it to make a difference for those who were truly mistreated and persecuted. "We have a responsibility to be worthy daughters of great and glorious women of the past," and she called on each chapter to join her in launching "a nationwide crusade against the evils which affect with particular severity, Blacks as American citizens. Push back the frontiers of ignorance, poverty, illiteracy, poor housing, and political indifference," she entreated.

Aware of the increasing delinquency among girls, Purnell sought and received a unanimous endorsement from the Executive Council to accept an invitation from the National Board of the Young Women's Christian Association to develop services or advocacy programs for high-risk girls from socially and educationally disadvantaged minority groups. The program was subsequently funded, and The Links received a $100,000 grant from the Department of Justice to prevent and treat delinquency among girls aged 11 to 17.

Purnell also formed other partnerships to provide a range of programming, including advocacy networks, political economics, and arts initiatives. Along with pushing domestic issues, Purnell embraced global

#7 Purnell with Connecting Link Clifton Purnell

assistance. In 1982, Links chapters donated $13,000 to fund the digging and purchase of water wells in Africa.

But Purnell's influence was most pronounced in The Links' structure and operations. Marshaling diagnosis, prognosis, prescription, and correction as arsenal, she forged a model for attacking internal issues. Purnell studied The Links' backbone and minutes from every Assembly to get her grounding and routing. "We evaluated where we were and what the mandates of the membership were through the years as recorded in the minutes," she said. Then Purnell enlisted a team of experts to evaluate areas specific to their discipline. The review was necessary not only to chart the course, but also to ensure that Purnell's vision for Linkdom was solidly anchored in policies and practices. Purnell characterized the evaluation as "somewhat of a summit in which for the first time, I suppose, committees of Links had a chance to meet and deliberate and project for the biennial." After determining what the organization's resources were and identifying its strengths and weaknesses, Purnell outlined the next step, which was "to prescribe where we need to go and how far we need to go, followed by correction," she said.

Purnell found the assessment on friendship particularly troubling. "We are mighty weak in that, mighty weak in that," she lamented. Decrying misinformation and disagreements as toxic, she encouraged dialogue: "Friendship is two-fold. It is empathy, it's sympathy, it's togetherness, and it's tolerance. I may not agree with you, but if we are friends, let us sit down and talk it out." As a correction, she pleaded, "Let judgments be made on the basis of facts ... and watch what we say and how we say it; because after you've said it, you can't take it back."

The attitude was consistent with Purnell's persona. She was an erudite woman who believed in the goodness and potential of humankind. "Women working together can surmount any barrier in improving the quality of life," she preached. For illumination and inspiration, she regularly injected truisms from philosophers and writers, interweaving quotes from the likes of Jesus, Martin Luther King, Shakespeare, Mordecai Johnson, Catherine Drinker Bowen, Rollo May, John Bunyan, Plato, Emerson, Melville, and more.

A second issue Purnell tackled was incorporation. In May 1980, Purnell advised the membership that The Links, Incorporated was no longer in compliance with the laws of New Jersey as a result of not having a resident of New Jersey on its Executive Council nor a Registered Agent. The Links had also failed to file as a foreign corporation in the District of Columbia, a mandatory requirement for organizations doing business in the District, though not incorporated there. Based on options proposed by "a highly reputable Washington, D. C. law firm," the Executive Council approved incorporating in the District, and the 22nd (1980) Assembly ratified the action.

Purnell also resolved the tax-exempt bottleneck for The Links Foundation. As early as 1968, The Links pondered ways to enable members to receive tax deductions for their Grants-in-Aid contributions, and in 1974, the general counsel recommended setting up a tax exempt fund. In her report to the 23rd (1978) National Assembly, Purnell noted, "Finally received 501 (c) (3) status in 1980." Ratification of *Bylaws* of the Foundation had been the final step.

Another weakness the review cited was the dearth in written procedures and guidelines. Purnell immediately moved to create "the basic documents that any organization needs." Among the publications completed during her administration was the first *Orientation Manual* for new members. Expressing her pride, Purnell told members, "You will note through our minutes as far back as you can read, we repeatedly stated a need for an orientation manual. Every set of minutes reflected this need ... we corrected this and now have an Orientation Manual."

The Purnell administration also published the first *Area Directors Manual*, and writing in the September 1979 *Link to Link* newsletter, Purnell outlined eight additional "documents and sets of guidelines that had been revised and sent to chapters" under her watch, including the *President's Manual*, *Chapter Program Manual*, and *Assembly Guidelines*. Touting the importance of communication, she further advised that more, including a current Membership Directory, were on the way; and in the end, the number exceeded a dozen.

The best testimony to the effectiveness of the publications came from Purnell's successor, 8th National President Dolly Desselle Adams (1982–1986). She prefaced her report to the 24th (1984) National Assembly by heralding the excellent state the organization was in when she received it in 1982.

I came to the helm of a well-organized, well-functioning growing organization, a group whose reputation, both nationally and internationally, commanded respect and regard. Our functions were clearly delineated in up-to-date Constitution and Bylaws and documented in manuals and guidelines. These continue to be used for smooth operation of the organization.

Showcasing all of the documents that had been completed throughout her term at the 1982 Assembly, Purnell said, "Today, I am happy to present to you seventeen (17) revised and new major documents for The Links, Inc." On parade with the publications were the authors of each. Making it clear that her success did not rest with her alone, Purnell confirmed, "The President is no stronger than those who work with her," she pronounced. As illumination, she borrowed a quote from Woodrow Wilson: "I used not only the brains I had, but all the brains I could borrow," she declared.

With its unveiling at the 23rd (1982) Assembly, *A History of The Links, Incorporated* marked a milestone in Linkdom as the first published account. Many attempts had been made to place an edition into circulation. The first unpublished manuscript of the Philadelphia Chapter was penned for the Second National Conference one year after incorporation on April 8, 1950, by National Historian Lillian Stanford; and as late as the 21st (1978) Assembly, where Purnell had been installed, an attempt to compile a yearbook was shelved. The Links now had a published history.

Purnell also saw the *Links Journal* as an essential, and she encouraged continued publication. At the May 1981 Executive Council and the Foundation Annual Meeting, she reminded members that prior to 1978, the last official *Journal* had been published in 1973, and she shared her chagrin that publication of The Links' organ had, again, been indefinitely suspended.

> At our conference [Lily Foundation Consultation] … in November, there were fourteen (14) National Presidents of major women's organizations. Every journal of those 14 presidents' organizations has carried our picture with a heading of what the Links have done. We have ceased publication of our Journal. We could only show our members the picture through the papers.

Purnell's hope was "to squeeze enough money" to resume publication. She reviewed the reasons for the tight budget in her final address to the 1982 Assembly: the new headquarters, the centralization of documents at the headquarters, the rescission of separate fees for Areas, and the advent of Nationally sponsored assemblies. She also pointed out that until 1978, The Links had perennially given away more

money than it had taken in. Nevertheless, "money has been used frugally," she assured them.

As proof, she shared the opinion of the auditor: "The Links, Inc. is in better financial condition than it has ever been." Purnell commended the Assembly for the gradual turnaround that had been made possible because the organization had stopped the hemorrhaging. "In 1978, dues were increased to $25.00 [from $20] and Grants-in-Aid was $25.00. Presently [1982], it is thirty-five dollars ($35.00)," she said.

In addition to placing the archives in a repository, commissioning a history, and reinstating the *Links Journal*, Purnell instituted other heritage markers. She placed photos of all former National Presidents at the National Headquarters, awarded plaques as recognition for 25 years of membership, and instituted the signet ring as the signature gift for a retiring National President.

As National President, Purnell gave birth to an unprecedented number of initiatives that she watched flourish, and she was still setting the stage for progressive moves as she prepared to pass the baton. Revealing findings from a study launched in 1979 that showed a negligible growth rate in membership, Purnell challenged the membership to do the math, and she further warned of the consequences of continuing business as usual.

#7 Purnell (left) and #8 Adams (right) flanking DC mayor Marion Berry and First Lady Barbara Bush at Black Women's Consultation in Washington, DC.

Linkdom has grown from a membership of eight (8) to a little more than five thousand (5,000+) ... Thus, the growth rate over the years averaged one hundred and forty-two (142) members per year or point seventy-eight hundredths (.78) members per chapter. How can we survive at this rate ... Without putting more emphasis on increasing membership (and younger members), we can anticipate an even faster decline in total membership as more members approach advancing years.

Purnell's transformative initiatives in programming, operations, and membership brought closure to drawn-out projects and placed policies and procedures in print. She was the strong clasp that assured security for the organization's precious links. Purnell not only expanded and fortified each link, but as noted by *Journal* editor Emma C. Walker at the closing banquet of the 23rd (1982) Assembly, "She [also] held together the pieces of the chain."

~ Earnestine Green McNealey, PhD

Julia Brogdon Purnell, LHD

Links Service
Southern Area Director
Charter Member and President, Baton Rouge Chapter

Impact During Tenure

- Relocated National Headquarters to a larger, more appropriate site, four blocks from the White House.
- Advanced Assembly approval to purchase a headquarters "with all deliberate speed."
- Steered ratification of the *Bylaws* of The Links Foundation, completing final step of establishment.
- Published first history of The Links, Incorporated.
- Instituted $101,000 Juvenile Justice initiative with US Department of Justice.
- Transferred The Links' incorporation from New Jersey to the District of Columbia.
- Produced and updated all manuals.
- Standardized guidelines for conducting National Assemblies, selecting honorary members, and identifying recipients of National Awards.
- Presented first awards of the National Achievement Scholarship Program.
- Instituted White Rose banquet as an Assembly staple.

Selected National Honors

- National President, Alpha Kappa Alpha Sorority
- Honorary doctorate in humane letters from eight universities
- Founder, Scott-Gilchrist Quality of Life Center, Baton Rouge (LA)
- Steering Committee, Status of Women in Louisiana
- Distinguished Service Citation, Allen University (SC)

Dolly Desselle Adams, PhD
Eighth National President (1982–1986)

Making History – Providing Hope

*Our cherished past has put us in place with all of the
resources to respond to the hope of our sisters and our people.*

WHEN THE LINKS' 8th National President took office at the 23rd (1982) Assembly, the world was in a transition between the industrial age and the information age. Alcohol education and drug education had expanded, bringing about movements such as Mothers Against Drunk Drivers, and Nancy Reagan's "Just Say No" campaign signaled from the White House that the widespread use of drugs among youth needed to be addressed. It was also the "Me" decade, and greed dominated. Social responsibility took a back seat to corporate excess. Time Magazine placed the computer in its coveted man of the year slot, family lifestyles changed, and the AIDS virus invaded.

With such a plethora of issues, deciding which ones to tackle could have consumed President Dolly Desselle Adams, but Adams did not have that problem. The Assembly had already mandated that she address two operational issues: the purchase of a National Headquarters and the start up of the foundation. Adams believed that The Links' worth was inextricably tied to the benefits the organization could generate for others, and her programming reflected that conviction. She reiterated this sense of purpose in a message carried in the *Journal*. "Our cherished past has put us in place with all of the resources to respond to the hope of our sisters and our people."

Providing hope became the guiding principle for Adams's administration, and she called on every Links member to help change the landscape of society. As a precursor, Adams immersed members in the organization's heritage in Philadelphia, the birthplace of The Links, and the site for the 24th (1984) Assembly, her first as National President. It was the first time The Links had returned to its roots since the group had become a National organization, and Adams capitalized on the setting to help members develop a deeper appreciation for Links' ideals and purposes. Members met and dialogued with Co-Founder Sarah Strickland Scott and other members of the founding chapter—Frances Atkinson, Lillian Stanford, Myrtle Stratton, and Dorothy Wright. The Assembly also endorsed a National observance day to commemorate The Links' founding and to encourage member to recommit to the goals of Linkdom.

Adams focused first on securing a permanent headquarters for operations. She believed that getting The Links' house in order was critical to developing and implementing programs. A key challenge was to find, purchase, finance, and furnish a national head-quarters, while developing and executing programs that addressed local, national, and international communities. "Tomorrow can be better than yester-day," she preached, and she called on Links to "build a place of our own where we can house offices and conference rooms, archives, computerized talent treasure, portraits of heroines of Links, Inc., and an Honor Roll of special contributors."

As directed by the 23rd (1982) Assembly, Adams had made acquisition of a central office a priority, but the task proved daunting. Reporting to the 24th (1984) Assembly, Adams noted a series of setbacks, but reassured the body of her resolve to make a headquarters a *fait accompli*: "We are determined to find a building, which reflects The Links' image in style and taste, which is within our means, and which will be large enough to serve our needs for the next 20 years," she said.

Adams presented a proposal that would fund the acquisition debt free. Describing the plan as "quite simple," Adams requested approval for a set aside of $100,000 from the unrestricted fund balance as of April 30, 1984, an allocation of $50,000 per year for a period of three years, beginning 1984–85, and a $100 per-capita one-time assessment that would also "ensure the upkeep of the building without the necessity of further taxation." The 24th (1984) Assembly overwhelmingly endorsed the plan.

A year later, Adams presided over the dedication of a debt-free, stately structure that stood within hailing distance of the center of government in the nation's capital. The specialness of the accomplish-ment was captured again in a 2019 interview, where she cited "dedicating the building" as the "most memorable moment" of her presidency. The message in the celebration program also rang as true as it had when she penned it three decades earlier. It reiterated Adams's belief that the building would facilitate the coordination and support essential for strengthen-ing programs. "This house will serve as a national Community Center from which people, projects, and programs are developed and empowered," she said.

Adams also reached the summit in program-ming, offering services of "historic proportions" in each of The Links' four facets. Julia Blanchard Smith, Adams's National Program coordinator, credited the achievements to Adams's previous service as a National Program director. "The experience of our National President as a National Program director provided her with insights, which have served well Links program direction and development."

Adams's commitment and zeal were also factors. Writing in the 40th anniversary issue of the *Journal*, The Links' magazine, Jamye Coleman Williams called Adams's dedication "inspiring," marveling that Adams carried out her responsibility as if it were a position from which she earned a livelihood. Being "dedicated and very energetic" was just part of the equation, however, noted Flavia Walton, Adams's Services to Youth director. "Her (Adams's) tireless support, patience, guidance, and infinite wisdom" were also keys in program implementation.

"Dynamic" was also a common descriptor for Adams, and under the international umbrella, she led the largest delegation (150-plus internationally known African Americans) that attended the end of the Women's Decade in Nairobi, Kenya. The Links also funded a Links Room in the Africare House, purchased water wells, and earned United Nations designation as a non-governmental organization (NGO). National Trends and Services received grants totaling $100,000 to expand Project Discovery, a pilot program funded by the Department of Labor, Women's Bureau, to help middle-aged, middle-income minority women enter the job market. Additionally, The Arts facet forged partnerships with professional Black arts personnel and guided the purchase of a sculpture by Elizabeth Catlett in memory of Co-Founder Margaret Rosell Hawkins. Adams also personally wrote a proposal that secured a $120,000 grant from the Lilly Foundation to host four consultations for Black women leaders, and she doled out the final payment on the $1 million pledge to the United Negro College Fund (UNCF).

The first "authentic national Umbrella Program" was also formulated and initially implemented with a $65,000 grant from the National Institute of Health, Office of Substance and Drug Abuse. "Considering the magnitude of the drug problem, this program portends to be one of the most important ever instituted by Links," Adams said in her final report to the Assembly.

Adams did not stop at making history—she also preserved it. Her administration completed the processing and placement of The Links' Archives. She also established the Legacy Council to ensure that collections reflected "the legacy of Links from the point of view of past National and Area elected and appointed officers."

Adams's educational preparation, missionary philosophy, teaching career, and organizational involvement engendered her sense of obligation to help others, especially children and young people. Links, she believed had a "great deal" and were, therefore, commanded to make tomorrow better than yesterday by responding "to the enormous needs of our people, and especially our youth." Her background beyond Linkdom also contributed to her ability to move programs beyond conceptualization.

As the wife of African Methodist Episcopal Bishop John Hurst Adams, Adams honed her skills as she worked to improve human conditions. In concert with Bishop Adams, she amplified the responses, and the duo became a force. Former Links historian Marjorie H. Parker noted the impact: "The two have formed a trained spiritually-oriented team which has made an indelible imprint on American life wherever they have lived."

In addition to having a magnanimous love-filled heart, Adams was loving, and she enjoyed being in the company of friends. She counted among the treasures of Linkdom the friendships she developed and strengthened, friendships she called, "many (and) enduring."

Relinquishing her command at the 1986 Assembly, Adams listed many of the innumerable

#8 Adams with Connecting Link, Bishop John Adams

voyages her team had powered. She noted that she was returning the ship fit, fully fueled, and ready for the next mission. Being president had been a full-time job, but her load had been lifted and lightened by a great team, the membership, and an efficient staff. While the tenure had been "exhilarating, exhausting, exciting, and productive," her work had been facilitated by a loving and supportive family—from the "best husband any woman could ask for" to three children who continually made her proud.

But the bonanza for gratitude and pride belonged to The Links, Incorporated. In honoring her values and pledge to do her best to help The Links, Incorporated make history and provide hope, Adams penned a legacy that will live and will keep hope alive in perpetuity. Anchored by Christ-like qualities and her desire to make the world better, she magnificently responded to the exigencies of the day and positioned The Links, Incorporated for an even "better" tomorrow. Her service made The Links proud.

~ Earnestine Green McNealey, PhD
~ Lucretia R. Payton-Stewart, PhD

Dolly Desselle Adams, PhD

Links Service:

National Director, International Trends and Services

Western Area Director, International Trends and Services

Inducted in Seattle (WA) Chapter; was a member of the Arlington (VA) Chapter when she assumed office; established Waco (TX) Chapter; current member of the Atlanta (GA) Chapter; has also been a member of the Angel City (CA), Columbia (SC), and Jacksonville (FL) Chapters

Impact During Tenure

- Purchased first National Headquarters.
- Initiated endowment for the maintenance of the National Headquarters.
- Completed The Links' first million-dollar gift, satisfying a $1 million pledge to the United Negro College Fund.
- Secured grants that included funding for the Black Women's Consultation ($120,000), Project Discovery ($100,000), and Project LEAD ($65,000).
- Purchased sculpture by Elizabeth Catlett in memory of Co-Founder Margaret Rosell Hawkins.
- Formed partnership with Africare that spurred the eventual creation of 75 water wells in rural African villages.
- Led Links delegation to Women's Decade Conference, Nairobi, Kenya.

Selected National Honors:

- President, Black Women's Agenda
- Board Director, United Negro College Fund, Operation Big Vote, Sickle Cell Disease Research Foundation, WHMR-TV, and I've Known Rivers, Inc. (Advisory)
- Episcopal District Supervisor, African Methodist Episcopal Church
- Obtained NGO status from the United Nations

THROUGH THEIR EYES

Excerpts from *The Links Oral History Collection*

Dolly Desselle Adams, PhD
On Her Tenure As
EIGHTH NATIONAL PRESIDENT (1982–1986)

January 2019 • Washington, DC

#8 Adams fielding interview questions.

Your Introduction to Linkdom

I was living in Seattle, Washington. There were a couple of ladies who became my friends, and they were members of the Seattle Chapter. We were all having babies at the same time, and our children were running around together, and we did all the other things together ... We all seemed to have the same kind of interests. Almost all of us were teachers or nurses; that was our profession. Now in Seattle at that time, there were no black teachers. So, when I say teachers, they were teaching either at a prep pre-, in another area, or at a private school. I became the first black teacher in the Seattle public schools. ... and they said, "Well, you ought to come into The Links." I wasn't too sure. I thought I had enough going on, but I liked the people who were in the group. So, I said, I'd like that; and, they invited me in.

Your Path to the Presidency

I transferred from Seattle to Angel City, which was in Los Angeles, and from Angel City to Waco, Texas, and then to the Arlington (VA) Chapter. I was married to an A.M.E. bishop in the beginning ... That's why I had so many jobs because you got a job wherever he would have a new place ... When I was a member of the Angel City Chapter, I was an area officer. When I came to the Washington area and became part of the Arlington Chapter, the National President, Julia Brogdon Purnell, made me National chairman of International Friends.

One day Julia, who had been my major professor in undergraduate school at Southern University, called me to her hotel room here in Washington, and said, "I want you to run for president." I said, president; president of Links? I was working church, and I had three children. Two of them were in college by that time. She said, "Your boss would be an empty nester ... You live here in Washington. There's a whole lot that has to be done with The Links in Washington, and I think you can do it." I said, I have to think about it. I went home and talked to my husband. And so, I decided I had to run.

Your Imprint on Linkdom

I think we were known for the fact that we bought that building and established the foundation.

My most memorable moment was dedicating the building. Julia Purnell's administration at the Assembly instructed that the new person coming in buy a house to house The Links and establish a foundation ... so I think that the greatest accomplishments were when I got those two things done ... when we bought the house, paid for it, renovated it, moved in, and furnished it; and we established the foundation at the end of the first two years.

Your Leadership Style

I tried to be open and honest and transparent so that people understood what I was doing. They didn't always accept or appreciate or even agree with it, but I had to stand by it if it was a decision that I thought I needed to make.

Your Biggest Challenge

My biggest challenge was meeting every problem as it came up, and there was a new one each day ... and then knowing who to go to, to get help.

Your "Lessons Learned"

- Leadership at each level prepares you for the fact that you don't know everything, and that there is a part of a structure with which you are not familiar because you've never been exposed to it ... So, it taught me first what the organization was about, but it also taught me that there was a great deal I did not know, and it helped me to find people who could help me.
- Basically, I learned from Links patience, and I learned the value of friendship... wherever I worked, cultivating friends and having a lot of patience, and loving other people so they can love you.
- One of the things I learned early on was to listen ... not just to people who had titles ... to sit down ... have a cup of coffee ... and listen ... and you find out so many things in a casual conversation about the organization and about the people in the organization.
- I learned to adapt to what the challenges were and what the problems were ... also learned how to ignore some of the problems, and it took me awhile to understand that in some instances, the best way to deal with people who created problems in order to be seen was to ignore them.

Your Advice for Future Presidents

You have to have a vision for what you are getting into, and you have to have the innate leadership skills ... the energy and interest and the common sense to get people to help.

~ From *The Links Oral History Collection*, Marcia Denise White, Editor

Regina Jollivette Frazier
Ninth National President (1986–1990)

Enhancing the Legacy – Fulfilling the Dream

We shall move forward with one accord to preserve our colleges, take the offensive in initiatives to ensure our rights, arrest the spread of drug addiction in our communities, and assure the survival of our families. All this and more, we shall accomplish together.

REGINA JOLLIVETTE FRAZIER was the youngest Link elected as National President of The Links, Incorporated and The Links Foundation, Incorporated, but the knowledge and experience she brought to Linkdom were vintage to the core; and she successfully guided The Links on "a voyage toward a harbor of service." Frazier considered her tenure to be an extension of the oath she had taken to Linkdom and a part of The Links' heritage. "Because we are the children of Sarah Strickland Scott and the late Margaret Hawkins ... we have everything we need to keep as indestructible—our bond of friendship, the commitment to serve, and the obligation to share," she said in her acceptance address to the 25th (1986) National Assembly on July 4 in Nashville, Tennessee.

The former National member-at-large, Southern Area director, and immediate past National vice president came with a portfolio, and she embarked with Thoreau's words as her guide: "We shall advance confidently in the direction of our dreams and endeavor to live the life we have imagined. We shall then meet with a success unexpected in common hours."

Frazier's ship flew the "Enhancing the Legacy—Fulfilling the Dream" flag, and as she set sail, she expressed gratitude for having been given a sound ship to steer:

Today is one of great celebration. The 210th anniversary of our country and the 100th anniversary of the Statue of Liberty. America has a great love for the "Lady in the Harbor." But it does not exceed the love we have for our eight ladies, the past national presidents who have stood at the helm of our organization and steered us safely on our voyage toward a harbor of service.

Frazier's vision was big and inclusive. She saw strength in numbers, and the rules of the ship required a focused and united effort designed to aid "the homeless, the illiterate, the poor and the helpless. Our collective obligation is to create a better world, and we shall do that together. We must constantly examine our communities, determine the wide range of possibilities and opportunities for service and act on them," she said.

Unveiling the travel manifest, Frazier declared:

> *We shall move forward with one accord to preserve our colleges, take the offensive in initiatives to ensure our rights, arrest the spread of drug addiction in our communities, and assure the survival of our families. All this and more, we shall accomplish together.*

As The Links' National member-at-large ten years earlier, Frazier had been charged with drafting public policy guidelines, and she was conscious of the positive impact that The Links' views expressed in the aggregate could wield when properly harnessed. So, it was natural that influencing public policy would be one of the rudders, and she welcomed the 25th National Assembly's resolution directing the establishment of The Black Family Institute of The Links, Incorporated. "We are fully aware that there is no problem more pressing toward which we can direct our energies than the survival of the basic unit of our society, The Black Family," Frazier said.

As a resident of Miami, Florida, Frazier had witnessed the "southern strains" on Blacks decried by W. E. B. Dubois: "Cities ripe with crime, drugs, and disillusionment." There was just one problem. While the National Assembly had adopted the resolution, it had made no provisions for funding it. Frazier attributed the act to "being propelled by the enthusiasm of the moment, created in the atmosphere of outstanding program ideas presented during our biennial deliberations." Nevertheless, she made it clear that this resolution would have life beyond the National Assembly. "We are … examining those facets of Black Family life where our impact can be most meaningful, measurable, and lasting," she said.

Frazier explored "options for seed money to launch the program," but left no doubt that somehow, The Links would strengthen the Black Family. "We shall, therefore, proceed with every means at our disposal, calling upon you to go that extra mile when necessary to ensure success. We have never failed in our programming efforts and we must not fail now," Frazier said. For the takeoff, Frazier called on ingenuity.

Using The Links' new umbrella programming approach, Frazier identified the Black Family as "the" hub for programming. Chapters were reminded that "our focus is the Black family. Whether a chapter goes with cancer prevention, artistic development, prevention of teenage pregnancy or hunger around the world, it is addressing preservation of the Black family."

The Executive Council also adopted a format change for the *(Links) Journal*, shifting from placing primary emphasis on chapter activities to highlighting programming centered on Black Family Life. The January 1987 *Link to Link* included an invitation to submit articles on 11 critical areas of concern, including The Back Family, Politics, Economics, Entrepreneurship, and Supplemental Education for Black Youth. Also included were Affirmative Action, Voter Participation, Health Care, Educational Voucher Systems, and Teen Pregnancy. Drugs/Crime, Black Youth Unemployment, and South Africa and African Americans rounded out the list.

A mighty wind thrust the ship forward. With a $938,000 grant from the Office of Substance Abuse and Mental Health Administration of the Department of Health and Human Services, The Links provided direct solutions through Project LEAD: High Expectations (PLHE). The three-year demonstration project (1987–1990) to prevent substance abuse, adolescent pregnancy, and sexually transmitted diseases among high-risk Black youth was an expansion of the concept of an earlier Links effort, Project LEAD (PL). Frazier's October 1988 newsletter pointed out, however, that unlike PL, PLHE was adequately funded.

Consequently, The Links would be able to provide "more systematic and effective training to prevent the onset of drug and alcohol use and adolescent pregnancy, training in values clarification, decision making, problem solving, vocational planning, and self-esteem."

To assist with the effort, Frazier formed and convened a national advisory panel consisting of the national presidents of eight major Black Greek-letter sororities and fraternities, as well as the graduate fraternity Sigma Pi Phi (The Boule) and Jack and Jill of America, Inc.

Frazier's sail for a better world moved another nautical mile with the 26th (1988) National Assembly designating the National Association for the Advancement of Colored People Legal Defense and Educational Fund, Inc. (LDF) as the recipient of The Links' second million-dollar-grant award. LDF had been key in securing liberties in education, economic justice, voter protection, and criminal justice, thereby offering an additional passageway for the Black progress Frazier sought. In so many ways, LDF's influence embodied the goals of Frazier's Black Family Institute.

In the 1980s alone, LDF was instrumental in decisions that denied exempt status to religious schools that discriminated on the basis of race, struck down the federal government's use of a written test that disproportionately disqualified Negroes and Latinos for employment, and overturned a Louisiana gerrymander intended to reduce African American voting strength. LDF also backed a North Carolina state ruling, later upheld by the US Supreme Court, that the at-large countywide election of state legislators illegally diluted Black voting strength, and it ordered the Department of Housing and Urban Development to spend $4 million to upgrade housing projects in the city and implement federal maintenance, tenant selection, and other procedures equitably.

#9 Frazier with Connecting Link Ronald Frazier

Frazier's concern for people of African descent was also reflected in initiatives in Zambia. She turned a personal invitation from the Zambian president, Kenneth Kaunda, into an opportunity to confer with the women of the country on projects with which The Links might cooperate. After meeting with the women, they identified cottage industries as their need for funding, and, subsequently, the 1990 Assembly approved a $10,000 grant.

To journey with her, Frazier issued a call not only for active members, but also reactivated members, new members, and new chapters. Two major changes during her administration had the potential for membership and chapter growth, and Frazier expected chapters and individuals to embrace them. The rulings by the 1988 Assembly, for the first time, offered former members who had resigned in good standing or forfeited membership for non-payment of dues the option to return within a two-year period, and special provisions had been added to facilitate the induction of daughters of Links. Chapters were also given greater latitude, with no restrictions on transfers during the first two years of membership. The membership cap was also raised to 55, exclusive of alumna members, and the ratio of inductees to transferees was no longer considered.

Frazier heralded the inherent potential of the changes and urged chapters to build on it:

> This is a plea to each chapter to carefully examine your membership, to evaluate talents needed that will complement your programmatic and administrative structure, and to aggressively seek the inclusion of women possessing those talents on your roster.

Contending that too many outstanding women were being excluded because of pettiness, jealousy, and class, she told members to "examine carefully the profiles of proposed members, [and] ask yourself if this individual will enhance your chapter. Then vote your convictions." She followed with a pithy bid on behalf of legacies. "Be sisterly and give more than perfunctory consideration to the applications made by Heir-O-Links to our chapters. Whether we know them personally or not, they know us. Many of them have grown up with Linkdom."

The many included Frazier, daughter of Platinum Link Frances Reeves Jollivette Chambers, also a member of the Greater Miami (FL) Chapter. In the 40-year history of The Links, she was the first Heir-O-Link to become National President, and she became their advocate. "What better legacy to The Links, Incorporated than the inclusion of our legatees?" she quizzed. Like Frazier, a pharmacist by trade, many were bright and successful professionals who would add value to The Links, and she urged chapters to let that worth to Linkdom be the determining factor: "It is our sincere hope that as each chapter pursues the membership process, voting will be based on the merits of the individual and the potential for increasing the stature of Linkdom," Frazier said.

With her expansion philosophy, Frazier, who was truly ahead of her time, also journeyed beyond the borders of the United States to enable other "extraordinarily capable women" to join the service voyage, establishing chapters in Nassau, Bahamas, and Frankfurt, Germany, in 1989 and 1990, respectively. She saw The Links as a global entity and wanted to bring to life the literal manifestation of the organization's logo. To her it was not just a virtual chain of service, but an actual one that encircled the globe, doing good for those who needed aid.

Along with service, the cardinal rule on Frazier's voyage was amity. She called on Links to "be instruments of good will, of love, of tolerance to all, regardless of race, religion or national origin." She further pressed, "As an organization founded on friendship, let kindness begin at home," and she knew the dispersion would follow.

> In 1987, we are in a critical period in our nation's history. A climate of intolerance seems pervasive. The generation gap, racial barriers, sexism, and economic stratification seem to divide us. It would seem that the words love and tolerance have an infrequent presence in today's world. It is, therefore, incumbent on us to begin the solutions to these problems. We can ill-afford to let the unique relations we enjoy be threatened by ill will. Chapter harmony is our goal … from that harmony we move to the larger world.

Frazier could count on vintage counsel for the first half of the voyage, but on July 4, two years to the date of Frazier's installation, the voice of Co-Founder Sarah Strickland Scott was stilled. Recapping Scott's life at a July 15, 1988, memorial service in Philadelphia, Frazier expressed her grief, but reaffirmed that she and her Links sisters would continue to heed the advice learned through the years, thereby perpetuating Linkdom. "Sorrow fills our heart, a sorrow that is deep and personal," she said, as she began her tribute; but, she rejoiced, "The dream lives on …. The one we love is gone, but The Links, Incorporated, the product of her ingenuity and that of the late Margaret Hawkins shall live for generations."

Continuing her tribute, Frazier illuminated the ways in which the vision was being realized:

> The dream lives and grows through a network that has survived more than four decades. The dream lives and grows in the more than 7,000 women across these United States that comprise our 228 chapters in 38 of the 50 states and the District of Columbia … We shall never forget because as Links, we are enhancing the legacy and fulfilling the dream. We are extending the hand of friendship and service. We have expanded our giving and contributions to the National Urban League, to the UNCF, to the Legal Defense and Educational Fund, Inc. in substantial ways, ever commemorating the spirit of giving which was the legacy of Link Margaret and Link Sarah.

It was a general assessment, but two years later, when Frazier returned her vessel to shore, the log provided a full account of the Frazier voyage toward a harbor of service and friendship. Her gallant steering not only kept the ship on course, but it also boldly moved Links into unchartered waters.

~ Rozalynn Suzanne Frazier
~ Earnestine Green McNealey, PhD

Regina Jollivette Frazier

Links Service

National Vice President
Southern Area Director
National Member-at-Large
Journalist and Secretary, Greater Miami (FL) Chapter

Impact During Tenure

- Instituted Project LEAD: High Expectations, a demonstration project for high-risk Black youth, designed to prevent substance abuse, adolescent pregnancy, and sexually transmitted diseases.
- Pushed adoption of successful membership measures aimed at growth, including provisions that enabled former members who had resigned in good standing or forfeited membership for non-payment of duties the option to return within a two-year period, encouraged the induction of daughters of Links, and increased the membership cap.
- Championed NAACP Legal Defense and Educational Fund as million-dollar grant recipient.
- Used modified Assembly format that resulted in $43,000 profit for Hawkins-Scott Memorial Manor fund, which was the initial contribution for the expansion of the National Headquarters into the Swiss Inn next door.
- Expanded international presence with the chartering of two international chapters (Bahamas and Germany) and collaborative projects with Zambia.
- Expanded presence within the United States, chartering 15 chapters, including the first in the state of New Mexico.
- Inducted American soprano Leontyne Price as an honorary member.
- Led The Links delegation during the Silent March on Washington in 1989.
- Produced two biennia in the black due to her fiscal conservatism.

Selected National Honors

- First Heir-O-Link to become National President
- National Parliamentarian for the Association of Black Hospital Pharmacists
- Board Chair, Miami-Dade County Zoning Appeals Board
- Board of Directors, United Negro College Fund, National Coalition on Black Voter Participation
- Executive Board, New World School of the Arts
- Executive Committee, Greater Miami United Way
- Life Member, YWCA, and Board Member, YWCA of Greater Miami and Dade County, Inc.
- Life Member, Orange Bowl Committee
- Life Member and Thanks Badge Recipient, Girl Scouts of the United States of America
- Honorary Chair, National NAACP Legal Defense and Education Fund Equal Justice Dinner, New York City
- Bronze Medallion, National Conference of Christian and Jews
- Leadership Award, Anti-Defamation League
- Women Who Make a Difference Award, Junior League of Miami, Inc.
- Leadership Miami
- AAUW Council of Presidents
- Life Member, Alpha Kappa Alpha Sorority, Incorporated

THROUGH THEIR EYES

Excerpts from *The Links Oral History Collection*

Regina Jollivette Frazier
On Her Tenure As
NINTH NATIONAL PRESIDENT (1986–1990)

January 2019 • Washington, DC

#9 Frazier fielding interview questions.

Your Introduction to Linkdom

My mother was a Link, and I was inducted into her chapter in 1970. She had asked me to attend a prior Assembly with her because you could have guests, but in my heart, I felt to go to the Assembly, I had to be a Link. So, when I was inducted, then I went to that Assembly. It must have been about three months later, and it was in Cincinnati. And I walked in the room and I said, these are my people. I have got to work with this organization because the women were so into it. They were providing service in their communities, and oh, they looked good. I said, maybe I can stay young looking at least if I participate in this organization. So, I went home, and I did. I got really busy. I got elected an officer in my chapter, and the rest is kind of history.

Your Path to the Presidency

Well, I went from being the recording secretary—that only lasted a few months because I had an appointment. Helen Edmonds, our fifth National President, talked with me at a subsequent Area meeting and wanted me to work with her, which was very interesting because I was the campaign manager at my first meeting for her opposition. Her room was right down the hall and I would peek out … kind of espionage, see what's going on, what I could use for our campaign. But she asked me to write a paper on the environment that was related to trees, planting trees around the country to help with the environment. I think she was really, really way ahead of her time, as she was in everything.

So, it went from there to service on different committees. And then I ran for National office, and we had an office called member-at-large. And I was running against my very good friend; she won that one. So, I ran again, and I won that one. After that, I ran for Southern Area director, and after that I ran for National vice president. I lost it on the first run and then I ran, again, and I got that. And then I ran for National President.

Your Leadership Style

I did believe in hearing what everybody had to say. But I also believed that the final decision was mine. I knew where I wanted to go with it … We are an organization of friends, but I was interested in making appointments for people who were well versed in the fields I needed. And so that's how those decisions were made. I didn't have to personally know them, but I had to know a lot about their reputations in programming.

Your Biggest Challenge

One of my challenges was not having a White Rose banquet. I was going to take the money and use it as the beginning money for buying another building for the headquarters. And that just happened not long ago, a few years back, but everybody thought it was terrible that I would do something like that. And I was frankly surprised at the concern over not having another chicken dinner.

Your "Lessons Learned"

I now call myself an organization woman because I am capable of joining any organization and knowing how to lead it if I choose to lead it. But at this point in time, I don't choose to lead it. It's very stressful to lead an organization like any organization, but an organization like The Links, Incorporated has no Indians. Everybody is a chief. I remember when I left office, I told my husband, my connecting Link, I said, you know, I don't ever have to be president of anything again the rest of my life.

Your Advice for Future Presidents

I would advise them first of all … to have a real fire in the belly or real passion for leadership, a real vision of where they want to take the organization. And then I would tell them, don't let anybody stop you.

~ From *The Links Oral History Collection*, Marcia Denise White, Editor

Marion Elizabeth Schultz Sutherland
Tenth National President (1990–1994)

Cherishing the Past – Cultivating the Present – Creating the Future

Stop for a minute and ask yourselves, Is what I'm doing kind? Is it helpful? Is it useful? Is it the way I would want to be treated? Then you will go a long way toward living up to the word friendship as embodied in the name Links.

"**M**Y NAME IS MARION (not Marilyn or Miriam) Elizabeth Schultz Sutherland (not Southerland) …. I'm five feet one and one-half inches tall and 115 pounds barefooted and soaking wet; the little grey-haired lady with the great big smile." The Links' 10th National President believed that prologue was necessary when she began her term (1977–1981) as Western Area director. Sutherland included the introduction in her booklet, *Personal From Me to Thee*, a collection extolling love and friendship. Her passion for amity not only colored her administration—it became her signature.

Outlining her vision in the January 1991 *Link to Link* newsletter, Sutherland advanced interpersonal relationships as the essential element in achieving the goals of her administration. "The most important aspect of my vision is a steady improvement in our relationships with each other," explaining, "It is imperative that we succeed in this area if all else is to be anything more than a game; a game we cannot win."

Noting her "acute awareness" of "how far from perfect" she deemed Links relations to be, Sutherland embraced rules as the elixir for helping members to get along:

Relationships in our organization are no different than those in the broader community, and while we can't legislate tolerance, love, and understanding, legislation can be used as a tool for encouraging us to treat each other with kindness and respect. Penalties for unseemly behavior have been set, and if we adhere to our rules, ugly is a word we can drop from our vocabulary.

As a supplementary tonic, Sutherland issued the first protocol manual (Josephine Stokes, author), and by the 29th (1994) Assembly, she declared that progress had been made and urged endurance: "Continue to strive to be Links in Friendship's Chain in a manner that would make our Co-Founders Margaret Rosell Hawkins and Sarah Strickland Scott proud." To gauge their actions, Sullivan offered her Golden Rule: "Stop for a minute and ask yourselves, Is what I'm doing kind? Is it helpful? Is it useful? Is it the way I would want to be treated? Then you will go a long way toward living up to the word friendship as embodied in the name Links," she said.

But Sutherland was by no means naïve. She knew that even with penalties, there would be some acrimony, so she counseled chapters to level the playing field by choosing women of quality. "I implore you to induct only those women who have good community service records, who have a reputation of getting along well with others and those whose skills and contacts can help make your chapter a better one," she said.

Sutherland concentrated Links service on "empowering the African-American Family for the 21st Century" through health, youth services, artistic linkages, and African aid. Initiatives focused on youth power: a platform for them to express their opinions on social and political issues, assertiveness training that provided another option to abuse; and motivational sessions that enabled them to see themselves as achievers, as persons who could soar like eagles, as ones who could exert internal control.

A number of Sutherland's initiatives were achieved in concert with The Links Foundation, so Sutherland's move to strengthen the tie between the two entities was a critical factor in programming. The 28th (1992) Assembly approved a bylaws change that fused foundation dues into the membership fee structure of The Links. Under a "Welcome to the Links Foundation" headline, Sutherland highlighted the new relationship in the May 1993 Link to Link. "I take this opportunity to tell you how pleased I am that all Links are now members of The Links Foundation, Incorporated. The two organizations, The Links Incorporated and The Links Foundation

are as close as Siamese twins and, until now, a part of us had been missing. We're delighted to have all Links aboard and moving in the same direction," Sutherland said.

The 28th National Assembly also approved a $30 per-member, per-year assessment to establish The Links' first program endowment housed under The Links Foundation. The fee, eventually termed Grants-in-Aid, was initially approved for a two-year period but became permanent, funding numerous projects, including The Links' legendary million-dollar grants.

In another move, the Assembly also voted to maintain Project LEAD: High Expectations as a major thrust. The initiative to prevent substance abuse, adolescent pregnancy, and sexually transmitted diseases among high-risk Black youth was initially funded through a federal grant that had culminated. Given the program's success, the Assembly approved up to $75,000 to retain the program in some form.

"Part of my vision for the program is that every chapter be involved in at least one portion of Project LEAD: High Expectations," Sutherland had said in 1992, and writing in the May 1993 Link-to-Link newsletter, she reaffirmed her resolve to do what was necessary to keep the program going, including making each module a "stand alone" Umbrella Program. To have one major program thrust that originates at the National level and filters down through all Areas and chapters was Sutherland's goal, and more than 100 chapters had participated in the program, which reached thousands during Sutherland's tenure.

Sutherland also tackled membership establishment, and in year two, she announced, "Well, I think we have made progress." She then shared the reason for her assessment.

> For as many years as I can remember, chapter establishment has been a very tender process for Links. There are territorial concerns, membership concerns and fund-raising concerns … We think we've got most of the bugs out of the thorny process.

The fix included defining commuting distance, setting boundaries for all chapters, and limiting the establishment of multiple chapters to areas that had a minimum population of 50,000 African Americans.

To facilitate a smooth process, Sutherland created a Chapter Establishment Manual but warned that vigilance and respect were required to get the process under control. Chapters should exercise their right to vote, but it was critical that they defer to the judgment of the Executive Council when there were conflicts. "They (the Executive Council) have all the information" and are in a better position to make the decision. Sutherland also assured members that "every effort has been made to ensure that new chapters will be groups which bring only honor to the name Links; that members of these groups are compatible, and they will work together toward achieving the goals of Linkdom."

Sutherland also welcomed the decision by the 28th Assembly to require only majority vote for daughters of Links: "That decision has had a far-reaching impact on our organization and leadership. It has given us renewed vim, vigor, and vitality," she said.

Sutherland's desire for a formal leadership academy did not materialize during her term. "In spite of our best efforts," she groaned, "We have been unable to find a way to finance a leadership enhancement academy." Nevertheless, she instituted an all-day leadership enhancement workshop at the 29th (1994) National Assembly and voiced her hope that the idea of training would continue. "We can't do our jobs to the best of our ability if we aren't trained." Sutherland saw the venture blossom ten years later at the Atlanta Assembly when the Scott Hawkins Leadership Institute held its first class.

In keeping with the heritage element of her theme, Sutherland commissioned the second edition of the history of The Links, secured the copyright on The Links' logo, and added an official Links flag. The history book was released in 1992, and the 28th (1992) Assembly made the purchase mandatory for new members. Announcing the release, Sutherland said, "No one who is interested in the life and times of African Americans should have to wonder, who

#10 Sutherland with Connecting Link Earl Sutherland

are, or what is, The Links? We know who we are, and others should be made aware of our outstanding accomplishments," she said.

Sutherland breathed a sigh of relief when The Links received the certificate of registration for The Links' trademark. "Finally, after years of waiting, calls to our senator, assistance from our lawyer, seemingly endless telephone calls, blood, sweat, and tears, we have received our certificate of registration for The Links, Incorporated logo," Sutherland said. Also, a flag designed by Carolyn Jennings Tate of the Plano North Metroplex (TX) Chapter was voted as the official flag at the 28th (1992) Assembly in Dallas, Texas.

Sutherland took great pride in the development of a strategic plan that she called "the plan for our future." Set forth in a manual by Leatrice Pride, the plan delineated The Links' core values—friendship, integrity, honesty, service, commitment, family relationships, courage, and respect for self and others. "These values carry the message of our shared purposes and standards. They give us a conception of what

Marion Elizabeth Schultz
BIRTH 3 JUL 1926 • Danville, Vermilion, Illinois, USA
DEATH 24 JUN 2015 • Bothell, King, Washington, USA

LifeStory   **Facts**   Gallery

Facts   Show ⌄
Name and gender ⌄

1926 (AGE)   **Birth**
                  3 Jul 1926 • Danville, Vermilion, Illinois, USA

1935 8   **Death of Father Clyde Mitchell Schultz** (1904–1935)
                  3 June 1935 • Springfield, Sangamon, Illinois

1971 44   **Marriage**
                  12 May 1971 • Las Vegas, Nevada
                     Earl Christian Sutherland
                     (1923–2014)
                     1 Source

1999 73   **Death of Mother Vella Cloyd** (1908–1999)
                  3 Sep 1999 • Springfield, Sangamon, Illinois, USA

2011 84   **Death of Husband Colie Raymond Merriwether** (1924–2011)
                  23 May 2011 • Kirkland, King, Washington, USA

2014 87   **Death of Husband Earl Christian Sutherland** (1923–2014)
                  19 Jun 2014 • Seattle, King, Washington, USA

2015 88   **Death**
                  24 Jun 2015 • Bothell, King, Washington, USA

future-facing, more able to reach the goals and ideals that were set long before we came on the scene.

When she took office, Sutherland promised to continue her predecessor's work to "Enhance the Legacy and Fulfill the Dream." She noted that the tasks and responsibilities would be greater than ever, but she promised to forge ahead. "We must be willing to take risks if we are to move to unlimited heights of accomplishment and service." She did that by cherishing the past, cultivating the present, and creating the future.

And she loved doing it! "I must tell you how much I enjoyed my job; you have made … my days as your president some of the most satisfying of my life," she gratefully acknowledged to the 28th (1992) Assembly. Two years later, the sentiments were the same: "I've had a wonderful time serving as your President … these past four years have been as sweet as honey, as fulfilling as a good marriage, and as loving as I dreamed."

makes Links membership worth attaining, and an idea of what makes the struggle to keep it worthwhile," she said. Also included were The Links' vision, mission, objectives, and ways to face challenges ahead.

Reviewing the process at the 29th (1994) National Assembly, Sutherland summarized the four-year effort. "The committee dealt with every aspect of Linkdom in a dispassionate and thoughtful manner: thinking only of what will be best for Linkdom in the long haul." Acknowledging the possibility of shortcomings, Sutherland said that the plan still merited endorsement. "Though it is not an unadulterated strategic plan, it is a good start; and it can be enlarged upon and amended as it is tested by time and practice." The Assembly agreed, approving the measure unanimously.

Summarizing her four-year term, Sutherland said that everything had been done for the posterity and preservation of Linkdom.

The various manuals, the Bylaw amendments, the strategic plan, leadership training, the Endowment fund, our history book, the journals, our books of poetry, music prayer, and meditations, all of them have been prepared to help us become more

In her introduction of Sutherland at the 28th National Assembly, 7th National President Julia B. Purnell, like Sutherland, alluded to Sutherland's size. But unlike Sutherland, Purnell did not focus on Sutherland's physical features. Describing Sutherland as "a package of efficiency and a bomb of energy," Purnell hailed her as "one whose inner and outward beauty of character and personality radiated quiet dignity and calmness, a balanced outlook on life, a deep sense of altruism, good judgment, and a model for all womanhood." Her ingenuity and productivity bolstered many areas of Linkdom, but galvanizing good relations was her priority; and that indelible imprint continues to strengthen the chain of friendship.

~ *Earnestine Green McNealey, PhD*
~ *Jessie M. Jones*

Marion Elizabeth Schultz Sutherland

Links Service

National Vice President

Area Program Coordinator

Western Area Director

Western Area Vice Director

Area Chairman, National and International Trends and Services

President, Seattle (WA) Chapter

Impact During Tenure

- Led effort to build program endowment fund through $30 assessment.
- Steered initiative to make The Links Foundation membership a corollary of Links membership.
- Secured approval for $75,000 Foundation grant to continue Project LEAD: High Expectations as a major program focus.
- Developed the first Strategic Plan.
- Pushed interpersonal relationships and published Protocol Manual that included fines for behavior unbecoming to a Link.
- Designated "African Americans and persons of African descent" as appropriate lingo to acknowledge members outside the boundaries of the United States.
- Imposed four-year moratorium on bylaws amendments.

Selected National Honors

- First National President from the Western Area
- Marion Schultz Sutherland Day, Mayor Norm Rice of Seattle, WA
- State of Washington Committee on Youth
- Board of Directors, Seattle Foundation
- Board, Seattle Opera
- President and Chair of the Board, Seattle First Baptist Church Corporation
- Author, *He Watches over Me*

Patricia Russell-McCloud, JD
Eleventh National President (1994–1998)

Linkages ... Toward the Possible

Few people turn away from ideas put forth by Links because they come with immediate credibility because of the history of Links and the power that Links hold in their communities.

"**M**OVE FORWARD WITH PURPOSE, passion, and principle." That was the mantra of 11th National President Patricia Russell-McCloud's administration. Russell-McCloud envisioned her task as a collective willingness to use the organization's multiple strengths and diverse networks to ensure that others, in large and small ways, would reach their full potential. Her interest in leading Linkdom sprang from her recognition of The Links, Incorporated as "a premier organization with power, purpose, and prestige."

As a result, Russell-McCloud crafted a vision, conceptualized a plan to achieve that vision, garnered resources to execute the vision, and delivered more than what some thought was possible. "To give service through friendship was a magnet for me and made me willingly commit time, effort, and resources to an organization moving forward with identifiable purposes," she said.

Her goal was to be intentional in thinking "sky," to go beyond the comfort zone, and shift the paradigm. In the Executive Council, she encouraged "epiphany thinking," "aha" thinking. That energy produced fresh ideas and a willingness to stretch. Her "Linkages ...

Towards the Possible" theme inferred, first, that the best efforts would work together for the common good, and second, that new program ideas would be explored to plan and implement program initiatives.

Members were encouraged to believe that their programmatic commitment to take creative, courageous, and bold steps in chapter and cluster programs would reach people at their point of need, without judgment. She developed methods to ensure that Links at all levels were involved, reaching out to neophytes and veteran members alike. Members like Anita Whatley, Dogwood City (GA) Chapter, were inspired by "this young leader's talents" and her conscious effort to include younger Links. "Link Regina Jollivette Frazier started it, and Link Pat embodied and accelerated it, representing a new generation of Links and new energy," Whatley said.

Russell-McCloud explained Whatley's perception, noting, "Our organization had been viewed as a seasoned membership, and some believed that there wasn't a place to champion the causes of younger Links. The younger Links were the daughters, the daughters-in-law, and the new and achieved young women in a community that became a Link."

Russell-McCloud's actions were grounded in her recognition of the prestige that Links have in their community and her belief that members could utilize that prestige to power service programs in their community in ways that no other organization could. "Few people turn away from ideas put forth by Links because they come with immediate credibility because of the history of Links and the power that Links hold in their communities," she said.

Russell-McCloud's assessment of The Links' technological structure also influenced her actions. "Communication is always essential, and The Links, Inc. did not have a firm technological infrastructure that would take us forward. Absent from our headquarters were a website, internet interaction with the membership, an electronic database with the capability for on-line registration for the National Assembly, and more," she said. As a result, Russell-McCloud aggressively moved The Links forward on technological actions that would ensure communication necessary not only for day-to-day operations, but also for the execution of the administration's key initiatives. Members adopted a $25 technology fee at the 31st (1998) Assembly.

Another factor that contributed to her success was Russell-McCloud's ability to get her leadership team and the organization to embrace partnerships with members and other organizations in ways that would empower and improve human kind. Leading

the charge was the Executive Council, particularly the Program team, under the leadership of JoAnn Brown, National Program director, with facet chairs Gwendolyn B. Lee, National Trends and Services; Betty Shabazz and Juel Shannon Smith, International Trends and Services; Gladys Gary Vaughn, Services to Youth; and Aaronetta Pierce, The Arts.

To achieve greater focus, Russell-McCloud modified the structure of National Trends and Services, adding three linkages—Education, Health, and Legislative Impact—to provide a broader outreach to the community, while giving greater definition to Links' endeavors. The acknowledgment of the need to shape children early in their educational process forged a partnership between the Education linkage and the Services to Youth facet. Russell-McCloud credits their untiring work for producing the signature program, Links to Success: Children Achieving Excellence.

Written by Gladys Gary Vaughn, the chair of Services to Youth, and Barbara Dixon Simpkins, National vice president and Membership chair, Links to Success was designed to provide early enrichment opportunities for pre-K to sixth-grade students and their families. The proposal won immediate endorsement from the Executive Council, and the 1998 Assembly added its seal of approval.

In the Health linkage, The Links—in concert with The Links Foundation—instituted the first corporate, community National Walk-a-Thon for health and hunger to provide free health screenings and encourage healthy lifestyles. Linkages to Life, a bone marrow and organ donor initiative that had its roots in the Southern Area, became a National campaign. Both programs achieved signature status.

Advocacy figured prominently in Russell-McCloud's administration. In response to requests from members for a forum that addressed hot topics in the society, and in Black America in particular, she convened The Links' first Leadership Summit. The meeting featured a cadre of leaders who understood and influenced issues impacting Black progress. Included were Kweisi Mfume, executive director of the NAACP; Dr. Julianne Malveauex, economist and syndicated columnist; Dr. Israel Tribble, educator;

Evern Cooper, executive director of the UPS Foundation; and Elaine Jones, counsel general of the NAACP Legal Defense Fund.

The face and circumstance of Kemba Smith, a Hampton University freshman wedded to the wrong group, also energized the Legislative Impact linkage. Convicted of being a "drug mule," Smith was sentenced to a 24-year sentence in a federal penitentiary, more years than she was old at that time. Her story wrought headlines, and it was heart wrenching.

It was particularly relevant to The Links because "our membership recognized that Kemba Smith could be a child of any one of our families," Russell-McCloud said, and at the 1998 National Assembly in Boston, The Links galvanized the Free Kemba movement. The efforts mushroomed during the next administration of The Links and subsequently culminated in President William Jefferson Clinton granting Smith full clemency in 2000.

Russell-McCloud's International Trends and Services programs also made an indelible imprint. Concerned about the plight and lack of educational progress in specific areas of Soweto, South Africa, The Links initiated Education across the Miles. In partnership with established initiatives, The Links established 10 elementary schools at the cost of $10,000 each. The effort led to the eventual funding for 51 schools, as well as supplementary support. All chapters got involved by donating $170 for School in a Box, funding the distribution of boxes of school materials in Africa. A further index that The Links was more than casually aware of global concerns was its mini summit at the United Nations, where members had an audience with UN secretary Kofi Anon.

Russell-McCloud's administration was equally deft in The Arts. The Elizabeth Catlett Award, the highest award that can be achieved in Linkdom for the program facets, was created, commissioned, and bestowed. Named for founders Sarah Scott and Margaret Hawkins and struck by Elizabeth Catlett, an internationally acclaimed sculptor, the award is a bronze female sculpture with extended arms, symbolizing the freedom to believe, achieve, and overcome.

Another feature of The Arts was The Living Legends: Wade in the Water, a traveling exhibit of Negro spirituals that reflected the various genres of music throughout the African American experience. The exhibit highlighted many of the outstanding voices in the African diaspora and featured acclaimed vocalist William Warfield as a central part of the exhibit.

Russell-McCloud's vision of the possible also spurred the first fundraising campaign for The Links Foundation. Launched to engender self-sufficiency for the foundation and to demonstrate Links' commitment to their foundation, the effort netted more than a half-million dollars. Extending the linkage to corporations, she simultaneously generated support by building or renewing partnerships to foster the common good.

Along with multiple program initiatives, Russell-McCloud presided over the 50th Anniversary commemoration of The Links during the 30th National Assembly in New Orleans, Louisiana, July 7–14, 1996. Her goal was to host an extravaganza that would be memorable and meaningful. The results pleased her. As The Links paid homage to the founders' vision, former presidents' leadership, and The Links' service initiatives, "we grew in our knowledge, understanding, and appreciation for our sisterhood," she said.

The conference also provided an opportunity to showcase technological improvements. Conferees registered within 15 minutes, in contrast to the hours the process had consumed in the past. The Links also offered warmth to needy families in the host city, purchasing over 5,000 blankets for distribution and sending cornucopia arrangements, filled with stable food items, to homeless shelters throughout the city.

Russell-McCloud was a committed, dynamic, caring, concerned, and conscientious leader who programmatically sought to engage the membership in reaching people at their point of need and who was directly involved in seeking to ensure creative programming ideas that would touch the head and heart of the membership. She achieved the possible by fusing the prestige of The Links' name, members' commitment, The Links' infrastructure, and corporate and community support.

When Link Russell-McCloud's administration came to a close at the 31st Assembly in Boston, the playing of Donnie McClurkin's song "Stand" set the stage for her farewell address as National President. It embodied her feelings about her four-year journey, with all that had been attempted, with all that transpired, with all that was accomplished—some with overwhelming support and some with questioning of why The Links, Incorporated should be doing this or that. And then came the refrain, "What can you do when you've done all you can? You just stand."

Likewise, Russell-McCloud's vision and actions culminated in programs that remain as vital linkages in The Links' quest … toward the possible.

~ *Janine P. Rouson*

Patricia Russell-McCloud, JD

Links Service
Inducted into the Arlington (VA) Chapter in 1976
Dogwood City (GA) Chapter
National Executive Council
National Nominating Committee
National Vice President

Impact During Tenure
- Generated broader outreach to the community by adding Education, Health, and Legislative Impact linkages to National Trends and Services structure.
- Instituted Schools in Africa initiative and funded the construction of three schools; the effort culminated in the purchase of 62 schools.
- Convened National African American Leadership Summit in association with the UPS Foundation (strategic planning on the issues that will affect people of African descent in the next millennium).
- Culminated first major fundraiser for The Links Foundation, netting more than $65,000.
- Revived purchase of chapter NAACP life memberships.
- Established signature programming with Links to Success: Children Achieving Excellence and Education across the Miles.
- Introduced School in a Box initiative for Rwanda.
- Introduced $25 technology fee and recommended standing committee status for Technology Committee.
- Led advocacy efforts for Kemba Smith in her fight for fair sentencing.

Selected National Honors
- First African American to serve as Chief Attorney for the Complaints Branch of the Federal Communications Commission, Washington, DC
- May 14, 1980, speech "If Not You, Who? If Not Now, When?" recorded in the congressional record of the United States (H3661)
- One of *Black Enterprise* magazine's Top Five Business Motivators in America
- Recognized in *Ebony* and *Essence* magazines
- Author, *A is for Attitude: An Alphabet for Living*

THROUGH THEIR EYES

Excerpts from *The Links Oral History Collection*

Patricia Russell-McCloud, JD
On Her Tenure As
ELEVENTH NATIONAL PRESIDENT (1994–1998)
January 2019 • Washington, DC

#11 Russell-McCloud fielding interview questions.

Your Introduction to Linkdom

I was a student at Howard University Law School … In my civic and academic pursuits, I was increasingly made aware to communities where I lived, worked and played. And there was a burgeoning need in an organization called The Links … they wanted to identify younger women who could carry the mission, mandate, and underpinnings of friendship and service to its optimum levels on a continuum of legacy.

Dr. Dolly Adams, the eighth National President, was in this area at the time and told the Arlington Chapter, "That child would be good … because she's able, and she's smart and she's a lawyer, too. So, you know, we should look at her." That's how I became more intimately involved and interested in their activities.

Your Path to the Presidency

Initially, they needed persons who had a clear understanding of *Robert's Rules of Order*, a parliamentarian. So different presidents, because of the ebb and flow of personal life, a person who might have had the appointment, and they cycled out or whatever. … Committee work moved me into board positions, where I sat and deliberated over the problems, issues, answers. It became apparent to them—this talk of the president.

Then I said, well, I could be vice president, and they thought that it would be worth the run … "They" were not only membership; it was persons in leadership … had even served in that capacity … felt that it was advantageous to give some consideration to that path. And because of the strong mentor relationships that existed with persons who are older, wiser, been there, done that, with tee shirt to show. I said, I'll run. And it was interesting because I think being the second-youngest president, there was a generational awareness that became my cause … If this occurs, this is a paradigm shift for an organization where the average age is 65 … I thank my mentor, Dr. Dolly Desselle Adams.

Your Imprint on Linkdom

I am a courageous leader. I am a change-minded leader. I am one, I'm a telecommunications lawyer. So, specificity would point to when I became president, we had no membership online. We were not able to register for conferences online. We were not technologically proficient, and we had 11,000 members; and they were still sending letters and filling out forms. And I'm from the FCC. So, I'm like, what are we doing? New Day, new day? And there's this young child; she doesn't even know that these people don't know or want to know a keyboard. So, they said, "You're going to leave half of your membership behind. And I know I'm going to take them into the 21st century. So, technology for Linkdom started under me.

I thought we needed partnerships because partners had more resources. So, from the top of my administration, I wanted to be certain that we had monies to best serve others that could go beyond. It's vital that we read to children, but I wanted a broader engagement. So, we had simultaneously a core group and Gladys Gary Vaughn is an expert in knowing the wording and the grantsmanship for that deliverable. So, all that was going on. There were monies and partners coming to pass that were value added, which gave me a broader ability to stretch into areas unknown, but a broader reach. Our partners included Kellogg, General Mills, AARP, Eli Lilly.

I was very proud of what we did in education and reading, very proud of Every Child Counts, very proud of Make Health a Habit. I like food, and increasingly, I was seeing too many African Americans impacted with diabetes, high blood pressure, and obesity … So, then I said, you know what? We need to look at health because it may not be everything, but without it, not much else is going to matter.

Your Biggest Challenge

I was in the very exciting throes of planning the 50th anniversary. I wanted it to be spectacular, exceptional, extraordinary, unforgettable. So, I had been intentional about the planning, flying back and forth from Atlanta, almost dual residences up here so much just planning my National Assembly. But the climate attitudes of the nation changed abysmally in '95 … the attitude was Blacks have had it, as a preference … Why is that relevant? Because Marc Morial was in New Orleans, the site of my National Assembly; and the ruling came down before my conference that affirmative action was up and over, that we are not going to give particular slots in the academy. We're not going to hold them for a minority, a number of entrances, and it was just falling and crumbling … I knew that it was catastrophic when Mark called and said, "Pat, we need to talk."

I met with my lawyer first before going and we as lawyers went over every console, every way by which we could say Yay, nay. And one thing … these commitments were made over eight years ago. These contracts were signed over eight years ago … You got over 3,000 folk coming that you can give up the ghost all on an ideological alignment even though it's our Black culture to say, I'll have to do that. Then doozy.

So legally, I told them we cannot take the hit. You will lose your shirt canceling the ACC conference because you don't align yourself with what's happening nationally. So, Mark said, I think Susan might not, bring it. Uh, Essence, I said, Susan is running the entertainment conference. I'm running a membership organization that gives service and friendship …. I said, I'm going to bring it in and I'm bringing it in by the grace of God; and if you don't help me, I'll make it anyway.

Your Advice for Future Presidents

There's one president at the time, and it is not us. We are yesterday's agenda. Sure example. We'll invite and ignite others who view her from a distance. So, it's important that she be the example and exemplary in the example that she sets. She must always look as beautiful as she does every day because they expect it; but more significantly, you are Links leader for 15,000 women globally. Be fair in your decision making. You must be consistent, and you must know that you are the leader of the towering and the tiny because everybody is not the Mack truck and going to go one to one with you. Some will be shy and introverted, but they, too, are your member, and they deserve your best inclusive attitude and opportunity to shine …. Fairness is your key to unlock and ensure celebration because you met me at my point of need and let me maximize my potential.

~ From *The Links Oral History Collection*, Marcia Denise White, Editor

Barbara Dixon Simpkins, EdD
Twelfth National President (1998–2002)

Yesterday's Courage, Today's Vision, Tomorrow's Hope

*The courage of those who have successfully led us in the past provides
a clear vision [for] today; [thereby offering] hope for tomorrow.*

CONGRESSWOMAN BARBARA JORDAN once asked the reflective question, "When do any of us do enough?" For 12th National President Barbara Dixon Simpkins, the answer was "Never." Simpkins believed in the interdependence of The Links chain and preached that continual performance was necessary to maintain and strengthen the connection.

After organizing and serving as the first president of the Prince George's County (MD) Chapter, in rapid succession, she added Area and National leader to her achievements. From secretary of the Eastern Area, Simpkins rose to director, and just 19 years after her election as a chapter president, she became the National head. Her selection was aided in part by her elevation to vice president by 11th National President Patricia Russell-McCloud following the death of then Vice President JoAhn Brown Nash in 1995. The position placed Simpkins up front and center, but it was her strong performance that got her elected as National vice president in 1996, effectively sealing her selection as National President at the 31st Assembly in 1998.

Simpkins approached the presidency with the belief that there were two essentials to a smoothly functioning organization: "effective and efficient leadership and followship. When both the leader and followers are committed to achieving the goals of the organization, leaders and members will enjoy the experience of friendship, while rendering services of quality to many people," she said.

Under the banner "Yesterday's Courage, Today's Vision, Tomorrow's Hope," Simpkins actualized The Links' mission of providing educational, civic, and intercultural activities to enrich communities. "The courage of those who have successfully led us in the past provides a clear vision [for] today; [thereby offering] hope for tomorrow," she said. For the "ongoing and uninterrupted journey of friendship and service," Simpkins chose a friendship plane with the caption "A Smooth Take Off into the Twenty-first Century," illustrating "the direction in which we hoped to move, and how we expected to effectively bridge the 20th Century and the 21st Century," Simpkins said.

While the vehicle differed from her predecessor's freedom train, Simpkins was committed to building on the foundation in place, and she "sustained many existing and proposed programs." As she summarized her first two years in the Spring/Summer 2000 *Link to Link*, she said, "We did not throw out the baby with the bath water." Having been an intricate part of the creations of the initiatives, Simpkins knew the value of each, and she maximized the potential.

Simpkins was also cognizant of the many unmet needs in communities, and she was not content simply to coast, so she added other initiatives that addressed the well-being and advancement of African Americans. She revealed the flight plan on takeoff—all 10,867 Links aboard, she said, would "embrace the vision, take ownership of plans, share in the decision-making process with harmony, and commit to supporting the efforts of the organization."

Touching down in San Francisco at the end of her first term in 2000, Simpkins declared, "It's time … to assess where we have been, where we are now, and where we are going as an organization of the new millennium." Crediting the membership for the successes, she noted, "As friends, we have worked shoulder-to-shoulder and side-by-side at the Chapter, Area, and National levels to achieve remarkable goals. We have focused on and actualized our mission," Simpkins declared.

As a final gauge, Simpkins evaluated the progress against the backdrop of the vision of the founders, querying, "Are we living up to the high expectations of our Co-Founders, Margaret Rosell Hawkins and Sarah Strickland Scott?" Her resounding response was "Yes." There was a crescendo in the answer at the end of her tenure in 2002. With pride, she heralded the honoring of The Links' mission.

Significant works have been done over the past four-year period by you … You kept the focus on our reason for being an organization, by enhancing the legacy of our fore sisters, by embracing the

legacy of friendship and service, and by demonstrating that programming is the heart of Linkdom.

Simpkins based her assessments on service delivery, enumerating accomplishments for the programs she had kept and innovations she had introduced. "We dreamed dreams that the National Program would be taken to greater heights—that we would soar and break new ground. We celebrate the realization of the dreams accomplished," she said.

Education across the Miles and Links to Success: Children Achieving Excellence took root in another administration, but Simpkins cultivated and maximize their potential. In her "Friend to Friend" message (Fall/Winter 1999), she highlighted the adoption. "It is significant that two signature programs began implementation in the month of October 1999." Further linking the initiatives to her program theme, Simpkins said, "Each of these programs is designed to give our youth both the skills they will need in the future and hope for tomorrow."

Education across the Miles was formally approved by the 31st (1998) Assembly as a Signature Program. As National vice president, Simpkins was part of the Governance Team and attended the groundbreaking ceremony for the first school in Soweto in May 1998. Roughly two months later, she took the reins of Linkdom, and her call for schools to educate "the underprivileged, underserved children in the remote villages and townships of South Africa" moved Links' contributions beyond expectation.

Surpassing both the first goal of 25 and the second milestone of 50, The Links, in partnership with the International Foundation for Education and Self-Help (IFESH), funded 52 schools. "It is evident that if the children of our motherland are to meet the challenges of the 21st century, education will be the answer," Simpkins said. Consequently, she did more than hand over a check for the construction. In February of 1999, Simpkins and a delegation of Links returned to South Africa for a site inspection "to ascertain firsthand, specifically the quality, location, appearance, and functional value of the two-room school buildings."

Simpkins also increased The Links' presence in South Africa by visiting existing schools, where The Links presented supplies and assisted with one-on-one learning activities. Simpkins and her entourage journeyed once more to South Africa in 2001 to tour the schools that had been completed. She also chartered the first Link chapter, providing a support base on the continent.

Simpkins was more intimately involved in Links to Success: Children Achieving Excellence (LSCAE), which was also approved as a Signature Program by the 31st Assembly. As National vice president, Simpkins co-authored the proposal, which was subsequently funded by the Kellogg Foundation, United Parcel Services Foundation, and the Exxon Foundation. She also maintained a presence in the Curriculum Development Committee and Lead Trainers workshops and employed evaluations to determine the program's effectiveness.

Through Summer Links Camp and Linkstowne, a school-year village, children with academic and social developmental needs received an array of mentoring and nurturing services, and companion services were available for their parents. A cadre of chapters conducted pilot studies in 1999, and many chapters duplicated the project in their communities.

In concert with an endorsement by the 31st (1998) Assembly, Simpkins continued The Links' support for the NAACP Legal Defense Fund's campaign (*United States v. Smith*) to have Kemba Smith released from a federal prison. A victim of mandatory sentencing laws, Smith was held for six years in a federal prison in Danbury, Connecticut, before President William Jefferson Clinton granted her clemency in 2000.

Simpkins's own initiatives wrought equally impressive results. Linkages to Life (LL), a concerted effort to increase awareness about organ, tissue, and bone marrow donation and encourage African Americans to become donors is still one of The Links' most effective and widely known programs. The effort, which emphasizes the disproportionate need for organ transplants by African Americans and the longer waiting time most endure, received the nod as a Signature Program at the 32nd Assembly in 2000. The

National effort was patterned on a successful model Simpkins had witnessed in the Southern Area.

Challenging Links to "fully understand that service is our obligation and not a special gift we give to others," Simpkins provided even more avenues for hands-on experiences, partnering with Habitat for Humanity to build houses at the 32nd and 33rd Assemblies. At the 32nd Assembly, The Links also introduced Youths Talk: Links Listen, and chapters established Youth Councils at the local level for students in grades 6 to 12. Additionally, a virgin art series was created to showcase unusually talented students. Simpkins called the series "quantitative and qualitative programs and activities that stimulated the creative minds of our youth and prepare them for the future."

The Links' philanthropy had supported other programs for African American youth and women, along with worthy causes, since 1954, and as the new millennium dawned in 2000, The Links shone, donating more than a half-million dollars in grants and other resources during the 32nd National Assembly. It was another example of The Links' mission in action. "We truly offer a lifeline to save and perpetuate those intrinsic values of the African American family and others of African descent," Simpkins said.

#12 Simpkins presenting a check at the 33rd (2002) Assembly.

Simpkins's mark on operations can be seen in many ways, but none has been more enduring than the "1 in 5" rule. "Linked in friendship, we, as members, strive to enhance the viability of the organization," she contended. Viewing an informed membership as essential to that vitality, Simpkins pushed the enactment of a one-in-five attendance requirement. Passed by the 32nd Assembly, the provision forced members to become part of the chain beyond their own chapter, requiring active members to "register and attend one Area Conference or National Assembly within every five (5) year period." The amendment was significant in and of itself, but it also had residual effects, germinating an era of increased member accountability, a 48-hour service requirement, and a Code of Ethics in the next administration.

On July 6, 2002, Simpkins guided the plane to a safe landing, but as the window on her presidency closed, the third component of Simpkins's triumvirate remained open— "Tomorrow's hope," she promised, would continue "to empower us individually and collectively, and keep Linkdom forging ahead with strengthened programs that impact the lives of those whom we serve—as well as our own." Reaffirming the impact, Simpkins detailed "all

my sister Links have done to help the organization achieve its long-termed and currently envisioned goals, for the period of July 1998 to the present."

"Thanks for the memories," she penned in her final "Friend to Friend" message. It had been a team effort, and everyone had played a vital role in helping The Links respond to the long-term and ever-emerging needs of the African American family:

> *As the curtains draw closed on this watch and all the players of the cast (the Executive Council and the Foundation Board) end their individual, collective, and unforgettable performances, I humbly and sincerely say, "Thanks for the Memories ... I thank you so much."*

For moving The Links "boldly into the new millennium" during her tenure, Simpkins singled out 1) her Program team for providing the direction and design and 2) chapters and members for the cooperation and work that made it a success. "We (were) each a small *strong* Link ... in a long unbreakable chain of friendship, love, and service," she said.

~ *Tracey Tolbert Jones*
~ *Earnestine Green McNealey, PhD*

Barbara Dixon Simpkins, EdD

Links Service

Vice President and National Membership Chair

Chapter Establishment Chair

Eastern Area Director

Eastern Area Secretary

Co-Author, Links to Success: Children Achieving Excellence

Organizer and first President, Prince George's County (MD) Chapter

Impact During Tenure

- Shepherded one-in-five attendance requirement.
- Established Linkages to Life as National Signature Program.
- Built 52 schools for the education of the underprivileged, underserved children in the remote villages and townships of South Africa.
- Held first Links University, focusing on technology training.
- Initiated Youths Talk: Links Listen.
- Executed Links to Success: Children Achieving Excellence.
- Presented $100,000 installment of million-dollar grant to NAACP Legal Defense and Education Fund.
- Continued efforts to free Kemba Smith.

Selected National Honors

- Board Member, International Foundation for Education and Self Help
- US Secretary of Education Exemplary Initiative Award

Gladys Gary Vaughn, PhD
Thirteenth National President (2002–2006)

Touching Tomorrow Today

From all those who accept the rare invitation to don the mantle of The Links, Incorporated, much is expected. We are required by the Constitution and Bylaws to be active members: attending and participating in Chapter meetings, participating in Chapter activities relating to the program facets, and paying all Chapter, Area, and National dues and assessments. Simply put, checkbook member and financial member are not categories of membership.

THE 13TH NATIONAL PRESIDENT chose "three simple words" to help members remember her theme, but it was charged with messaging and action. "It was my attempt to get the members and the organization in its totality to understand that everything we did as an organization now would impact the organization in the future, and we should do what we could to get it right." Gladys Gary Vaughn engineered two transformative measures that dramatically changed The Links culture: a 48-hour service requirement and a binding Code of Ethics.

Vaughn believed in the power of dialogue to shape the future, and she used "Conversations for Change" to engage and involve members in structured discussions that would close the gulf between governance and membership. "Links actions would become what we did, as opposed to what the administration did," she said. Vaughn hoped to spur "reflective, futuristic thinking and planning" within parameters that would define the organization for generations to come:

What do we want to be in the 21st Century? How can we interface technologically? How can we ensure more effective delivery of our services to our members and to the underserved and unserved? How can our organization encourage spirited involvement and creative performance of

ALL of its members? How can we effect better use of the extraordinary expertise and networks resident in chapters?

The talks began in 2002 at a joint meeting of the Executive Council, National Committees, and The Links Foundation, and Vaughn took them on the road to 2003 Area Conferences and the "first-ever Area Officers Orientation." Chapters also held sessions during the 2003–2004 year. Emphasizing the importance of the discourse, Vaughn said, "The stage is being set for how we will invest in our own future, for how we will touch tomorrow today."

Four common perspectives evolved as connectors: a mandatory level of service, a Links Code of Ethics, structured leadership training, and excellence in programming. Having observed and participated in Links decisions for 18 years before she assumed the presidency in 2002, Vaughn knew the quartet in its entirety was essential in positioning The Links as the "progressive, elevating, and inspiring seed" hailed by Anna Julia Cooper, an icon Vaughn often quoted. "The Links, Incorporated, is indeed, the entity where new triumphs for communities of color will be dreamed, incubated, planned, and unfolded," Vaughn declared, and she actualized the claims.

While both changes were monumental, the 48-hour service mandate quantified what constituted service. The 34th (2004) Assembly approved the measure, which required each member to perform a minimum of 48 hours of service under The Links banner in order to maintain membership. The passage came fresh on the heels of a "1 in 5" attendance requirement approved by the 32nd Assembly in 2000.

Some members vehemently opposed the move from the outset, arguing that while they subscribed to service, the number of hours donated should be a matter of choice. "Legislating a minimum number of hours impugns our veracity and treats us as employees, rather than volunteers," became the rallying retort. Others maintained the move was a veiled attempt to excise members. The majority, however, shared Vaughn's beliefs and wanted a standard, so much so that the actual proposal did not originate

with Vaughn—it came forth as a bylaw amendment from a chapter, a clear indication that Vaughn's conversations for change had resonated.

To Vaughn, being a member meant more than just paying dues, and she hammered the idea with the expression, "We don't have check book Links."

From all those who accept the rare invitation to don the mantle of The Links, Incorporated, much is expected. We are required by the Constitution and Bylaws to be active members: attending and participating in Chapter meetings, participating in Chapter activities relating to the program facets, and paying all Chapter, Area and National dues and assessments. Simply put, checkbook member and financial member are not categories of membership.

Vaughn promoted member involvement as integral to program excellence: "Our ability to conduct meaningful, well-designed and science-based programs is tied to the service rendered by our members. It takes all members to make a significant and sustainable impact upon the communities we serve," she said. Vaughn's approach was to dialogue. Among the benefits she delineated were work and support from the full membership, enhancement and enlargement of outreach efforts, and vital documentation of Links' involvement for tax compliance and corporate support. Even after its passage by a 233-24 vote, however, Vaughn found herself two years later having to stave off an attempt to rescind the requirement.

This time, as opposed to theories about the efficacy of the change, she had preliminary results; and again, she prevailed. Two years of impact studies showed that the requirement had indeed increased attendance and participation, strengthened programming, and increased collaborations with other groups. Additionally, constant contact had improved member relations and The Links' credibility as a viable service organization had been enhanced.

It took Vaughn a little longer to pass the Code of Ethics, but its imminence in her administration was also certain. It was an integral part of her campaign for the presidency. In her "Statement Regarding Candidate's Concept of The Links, Incorporated," Vaughn articulated the framework:

That we understand our mission and goals, know our responsibilities, rights, and privileges, understand and appreciate the special Links culture, and foster the special networks that are continually being nurtured and established, and that our practices are clear, policy driven, consistent and accurate.

When the Code of Ethics was first presented during Vaughn's first term, the margin of defeat was not large. Without any coordination, several members tried to revive the measure on the floor, but Vaughn decided to wait until the next Assembly. That will give us time to address the concerns that have been raised here and we can have a better proposal," she recalled in a 2019 interview. In Philadelphia, "the proposal passed with hardly a whimper, [thereby] setting a framework for ethical behavior for the organization." Reiterating the import of the Code of Ethics, Vaughn said, "My point of view then and now is that if you're an organization worth two cents, you have to have an ethical framework."

In another history-making move, Vaughn established a leadership academy to nurture young leaders "willing to use their talents and expertise to help ensure promising futures for Black women's organizations." The Scott-Hawkins Leadership Institute (SHLI) premiered at the 34th Assembly and introduced its second class at the 35th Assembly. Praising SHLI's effectiveness in "identifying, developing, mentoring, and training Links aged 21–45 to assume leadership roles in fraternal, civic, and cultural organizations serving the African American community," Vaughn's successor, 14th National President Gwendolyn B. Lee, retained the program, as did the three National Presidents who followed Lee. By naming the institute Scott-Hawkins, Vaughn also achieved her objective of having members honor and revere The Links' heritage. "We have a responsibility to pass on the legacy of Sarah Strickland Scott and Margaret Rosell Hawkins," she said.

Vaughn was also a program guru widely recognized for program design, grant writing, and administration. Her programming approach was informed by her tenure as Services to Youth director and Grants-in-Aid chair, and further seasoned by her experience as a National Program leader in the Cooperative State Research, Education and Extension Service of the United States Department of Agriculture. She introduced several innovations that earned kudos at home and abroad.

Among the programs honored was The Links' signature art project for the 2002–2006 biennium. Featuring the Ritz Chamber Players (RCP), the nation's first chamber music ensemble series comprised solely of accomplished musicians spanning the African diaspora, the program was successful in introducing audiences to classical music and promoting young Black artists. In addition to sponsoring RCP at Assemblies, Area Conferences, and chapter events, The Links also feted the group in a special 2006 Mother's Day performance in Jazz at Lincoln Center and sessions at two public schools and the Metropolitan Museum of Art, achieving mainstream coverage from media, including NBC News, which interviewed Vaughn.

The Links also received the Organization of the Year designation by the United Nations for its unique and creative international programming—from MAAMA Birthing Kits to Education across the Miles. Additionally, national acclaim was bestowed for a series of ads developed in partnership with Roche to promote The Links' signature National Trends and Services project, Linkages to Life. The Links' largesse, particularly the million-dollar grants, continued to garner attention as well. Under Vaughn, the pledge to the National Association for the Advancement of Colored People Legal Defense Fund was also completed at the 34th Assembly, and the new grantee, the National Civil Rights Museum of Memphis, received the first installment of the million dollars it will receive over an eight-year period.

Because Vaughn stressed excellence in chapter programming, she used incentives to salute programs that stood out. It was the beginning of cash prizes for the best-of-the-best programs, and the funds also helped chapters expand their offerings, increase the number of people being served, expand the territory, and/or continue the service. An added value was the publication of a Promising Practices/Best Practices guide that chronicled the programs and served as a model for other chapters.

Through a new category of membership and a special salute at the 60th Anniversary Closing Banquet, Vaughn also paid homage to Links who were 80 years old, had rendered service to Linkdom for at least 30 years, and were active. Platinum status was approved by the 34th (2004) Assembly, and

Vaughn issued a special invitation to all 343 to attend the 35th (2006) Assembly in Philadelphia, where The Links celebrated its roots and—in the midst of celebrating the founding group—also recognized those who had been part of the chain for four decades.

In Philadelphia, Vaughn also took her final bow for the enduring triumphs she had achieved. She thanked members for staying the course with her. Together, they began focused conversations about critical dimensions of Linkdom that needed change and they transformed the organization with practices and programs that will permeate many tomorrows.

~ *Earnestine Green McNealey, PhD*

Gladys Gary Vaughn, PhD

Links Service

National Vice President and Membership Chair

National Director, Services to Youth

National Chairman, Proposals, Foundations, and Grants

Co-Author, Links to Success: Children Achieving Excellence

Member, Strategic Long-Range Planning Committee and Project LEAD: High Expectations

Charter President, Potomac (VA) Chapter

Impact During Tenure
- Established 48-hour service requirement.
- Engineered Code of Ethics.
- Instituted Scott-Hawkins Leadership Institute.
- Developed Leadership Institute for Chapter Officers.
- Added Platinum to membership category.
- Presented final installment of million-dollar payment to NAACP Legal Defense and Education Fund.
- Accepted Links' award as Organization of the Year from the United Nations for international programming from the MAAMA Birthing Kits.
- Presented first installment of $1 million grant to the National Civil Rights Museum of Memphis.

Selected National Honors
- Hall of Fame, School of Agriculture and Home Economics, Florida A & M University
- Co-Founder, National Coalition for Black Development in Home Economics, US Department of Agriculture
- Outstanding Performance Award, Association of Family and Consumer Sciences
- Superior Performance Award, US Department of Agriculture
- Board Director, Black Women's Agenda, National Consumers League, Black Patriots Foundation
- Home Economics Association for Africa
- Delta Sigma Theta National Social Action Commission, Mission Center, and American Baptist Churches of the South

THROUGH THEIR EYES

Excerpts from *The Links Oral History Collection*

Gladys Gary Vaughn, PhD
On Her Tenure As
THIRTEENTH NATIONAL PRESIDENT (2002–2006)
January 2019 • Washington, DC

#13 Vaughn fielding interview questions.

Your Introduction to Linkdom

My actual first introduction to The Links was when I was a child reading *Jet* and *Ebony* magazines. And particularly in *Jet*, there were almost weekly pictures of these black women who were giving $1,000 scholarships and $1,500 scholarships and contributions to the Urban League. That's where I first saw the word Links and it was Links, then; not The Links. I was introduced to The Links, Incorporated much later in my life when I received invitations from Jacqueline Robinson to attend social events of the Arlington (VA) Chapter. She and I got to be very dear friends, and from there, she introduced me to other individuals.

Mrs. Robinson called me one day … She was a nurse, and I thought she wanted me to help her to establish a group of kids somewhere in the District, or to help her with some program in nursing. I was stunned when I learned later that she was estab-lishing an interest group for The Links, Incorporated. So, I told her, in no uncertain terms was I interested in becoming a Link. And she said, "You are, and you will be." … And so, I said, I'll join the group. But what I did not know is that she intended me to lead the group. To make a long story short, through Jackie's direction, I served as the president of the Beltway Women's League, our little interest group, comprised of women who lived in and around the Washington, DC, beltway. I'm really glad that I listened to her.

Your Path to the Presidency

Link Jacquelyn was the National Chapter Establishment officer, and she was a part of the board of Link Dolly Desselle Adams, National President. During the time that we were an interest group, we periodically met with Mrs. Robinson, but sometime Dr. Adams would also come to the meetings. Toward the end, the National vice president, Regina Jollivette Frazier, would also come. And so, I had these three ladies pretty much monitoring everything I did, and they were very pleased with what our chapter did. For example, I remember calling Jackie asking her if she would send me a copy of the guidelines for chapter establishment … and she said, "I'm counting on you to help write the guidelines."

She was serious. We had to submit a report. She called me one day and said, "Gladys, you're going to hear about this, so, I'm telling you now. I'm taking the report that the Beltway Women's League submitted. … I'm clean-ing it up just a little bit for my purposes, and that's going to be my report." I said, "That's fine." On the night that we were actually inducted, we wound up as the Potomac Chapter. Link Dolly was there, Link Regina was there, and Link Jackie was there.

It's about one year from the time my chapter is The Links Chapter from the time that Link Regina becomes president, but when she does become president, I receive a call … and she tells me that she wants me to serve on her board of directors; she has heard that I was a grant writer, and she wants me to write grants so that she can get external funds for research-based programming … I said to her, I think maybe you might have misdialed; you have reached the wrong Gladys. I'm Link Gladys Gary Vaughn with the Potomac Chapter, and we have just recently become a chapter.

Link Regina was livid. "I have not misdialed. I know what I need, I know what I'm asking." But I can't serve on the board, I said. You have to have been a Link 20 or 30 years before you get to the level of serving on the board. And she replied, "That may be your impression Link Gladys, but I am asking you to serve on the board and to help me to get grant funds for programming for The Links. Can you do this?" I said, yes, I can. And that's what I did. The first grant I wrote ... was for $985,000 for a program called High Expectations. Link Marion (the 10th) asked me to serve on a strategic planning committee. Link Pat (the 11th) gave me two options ... I said to her, well, I've done the grants thing, so I'll try Services to Youth.

I'd never run for an office in The Links. I'd been appointed to everything .... But people were beginning to ask if I would run for office. And so, I began to give it some consideration. I was married to a gentleman who was a non-joiner ... but he never got in my way. I asked him what was his opinion about my running for the vice presidency of The Links? "Well, if you're interested, I'll support you." And so ... I turned in my application ... and I won the election. Some of my Links friends urged that I run for the presidency because I had had a successful vice presidency ... I did run. My name was the only one on the ballot ... a member of my chapter stood on the floor and said, "Since Link Vaughn's name is the only one on the ballot, can we now elect our president?" And so, I became the only president to be elected as president unanimously from the floor.

Your Imprint on Linkdom
Established ... the governance structure, a program created to bring in all of the individuals who served at the National level and at the Area level and had a common function.

Created an institute for members ... between the ages of 21 and 40 ... to get them to stay with us ... to offer them an opportunity to learn about the history of the Black Club women's movement and the role of black women's organizations ... in maintaining the black community.

Created platinum members to recognize women in the organization who had reached age 80 and had given 30 years of service as active members.

Set a framework for ethical behavior for the organization (Code of Ethics).

Revamped our program planning and review process.

Your Biggest Challenge
Member engagement and the fact that there were a lot of cracks in the organizational structure that had to be addressed. And so, my first challenge was to make sure that all components of the organization were fully aligned. Our structure is that we have a National body, which is the core; and part of the core is four Areas and all of the chapters. But everybody was doing their own thing. And you can't, that's no way to run a railroad. I think we did very well with that and in establishing policies that govern the organization in its entirety.

Your Advice for Future Presidents
And what I would suggest to anybody who wants to lead is that you need to look for good people. But people who would tell you the truth, and if you do that, you pretty much will be successful. If you listen to what they tell you, if you believe in what they're telling you.

~ From *The Links Oral History Collection*, Marcia Denise White, Editor

Gwendolyn Byrd Lee, PhD
Fourteenth National President (2006–2010)

We will be the change that we want to see in the world.

WHEN THE LINKS' 14TH NATIONAL President posited "Seizing the Opportunity to Provide World-Class Leadership, Friendship & Service" as the theme for her administration, Gwendolyn Byrd Lee visualized a chain of close-knit friends driven by a common purpose, exceptional programming propelled through partnerships, and unprecedented service keyed to community needs. Her goals even included "transforming The Links' National Headquarters into an organizational structure that is respectful, resourceful, and most importantly, responsive."

Never in her wildest dreams, however, had Lee envisioned crafting a grand edifice befitting the organization she planned "to take … from good to great." But when obtaining the building next door to The Links' current headquarters became a possibility, Lee embodied her mantra, and she grabbed the opportunity to upgrade The Links' operations hub, simultaneously elevating The Links' presence in the nation's capital.

"We have a wonderful opportunity," Lee told Links in a June 21, 2007, letter, and on the first vote at the 36th (2008) Assembly, delegates agreed. They not only ratified purchasing the building as part of an expansion and renovation effort, but they also approved a funding package. When Lee left office in July 2010, "all contracts for the renovation, restoration and renewal had been finalized," and within hailing distance of the United States capitol, two buildings with two addresses on Massachusetts

Avenue were being merged and transformed into the $20 million grand edifice of The Links Incorporated, 1200 Massachusetts Avenue, NW.

As a precursor to delivering service, Lee engendered a harmonious membership that actively participated in chapter events and functions. "The cornerstone of our great organization is friendship, [and] the power to positively impact critical issues," she declared, rested in cementing "a circle of loving friends." To increase the bonds, Lee declared November as Friendship Month, and she encouraged members to celebrate each other. "I'm proud to say this has been a resounding success," she rejoiced after

the 2006 debut; and the three administrations that followed have continued to place friendship at the center of everything Linkdom.

Throughout her tenure, Lee increased communication at all levels, incorporating frequent newsletters, a "Calling Post" service, telephone calls, personal appearances at events, Wednesday and Sunday Presidents' Chats, and timely responses to e-mail. The byproduct was a circle of chapters and members who felt good about themselves and their leaders. "From all indications, there appeared to be an increased feeling of inclusiveness." Over the four-year journey, Lee always praised chapters for the "tremendous commitment we have to our communities."

The work was reflected in programs and community engagement. Lee orchestrated "the delivery of successful solutions to people of African descent" across the United States and on the Ivory Coast. The missions included the revitalization and expansion of The Links' signature programs for youth and women, aid for African schools, published positions on hot topics, and continued funding for causes that paralleled The Links' way.

Revamped signature programs were focal conduits for the "hope and relief" programming that Lee championed. "Our signature programs will once again find prominence at the heart of our programming agendas, Lee said. Among the modifications was the rebranding of LEAD to Links Educate, Accommodate and Develop Classics and curriculum modifications, which addressed the evolving challenges—financial literacy, career awareness, and mentoring for grades 4 to 8. Links to Success: Children Achieving Excellence was also redesigned to target literacy in grades pre-K through 3, and Lee determined that "to see what was going on with our schools," she led a delegation of 112 Links to South Africa, where they toured the last of the 62 schools The Links had established through its Education across the Miles initiative, which began in 1996.

The Walk for Healthy Living and Linkages to Life were subsumed under a new, expansive signature initiative addressing heart disease, the number one killer of African American women. Dubbed HeartLinks, the initiative was approved by the 36th (2008) Assembly. Health services received another shot when and the 37th (2010) Assembly created Health and Human Services as The Links' fifth facet.

Lee embraced other staples as well. Pleased by the Scott-Hawkins Leadership Institute's success in developing emerging and aspiring leaders, Lee expanded leadership development offerings and championed aid to historically Black colleges and universities (HBCUs), a Links cause célèbre since the 1970s. The Links' four Areas carried the banner for endowed scholarships, with Lee's earmark of $50,000 signaling the importance of the venture.

During the 2006–2007 program year alone, The Links established HBCU endowments of one-half-million-plus. The Links also awarded its standard Assembly Grants-in-Aid, presenting $420,000 to community groups in 2008 and $450,000 in 2010, along with million-dollar-installment payments: $225,000 to the National Civil Rights Museum and $500,000 to Susan G. Komen for the Cure (2010).

Lee also ensured that The Links' voice on public issues was heard! The first African American women's organization to condemn Don Imus's derogatory comments about Rutgers' women's basketball team in 2007, The Links flooded the airways and used print media and e-mail blasts to call for Imus's firing. The Links also held a public forum to examine reauthorization of "The No Child Left Behind" (2007) and opposed "the illegal immigration laws of Arizona" (2010).

Via collaborations with corporations and institutions, Lee buttressed the ability of chapters, Areas, and National to impact communities. Capitalizing on The Links' reputation for getting things done, Lee formed strategic alliances with Komen for the Cure, the National Cares Mentoring Movement, and Heart Promise—partnerships that transcended the paper. National Cares Mentoring Movement Director Susan Taylor was so pleased by The Links' delivery that Lee was invited to join her in a promotional segment on the *Oprah Winfrey Show.*

Lee also pushed an "effective and efficient National Headquarters." From files to personnel, she put in place a framework that engendered "world-class" member services and support for chapters, officers, and committees. An enhanced, user-friendly website with vital, up-to-date information was rolled out in 2007, and members received digital copies of new, blended, and revised documents at the 36th (2008) Assembly.

"A lot has been accomplished since July 6, 2006," Lee declared as she expressed gratitude to the 36th Assembly for the opportunity: "Link Sisters, I sincerely thank you, again for entrusting me with your confidence to lead this organization to new heights." The Assembly exuberantly responded by unanimously reelecting her for two more years. Rating Lee's performance as she prepared to relinquish her office in 2010, the Assembly commended Lee for her "superlative, most meaningful and effective leadership."

"With distinction and with an emphasis on strengthening friendship and organizational linkages," Lee delivered on the promise to her sisters: "We will be the change that we want to see in the world." Her masterful orchestration lifted friendship, program, and operations to noteworthy heights.

~ *Earnestine Green McNealey, PhD*
~ *Yvonne Roulhac Horton, PhD*

Gwendolyn Byrd Lee, PhD

Links Service

National Vice President, Recording Secretary and Member-at-Large

Chair, National Nominating Committee

National Director, National Trends and Services

Chair, Central Area Services to Youth

Charter Member, Corresponding Secretary, and President, South Suburban Chicago Chapter

Impact During Tenure

- Spearheaded purchase of 1204 Massachusetts Avenue, and secured funding package to cover the expansion, renovation, and integration with 1200 Massachusetts.
- Pushed Health and Human Services as fifth program facet.
- Introduced HeartLinks and Classics through the Ages as signature projects.
- Published the third official history of The Links, Incorporated.
- Endorsed retention of the 48-hour service requirement.
- Presented second installment ($225,000) of million-dollar commitment to the National Civil Rights Museum and $155,000 in Grants-in-Aid to other recipients.
- Championed bylaws amendments promoting growth, including reducing reinstatement fees from $2,000 to $500 for members who resigned in good standing and exempting daughters of Links in computing the total number of members in chapters that reach maximum size.
- Provided financial and human resources in weather crisis (Hurricane Katrina).

Selected National Honors

- Illinois Administrator of the Year
- Illinois Women Administrators Dare to Be Great Award
- South Suburban Illinois Association for Supervision and Curriculum Development Shared Leadership Award
- Excellence in Educational Award
- Two-time IPA Region VII, Principal of the Year
- Consultant, National Board for Professional Teaching Standards in Illinois
- Master Consultant, QLD Learning Corporation

THROUGH THEIR EYES

Excerpts from *The Links Oral History Collection*

Gwendolyn Byrd Lee, PhD
On Her Tenure As
FOURTEENTH NATIONAL PRESIDENT (2006–2010)
January 2019 • Washington, DC

#14 Lee fielding interview questions.

Your Introduction to Linkdom

Well, I was first introduced to Linkdom by a very dear friend's mother. Her mother happened to be very good friends with our Co-Founders. She was in the Philadelphia Chapter, and they were all members of The Links and Jack and Jill. She happened to have been the national president of Jack and Jill. She wanted her daughter to be a Link, but her daughter was way off in Illinois, outside of Chicago with me. She said, "Just go ahead and figure this out so we don't have to have a chapter. My daughter can be a member where she was good friends with, at that time, the Chapter Establishment officer, Anna Julian. Anna, I need a chapter in the southern part of the Chicago land area." So my daughter can be a Link was pretty much the way it went.

She said, "Talk to your chapter," which happened to be the Chicago Chapter, and see if they will sponsor the chapter because you had to be sponsored back then. And so, she invited us all to a luncheon .… I'd say there might've been maybe 10 or 12 of us. We didn't really know what we were getting into. Yvonne's mother is coming; her name was Dr. Nellie Roulhac. Okay. She wants to talk to us about a group. Okay. So, we all showed up … at the time in our early 20s and we had a great lunch, great conversation. That's when she said, um, I want you all to think about starting a Links chapter. Now she asked us politely, but we already knew we were going to start a Links chapter.

Your Path to the Presidency

I wanted to be the Supreme Basileus of Alpha Kappa Alpha Sorority. I had come up through the ranks. I had been president of my undergraduate chapter on campus. I was AKA all the way. And then, when I was asked to be a part of The Links, because it was so small, I had to assume many roles. So, I was rather immersed into leadership positions very early on, and it consumed me. I couldn't do both and raise a family; so, I selected The Links because it was in its infancy, my chapter. I was considered to be a charter member, so it was important for me to make sure that we kept the legacy going.

I never in my wildest dreams thought I would become the National President, though. Usually if I'm involved or engaged in anything, I emerge as a leader because I will see where things are falling apart and try to put it together. I think when I was recording secretary was when I finally made up my mind that I was going to move on. And you have to do that early on. You can't just wait and wake up one night. Oh, I think I'm going to be president. For me, it started when I was recording secretary.

I started just thinking, you know what, I think I could do this. And then I was encouraged every step of the way, you know, let me start here and work hard here and move on up, you know; because that's basically what I had always been told. They didn't necessarily like people just coming out of the blue running for an office. They liked for you to have some experience and before taking on a position. I started off with a position they no longer have. I went from member-at-large to the National Nominating Committee chair … to recording secretary, and then I became the director of National Trends and Services. Then, I was National vice president, and finally, the president.

Your Biggest Challenge

I'm just coming into my tenure as National President, and I'm at the Central Area Conference, and I get a telephone call from headquarters saying the gentleman that owns the building next door wants to talk with me. He had promised Link Dolly Desselle Adams that before he would ever sell the building, he would give us the right of first refusal. When I had the conversation with him, he says, "Yes, I need to sell it and I want to do it in a hurry." Within two weeks, I had to pull money together. That's why I say The Links, Incorporated and the members in this organization are phenomenal, phenomenal. Picked up the phone, call, put it out there. Thank God, we had email at that time, um, sent out emails in my email blast, called people, and I had money for a deposit. Money for the down payment, cash money.

I had to get a loan because it was construction, because unfortunately, they had to demolish most of the building. However, it was in a historic district. So, some of the original things had to remain. I just can't even tell you how difficult it was trying to get through that whole process. So, my first year in office, this is what I faced, having to look at the building next door, and then do reconstruction. That meant I had to also in many ways, uh, demolish part of the first building because they weren't equal. So, then we had to make the two buildings equal in size. So, we had to put stairs to lead up to the next area so that this part which was here could match up to this part. That was, it was unbelievable. And, when you go downtown and you have to get the, um, um, uh, the permits in Washington DC! I've never had anything this horrific or horrendous in my life. I said I would do better going to a foreign country, record and speak the language, and I probably would get a permit quicker than I would in DC.

But you know, again, there's a blessing in a silver lining. A Links sister who had a lot of clout. What permits do you need? Boom, boom, boom. No problem. Two to three weeks. I hit my permits. That's how it works. That's how it works, Links is a phenomenal organization. Women who will pull together and do what they need to do. So, we got our permits, we wanted to use an African American architect. So we put bids out for that. And uh, we finally we found one. And then, getting the renderings, the drawings and determining; and then having the group approve it; to say, oh yeah, this is how we want the building to look, or no, this is not. And then finally getting the organization to agree to pay for it. Because even though we had a loan, you got to pay off the loan. And so when you start talking about assessing people does not go over very well. And I was just amazed, amazed at how I'd say 90 percent of the women in this organization …. I said, If you want it, we'll pay for it. And they did.

Your "Lessons Learned"

You assume that people know who the officers are. The National vice president, Margot James Copeland, and I had just been newly elected. I think we'd been to San Diego with the Western Area Conference. "I was so proud. We're so happy!" We are walking down the hallway, and we see a group of ladies with The Links symbol. They had a camera. It was a whole group of them. They said, "Do you mind?" We said, "Of course not." And they handed us the camera to take the picture of them.

~ From *The Links Oral History Collection*, Marcia Denise White, Editor

Margot James Copeland
Fifteenth National President, 2010–2014

Leading With Excellence, Serving With Grace

*You lead with excellence, knowing that each and
every time that we step forward in the community,
we are stepping forward with our best.*

IN SELECTING "LEADING WITH EXCELLENCE, Serving With Grace" as the theme or her administration, 15th National President Margot James Copeland wanted to send a message to the membership. "We are leaders, but it's not enough to be in charge," she noted. "You lead with excellence, knowing that each and every time that we step forward in the community, we are stepping forward with our best. Know that our greatest bonds and connections are formed and framed within this organization." A model of servant-leadership, Copeland was ever-mindful of her predecessors yet forged her own path during her presidency.

As National President, Copeland sought to honor the work of past presidents and address any unfinished business, whether it was the ongoing renovation and expansion of National Headquarters or the fulfillment of philanthropic pledges and partnerships. Copeland's six National Strategic Priorities cascaded to all levels of the organization, designed to enhance its visibility, operation, and membership growth:

- Delivering and Sustaining Transformational Programs
- Enhanced Member Services and Engagement
- Fund Development and Fiscal Responsibility
- Organizational Assessment and Alignment
- Leadership Development
- Promoting the Links Brand

Her highest priority, however, was sisterhood and friendship. Copeland fostered an inclusive relationship among members of her governing team and kept members at the forefront of the work of leadership, the Executive Council, and the chapters. She developed mechanisms to support Links at all membership levels and established committees and communications to make operations and leadership more transparent. "Every decision will be made with the member in mind, putting her first," she stated.

The Links' gala anniversary celebration the following year offered a grand stage to display 65 years of friendship and service. Held in November of 2011, the gala anniversary weekend celebration in Washington, DC, included a rededication of the National Headquarters—renovation of the state-of-the art LEED® Gold-certified building was completed within budget. More than 500 Links lined the streets in front of the Massachusetts Avenue headquarters to celebrate and tour the modernized facility. Copeland could not have been prouder. While much of the concept and design work for the building's expansion was completed prior to her installation, the construction had to be completed. Once finished, she wanted every Link to feel at home. "I wanted our members to have a real, live connection with the property because they owned it," she said. "We did not use one outside dollar. We purchased that property and funded it ourselves."

Another anniversary highlight was the presentation of the inaugural Links Medal, the highest honor, to *Ebony* magazine. Linda Johnson Rice, former Johnson Publishing Company president and CEO, came to accept the award in person. In all, the gala celebration raised more than $600,000. Copeland took a moment to reflect: "This has been a historic moment for our organization as we honor our past. We have challenges in our community, but you can count on the Links to be there to fill the gap, to be there for our people in health, in education and for our young people across the board."

Filling that gap through strong programming and philanthropy remained key areas of focus throughout her tenure. For The Links to not only maintain, but grow its stature and influence, Copeland pushed to make programming more impactful and sustainable. She set the tone for heightened community impact through organizational alignment and transformational programming. She focused her attention on strengthening and expanding current programs. Importantly, she raised the status of chapter program directors, sending a clear message about the relevance of programming—and the expected higher level of excellence in delivery.

Mirroring her own roots, National initiatives were created in support of historically Black colleges and universities (HBCUs) and science, technology, engineering, and mathematics (STEM) education and careers. Funded by the Lumina Foundation, the National HBCU Initiative established partnerships with local community colleges and HBCUs to increase postsecondary access, matriculation, retention, and completion. She expanded the organization's STEM footprint by forging partnerships with NASA and technology and energy sector companies. A partnership with Chevron provided grants to the highest-performing chapters in STEM education.

Copeland spurred groundbreaking youth service efforts by elevating involvement in efforts to combat childhood obesity. The programming around childhood obesity garnered national recognition from First Lady Michelle Obama, whose own signature initiative, Partnership for a Better America, also advanced nutrition, wellness, and physical fitness for youth.

Copeland also led her team to proactively develop strategic collaborations in alignment with historical organizational strengths. These partners included Achieving the Dream, Africare, American Heart Association, Partnership for a Healthier America, and Mayo Clinic. Additionally, The Links and the NAACP partnered to advance voter education, registration, and turnout. The success of that initiative led to another highly successful partnership with Sigma Pi Phi Fraternity to address anti-voter suppression and voter advocacy at the national level. Such collaborations helped The Links leave a lasting imprint. "It was a time where we went from 'who are the Links' to 'what do the Links think,'" recalled Copeland. "It was a glorious time, a time of great connection, time of hope, a time of great optimism, a time that we could see where we fit into the fabric of greater society."

Copeland credited the milieu of the first National Assembly of her administration with refining the organization's voice. Members gathered for the 39th National Assembly in Orlando amid the national outcry over the tragic shooting death of Trayvon Martin, an African American teenager, by a white neighbor in nearby Sanford months earlier. His parents, Sybrina Fulton and Tracy Martin, were invited to an open forum at the Assembly. Copeland recalled, "There were 3,000 chairs set up in that ballroom. There was not an empty seat. … It was stone quiet, and everyone stood in respect and in silence as we walked into the room. It was a powerful moment at the National Assembly. It was a powerful moment in Linkdom, and I do think where we got our footing and our voice. This is something we want to lift up."

For the duration of her tenure, she continued to leverage opportunities for the Links to rise and meet the challenges of the day, lending her platform to social justice issues. Copeland was at the White House for the launch of President Barack Obama's My Brother's Keeper initiative in February 2014 to address persistent opportunity gaps facing boys and young men of color. She hosted public forums around the education achievement gap between minority students and their peers and the impact of violence on children and communities.

Building upon The Links' rich legacy of global service, Copeland expanded the reach and promise of international programming to greater numbers of women and children. Copeland led a delegation of members to West Africa, where four Liberian schools—Ann Sandell, Todee Mission School, AME University, and School for the Blind—were built and sponsored by The Links. The delegation shared information on best practices and teacher development with Liberian educators. The Links also funded construction of two wellness centers for expectant mothers in partnership with Africare.

In a poignant and historic moment, Copeland presided over the first honorary member induction ceremony held outside of the United States, welcoming the Liberian president, Ellen Johnson Sirleaf (the first woman president elected in Africa), into the Circle of Friendship.

Organizationally, Copeland established processes that would ensure fiscal discipline, accountability, and financial management at the National level. With her fundraising prowess, the Links reached greater philanthropic heights during her administration. A strong fund development program was instituted, as well as a plan to rebuild the structure of The Links Foundation, Incorporated. Copeland launched the Vision 2020 fundraising campaign with the goal to raise $10 million for The Links Foundation by 2020. By the end of 2011, the campaign was nearly halfway to meeting its goal.

Under her administration, the Links presented the final installment of a $1 million grant to the National Civil Rights Museum in Memphis and pledged $1 million to the Smithsonian National Museum of African American History and Culture in Washington, DC. As the first African American organization to pledge a seven-figure gift to the institution, the Links' gift encouraged others to follow suit.

Copeland also sought to address a longstanding administrative challenge: determining and reconciling the exact chartering dates of several chapters. The chartering list compiled during her tenure stands today as the document of record. Additionally, she drove the expansion of The Links' social media presence and spearheaded the launch of two new online publications: the biannual news magazine, *LINKED*, in 2011, and a digest of members' newsworthy achievements, *Links in the Spotlight*, in 2014.

She also established new committees on the Executive Council, including Organizational Effectiveness, Alumna and Platinum Affairs, and Philanthropy and Strategic Partnerships, and she chartered seven new chapters (Greater Denton County, Texas; Mississippi Delta, Mississippi; Greater Rappahannock, Virginia; Lone Star, Texas; Greater Bronx, New York; Greater Pearland Area, Texas; and Patuxent River, Maryland). She inducted the former US secretary of state, Condoleezza Rice, into honorary membership and awarded her The Links' Lifetime Achievement Award. The second Links Medal was awarded to the National Urban League in 2014. The Links Leadership Academy (LLA) was also launched during her tenure.

To those who know her best, Copeland's Links leadership journey was in divine order. She was born into Linkdom: Her mother, Thelma Taylor James, was sponsored by Links Co-Founder Margaret Rosell Hawkins's sister-in-law into the Petersburg (VA) Chapter. Copeland's godmother and name-sake was Marietta Hall Cephas, composer of "The Links Song," another Petersburg Link. Family friend Mildred Hayes recalled: "The organization is the impetus for all she has done."

A visionary strategist and unrelenting optimist, Copeland brought a lifetime of experiences to full bloom as National President, with her faith in the power of Linkdom and loyalty of members unstinting. "We can become whatever we seek to become, if each of us continues to be 'the link in friendship's chain.'"

~ *Raven L. Hill*
~ *Sadie Winlock, DM*

Margot James Copeland

Links Service
National Vice President
Central Area Director
President, Cleveland (OH) Chapter

Impact During Tenure
- Established four new National initiatives in support of historically Black colleges and universities, STEM education and career readiness, combating childhood obesity, and Achieving the Dream.
- Increased emphasis on strong programming and philanthropy: Developed strategic partnerships with national organizations, embarked on Vision 2020 fundraising campaign, awarded final installment of $1 million to National Civil Rights Museum, and pledged $1 million to Smithsonian National Museum of African American History and Culture.
- Completed the renovation and occupancy of National Headquarters within budget.
- Commemorated 65th anniversary with gala weekend celebration.
- Oversaw the first honorary member induction outside of the United States: Liberian President Ellen Johnson Sirleaf.
- Expanded social media presence and new communications tools.

Selected National Honors
- Goddaughter of "The Links Song" composer Marietta Hall Cephas
- 2013 Alumni of the Year, Hampton University
- Esteemed Alumni, The Ohio State University/100 Years of African American Achievement
- Delta Sigma Theta Sorority, Inc., Community Service Award
- Vice Chairperson, Cleveland Bicentennial Commission and Cleveland Millennium Commission
- Chair, Cleveland Mayor Michael R. White Inaugural Committee
- Torchbearer Award, United Negro College Fund
- "Top Influential Women in Corporate America," *Savoy Magazine*

THROUGH THEIR EYES

Excerpts from *The Links Oral History Collection*

Margot James Copeland
On Her Tenure As
FIFTEENTH NATIONAL PRESIDENT (2010–2014)

January 2019 • Washington, DC

#15 Copeland fielding interview questions.

Introduction to Linkdom

I was born into Linkdom. My mother was a link, Thelma Taylor James, from the Petersburg, Virginia, chapter. Ironically, her sponsor was the sister-in-law to Margaret Hawkins, one of our Co-Founders. I remember playing with the children from the Hawkins Brown family when they would visit Petersburg, which is one of the older chapters of Links. So, I was an Heir-O-Link back in the day when they called us Bob-O-Links. And growing up there, I've since obviously become a Link, and I'm the mother of a Link. So, we are three generations of Links in our family. I grew up in Petersburg and knew the Petersburg Links, and went on to graduate school in Ohio and subsequently moved to Cleveland, where I was inducted into the Cleveland Chapter in 1982.

What we are really good about at Links is when our children move to places beyond our arms' reach, we have friends in those communities. What we want is a watchful eye on our adult children, although our children don't know that. My mom and my godmother, who was Marietta Cephas, the composer of The Links song, had some friends in the Cleveland area who she wanted to make sure kept a watchful eye on me. And subsequently you get to know others. And then, one day someone invites you to join our beloved organization.

Your Path to the Presidency

My first few years as a Link, in fact, my first 13 years as a Link, I spent in leadership roles at my door and my chapter, understanding how to connect the work of Linkdom to the greater Cleveland area …. That work was recognized by National and Area organizations along the way, and our chapter got a bit of attention through the National Office and National leadership. So, others that came after Link Dolly saw this young Link, who was president of the Cleveland Chapter. Although she never became president because she passed away prematurely, Link JoAhn Brown-Nash was the Central Area director, and she really positioned me in the Central Area; and I subsequently became Central Area director, where I could take this whole engagement and service. My theme then was Leadership, Legacy, and Love. I took it really quite frankly, a page out of her book; and also, you go from running one chapter to running 69 chapters across the heartland of America and making sure that we are engaged, and we are the best that we can be.

After I stepped down as Central Area director, I was happy for the break. It's a busy job, very time consuming, a lot of travel, great engagement with members, but it's a very, very busy job. I wanted to stay engaged …. Gladys Gary Vaughn found a pathway to keep me connected with the organization, but I wasn't so sure that leadership in elected office was my path. I preferred in my mind to think that I could be a better fit, you know, in a senior appointed role … envisioned myself as a National director of Programs or the Chapter Establishment officer. I didn't want the ultimate responsibility of actually being elected to office or running for it. But it ended up being a path that I did end up taking. At the end of 2006, I tossed my hat in the ring among some very worthy candidates, and we remain friends to this day.

Your Most Memorable Moment

I am proud of many of the things that we accomplished during my administration, not the least of which is The Links Foundation million-dollar gift that went to the Smithsonian African American Museum of History and Culture; that was historic. We were the first African American organization to pledge a seven-figure gift to the museum, and they will tell you from that point on, other African American organizations began to follow suit. That was important to set the stage. We can't expect others to do this for us. We have to do it for ourselves. This is our place, our history. And it was very, very prideful.

We also commissioned The Links Medal and Ed Dwight, the renowned sculptor, was commissioned to do that … and the first recipient of the sculpture was *Ebony* magazine. Linda Johnson came to Washington, DC, to celebrate with us. That was a big moment because who didn't grow up with *Ebony* magazine on their parents' coffee table and understanding that we are giving that to organizations that quite frankly transformed how the African American image was presented to the larger world and culture, and who better than Ebony to receive that.

The Links has a proud tradition of serving on the continent of Africa. I believe just about every president has had some type of connection and work and engagement with the continent. And we went to Liberia. The president of Liberia is an honorary member of The Links, and we had the first induction of an honorary member on foreign soil, where we inducted Ellen Johnson Sirleaf. While In Liberia, we opened maternal waiting rooms. We renovated or supported schools. We had teacher training for our educators who were with us. We worked with teachers in Liberia and on and on and on.

Kellogg gave us a wonderful grant to initiate "I'm my Brother's Keeper" initiative, and I had the distinct privilege of going to the White House the day that Barack Obama signed the "My Brother's Keeper" initiative …

I could go on and on and on. There were others, but it was a glorious time, a time of great connection, time of hope, a time of great optimism, a time that we could see where we fit into the fabric of greater society. Our partnership with the Boule and NAACP around a voter impact and a voter recognition and voter registration, getting people working with other organizations like ours to, to take that further. Even with voter suppression, having attorneys from our respective organizations there to work the polls to make sure people weren't turned away.

These were big and bold efforts that we did because you can't do everything yourself. So, you look for those opportunities where you're going to work with colleagues across the field and accomplish things. It was a time of hope and aspirations. It was a time when we went from Who are The Links to What do The Links Think? We have a voice. We gave clarity to that voice and advocacy. We knew that people wanted to know what we thought on given issues. So, we had position statements that came out on a regular basis on various topics, not the least of which around the murder of our black boys.

~ From *The Links Oral History Collection*, Marcia Denise White, Editor

Glenda Newell-Harris, MD
Sixteenth National President (2014–2018)

Building a Healthy Legacy: A Prescription for the Future

*We have done better than good, in all the ways and places
that we should, and for all the people we could. And yet,
we know that there is so much more work to do!*

THE FIRST PHYSICIAN TO ASSUME the helm of The Links, Incorporated, 16th National President Glenda Newell-Harris, came into office with a prescription for success. Working under the theme "Building a Healthy Legacy: A Prescription for the Future," she focused not only on the organization's foundational areas of membership, operations, programming, and philanthropy, but emphasized the need for members to prioritize their own physical, mental, and emotional health. Doctor's orders for individual members and the collective organization: *Stay healthy*—in mind, body, spirit, and philanthropy.

The message resounded with Links around the world. Over her four-year term, she turned the spotlight on health, elevating the organization's work in addressing chronic health disparities while seeking to chart a solid course towards the future. "I felt compelled as a physician to infuse more health-related topics," Newell-Harris noted. "I picked a lot of topics that were on the edge, kind of controversial."

Signature initiatives included HIV and hepatitis C education and awareness. Oral health was introduced as a National initiative in partnership with Colgate-Palmolive. A toolkit was developed to help destigmatize mental health conditions. Health disparities programming continued, targeting diseases that disproportionately affect women, such as breast cancer and heart disease awareness. The doctor was not shy either about sharing her own experiences as a patient getting mammograms and colonoscopies.

The Black Lives Matter movement and human trafficking were also adopted as signature initiatives. After a spate of highly-publicized killings of unarmed African Americans at the hands of law enforcement,

The Links organized a three-month Black Lives Matter webinar series to arm members with facts around voter rights and registration, inequality in the prison system, and police brutality so they could translate the movement into effective programming and concrete messaging. Local chapters were encouraged to host Black Lives Matters educational symposiums to provide youth with tips and strategies for community organizing and engagement with law enforcement. The Links also implemented programming around human trafficking and the Flint, Michigan, water crisis.

For Newell-Harris, a pioneer in her own right as the first African American to integrate the prestigious Miss Porter's School in Connecticut, the focus on these issues was vital to The Links' relevance. "For the organization to continue to be progressive, we've got to keep ourselves laser-focused on the hot topics at the time and continue to move the organization [forward]."

Progressivism was not limited to domestic issues. Internationally, a global service delegation of members employed a "boots on the ground" approach as part of a three-year commitment to enact transformational service in Montego Bay, Jamaica. Utilizing an integrated service delivery model led by International Trends and Services, programming efforts in the areas of health, STEM, and the arts focused on three partner schools—Mt. Zion Primary School, Watford Hill Primary, and St. Mary's Preparatory and Kindergarten School—and Cornwall Regional Hospital. "The harsh reality of the lives of the children and their families coupled with the challenges they face each day in their quest to receive an education was especially moving to the delegation," noted Carolyn Glenn from the Bradenton/Sarasota (FL) Chapter, recalling the 2016 trip to Watford Hill Primary School.

"One member … witnessed a parent collecting leftovers from the plates of the children. The parent was quick to explain that he planned to take this 'good food home' to the rest of his family." By the end of the third mission trip, the Links had given more than 5,000 service hours and exceeded $1 million in economic support and $550,000 in monetary support and in-kind donations. The organization provided dental screenings and education on STEM and nutrition to more than 1,200 youth.

During the 40th National Assembly in Las Vegas, Newell-Harris issued a positive prognosis: Membership had increased to nearly 15,000, and attendance at national events and conferences was also on the rise. There were new partnerships with the NAACP, Africare, the National Society of Black Engineers, and the Centers for Disease Control and Prevention, grants from the National Institutes of Health and Bristol-Myers Squibb, and the relaunch of Classics through the Ages. The Links Medal, the organization's highest honor, was presented to the NAACP in recognition of its ongoing work to improve African American progress. The Links also hosted two community service projects: A Summer for Smiles dental van screenings for children in partnership with Colgate-Palmolive and volunteering at Three Square food bank.

In November 2016, members commemorated The Links' 70-year legacy in the organization's city of origin. The daylong event included leadership workshops and panel discussions along with a donation to the Philadelphia Salvation Army for its work to combat human trafficking. "Meeting in our founding city of Philadelphia is the perfect backdrop to celebrate 70 years of friendship and service," Newell-Harris remarked. "We continue our legacy of providing transformational global impact in the communities we serve."

To bolster the group's work, Newell-Harris pushed for The Links to have a more visible presence in Washington, DC, home to the organization's headquarters. "We believe wholeheartedly in the ideals of justice and equality," she said. "And we will work closely with those who understand that our communities are under siege and need a voice to lift their cause." The inaugural Pumps on the Hill Day of Action and Links Legislative Luncheon events were held during the 2017 Congressional Black Caucus Annual Legislative Conference, which attracts movers, shakers, and policymakers each fall.

During Pumps on the Hill, nearly 300 members met with congressional members, key legislators, and representatives to strengthen support for The Links' legislative priorities, including working families, women and children, educational equity, voter

Newell-Harris (center), National officers, and local Links officials visit St. Jude.

suppression, the prison industrial complex, and health care. Over the course of her term, Newell-Harris hosted public issues forums to explore challenges and solutions around mental health issues and dementia, violence prevention in communities of color, and the declining number of African Americans in the medical profession, anchoring the discussions around women.

The Links continued to weigh in on the issues of the day with the release of public statements decrying racial incidents at American University and in Charlottesville, Virginia, seeking support for victims of national disasters and uplifting Congresswoman Frederica Wilson, a Links member and a target of "character assassination" by President Donald Trump's administration. "Our commitment to service and uplifting our communities has never been more important. If not now, when?"

At the same time, The Links found new ways to call attention to health issues, such as the need to diversify the medical profession. The Links Scholars

#16 Newell-Harris with Connecting Link, Attorney Robert Harris

in Medicine scholarship program was launched to help defray the cost of medical school, awarding a total of $250,000 in scholarships to five female medical students over two years. A million-dollar Legacy Grant, the organization's fifth, was awarded to St. Jude's Children's Research Hospital for three sickle cell disease initiatives: the development of a community health worker program in Nigeria, an age-appropriate app to assist in the transition from pediatric to adult care, and research to increase knowledge of cognitive deficits in children with sickle cell disease.

"St. Jude is an organization whose mission and vision align with ours when it comes to the health of African American children," said Newell-Harris, "and we greatly admire its deep and longstanding commitment to children with life-threatening diseases like sickle cell disease."

In addition, fundraising continued at a healthy pace towards the Links Foundation's Vision 2020 $10 million campaign, bringing in more than $2 million during her term. A new donor circle was introduced—the 1946 Society, composed of members who contributed a minimum of $25,000 over a designated period.

Meanwhile, membership climbed to more than 15,800 and chapter growth continued in all four areas and "across the pond": Mount Rose, Maryland; Katy-Richmond Area, Texas; Colorado Springs, Colorado; Hilton Head, South Carolina; Northwest Arkansas; Central Massachusetts; two in Mississippi, Gulf Coast and Mississippi Roses; and London, United Kingdom. Senator Kamala Harris of California, only the second African American to serve in the United States Senate and the first South Asian American, was inducted as the tenth honorary member.

At the National Headquarters, the administration retired the remaining $1 million in building debt and focused on human resources. Newell-Harris hired director-level leadership in communications, programming, membership, technology, and fund development. On the operations side, the administration took a closer look at branding and marketing in terms of merchandising and membership.

As part of an effort to exercise greater control over the organization's brand, the Links Boutique opened in May 2018 with high-quality products designed to provide greater financial support to members, chapters, and communities. An official Links pin was introduced. "When you are adorned with this pin, there is nothing else needed except your expression of love and friendship for one another," she noted.

Newell-Harris also encouraged consideration of younger women's perception of The Links' brand. In her previous role as National vice president and Membership chair, Newell-Harris had developed a keen interest in the next generation of members. As National President, she created the Next Generation Committee to help chapters more successfully identify, recruit, integrate, and retain members under the age of 50. She urged chapters to be intentional about bringing millennials into the fold and to consider their own daughters, nieces, and granddaughters as immediate candidates for membership—and not just one or two at a time.

In looking towards the organization's future, she assembled a Brain Trust Task Force to navigate various spheres: membership, programming, strategic planning, headquarters staffing, fund development, governance, and others. Based on their work, the organization invested in Fund Development staff at headquarters. The existing Service Delivery Model was validated for continued usage. And a new mission statement was approved: "Friends transforming communities through service."

After the 41st National Assembly in Indianapolis, Newell-Harris's delivered a final prognosis in a message to members: "'Building a Healthy Legacy: Our Prescription for the Future' was more than a theme. It was a challenge to us as individuals to keep our physical, mental, emotional, and spiritual health at the forefront of everything that we do. And as an organization it was a call for us to thrive, stay relevant, and be solvent after 71 years of age. … We have done better than good, in all the ways and places that we should, and for all the people we could. And yet, we know that there is so much more work to do!"

~Raven L. Hill

Glenda Newell-Harris, MD

Links Service

National Vice President

Chair, National Nominating Committee

Chair, Health and Wellness Linkage

Impact During Tenure

- Established four signature initiatives: HIV and Hepatitis C education and awareness, Black Lives Matter, and Human Trafficking.
- Elevated programming around personal health, chronic health disparities and social justice while focusing on long-term organizational growth.
- Raised more than $2 million towards Vision 2020 fundraising campaign; launched 1946 Society.
- Awarded $250,000 through Links Medical Scholars Program and fifth million-dollar Legacy Grant to St. Jude's Children's Research Hospital.
- Retired mortgage on National Headquarters.
- Held 70th anniversary celebration in Philadelphia.
- Inducted US Senator Kamala Harris as tenth honorary member and oversaw chartering of 10 chapters, including London, United Kingdom.

Selected National Honors

- First African American student to attend Miss Porter's School, a private girls college-preparatory school
- Scroll of Merit Award, National Medical Association
- Author, *Focus on YOUR BEST HEALTH*
- Past President, Sinkler-Miller Medical Association

THROUGH THEIR EYES

Excerpts from *The Links Oral History Collection*

Glenda Newell-Harris, MD
On Her Tenure As
SIXTEENTH NATIONAL PRESIDENT (2014–2018)
January 2019 • Washington, DC

#16 Newell-Harris fielding interview questions.

Your Introduction to Linkdom

My mom introduced me to the Links, Incorporated. As a young child, I do remember hearing about The Links doing things in my community. I was born in Raleigh, North Carolina, and then moved to Winston-Salem. But my mom was really the motivation. Mom became a Link and just kept encouraging me and telling me the things that they were doing. And then at a certain point, she just told me that it was something that I needed to do. I must admit I had reluctance. I didn't really know what the Links did. … From my perspective at that time, I felt that they were a bit more senior, and I wasn't quite sure what mom thought I could gain from that. But most of my life was driven by my mother. And so I was an obedient daughter. And when she said it was time to do it, I said, okay.

Your Path to the Presidency

I was really young when I started into this organization. When I became a link, I was 32. And so I have to say that when I joined, I had absolutely no desire, no aspiration or interest in leading. I really didn't have that interest for a very long time. But, after being a Link for about eight or 10 years, I was fortunate to be appointed by Link Barbara Dixon Simpkins, who at the time was the National President … as the chair of the health and wellness linkage.

I was the second person to hold that position. And it was something that I was comfortable doing because it was right in my area of expertise. It didn't even, in my opinion, require that I get to know a lot about The Links. And so, she allowed me to be able to get into the organization in a leadership role to function in something that I was comfortable in. I stayed in that role as chair of the health and wellness linkage for four years.

After that, I had an opportunity to actually do in that, in that role, at that time, what I considered the big table where all of the decisions or many of the decisions were being discussed and made. As a very young Link, I was fascinated. As a physician, I had not followed a business route. So, I didn't truly understand, HR. I didn't even know what human resources really was … had not been trained about budget and finance and team building; those were all very foreign terms to me.

After the four years, I was very intrigued by that, and it was a trajectory of learning that I thought was of interest. I didn't know anything about it, and the best way to learn more about it was to stay involved. Rather than wait to see if you might be tapped by another president … I decided to do the rough thing and go ahead and throw my hat in the ring. The first position that I ran for was the Nominating Committee, representing the Western Area, and I won that four-year position. I got a chance to see the organization from a slightly different pair of lenses, because it was more at the Area level.

After that, I ran for chair of the National Nominating Committee. I was very lucky, and I won that position that put me back at the Executive Council table. By that time there were a brand-new group of people doing it. So, I had new people to get to know and learn. I had to understand fully my area is nominating chair and then some of the terminology. I became more comfortable, and I served in that position for four years. It was right around the end of that third and fourth year that I began to get feedback from folks saying, what are you going to do next? I really didn't have a lot of thought about, I was just enjoying what I was doing, but I did make a decision to run for National vice president. That was a very tough race. There were a lot of people running. I was coming from the West, the smallest area, the least number of chapters and I was not well known because I was from the West and it was so far from where all the power is in this organization. We believe that the power is in the South and in the East, and I'm all the way on the other side of the country. While I ran for that position and I won, I was very lucky. When it was time to run for National President, I did not have an opponent and I was voted on sort of a unanimous ballot, which was kind of a surreal kind of a situation.

So, it just projected along, and I found myself there; and that's one of the more fascinating aspects about this. My mother is 101 years old. She is still alive and well and not only was she there for my election, but she was there when I was installed. The entire time I was president, I was always able to pick up the telephone and reach out to get a word of advice, comfort, support, or to tell me, "That's one you don't need to touch; leave that one alone." So I was really blessed to have that happen during my presidency as well.

Your Biggest Challenge

I think there were two significant challenges. One is, whether we would want to admit it or not, there are politics in this organization and, I think when I came in, I was very naïve about that; but I'm a fast learner, and so I had to learn how to maneuver and navigate …. But if at the end of the day, if you can always remember that your goal needs to be focused on what's good for the organization, then I think you'll generally be led to making the right decision. The other big challenge for me was work life balance. I am and continue to be a physician practicing medicine. About two weeks before I was elected National President, I actually was given the opportunity to walk into what I consider a dream job as a doctor, a job that I had probably wanted to have a lot earlier in my career, but it wasn't made available to me, and I took very, very different kinds of jobs as a younger physician so that I would have more flexibility with my children.

But, trying to be able to work this nonpaying, full-time Links job and then work my paid job as a regional medical director was a challenge; but I love them both. And so, I think when you have a passion for something, you just do it. I had a lot of late nights working seven days a week for both The Links and for my job because I knew that it was important that I keep my day job because that's what paid my bills before I moved totally into my structure. And what might have made me as successful …. I can't leave this subject without talking about my supportive family. My husband, who had already served as national president of three other organizations, was really a rock for me. He understood the need for the time away, the hassle periodically, the travel. And I had two children that were at home, but really, they were grown. So, I didn't have anybody at home. I really think that when you step into this kind of role, you've got to have a supportive family. And I'm delighted and I'm grateful that I had that.

~ From *The Links Oral History Collection*, Marcia Denise White, Editor

Kimberly Jeffries Leonard, PhD
Seventeenth National President (2018–   )

We have so much to achieve and to look forward to accomplishing.

KIMBERLY JEFFRIES LEONARD came to the presidency clad in a sense of boldness—Bold Legacy, Bold Impact, Bold Visionary, Bold Results. Leonard envisioned the National President and members "making bold moves together" to effect change. "Step forward boldly and strategically on the issues we address, the battles we fight, and the way we use our voice," she entreated them.

Leonard would lead. It was an opportunity she had staked out two decades earlier when she and her mother attended the 31st (1998) Assembly in Boston, Massachusetts. "So impressed by all that went on and the ladies who belonged," Kim told Dr. Mary Jeffries, "Mama, I want to be National President." Beaming following Leonard's election 20 years later at the 41st (2018) Assembly in Indianapolis, Jeffries said she was "a proud mama," but she confessed that while she acknowledged her daughter's wish with "Yeah, hmm," she "never thought that much about it coming to fruition."

While the notion of becoming National President did not consume Leonard, it also did not go away. As she built relationships throughout Linkdom, rendered service at every level, and gradually traversed the governance structure, Leonard realized that her wish had been a harbinger of her destiny with The Links. So much of The Links' agenda also paralleled her professional calling as a health and human services professional and advocate, ties that would

subsequently play a role in The Links doing something that had not been done since 1978.

Leonard grabbed every opportunity to ready for the time she knew would come. She served as recording secretary for her chapter, earned a spot in the inaugural (2004) class of the Scott Hawkins Leadership Institute, and chaired several health-related committees on the Area and National levels. Her penchant for putting all her talents to work to deliver unmatched outcomes led to eventual appointments and elections to the National Executive Council, where she gave 14 years of uninterrupted service prior to her ascendancy.

In both appointed and elected positions, Leonard powered enduring movement. She launched the Chapter Secretarial Tool Kit, which created a one-stop resource with operational guidelines and "a

President Kimberly Jeffries Leonard (center) with former National Presidents at The Links' 2018 Legislative Luncheon. Left to right: #14 Gwendolyn Byrd Lee, #13 Gladys Gary Vaughn, #8 Dollie Desselle Adams, and #9 Regina Jollivette Frazier.

form for everything," thereby fostering compliance, common procedures, and alignment across chapters and Areas. She followed up by developing and conducting webinars that helped chapters make the transition.

Leonard's expertise and formal relationships with health giants like the National Institutes of Health, the National Heart, Lung, and Blood Institute, and Heart Truth fueled the lift for the HeartLinks signature program and so many other health initiatives that 14th National President Gwendolyn Lee deemed an independent facet essential. As a result, the 37th (2010) Assembly endorsed Health and Human Services as the fifth facet, modifying the four-pronged program paradigm that had been in place for 32 years.

As National vice president and Membership chair, Leonard also anchored efforts to strengthen membership—from targeting potentials under 40 to developing and implementing a certification process that helped small chapters retain their viability as a Links unit. Through alignment and enhanced communications, the Membership Committee also effected a

reduction in membership forfeitures and resignations, as well as increases in member inductions.

So, when President Kimberly Jeffries Leonard took the reins on June 30, 2018, she brought boldness: an in-depth knowledge of internal and external operations and programming, an ardent understanding of and appreciation for The Links' legacy, and a plan to strategically position Links to save lives and improve communities amid a changing society and in villages with changing needs. But friendship would be recognized as "the primary tenet" of The Links, Incorporated. "Our focus is service, but we are an organization based on friendship," she pronounced, and she pledged "to make 'Friendship First' a major focus and core value."

The promise was made in her campaign literature, reiterated in her acceptance speech, stressed in her 2019 State of the Organization address to Area Conferences, and interlocked in all aspects and segments of Leonard's administration. In concert with the "service through friendship" model the Co-Founders had designed, service would remain a tenet, but friendship would be at the forefront. Along with the focus on friendship and service, Leonard's commitment included four additional tasks: aligning programming, stabilizing the National Headquarters, updating technology, and leveraging membership.

Nine months into her tenure, Leonard provided an assessment of her team's progress: "We have accomplished much," she said, and she detailed the processes underway in some areas, and outlined the improvements made in others. On the friendship front, a new Links, Incorporated app that would encourage and facilitate interaction and bonding was in development, the context and process for recognizing milestone anniversaries in Linkdom had been created, a National Day of Service that would bring Links together as one organization was being finalized, and a survey to assess members' needs and engagement had been completed.

True to her forthright and transparent modus operandi, Leonard also called out behavior that had deflected The Links' mission and was detrimental to the organization, as it "did not reflect the true meaning of friendship." Always mindful of the need to have a united sisterhood to continue the work of empowering communities, Leonard declared, "Unity is our aim now. Our differences can be put aside, and we can move on."

To align programming, "relevance and account-ability" success metrics are being employed. "We have a voice, and we are using it," Leonard said, as she recapped some of the rapid response resolutions and statements that The Links had issued to address issues of the day that included a Call to Action on the 2020 census. Leonard had also increased collaborative partnerships to buttress the number of sustainable and measurable programs and extend the reach of existing initiatives to communities with the greatest need. New partnerships included a collaboration with Dove that will increase social justice engagement, an alliance with the March on Washington Film Festival that will offer film internships to students outside its traditional feeder pools, and a collaboration with the National Wildlife Federation that will further enhance STEM programming. Leonard also maintained exiting alliances that include AARP, Africare, Colgate Palmolive, and the National Society of Black Engineers.

Leonard assured members that National Headquarters was "moving forward" with an interim director at the helm: staff "workloads had been streamlined for increased effectiveness, and the precise tools staff members needed to be productive" had been provided. The Membership Department had been restructured to improve response time and productivity, access protocols for the website had been simplified, and designs had been tweaked to make navigation user-friendly. The vendor program had also been updated to facilitate the purchase of branded items from authorized vendors and simulta-neously protect The Links brand.

Leonard made celebrating and preserving The Links' legacy a priority—oil portraits of the founders were installed at the National Headquarters, the oral history collection now included interviews with the former National Presidents, the fourth edition of the history of The Links was on track for release at the Leadership Summit, and Estate and Legacy planning had been added as a category in the 1946 Society.

Leonard also carried forth The Links' tradition of having a presence where decisions are being made as a means of assuming our role as "effective gatekeepers of justice in our communities." From meeting one-on-one with civil rights icon Congressman John Lewis (D-GA) to attending congressional hearings on social justice to keynoting forums on hot button issues, Leonard has focused the agenda on actions that will empower purposeful lives and strong communities. "This is what Links do; this is who we are," she proclaimed.

Further illuminating The Links' commitment, and emoting unrestrained enthusiasm in her manifes-to's ability to honor it, Leonard avowed:

> We have an obligation to support the least and the lost, women and children who live on Life's tenuous margins. That is where I want to lead us … We have so much to achieve and to look forward to accomplishing.

With her audacious start, the finish will no doubt be equally bold.

~ Earnestine Green McNealey, PhD

Kimberly Jeffries Leonard, PhD

Links Service

National Vice President

National Recording Secretary

National Director, National Trends and Services

National Chair, Mental Health Initiative

National Chair, Heart Truth Initiative

Eastern Area Chair, Health Linkage Committee

Member, Eastern Area Services to Youth Committee

Co-Chair, Arlington (VA) Chapter, Strategic Planning Committee

Recording Secretary, Arlington (VA) Chapter

Impact During Tenure

■ Maintained and expanded collaborative partnerships that provide thousands of dollars in additional resources and assistance for National programs. Alliances include STEAM, the National Society of Black Engineers, General Motors, and the National Wildlife Federation; health, Colgate, Partnership for a Healthier America, and the National Dental Association; HBCUs, Achieving the Dream, Inc.; Aid for Africa, Africare, and the Sullivan Alliance; social justice, the NAACP and Dove; and financial literacy, Ally.

■ Enhanced National Headquarters operations and service delivery via personnel changes and technological upgrades.

■ Published the fourth edition of the official history of The Links, Incorporated.

■ Commissioned and installed oil portraits of the Co-Founders at National Headquarters.

■ Expanded oral history collection with interviews of former National Presidents.

Selected Honors

■ Chair, The Commission on African American Affairs, District of Columbia, 2017–

■ AARP African American Change Maker, 2015

■ Vice President for Administration, The Black Women's Agenda, Inc., 2013–present

■ Recipient, The Chancellor's Medallion, Fayetteville State University, 2017

PART V

Force Fields

Area and Chapter Conduits

By 1952, the Philadelphia Club had become a National organization of more than 50 chapters. Area units, led by an Area director, were instituted to administer programs, strengthen ties among chapters, and streamline operations under the direction of an Area director.

By 1952, the Philadelphia Club had become a National organization with more than 50 chapters. Smaller configurations of the whole were instituted to administer programs, strengthen ties among chapters, and streamline operations. Area chairmen were licensed as liaisons between the chapters, Areas, and National, and as program specialists and operations coordinators. The 4th (1952) Assembly approved operating expenses of $10. Based on a recommendation from Western Area Coordinator Loraine Rickmond, Area coordinators were also added to the Executive Council, and the title was changed to Area director.

From the outset, the Eastern Area was dominant in the makeup of chapters. Ten of the 14 chapters that formed National Links were located in the Eastern Area, with two situated in both the Central and Southern Areas; but there was no presence in the West. The chartering of three California chapters (Los Angeles, Oakland Bay, and San Francisco) in

1950 brought a Western division into play, and the 6th (1954) Assembly approved a four-Area configuration: the Eastern, Southern, Central, and Western Areas.

The delayed genesis in the Western Area, coupled with a smaller contingent of potential Links members, resulted in a noticeably smaller number of chapters and members. Reconfiguring the Areas for a more even distribution of members and chapters was a thorny issue, first addressed by a geographical realignment in 1953 that moved Denver from the Central Area to the Western Area. Further relief was provided by the (1955) Assembly, which approved a fifth Area (for one year) to foster proportional distributions.

Additional efforts to address the imbalance included a realignment in 1965 that sent three Southern Area states to the other three Areas: Virginia to the Eastern Area, West Virginia to the Central Area, and Texas to the Western Area. Yet, rapid growth in the South persisted because

Newly elected Area Directors with National President Kimberly J. Leonard (center). Left to right: Lorna Hankins, Western; Sylvia Perry, Southern; Shuana Tucker-Sims, Eastern; and Monica Boone Allen, Central.

the establishment of chapters was not regulated. Concerned by the growth, the 18th (1972) National Assembly vested the authority and responsibility for creating chapters with National, and National President Helen Edmonds named a Chapter Establishment officer.

Anna Rosell Julian, former National Membership chair, monitored growth, completed a demographic analysis of the membership and identified cities ripe for colonization as a means of formulating guidelines. During 1977 and 1978, chapter establishment was limited to the Western Area, but when only four chapters had been established during that period, the Executive Council relaxed the restriction; the four-Area configuration has prevailed.

Given the variations in size and resulting costs, a call to disburse Area allotments on a per-capita basis was eventual. The proposal came at the 36th (2008) Assembly, where it was defeated in large part by a special committee that had determined passage would infringe on the governance process. "Our representational governance for Areas gives each chapter equal voice and vote in our National Assembly and Area meetings (i.e., a Senate vs. a House of Representatives); one chapter, one vote," said Mary Currie, Southern Area director and chair.

Because the largest pool of potential members is concentrated in the Eastern and Southern Areas, the unevenness has persisted; but the gaps have narrowed. The West, which perennially has been at the bottom in both the number of chapters and members, captured a 20 percent market share in chapters and membership in 2010. Of the 270 chapters, the Western Area had 54, and 2,109 of the 10,045 members were members of the Western Area. The 20 percent share held for chapters during FY 2018–2019, with 60 of 288, but dipped slightly to 19.6 percent for the number of members: 3,066 of 15,615.

An even better indicator of the progress in distribution was the combined share for the Southern and Eastern Areas was only 4 percent more than the yield for a perfect distribution. The two Areas have been the leaders, with each having a slight edge in chapters and membership, respectively. For FY 2018–2019, Southern had 80 chapters and Eastern had 78. Their combined number (158) was equal to 54 percent, or 4 percent more than equity. The membership share was slightly higher: Eastern had 4,462 members to the 4,388 members in Southern, totaling 8,850 or a share of 56 percent.

The makeup (states, territories, countries, or subdivisions thereof) of the Areas is prescribed in Article III of the Bylaws. While all 50 states were assigned to an Area, The Links has established chapters in only 42. The placement of international territories, prescribed for the Area closest to the chapter, was made accordingly. London, United Kingdom, established in 2018, became part of the Eastern Area, and the Nassau, Bahamas Chapter, established in 1989, was placed in the Southern Area.

On purpose and delivery, however, with guidance, motivation, and support from the Area director, each chapter and each Area have been friendship generators and service originators—strengthening each other and magnificently promoting civic, educational, and intercultural activities that have enriched the community. The spirit of competition has further spurred the innovations and levels of delivery.

Area Conferences have served as the venue for the election of the Area director and other officers, as well as updates on the state of the Area and the National organization and forecasts for the future. Training, hands-on service, and renewal have also become staples, with emphasis on governance, program development, organizational training, community service engagement, and celebration of The Links, its members, and its service. Area Conferences were held annually at the site of the Assembly until 1974, when they moved to a biennial schedule, convening during non-Assembly years.

Area directors not only have coordinated the conferences, but they have fulfilled a myriad of additional responsibilities. They have served as liaisons between the chapters and the Areas and between the Areas and National. They have been the voice for chapters and Areas, as well as the messengers and administrators, executing duties prescribed in the Bylaws.

Left to right: Former Area Directors Barbra Ruffin-Boston, Western Area; Bishetta Merritt, Eastern Area; Mary Currie, Sothern Area; and Teree Caldwell-Johnson, Central Area.

- To convey the intent of the National Program to the individual chapters in the Area;
- To participate in the development and promotion of the policies and programs of The Links, Incorporated;
- To assist the chapters in promoting civic, educational, and intercultural activities that will enrich the community;
- To facilitate the resolution of civic and social problems, and to work together toward achieving common goals; and
- To unite the chapters within a geographical area to accomplish the goals of the National organization through the exchange of ideas,

methods, and techniques to implement the National Program.

The dexterity with which each Area director has executed her charge has been reflected through members and chapters who honor the tenets of Linkdom. They have been the friendship generators and service originators, offering the kindness, encouragement, and support that power close bonds, and implementing transformational programs that empower strong communities.

~ *Earnestine Green McNealey, PhD*
~ *Barbara Trotter, EdD*

AREAS AND CHAPTERS

Area	Territory	# of Chapters		# of Members	
		FY 2009–2010	FY 2018–2019	FY 2009–2010	FY 2018–2019
EASTERN	*12 states and two territories* Connecticut, Delaware, Maine,* Maryland, Massachusetts, New Hampshire,* New Jersey, New York, Pennsylvania, Rhode Island, Vermont,* Virginia, District of Columbia, and the United Kingdom.	73	78	2,599	4,462
SOUTHERN	*7 states and a territory* Alabama, Florida, Georgia, Louisiana, Mississippi, North Carolina, South Carolina, and Nassau, Bahamas.	74	80	2,843	4,388
CENTRAL	*17 states* Arkansas, Illinois, Indiana, Iowa, Kansas, Kentucky, Michigan, Minnesota, Missouri, Nebraska, North Dakota,* Ohio, Oklahoma, South Dakota,* Tennessee, West Virginia, and Wisconsin.	69	70	2,494	3,763
WESTERN	*14 states* Alaska, Arizona, California, Colorado, Hawaii, Idaho,* Montana, Nevada, New Mexico, Oregon, Texas, Utah,* Washington, and Wyoming.*	54	60	2,109	3,066
Totals		270	288	10,045	15,589

*No chapters

Data (April 20, 2019) provided by National Headquarters. Chart does not include 2019 inductees.

CHAPTER 9

THE EASTERN AREA:
The First

*I*t all began in the East—the idea, the vision, the dream, the plan … the hope. When Margaret Hawkins's vision of a club of friends serving their communities was realized as the Philadelphia Club on November 9, 1946, it was the first step in the creation of National Links. The single club germinated into 14 distinct clubs, which linked to form a National body of chapters in 1949. By 1950, the number of chapters had increased to 30, with three from the Western Area.

The additions set the stage for informal divisions created in 1952 with the appointment of Area coordinators and formalized in 1954 when The Links decentralized into four geographical Areas by vote of the 6th Assembly. As the home of the Philadelphia Chapter, the Eastern Area became the premier Area. Reverence has naturally been bestowed on the Area because of its heritage, but illustrious leadership and exceptional programming have also contributed to the Area's prominence and the imprint it has made in communities.

Growth has been steady, but efforts to make the four Areas more equitable have been successful. When decentralization was instituted, Central was dominant with 16 of the 30 (53 percent) chapters. During FY 2018–2019, the Eastern Area still had the highest number of chapters, but distribution across the Areas had become more proportionate. Of the

Shuana Tucker-Sims, Eastern Area director

288 active chapters of The Links, 78 (27 percent) were located in the Eastern Area. Territories include the states of Connecticut, Delaware, Maryland, Massachusetts, New Jersey, New York, Pennsylvania, Rhode Island, and Virginia, as well as the District of Columbia and London, England, the last chapter chartered (2018).

At the heart of decentralization was the addition of smaller Area units, designed to administer programs and streamline responsibilities and duties under the direction of an Area director elected at the Area Conference. The first Eastern Area Conference

191

was a return to the seat of Linkdom, and the 24 chapters present in Philadelphia elected Madeline Broaddus, Central New Jersey Chapter, as the first Eastern Area director.

Sixteen others were chosen, with Shuana Tucker-Sims becoming the 17th Eastern Area director at the 45th Area Conference, held in Atlantic City, New Jersey, in April of 2019.

Charged with fostering friendship and supporting the programs and operations of the National body, Eastern Area directors embraced the mantra, "While we cannot do everything, we certainly do everything we can." They donned the very best mantles of leadership. They inspired, challenged, and guided their chapters and members in accomplishing amazing things.

Area Conferences served as venues not only for electing officers, but also for reviewing programs and operations, evaluating the organizational structure, and recommending ways to strengthen Linkdom at the Area and National levels. The conferences also spawned closer relationships and buttressed the commitment to Linkdom.

From 1952 to 1971, Eastern Area Conferences were held annually at sites in the Eastern Area. Beginning in 1973, Area Conferences were held biennially on an alternating schedule with the National Assembly. Consistent with the National practice of hosting Assemblies, individual chapters served as hosts until 1989, when the cluster host concept was introduced. More than 1,000 Links and their families attended the Atlantic City, New Jersey, event.

AREA DIRECTORS, THEMES, AND KEY INITIATIVES

Madeline Broaddus (1952–1957)
Central New Jersey Chapter

"Link Women in Today's World"

Set the tone and focus for the scope of service, noting, "Our challenge in this generation is to discover our common interests, the terrain of possible collaboration, the overlapping areas of sympathy and understanding, of aspiration and mutual advantage, that binds mankind together regardless of political, faith, race, creed, or color." Also sponsored an Area-wide youth talent search.

Prudence Irving (1957–1961)
Boston (MA) Chapter

Pushed economic savvy with efforts that included a conference discussion, "Our Link Dollar – Past, Present and Future."

Bessie Hill (1961–1965)
North New Jersey Chapter (charter member)

Created "Christmas Card Plan," which raised $41,000 for the NAACP and National Urban League. The fundraiser became a National Links project.

Beatrice Butler (1965–1969)
Baltimore (MD) Chapter (charter member)

"Collective Strength for Organized Action"
"The Beauty of Blackness – Channeling Black Hope"

Initiated the Daisy Lampkin Award to recognize Links who had made significant contributions in projecting the Black image and the heritage of African Americans. Chapters also supported scholarships, testing and tutorial programs, vocational training, guidance counseling, unwed mothers, sponsored art workshops, and exhibits.

Millicent Smith (1969–1973)
Connecticut Valley Chapter (charter member)

Encouraged chapter programming that addressed preparing, educating, and supporting youth. "It is my fervent wish that we maintain an intensive focus on educating youth."

Thelma Ayers Hardiman (1973–1979)
Buffalo (NY) Chapter (charter member)

"Friendship With Purpose" (Roanoke); "Reach Out and Touch" (Bucks County); and "Serve with Love" (Arlington, VA)

Published the history of the Eastern Area (Barbara L. Stokes, Delaware Valley Chapter) and recommended Marion Anderson as an honorary member. Also modeled and encouraged acts of "friendship" for Co-Founder Sarah Strickland Scott, "giving her the love and friendship that she so aptly deserved."

Mignon Bolden Johnson (1979–1983)
Arlington (VA) Chapter (charter member)

"Excellence through Member Participation"

Endorsed the African Water Wells Project and initiated the Paragon Award for non-Links who best exemplified and/or supported any facet of Linkdom. Also initiated the office of sergeant at arms to ensure smooth business operations and appointed the Eastern Area representative for the 1970 White House Conference. "I tried to develop and maintain a climate of creativity, unity, positive commonality based on respect, love, and high expectations in pursuing Link programs."

Rachel M. Hill (1983–1987)
Delaware Valley Chapter

"The 3 R's – Recapturing the Past, Revitalizing the Present, Refocusing for the Future"

Stressed three priorities: Membership, funds for National Headquarters, and program excellence.

Betty King Obiajulu (1987–1991)
Greater New York Chapter

"The A Team – Renewing Our Heritage – The Black Family"

Established the Area newsletter (*Linkage*); started the Eastern Area Scholarship Fund, setting aside $20,000 in the Area treasury at the end of her term; established the Hardiman-Johnson Rotating Chapter Award for Excellence in Programming for outstanding Umbrella Projects; funded the first Eastern Area scholarship to be awarded at the Area Conference; created the Area newsletter; and organized chapter clusters.

Barbara Dixon Simpkins, EdD (1991–1995)
Prince George's County (MD) Chapter organizer and first president

"Strengthening the Black Family through Friendship, Love and Service" (1993)
"Linkages of Service in Friendship and Love" (1995)

Initiated biennial retooling session (1992 and 1994) for effective chapter leadership; awarded scholarships valued at $2,000 to universities in Virginia and New Jersey (locations of Area Conferences); introduced the use of computer technology for registration and on-site record-keeping for the 33rd Eastern Area Conference; Broke ground in South Africa for LINKS/IFESH schools; composed the Area Conference theme song; and sponsored the South African Links Chapter.

Cecelia Brown Henderson (1995–1999)
Buffalo (NY) Chapter

"Serving Up Success"

Funded construction for 10 schools in South Africa; published Area newsletter (*Serving Up Success*); held leadership summits for chapters in 1995 and 1997; traveled to South Africa to distribute supplies to children in the Education across the Miles project; held program workshops and town meetings at Area Conferences; and developed and implemented a "Friendship Communication Chain" for chapter information delivery. Also, presented Heart Power Kits, an educational health and wellness curriculum, to the school systems of Philadelphia and New York City; created and unveiled the 50th Anniversary Quilt; produced the first "Video of Success: Some Good Each Day"; secured site for the Eastern Area Archives; and held on-site retreat with the Frankfurt, Germany Chapter and the Eastern Area Executive Committee. The Area also won the first Project Walking Fete Poster Art Contest during her tenure.

Alethia L. Spraggins, PhD (1999–2003)
Washington (DC) Chapter

"Building a Foundation for the Future through Leadership, Labor and Love"

Established divisional leadership with three Peer Assisting Leaders (PALs) to expedite materials and services to chapters; set up the Area website, www.eastlinks.org; and obtained a $5,000 grant from the District of Columbia government for the C-L-O-N-E-S (Connecting Links Offering New Experiences to Sons) Project, which uses Connecting Links to mentor African American boys ages 9–11 at Birney Elementary School, DC Public School System. Also, funded five $3,000 grants to enhance chapter programs; installed the Eastern Area Archives at the Historical Society of Pennsylvania in Philadelphia; held Area's first Legacy workshop; grouped 75 chapters into 12 clusters for Conference hosting; developed a handbook on Eastern Area directors: *Living Treasures: Thirty Years of Eastern Area Stars, 1973 to 2003*; funded statues of Links Co-Founders Margaret

Eastern Area 2019–2021 officers and (second from the right) National President Kimberly Jeffries Leonard. Right to left: Shuana Tucker-Sims, Eastern Area director; Leonard; Lisa Loury Lomas, Eastern Area vice director; Barbara Burton, Eastern Area secretary; and Norma B. Hutcheson, Eastern Area treasurer

Hawkins and Sarah Scott in the Great Blacks in Wax Museum in Baltimore, Maryland; and composed the Eastern Area Closing Hymn.

Joyce C. Lowe (2003–2007)
Boston (MA) Chapter

"We Are the Power of Many … We Will Light the Way!!!" (2005) and "We Are the Power of Many … We Can, We Will, We Must Light the Way to Touch Tomorrow Today" (2007)

Prepared and distributed "Maama Kits" (sanitizing kits for pregnant women) to Africa; partnered with Roche Pharmaceuticals and African American transplant surgeons in the Eastern Area to advance organ and tissue donations in African-American communities. Also, established two centers for African American Life and History at Hampton University and Norfolk State University, donating over 1,000 books and DVDs from Eastern Area chapters; increased the use of umbrella projects; implemented the chapter advocacy program hotline for tactical support to chapter presidents on critical matters (boundary and intake issues); worked toward endowment with HBCUs in the Eastern Area; published the *Eastern Area Beacon* newsletter; and sponsored Poster Art Contest, which was later adopted as a National Program.

Bishetta D. Merritt, PhD (2007–2011)
Washington (DC) Chapter

"Circle of Friends"

Developed the dental health program, Links to Oral Health (kickoff at Seattle National Assembly with Congressman Elijah Cummings as the speaker); created Cares Circles, opportunities for community leaders to share best practices for turning underserved schools into successful, safe learning environments; continued the Links Go Green in the East poster art contest from the previous administration; prepared tool kits for Eastern Area schools in South Africa; developed an international pen pal program with 18 Eastern Area schools in South Africa; and used completed surveys on the impact of membership in the

The Eastern Area of The Links, Incorporated
United By Our Commitment To Serve Our Communities

Eastern Area message

"sandwich generation" on leadership in the Eastern Area to create workshops at the Area Conference. Also, developed partnerships with MoMA, the National Dental Association, AARP, National Black Nurses Association, DC Teachers Federal Credit Union, Odyssey Media, MEDCO, and Colgate for program funding and in-kind services; created a video on the first 40 chapters; commissioned artists from the Blue Ridge-Piedmont Cluster to create pieces of art to donate to the Harrison Museum, an African American museum in Roanoke, Virginia. The Eastern Area won 14 program awards at the Seattle (2008) and Detroit (2010) National Assemblies.

Dianne Smith Hardison (2011–2015)
Old Dominion (VA) Chapter

"Leveraging the Legacy of Friendship and Service"

Developed the Young Master Writers Program and the Mental Health Initiative (became a National Initiative in 2015); developed a partnership with the American Cancer Society; developed an Entrepreneurship Initiative and the Eastern Area Green Book (Link entrepreneurs providing goods and services to other Links chapters); produced a quarterly *White Rose Chronicles* newsletter; created the Leveraging the Legacy of Friendship and Service Award to honor

members who exemplified outstanding service and friendship; acknowledged service to the organization (less than 25 years of service, and 25 to 39 years of service); continued the Oral Health Initiative, which became a National Initiative in 2014.

Natalie H. Fant (2015–2019)
Reston (VA) Chapter

"United by Our Friendship and Our Commitment to Service Our Communities"

Expanded implementation of the Service Delivery Model (SDM) and Umbrella Programming at the Area level to encourage chapter-level implementation. The most significant service was the Umbrella Program, the Inaugural Health Equity Ambassadors Mission, which was delivered in Nassau, Bahamas, in March 2017 using the SDM. The Links, Incorporated adopted two Eastern Area programs at the National level—the Health Equity Ambassadors (HEA) Program and the Young Master Writers Program (YMWP).

Shauna Tucker-Sims, PhD (2019 –)
Fairfield County (CT) Chapter

"Embracing our Legacy, Cultivating our Future" Programming has also set the Eastern Area apart. Seven Area programs were exceptional enough to become National programs:

- Christmas Card fundraiser for the NAACP and the National Urban League – Bessie Hill (1961–1965)
- Water Wells in Africa – Mignon Johnson (1979–1983)
- Poster Art Contest – Joyce C. Lowe, (2003–2007)

- Mental Health – Dianne Smith Hardison (2011–2015)
- Oral Health – Dianne Smith Hardison (2011–2015)
- Young Master Writers Program – Natalie H. Fant (2015–2019)
- Health Equity Ambassadors Mission – Natalie H. Fant (2015–2019)

Chapter programming has also loomed large and grand. Ten noteworthy (randomly selected) initiatives are listed below.

Program & Chapter	Focus
Links to Health Smiles Washington (DC)	Dental health care for youth within the Washington, DC, metropolitan area, partially supported through a $25,000 grant from AETNA.
The Achievers Program Wilmington (DE)	An eight-month program to groom African American young men for academic, business, and social success. Each participant also received a scholarship.
Operation Achieve Brooklyn (NY)	Academic and social skills sessions for high school students.
Women of Color and Cancer Buffalo (NY)	A series of conferences designed to increase awareness and identify resources.
Sister, Will You Help Me Newport News (VA)	A support group for breast cancer survivors.
Linking With the Library Essex County (NJ)	A summer reading program for children ages 4–9.
Sundays at Four Farmington Valley (CT)	Talks and workshops on topics of international significance.
From Aunt Jemima to Attorney Claire Huxtable Boston (MA)	Series on images of African American women on the screen.
Project Praise (Providing Resources Aimed at Independence and Self-Empowerment) Harbor City (MD)	Ongoing initiative focused on the well-being of women and children at the Springhill Transitional Housing Program in Baltimore City.
Project Rural Reach Potomac (VA)	A family planning program for rural women in Tanzania, East Africa.

Links from the Eastern Area have also played key roles in governance, program and operations at the National level, serving as National President, Executive Council members, and National Headquarters staff. Eight of the 17 National Presidents were residents of the Eastern Area when they were elected: Sarah Strickland Scott, Philadelphia (PA) Chapter (1949–1953), Margaret Rosell Hawkins, Philadelphia (PA) Chapter (1953–1957), Margaret Pauline Fletcher Weeden Maloney, Lynchburg (VA) Chapter (1957–1962), Pauline Allen Ellison, Arlington (VA) Chapter (1974–1978), Dolly Desselle Adams, Arlington (VA) Chapter (1982–1986), Barbara Dixon Simpkins, Prince George's County (MD) Chapter (1998–2002), Gladys Gary Vaughn, Potomac (VA) Chapter (2002–2006), and Kimberly Jeffries Leonard, Arlington (VA) Chapter (2018–present).

By virtue of their offices, National Presidents and Area directors also served on the Executive Council. Other Eastern Area members of the Executive Council included Thelma Ayers Hardiman, Buffalo (NY) Chapter, National vice president, Chapter Establishment officer, and chair of the National Links Legacy Council; Beatrice Butler, Baltimore (MD) Chapter, first National recording secretary and National treasurer; and Marjorie H. Parker, Washington (DC) Chapter, National archivist and author of the first and second editions of The Links' history.

Other vice presidents included Allie Latimer, Washington (DC) Chapter; Lottie Dinkins, Central New Jersey Chapter; and Bessie Hill, North Jersey Chapter. Additional members who served were Katie Greene, Philadelphia (PA) Chapter, chair, Handbook and Public Relations; Lillian Brown, Pittsburgh (PA) Chapter, chair, Membership; Jessie M. Vann, Pittsburgh (PA) Chapter, chair, Public Relations; Claudine Lewis, Central New Jersey Chapter, chair, Publications and Journalism; Barbara Stokes, Delaware Valley (PA) Chapter, first National archivist; and Myrtle Manigault Stratton, Philadelphia (PA) Chapter, corresponding secretary.

Others who served were Lillian Stanford, Philadelphia (PA) Chapter, National historian; Dorothy Reed, Eastern Long Island (NY) Chapter,

National treasurer; Gloria Massie, Prince George's County (MD) Chapter, National journalist; Jacqueline Bontemps, Hampton (VA) Chapter, National secretary; Vivian Pinn, Boston (MA) Chapter, member-at-large; June Banks, Norfolk (VA) Chapter, member-at-large; and Ethel Lowry, Greater New York Chapter, National financial secretary.

Hazel Reid, Newport News (VA) Chapter, served as National financial secretary; Janet Ballard, Richmond (VA) Chapter, was National parliamentarian; Frances M. Flippen, Capital City (DC) Chapter, served as National treasurer; and Cecelia B. Henderson, Buffalo (NY) Chapter, was National secretary. Other members of the Council were JoAnne L. Bates, Pittsburgh (PA) Chapter, chair, National Nominating Committee; Brenda R. Metze, Fairfield County (CT) Chapter, National journalist; Bishetta D. Merritt, Washington (DC) Chapter, chair, National Nominating Committee; and Margaret Elaine Flake, Greater New York Chapter, chaplain.

F. Denise Gibson, Arlington (VA) Chapter, served as National chair, Awards/Recognitions; Michele V. Hagans, Capital City (MD) Chapter, chaired the Building Operations Committee; and Rozalynn S. Frazier, Metro-Manhattan (NY) Chapter, was chair, Communications Committee. Also serving were Caroline R. Lang, Prince George's County (MD) Chapter, chair, Evaluations Committee; Stephanie Mays Boyd, Philadelphia (PA) Chapter, chair, Strategic Partnerships Committee; Barbara Nance McKee, Patuxent River (MD) Chapter, director, International Trends and Services facet; and Nicholette M. Martin, Arlington (VA) Chapter, director, Health and Human Services facet.

Chief administrative officers in the National Headquarters included Susie Verdell, Petersburg (VA) Chapter, the first, and Mary P. Douglass, Prince George's County (MD). Also of note, both the National Headquarters and the National Archives are located in the Eastern Area.

~ Alethia L. Spraggins, PhD

EASTERN AREA DIRECTORS

1	Madeline Broaddus	1953–1957
2	Prudence Irving	1957–1961
3	Bessie Hill	1961–1965
4	Beatrice Butler	1965–1969
5	Millicent Smith	1969–1973
6	Thelma Hardiman	1973–1979
7	Mignon B. Johnson	1979–1983
8	Rachel Hill	1983–1987
9	Betty Obiajulu	1987–1991
10	Barbara Simpkins	1991–1995
11	Cecelia Henderson	1995–1999
12	Alethia Spraggins, PhD	1999–2003
13	Joyce C. Lowe	2003–2007
14	Bishetta Merritt, PhD	2007–2011
15	Dianne Smith Hardison	2011–2015
16	Natalie H. Fant	2015–2019
17	Shauna Tucker-Sims, PhD	2019–

Area Director Tucker-Sims and National President Kimberly Jeffries Leonard (fourth and fifth from the right) with Greater Queens (NY) Chapter

EASTERN AREA CHAPTERS (78)

FY 2018–2019

Albany District (NY)	Clifton Park	NY
Annapolis (MD)	Silver Spring	MD
Arlington (VA)	Haymarket	VA
Atlantic City (NJ)	Atlantic City	NJ
Baltimore (MD)	Baltimore	MD
Bergen County (NJ)	Riverdale	NY
Boston (MA)	Watertown	MA
Brooklyn (NY)	Brooklyn	NY
Bucks County (PA)	Chalfont	PA
Buffalo (NY)	Buffalo	NY
Capital City (DC)	Washington	DC
Central Massachusetts (MA)	Shrewsbury	MA
Central New Jersey (NJ)	New Brunswick	NJ
Charlottesville (VA)	Louisa	VA
Chesapeake/Virginia Beach (VA)	Virginia Beach	VA
Columbia (MD)	Ellicott City	MD
Commonwealth (VA)	Richmond	VA
Danville (VA)	Blairs	VA
Delaware Valley (PA)	Philadelphia	PA
Dover (DE)	Dover	DE
Eastern Shore (NY)	Dix Hills	NY
Erie County (NY)	Buffalo	NY
Essex County (NJ)	South Orange	NJ
Fairfield County (CT)	Stamford	CT
Farmington Valley (CT)	Canton	CT
Greater Bronx (NY)	Bronx	NY
Greater Hartford (CT)	Farmington	CT
Greater Hudson Valley (NY)	Cortlandt Manor	NY
Greater New York (NY)	Oakland Gardens	NY
Greater Providence (RI)	East Providence	RI
Greater Queens (NY)	Jamaica	NY
Greater Rappahannock (VA)	Spotsylvania	VA
Greater Springfield (MA)	Wilbraham	MA
Hampton (VA)	Hampton	VA
Harbor City (MD)	Towson	MD
Harrisburg (PA)	York	PA
James River Valley (VA)	Richmond	VA
London (UK)	London	UK
Long Island (NY)	Uniondale	NY
Lynchburg (VA)	Forest	VA
Metro-Manhattan (NY)	New Rochelle	NY

Metropolitan (DC)	Mitchellville	MD
Middlesex County (MA)	Boston	MA
Milford (CT)	Milford	CT
Montgomery County (PA)	Chester Springs	PA
Morris County (NJ)	Union	NJ
Mount Rose (MD)	Mitchellville	MD
New Haven (CT)	New Haven	CT
Newport News (VA)	Carrollton	VA
Niagara Falls (NY)	Getzville	NY
Norfolk (VA)	Virginia Beach	VA
North Jersey (NJ)	Somerset	NJ
Old Dominion (VA)	Ashburn	VA
Patapsco River (MD)	Owings Mills	MD
Patuxent River (MD)	Silver Spring	MD
Penn Towne (PA)	Philadelphia	PA
Petersburg (VA)	Petersburg	VA
Philadelphia (PA)	W. Conshohocken	PA
Pittsburgh (PA)	Mars	PA
Portsmouth (VA)	Portsmouth	VA
Potomac (VA)	Fulton	MD
Prince George's County (MD)	Upper Marlboro	MD
Princess Anne (MD)	Salisbury	MD
Rancocas Valley (NJ)	Burlington	NJ
Raritan Valley (NJ)	Plainfield	NJ
Reston (VA)	Oak Hill	VA
Richmond (VA)	Midlothian	VA
Roanoke (VA)	Roanoke	VA
Rochester (NY)	Rochester	NY
Silver Spring (MD)	Silver Spring	MD
South Jersey (NJ)	Voorhees	NJ
Southern Maryland Chain (MD)	Indian Head	MD
Suffolk (VA)	Suffolk	VA
Syracuse (NY)	Syracuse	NY
Washington (DC)	Washington	DC
Waterbury (CT)	Waterbury	CT
Westchester County (NY)	White Plains	NY
Wilmington (DE)	Landenberg	PA

Data provided by National Headquarters

EASTERN AREA CONFERENCES 1952–2019

Year	Locale
1952	Philadelphia, Pennsylvania
1953	Boston, Massachusetts
1954	North Jersey, New Jersey
1955	Albany District, New York
1956	Baltimore, Maryland
1957	South Jersey, New Jersey
1958	Wilmington, Delaware
1959	Washington, DC
1960	Hampton, Virginia
1961	Pittsburgh, Pennsylvania
1962	Richmond, Virginia
1963	Connecticut Valley, Connecticut
1964	Philadelphia, Pennsylvania
1965	Petersburg, Virginia
1966	Syracuse, New York
1967	Buffalo, New York
1968	Lynchburg, Virginia
1969	Central New Jersey, New Jersey
1970	Annapolis, Maryland
1971	Danville, Virginia
1973	Delaware Valley, Pennsylvania
1975	Roanoke, Virginia
1977	Bucks County, Pennsylvania
1979	Arlington, Virginia
1981	Niagara Falls, New York
1983	Norfolk, Virginia
1985	Ocean City, Maryland (hosted by Princess Anne, Maryland Chapter)
1987	Williamsburg, Virginia (hosted by Newport News, Virginia Chapter)
1989	Atlantic City, New Jersey
1991	Stamford, Connecticut
1993	Richmond, Virginia
1995	East Rutherford, New Jersey
1997	Philadelphia, Pennsylvania
1999	New York, New York
2001	Buffalo, New York
2003	Baltimore, Maryland
2005	Norfolk, Virginia
2007	Crystal City, Virginia
2009	Roanoke, Virginia
2011	Atlantic City, New Jersey
2013	Boston, Massachusetts
2015	Foxwoods, Connecticut
2017	Richmond, Virginia
2019	Atlantic City, New Jersey

CHAPTER 10
THE CENTRAL AREA:
The Heartbeat of Linkdom

*I*n the great land of Linkdom, between the coasts are mountains, rivers, streams, and the heartbeat of The Links, Incorporated, the Central Area. The Links' heart beats through 69 established chapters that stretch across 15 great states situated in the middle of the United States: Arkansas, Illinois, Indiana, Iowa, Kansas, Kentucky, Michigan, Minnesota, Missouri, Nebraska, Ohio, Oklahoma, Tennessee, West Virginia, and Wisconsin. The beat resonates through 3,763 Links whose rhythms have created initiatives that have transformed communities. As the "Heart of Linkdom," the Central Area has provided leadership and service designed to address the issues of Black America for the day, the decade, and the year. The Central Area has delivered services designed to help underserved communities become better.

The first heartbeat sounded in St. Louis, Missouri, in 1948. It was a time of unrest. In the 1940s, the Ku Klux Klan planted a 10-foot cross and a white hood bearing the letters "KKK" on the Buder playground, a recreation area that had been previously restricted to white children. Until 1944, St. Louis' two major league baseball teams, the Browns and the Cardinals, restricted Negroes to the bleachers and pavilion at Sportsman's Park. In 1947, Jackie Robinson entered the major league as the first black player in the game, supported by Missouri baseball icon Branch Rickey. However, the St. Louis Cardinals threatened to strike if Robinson came to their baseball field.

The incidents were typical of the injustices that the St. Louis (MO) Links club organized to combat. Eager to bring The Links' civic, charitable, and intercultural focus to their city, the "St. Louis Ladies" organized February 20, 1948, at the home of Blanche Sinkler, sister to Frances Vashon Atkinson, a member of the Philadelphia Links, the original club. Two months later on April 15, Atkinson used the organization's first installation service to induct the women, making St. Louis the fourth club and first contingent of what became the Central Area.

The chartering group was composed of eight members: Blanche Sinkler, president; Olive Carpenter, vice president; Mary Evans, recording secretary; Joy Blanche, treasurer; Charlotte Ford, Alice Harding, Anna Lee Scott, and Melba Sweets. The club immediately became an integral part of the fight for equal rights. After receiving a letter from the NAACP, the club made a donation to the education fund to open the University of Missouri to Negroes.

The chapter also held fundraisers to foster Negro progress. Activities included Sunday evening waffle suppers and teas, complete with a fashion parade, and the annual rummage sale and Lucky Tally Bridge. On October 2, 1959, the chapter's Gifted Student Project was established to encourage Negro students to achieve and aspire to higher levels. The chapter purchased a life membership in the NAACP to aid the group's redress against Jim Crow laws.

Thirteen months following the St. Louis installation, the Dayton Club debuted on May 28, 1949, with 13 charter members: Letitia Rose, president; Lillian Taylor, Viola Finley, Lucie Taylor, Remitha Ford, Beatrice Darnell, Melissa Bess, Bessie Jones, Margaret Robinson, Cora Peters, Ruth Smith, Hortense Campbell, and Ruth Lewis. It was the last

Central Area group chartered before a convention was called to nationalize the group. On June 4, 1949, the St. Louis and Dayton Clubs joined 12 other Links clubs in Philadelphia to form National Links with units that would now be called chapters.

Approximately 15 years after the Supreme Court (1944) declared all-white primaries illegal, Blacks registered to vote at one of the highest levels in history (1,250,000 in 1958). "The Civil Rights Act of 1957, the first federal civil rights legislation to be passed since 1875, authorized the federal government to take legal measures to prevent a citizen from being denied voting rights." Six Links chapters were chartered in the Central Area during the 1950s, extending the link of service to Columbus and Cincinnati, Ohio; Chicago, Illinois; Omaha, Nebraska; and Cleveland and Wilberforce, Ohio.

The Columbus (OH) Chapter was chartered on March 26, 1950, followed by the Cincinnati (OH) Chapter on March 30, the Chicago (IL) Chapter on May 21, the Cleveland (OH) Chapter on October 28, the Omaha (NE) Chapter on September 30, and the Wilberforce (OH) Chapter on November 11.

Early programming included the Omaha (NE) Chapter hosting cotillions that introduced young Black college women to the community. The Cleveland (OH) Chapter, in cooperation with The Girl Friends, Inc., recognized honor students from the Cleveland public high schools, presented Janet Collins, the first Black prima ballerina for the Metropolitan Opera Company, donated $1,500 to the NAACP, and sponsored scholarships for students at the Cleveland Institute of Music. Many chapters volunteered at nursery schools, supplied needed items to community centers, supported existing programs at YMCAs, and established youth programs at their churches.

In 1951, six chapters were chartered in the Central Area: Southern West Virginia, Detroit (MI), Indianapolis (IN), Charleston-Institute (WV), Greater Kansas City (KS), and Louisville (KY). Chapters were still fighting to enjoy rights that had been granted by the courts. In 1954, the Greenbrier County Board of Education ignored the law and maintained segregated schools until 1956, and Indiana, home to the Ku Klux

Monica Boone Allen, Central Area director

Klan, continued to lynch Negroes for questionable crimes. Many communities were underserved, Negroes were disproportionately affected by disease, and there were limited opportunities for youth development.

Responses by chapters were based on the particular needs of the community. The Detroit (MI) Chapter donated food baskets filled with gifts for elderly ladies at the Phyllis Wheatley Home Association, adopted the West End Day Care Center, stuffed toys for young patients at the Children's Hospital, and collected magazines for patients at the Veterans Hospital.

By 1958, the Central Area had 24 chapters, and over the next two decades, 21 more chapters were added. The social and economic climate also began to ameliorate. Realizing the value of the Black consumer, corporations began to partner with The Links and other social action groups. With additional support, chapters strengthened their programming.

Another boost to programming came via Area Conferences, which began as annual events in 1952, but have met on a biennial schedule since

1975. Conference workshops and sessions fostered knowledge about program and operations, facilitated bonding between chapters, and celebrated The Links' heritage and legacy. Areas were established to decentralize operations, programs, and duties; so, the election of an Area director and other officers is a core requirement. Twenty Area directors have kept the Central Area's heartbeats in rhythm.

The Central Area has also established a tradition of being in the vanguard relative to the level of support given to National service initiatives. Central Area was the first to sponsor Leadership Summits for chapter members, offering training in chapter management, leadership, programming, and resource development. At the 1993 Area Conference in Indianapolis, 13th Central Area Director JoAhn Brown-Nash created the first community outreach project, a practice later adopted by the 29th (1994) National Assembly.

The Central Area also has a long tradition of providing financial support to offer and expand opportunities that enable African American youth to develop, flourish, and experience success. The Area has contributed $140,000 to The Links Foundation. At the 2007 conference, the Central Area also gave $15,000 for mammograms for women not covered by insurance in Kansas City and hundreds of cuddly teddy bears to the Samuel Rodgers Community Health Center. A $5,000 donation was also made to Black Coalition Health Care to support related educational programs in the Kansas City community.

In 2001, the Central Area dedicated the JoAhn Brown-Nash Reading Room at the Cornelia Crenshaw Branch of the Memphis-Shelby County Public Library System, symbolizing the 29 reading rooms Central Area had created across the Area. To date, 45 chapters have established reading rooms, where more than 250,000 children have discovered new worlds and new ideas through the 18,660 books given by members of Central Area. The project, named for Area Director Nash, followed Central Area's establishment of a $100,000 scholarship fund in her honor at Fisk University in 2000. As she presented the gift, 15th Central Area Director Margot James Copland said of Nash, "She … committed herself to use her talents in whatever way she (could) to help fulfill the hopes and dreams of others."

Central Area, also referred to as the "Heart of America," further demonstrated where its heart was through its support of historically Black colleges and universities (HBCUs). Awards to HBCUs since 2001

Central Area leadership 2017–2019

2019–2021 Central Area Officers Central Area Director Monica Boone Allen, Windy City (IL) (center), with other newly elected Area officers (left to right) Joel-lyn A. McCormick, Nominating chair, Tulsa (OK); Lauren Hicks Barton, MD, secretary, Oakland County (MI); Sheila R. Brown, vice director, Lake Shore (IL); and Chalon Edwards Anderson, PhD, Foundation representative, Oklahoma City (OK)

have totaled more than one-half million, including $182,000 in 2005. Such support brought to fruition the vision of 16th Director Jeannine Quick-Frasier, who told members: "Sisters, we can have a profound impact upon the lives of countless scholars who will be the professionals of tomorrow … ensuring a bright future for many through our collective presence defined by a singular significant act of generosity." Seventeenth Area Director Teree Caldwell-Johnson raised over $250,000 for an HBCU-endowed scholarship program with her "Heart of Linkdom HBCU – Give-Reach-Grow" initiative.

The Central Area has continually sought ways to improve programming. Monetary incentives, which have enhanced and strengthened chapter efforts for more than a decade, still spur creativity and program expansion. The Cleveland (OH) Chapter won an award for its Andrew J. Rickoff School project, a three-year effort that enhanced proficiency scores and increased members' desire to serve; the chapter also opened a computer laboratory. Other exemplary programs include The Tulsa (OK) Chapter's adoption of 10 girls, called the "Chainettes." The girls' immersion in "social, cultural, and educational opportunities" led eight of them to college—and they graduated.

The Youngstown (OH) Chapter has encouraged cultural awareness through the sponsorship of dance troupes. The Modern Dance Group of West Virginia State University was one of the first groups. Through the years, the chapter presented the Harlem Boys Choir, The Alvin Ailey Repertory Ensemble, and The Dance Theatre of Harlem, which featured an Heir-O-Link, Stephanie Dabney, as the lead dancer.

International programming heartbeats have also been in rhythm. Chapters have provided professional expertise in curriculum and lesson plans development to schools in Liberia. The Maternal Waiting Home program helps to alleviate the complications and health issues in mothers and newborns due to deliveries without the assistance of trained medical professionals. The River City (TN) Chapter supported "Linkage to Jamaica" by identifying local Jamaicans and forming an association that meets to review programs and projects.

The Dayton (OH) Chapter adopted a children's home in Sierra Leone, West Africa. Yearly, support is given to the Society for the Advancement of Culture and Welfare in Sierra Leone. The chapter also participated in "Education across The Miles." The Memphis (TN) Chapter impacted the lives of people of the African diaspora by serving in five different countries. In 1999, the chapter, together with the Central Area Arkansas-Tennessee Cluster, built a school in the KwaZulu-Natal District of South Africa.

Area programs have been exceptional. Initiatives have run from scholarships and endowments for HBCUs, which have become staples, to "Through the Eyes of a Child," the Signature Program of 19th

Area Director Glenda Masingale Manson. Area directors have also introduced operational measures that have improved efficiency and fostered friendship through legacy events and member recognition.

AREA DIRECTORS

Portia M. Searcy (1952–1954)
Chicago (IL) Chapter

The first Central Area director was Portia M. Searcy. She was the organizer of the interest group that became the Chicago Chapter of The Links. She held the first Central Area Presidents' Dinner at the first meeting of the Area in Chicago. Searcy chartered the Memphis and Nashville (TN) Chapters, increasing the number to 15 chapters with some 5,000 members.

Blanche Sinkler (1954–1956)
St. Louis (MO) Chapter

The second Central Area director was Blanche Sinkler. She was a charter member of the St. Louis Chapter. She chartered two chapters: Huntington (WV) in 1955 and Youngstown (OH) in 1956.

Bess Simpson (1956–1958)
Indianapolis (IN) Chapter

Bess Simpson was the third Area director. She focused on programming involving youth, academic excellence, civic and public service, and the promotion of cultural enrichment to the disadvantaged, all befitting these particular times and trials of Black America. Four chapters were chartered during her directorship: Springfield (OH) and Little Rock (AR), both in 1956; Des Moines (IA) and Oklahoma City (OK), both in 1957.

Vivian Beamon (1958–1960)
Cincinnati (OH) Chapter

Vivian Beamon was the fourth Central Area director. She led the Area into the 1960s. Two chapters were chartered during her tenure: Northern Indiana, 1958, and Topeka (KS), 1959. Beamon was also the fourth National President.

Lillian Mosee (1960–1964)
St. Louis (MO) Chapter

Lillian Mosee was the fifth Central Area director. She served two terms. One chapter was chartered under her leadership: Milwaukee (WI).

Laura Jones (1964–1966)
Dayton, (OH)

Laura Jones was the sixth Central Area director. She was the first Area director to meet the NAACP Legal Defense Fund quota. The Central Area supported African American Mississippians who were fighting for their rights and provided programs for the gifted, as well as disadvantaged, youth. The Area also presented John Griffith, the author of *Black Like Me*. Two chapters were chartered during Jones's tenure: Jackson (TN) and Tulsa (OK), both in 1964.

Evelyn Harper (1967–1972)
Topeka (KS) Chapter

Evelyn Harper was the seventh Central Area director. She finished the unexpired term of 6th Area Director Laura Jones and won a term of her own. Harper used the news media to promote the work of The Links. She gave time and energy to advancing the friendship element of the organization and worked closely to engage Connecting Links to ensure their skills and talents were utilized towards achieving goals. Four chapters were chartered during her tenure: Wichita (KS), 1968, Frankfort–Lexington (KY), 1968, Pine Bluff (AR), and Knoxville (TN).

Willie Stevenson Glanton, Esq. (1972–1974)
Des Moines (IA) Chapter

Glanton was the eighth Central Area director. She focused on operational efficiency, conducting workshops on membership, the *Constitution and Bylaws*, and National Program areas. Glanton also developed a kit to prepare new members for their roles in Linkdom. Four chapters were chartered during Glanton's tenure: Toledo (OH), Lansing/East Lansing (MI), North Shore (IL), and Minneapolis/St. Paul (MN).

Roberta Basnett (1974–1979)
Columbus (OH) Chapter

Roberta Basnett was the ninth Central Area director. Basnett's accomplishments included the establishment of the Sarah S. Scott Founder's Award, which came with $1,000 awards to Wilberforce and Central State Universities, as well as Payne Seminary. The award was used to purchase books destroyed during the 1974 Xenia, Ohio, tornado. In 1979, the second Sarah S. Scott Founder's Award was presented to the Nashville (TN) Chapter to support a scholarship for youth for the John Work Music Award, and it provided seed money for the exhibition Forever Free – Art by Afro-American Women. Basnett also produced the *25th Anniversary Journal* and established the Central Area newsletter. Eleven chapters were chartered during her tenure: Normal-Champaign (IL), South Suburban Chicago (IL), West Towns (IL), Kent Area (OH), Quad Cities (IL), Hendersonville (TN), Ann Arbor (MI), Chattanooga (TN), Flint Area (MI), Missouri City (MO), and Fort Wayne (IN).

Fannie Wilson Ellis (1979–1983)
Northern Indiana Chapter

Fannie Wilson Ellis was the 10th Central Area director. She believed in the ideals of program activities, and she worked to engage members. Ellis chartered five chapters: Tri-City (MI), Oakland County (MI), Greater Wayne County (MI), Jackson County (MO), and Music City (TN).

Marjorie Joyce Mims (1983–1987)
Chicago (IL) Chapter

Marjorie Joyce Mims served as the 11th Central Area director. She initiated the "Marjorie Joyce Mims Umbrella Program Award," commissioned the writing and publication of the history of the Central Area, and she awarded "Certificates of Service" to outgoing chapter presidents. Mims installed five chapters: Hoffman Estates (IL), Shelby County (TN), Paducah (KY), Madison Metropolitan (WI), and Gateway (MO).

Marion Ridley Sweeney (1987–1991)
Las Vegas (NV) Chapter

Marion Ridley Sweeney was the 12th Central Area director. Under her leadership, the Central Area took first place in four program facets at the 1990 National Assembly. She chartered seven chapters: Windy City (IL), Western Reserve (OH), Renaissance (MI), Twin Rivers (OH), Parthenon (TN), Cream City (WI), and South Bend (IN).

JoAhn Brown-Nash (1991–1995)
South Suburban Chicago (IL)

JoAhn Brown-Nash was the 13th Central Area director. Brown-Nash selected as her theme: "A-Train: Action, Acceleration, Accomplishment, Attainment and Affection." She introduced the idea of community outreach in the cities where conferences or Assemblies are held. That idea has become a mainstay of the organization. She chartered the Great Lakes (MI), River City (TN), Archway (MO), and Harbor Lites (IL) Chapters.

Delores Henderson (1995–1999)
Minneapolis/St. Paul (MN) Chapter

Delores Henderson was the 14th Central Area director. Her leadership theme was "Love and Affection." Henderson filled Link Nash-Brown's term when she was elected to the National Executive Council. Henderson established Area clusters, as well as JoAhn Nash-Brown Reading Rooms in Chattanooga, Detroit, and Cleveland. She continued the community outreach program and developed partnerships with General Motors, General Mills, the Kellogg Foundation, and the Pillsbury Foundation. She held the first Summit meeting, and she was the first Area director to utilize technology, adding color to the Cleveland, Ohio, and Little Rock, Arkansas, conferences. She chartered the Circle City (IN) and Lake Shore (IL) Chapters.

Margot James Copeland (1999–2003)
Cleveland (OH) Chapter

Margot James Copeland was the 15th Central Area director. Her theme was "Leadership, Legacy and Love." She expanded the JoAhn Brown-Nash Reading Rooms to 42 across the Central Area, and she established an endowed scholarship in Brown-Nash's honor with the Middle Tennessee Foundation in Nashville and Fisk University for $100,000. (More than 40 students have received support). Copeland also introduced Organizational Effectiveness in the Central Area with a Chapter Enhancement and Resolution workshop, and she also established a Fund Development Campaign that left a surplus of $105,000 in the Central Area treasury. Chapters chartered under Copeland included Kalamazoo (MI) and Macomb (MI).

Jeannine Quick-Frasier (2003–2007)
Columbus (OH) Chapter

Jeannine Quick-Frasier was the 16th Central Area director. Leading with her theme, "Affirming Friendship," Frasier continued the programs of her predecessors and directed the work of the Area towards challenges that people of color faced in the 21st century. She honored chapters for excellent demonstrations of community service through programming, and she supported those programs financially for continuity of deliverables. Chapters began to realize financial support in amounts from $1,000 to $10,000, enabling them to give more in time, effort, and resources to serve. She chartered the Queen City (OH) Chapter.

Teree Caldwell-Johnson (2007–2011)
Des Moines (IA) Chapter

Teree Caldwell-Johnson was the 17th Central Area director. Her theme was "Powering the Promise." She continued the commitment The Links, Incorporated made to historically Black colleges and universities (HBCUs). She established "Heart of Linkdom HBCU – Give-Reach-Grow," which raised over $250,000 for an endowed scholarship program. Caldwell-Johnson also

established the Central Area National Headquarters Naming Right Agreement, Central Area Boutique, and the Central Area Signature Project, Linking to Close the Gap. She continued her work by administering two Central Area Assessment Surveys during her four years as Central Area director, creating the Inter-Generational and Capacity Building Task Force, and preparing the Area for the future by identifying the sites/states for Central Area Conferences through 2027.

Alice Strong Simmons (2011–2015)
Oklahoma City (OK) Chapter

Alice Strong Simmons was the 18th Central Area director. "Excellence, Elegance, Ethics" was her theme that supported her drive towards enhancing long-standing programs of The Links, Incorporated. She established a "central" focus for the Area using the Signature Program, "Closing the Achievement Gap." Strong Simmons created continuity among the 69 and improved the reading skills of pre-K–3rd-grade children. Partnering with Kettering Foundation, Strong Simmons galvanized The Links, organizing focus groups and team leaders, and she began chapter community forums to analyze the educational issues in communities across a 15-state area. Tools were identified to assist Central Area chapters in addressing the reading readiness in the early education years and improving reading skills across the middle and high school years.

Glenda Masingale Manson (2015–2019)
Central Illinois Chapter

Glenda Masingale Manson was the 19th Central Area director. She preached self-reflection: "Be the change you want to see in the world." With the theme "The Power of 1," she urged members to use their talents to make a difference. Manson practiced inclusion and demonstrated ways to collaborate and create. Her signature project, "My Community Through the Eyes of the African American Child – Linking Images," provided ways to empower children by engaging them creatively through the visual arts. Children were given a camera and encouraged to capture what was beautiful and identify what they would like to change. Manson also instituted "LinkSheroes" to recognize the contributions of members who had served or were active in the military. She continued past initiatives that included support for historically Black colleges and universities. She chartered the Central Missouri Chapter.

Monica Allen (2019–)
Windy City (IL) Chapter

Monica Allen, vice chair of the Central Area, was elected as the 20th Central Area director at the 2019 Area Conference. The mantle of leadership was passed to her to continue the legacy, pride, dignity, and class initiated by the 19 former Central Area directors.

Other members of the Central Area also helped to fulfill The Links commitment to friendship and service via leadership and service on the Executive Council. Central Area has produced three National Presidents: Vivian Beamon, Cincinnati (OH) Chapter; Gwendolyn Lee, South Suburban Chicago (IL) Chapter, and Margot James Copeland, Cleveland (OH) Chapter. These women inspired members in Central Area and throughout Linkdom.

Former presidents Beamon, Lee, and Copeland also served as National President, and Lee was member-at-large. Other National officers were Anna Julian, Chicago (IL) Chapter, National vice president, National treasurer, and Chapter Establishment officer; JoAhn Brown-Nash, South Suburban Chicago (IL) Chapter, National vice president and Chapter Establishment officer; Letitia Rose, Dayton (OH) Chapter, National vice president; Alice Jones, Chicago (IL) Chapter, National recording secretary; Bernice McAllister, Cleveland (OH) Chapter, National recording secretary; Ruth Williams Chicago (IL) Chapter, National recording secretary; Louise Quarles Lawson, Chicago (IL) Chapter, National treasurer; and Faye H Price, Chicago (IL) Chapter, National parliamentarian.

All Area directors were members of the Executive Council during their tenure. Program directors and operational chairs included Alma Dodd, Windy City (IL) Chapter, National Program director and Services to Youth chair; Wendy Thomas, Huntington (WV) Chapter, Services to Youth director; Yvonne Robertson, Cincinnati (OH) Chapter, Arts director; and Alpha Blackburn, Indianapolis (IN) Chapter, National Arts director. Anne S. Pruitt Logan, Columbus (OH) Chapter, served as National Program coordinator, Margaret Hough, Cincinnati (OH) Chapter and Adrienne Jones, Cleveland (OH) Chapter, led the National Arts facet, and Inez Brewer, Northern Indiana Chapter, directed National Trends and Services.

Also serving were Christine Branche, Cleveland (OH) Chapter, National Trends and Services director; Etta Moten Barnett, Chicago (IL) Chapter, International Trends and Services director, Inez Brewer, Northern Indiana Chapter, National Program facet director, and May Alice Ridley, Parthenon (TN) Chapter, Education Linkage.

Current members of the Executive Council from the Central Area include Monica Allen, Windy City (IL) Chapter, Central Area director; Crystal L. Kendrick, Queen City (OH) Chapter, National recording secretary; Gwendolyn B. Lee, South Suburban Chicago (IL) Chapter, chair, Council of Presidents; Joan Prince, Milwaukee (WI) Chapter, chair, International Trends and Services; Patricia Pearman, Milwaukee (WI) Chapter, Health and Human Services chair, Alice Strong Simmons, Oklahoma City (OK) Chapter, Ethics and Standards chair; Karen Jefferson Morrison, Columbus (OH) Chapter, chair, Legislative Issues, Public Affairs, and Resolutions Committee; Jarnell Burks-Craig, Indianapolis (IN) Chapter, chair, Elections Committee, and Larnell Burks-Bagley, Indianapolis (IN) Chapter, chair, Protocol Committee.

The Central Area has been a vital Link in building and strengthening The Links. Through friendship, service, and operations initiatives in the great land of Linkdom, between the coasts are mountains, rivers, and streams … the heartbeat of The Links Incorporated, the Central Area is strong.

~ *Delores Henderson*
~ *Alice Strong Simmons*

CENTRAL AREA DIRECTORS

Director	Tenure	Chapter
Portia Searcy	1952–1954	Chicago (IL) Chapter
Blanche Sinkler	1954–1956	St. Louis (MO) Chapter
Bess Simpson	1956–1958	Indianapolis (IN) Chapter
Vivian Beamon	1958–1960	Cincinnati (OH) Chapter
Lillian Mosee	1960–1964	St. Louis (MO) Chapter
Laura Jones	1964–1966	Dayton (OH) Chapter
Evelyn Harper	1967–1972	Topeka Chapter
Willie Glanton	1972–1974	Des Moines (IA) Chapter
Roberta Basnett	1974–1979	Columnus (OH) Chapter
Fannie Wilson Ellis	1979–1983	Northern Indiana Chapter
Marjorie Joyce Mims	1983–1987	Chicago (IL) Chapter
Marion Sweeney	1987–1991	Dayton (OH) Chapter
JoAhn Brown-Nash	1991–1995	South Suburban Chicago (IL) Chapter
Delores Henderson	1995–1999	Minneapolis/St. Paul (MN) Chapter
Margot James Copeland	1999–2003	Cleveland (OH) Chapter
Jeannine Quick-Frasier	2003–2007	Columbus (OH) Chapter
Teree Caldwell-Johnson	2007–2011	Des Moines (IA) Chapter
Alice Strong Simmons	2011–2015	Oklahoma City (OK) Chapter
Glenda Masingale Manson	2015–2019	Central Illinois Chapter
Monica Allen	2019–	Windy City (IL) Chapter

CENTRAL AREA CHAPTERS

Ann Arbor (MI)	Ann Arbor	MI
Archway (MO)	St. Louis	MO
Central Illinois (IL)	Normal	IL
Central Missouri (MO)	Jefferson City	MO
Charleston-Institute (WV)	Dunbar	WV
Chattanooga (TN)	Ooltewah	TN
Chicago (IL)	Chicago	IL
Cincinnati (OH)	Cincinnati	OH
Circle City (IN)	Indianapolis	IN
Cleveland (OH)	Shaker Heights	OH
Columbus (OH)	Westerville	OH
Cream City (WI)	Brookfield	WI
Dayton (OH)	Dayton	OH
Des Moines (IA)	West Des Moines	IA
Detroit (MI)	Detroit	MI
Flint Area (MI)	Flint	MI
Fort Wayne (IN)	Fort Wayne	IN
Frankfort/Lexington (KY)	Lexington	KY
Gateway (IL)	St. Louis	MO
Great Lakes (MI)	West Bloomfield	MI
Greater Kansas City (MO)	Lee's Summit	MO
Greater Wayne County (MI)	West Bloomfield	MI
Harbor Lites (IL)	Waukegan	IL
Hendersonville Area (TN)	Nashville	TN
Hoffman Estates (IL)	Arlington Heights	IL
Huntington (WV)	Huntington	WV
Indianapolis (IN)	Indianapolis	IN
Jackson (TN)	Jackson	TN
Jackson County (MO)	Lee's Summit	MO
Kalamazoo (MI)	Kalamazoo	MI
Kent Area (OH)	Hudson	OH
Knoxville (TN)	Knoxville	TN
Lake Shore (IL)	Chicago	IL
Lansing/East Lansing (MI)	East Lansing	MI
Little Rock (AR)	Little Rock	AR
Louisville (KY)	Prospect	KY
Madison Metropolitan (WI)	Franklin Park	IL
Memphis (TN)	Collierville	TN
Milwaukee (WI)	Milwaukee	WI
Minneapolis-St. Paul (MN)	Mendota Heights	MN
Music City (TN)	Whites Creek	TN
Nashville (TN)	Nashville	TN

North Shore (IL)	Evanston	IL
Northern Indiana (IN)	Gary	IN
Northwest Arkansas (AR)	Rogers	AR
Oakland County (MI)	West Bloomfield	MI
Oklahoma City (OK)	Oklahoma City	OK
Omaha (NE)	Omaha	NE
Parthenon (TN)	Brentwood	TN
Pine Bluff (AR)	Dumas	AR
Quad Cities (IL)	Davenport	IA
Queen City (OH)	Cincinnati	OH
Renaissance (MI)	Farmington Hills	MI
River City (TN)	Memphis	TN
Shelby County (TN)	Memphis	TN
South Bend Area (IN)	South Bend	IN
South Suburban Chicago (IL)	Olympia Fields	IL
Springfield (OH)	Springfield	OH
St. Louis (MO)	Overland	MO
Toledo (OH)	Sylvania	OH
Topeka (KS)	Topeka	KS
Tri-City (MI)	Midland	MI
Tulsa (OK)	Owasso	OK
Twin Rivers (OH)	New Albany	OH
West Towns (IL)	Bartlett	IL
Western Reserve (OH)	Richmond Heights	OH
Wichita (KS)	Wichita	KS
Wilberforce (OH)	Xenia	OH
Windy City (IL)	Calumet City	IL
Youngstown (OH)	Youngstown	OH

CHAPTER 11

THE SOUTHERN AREA:
The Leader

*T*he tagline "Southern Area Leads!" was declared by Julia Brogdon Purnell, the seventh Southern Area director, and it has continued to define the Area. Leaders, chapters and members of the Southern Area and The Links, Incorporated have borne out this slogan. Ten National Presidents were either elected while residing within Southern Area boundaries or have southern roots; two National Presidents served as Area directors, and numerous Sister Links have served on the National level. The Southern Area has played an essential role in helping to shape the development and character of The Links, Incorporated.

These two entities were conceived in the turbulence of the 1940s. World War II had ended, and the Great Migration continued with Negroes moving North and West. Servicemen were returning home and reveling in America's victory with the surety that they too would partake of the nation's prosperity and success. It quickly became apparent that the dreamed-of scenario was a delusion. Systemic racism permeated the American landscape. Housing, employment, education, and interstate travel were of great concern for Negroes. Nowhere was this more evident than in the Deep South.

During this period, most of the states that would comprise the Southern Area were 35 percent Negro, and some, namely Louisiana, Mississippi, and South Carolina, had a Negro population significantly larger. The area was fertile for the formation of an organization responding to the unmet needs of educated Negro women and a large underserved population.

1948–1979

The Co-Founders of The Links, Incorporated, Margaret Rosell Hawkins and Sarah Strickland Scott, along with the other members of the Philadelphia Club, concluded the time was right to extend their hand of friendship and service into the South. Hence, plans to organize a sixth club began. Julia Delaney of Raleigh, North Carolina, was contacted, and she, in turn, spoke with her daughter, Nan Delaney Hines, who felt the eastern portion of North Carolina was an ideal place for the sixth club to be formed. With the assistance of Ann Armstrong, the idea took root. At 1:00 pm on April 19, 1948, the Rocky Mount-Wilson-Tarboro Club was formed. The sponsors were Julia Delaney and Doris Reynolds, representing the Philadelphia Club. The club's name was later changed to Wilson-Rocky Mount-Tarboro in deference to Nan Delaney Hines, one of the organizers and first president. The club immediately established a presence in their communities by donating furnishings for the new YMCA and helping the Girl Scouts furnish the recreation room in their cabin.

On April 18, 1949, Julia Delaney, representing the Philadelphia Club, conducted the chartering ceremony in Raleigh, North Carolina, and took the reins as the first president. In addition to Delaney, the charter members included Blanche Daniels, Ruby Fisher, Amelia Hamlin, Ernestine Hamlin, Gertrude Harris, Nannie Inborden, Willie Kay, Mamie McCauley, Louise McClennan, Louise Perrin, Mildred Taylor, Gertrude Trigg, and Marguerite White.

Notably, the club obtained markers for Black historians and was instrumental in establishing story hours at local libraries. These two clubs, respectively, were the sixth and 10th clubs chartered before the organization was nationalized in 1949, when Sarah Scott was elected the first National President. Interestingly, Delaney served as the organization's legal advisor (1949–1950), and after the organization was nationalized, she served as Area chairman.

Rocky Mount-Wilson-Tarboro (NC) Chapter Charter Members

Ann Armstrong	Rocky Mount, NC
Marguerite Armstrong	Rocky Mount, NC
Sallie Armstrong	Rocky Mount, NC
Nancy T. Bowens	Rocky Mount, NC
Esmeralda R. Hawkins	Rocky Mount, NC
Jessie H. Pash	Rocky Mount, NC
Grace W. Artis	Wilson, NC
Addie D. Butterfield	Wilson, NC
Ethel Hines	Wilson, NC
Norma Darden	Wilson, NC
Nan Delaney Hines	Wilson, NC
Vera Shade	Wilson, NC
Helen G. Quigless	Tarboro, NC

As the Southern Area mapped its direction, societal concerns about civil rights, education, and employment persisted. The country also continued to witness the Second Great Migration (1940–1970). In the 1940s, the migration brought almost 1.4 million Negroes from predominately rural areas in the South to the North and West. In the 1950s, 1.1 million Negroes continued the southern exodus. In keeping with the tenor of the times, at the 4th Assembly in 1952, the organization adopted its first National project.

In 1954, the Assembly voted to divide the National organization into four geographical areas: Eastern, Southern, Central, and Western. The original Southern Area configuration included Virginia, West Virginia, North Carolina, South Carolina, Georgia, Florida, Alabama, Mississippi, Louisiana, and Texas. The first Southern Area chairman was Julia Delaney.

Bernice Martin was the first Area Director (1955–1957). She inspired and charged the delegates

at the Area Meeting hosted by the Wilson-Rocky Mount-Tarboro (NC) Chapter in 1956 to remember: "You are all Links! In our organization, each member has an obligation, a responsibility—his own unique contribution to make—towards our understanding of life and our club."

Between 1957 and 1979, six Links donned the banner of Area director to lead, guide, and inspire members of the organization. The second Area director, Georgia Schanek (1956–1957) built on Link Martin's call for accountability and challenged members to rank themselves.

We have recognized the need for ethical relations. Let us begin today, now, at home, in our chapters, with ourselves to live up to the term "ethical" in our literature. Let us make it a real and living word—not just a space filler. If we correct this fallacy at home, then our Area and the Nation will reap the benefits, quietly and effectively. Let us practice friendship, really live it—go back to our ritual and read it through, really, really read it. Then ask yourself, "How do I rate."

The third Area director, Esmeralda Rich Hawkins (1958–1961), was a charter member of the Wilson-Rocky Mount-Tarboro (NC) Chapter and a teacher and pioneer in television teaching. She stressed, "Sister Links must demand excellence from the youth they reach."

In addition to serving the organization nationally, Southern Area Links chapters implemented stellar local programs and community initiatives that included a Black Arts Festival by the Charleston (SC) Chapter and a Debutante Cotillion and Lyceum Series by the St. Petersburg-Tampa (FL) Chapter, and they volunteered and financially supported a segregated daycare center by the Atlanta (GA) Chapter. The Greater Miami (FL) Chapter sponsored cancer institutes to educate the public about cancer. The New Orleans (LA) Chapter adopted a school, volunteering and providing financial support. Similarly, the Durham (NC) Chapter began a milk fund for children who needed extra nutrition.

Linda Reddick, fourth Area director (1961–1965), implemented "The New Link Image," embracing cultural, religious, and educational growth. She initiated a $1 per-capita tax and instituted the Outstanding Chapter, Outstanding Project, and Outstanding Links Awards for the Area.

As the civil rights movement was achieving its greatest legislative gains, the Southern Area was actively engaged. Chapter initiatives included the Columbus (GA) Chapter helping to fund the legal defense for a group of young women who organized to integrate the lunch counters and buses and the Jacksonville (FL) Chapter adopting the Lackawanna Elementary School.

In 1965, the geographical Areas were reconfigured, moving Virginia to the Eastern Area, West Virginia to the Central Area, and Texas to the Western Area. Continuing to inspire, Maude K. Reid, fifth Area director (1965–1969), began the practice of convening presidents prior to the opening of the first business session of an Area Conference. She also opened selected conference events to the public to help project the image of The Links, Incorporated in the communities being served. Link Reid established the first protocol procedures, developed criteria for qualifications for Area officers and election procedures, which became National models.

At the beginning of the new decade, Gladys D. Woods was elected sixth Area director (1969–1973). "Priorities in the 1970s" set the agenda for Woods. "It is my deepest desire that we begin with reflections on the structure of Southern Area Links. Let us re-examine our total organization by looking for new ways of reaching the goals of the threefold purpose of Links, Incorporated," she said.

Julia Brogdon Purnell, seventh Southern Area director (1973–1978), coined the Southern Area slogan, "Southern Area Leads." Additionally, she encouraged organizational structure and program growth, enhanced communication, and practiced positive group dynamics and human relations. To that end, she conducted seminars via mail with new chapter presidents, authored a president's handbook, held a meeting with chapter presidents at the beginning of each Area Conference, and instituted a chapter honor roll. By June of 1979, there were 41 chapters in the Southern Area providing exemplary programs and services in their communities.

1980–1999

The 1980s dawned with many societal changes, particularly socioeconomic and technological. The war on drugs accelerated, the AIDS epidemic was recognized, and the Cold War was ending. First Lady Nancy Reagan championed the "Just Say No" campaign. Many Southern Area chapters sponsored activities within that framework, as well as HIV/AIDS awareness and support information. Markedly, the Bold City (FL) Chapter, with a grant from the City of Jacksonville Ryan White Foundation, published three annual HIV/AIDS Service Directories for victims and

Southern Area Director Sylvia Perry (foreground) with her 2019–2021 leadership team.

caretakers. Bold City also funded the building of the first school in the Education across the Miles initiative.

Programmatically, the Southern Area chapters continued to inspire. The Orangeburg (SC) Chapter was recognized on a National level for its Project LEAD: High Expectations activities, Adopt a School Program, and Global Investment in Women and Youth Initiative. On the National and Area levels, they received awards for Sisters in Sync Program, Youth Summit, Health Disparities Initiatives, and The Rosenwald Schools Program. The Nassau, Bahamas Chapter began The Straw Project, introducing students to a viable and lucrative business. The Baton Rouge (LA) Chapter formed a successful mentoring program for young boys at Capitol Middle School, maintaining it for seven years.

Juanita Johnson, eighth Area director (1979–1981), assumed the mantle of Southern Area director. "Improving the Quality of Life by Linking People to People" was her focus. Additionally, she assisted in revising the manual *Archives Briefs for Southern Area.*

Regina Jollivette Frazier, ninth Area director (1981–1984), authorized the printing and distribution of the Area bylaws and focused on networking to achieve the maximum impact on improving the human condition. She initiated a Southern Area Scrapbook for the biennium and held a Southern Area arts camp for young artists in Montgomery, Alabama.

Tenth Area director Martha Boone (1984–1985) planned and executed the 28th Southern Area Conference in Daytona Beach, Florida, and encouraged chapter and individual service by providing achievement incentives.

Carolyn Washington, 11th Area director (1985–1987), primarily focused on the heritage and growth of Linkdom. In a letter to the 29th Southern Area Conference attendees in Charlotte, North Carolina, she said, "The work that you do and the decisions that you make will be unparalleled in the historical significance to the growth and success of our organization as we embark upon the new millennium."

Barbara Moore, 12th Area director (1987–1991), stated, "We must not rest on our laurels … for it is our charge and sacred duty to meet the challenges before us. The greater the challenge, the bigger the opportunity; it is our responsibility to meet the challenges that confront us because these are our opportunities to serve."

Katie R. Bell, 13th Area director (1991–1995), ushered in the new decade with a focus on health, the Black family, and self-esteem. The theme of her administration, "Living the Dream," saw the implementation of community-based programs, including Teddies for Tots month. More than 1,000 teddy bears were distributed to hospitals and police departments to share with children traumatized by violence, illness, or loss.

On the precipice of the new millennium, 14th Area Director Joyce Martin Dixon (1995–1999) held the first Southern Area Summit under the theme "Launching Linkages" at the 30th (1996) National Assembly. Dixon also updated the Southern Area history and introduced "Linkages to Life," the forerunner of the National Signature Program of the same name approved at the 32nd (2000) National Assembly. She presided at the Southern Area's 50th anniversary celebration in Charlotte, North Carolina. At the end of the millennium, there were 73 Southern Area chapters, including the first international chapter in Nassau, Bahamas.

2000–Present

At the dawn of the new millennium, the United States and the world were very different than in the 1940s when The Links, Incorporated and the Southern Area were born. Economic growth had considerable social and environmental consequences. The internet contributed to globalization, and the people of the world were instantly connected. September 11, 2001, saw the single deadliest terrorist attack in our history. In 2005, Hurricane Katrina flooded the entire city of New Orleans with devastating effects, and 2008 saw the election of the first African American president, Barack Obama.

As the world evolved, so too did programming efforts in the Southern Area. The Wilson-Rocky Mount-Tarboro (NC) Chapter partnered with the American Heart Association, co-hosting

National President Kimberly Jeffries Leonard with former Southern Area directors. Left to right, seated: Leonard, #19 Anne Turner Herriott, and #9 Regina Jollivette Frazier; left to right, standing: #18 Eneid A. Francis, #17 Director Mary F. Currie, and #14 Joyce Martin Dixon.

the "Go Red for Women" Community Luncheon and Discussion, tutored elementary children, and sponsored an African American art exhibit. The Birmingham (AL) Chapter served as the Area host chapter for the Linkages to Life program and received an award in 2009 for work done with the Pathways Homeless Shelter. The Ft. Lauderdale (FL) Chapter actively supported the Childhood Obesity Prevention initiative and STEM career infusion activities.

The Greenville (SC) Chapter championed the arts and a long-established partnership with the Greenville County Schools Fine Arts Center with the inauguration of "A Classical Education" program. This program planted a seed in the National Arts Committee as it developed the first signature arts program, "Classics through the Ages." For 11 years (2002–2013), the Durham (NC) Chapter spearheaded a recognized Umbrella Program, "Healthier Families: Changing Our Lifestyles," to address the community issue of homelessness and precariously housed individuals. The Magnolia (GA) Chapter adopted the Coretta Scott King Young Women's Leadership Academy. The Southern Area chapters were invested in many more impactful and transformational programs and initiatives to improve and enhance the lives of people in their communities.

The 15th Area director, Nancy Shade Anderson (1999–2003), was elected on the cusp of the new millennium. Her administration's theme, "Celebrating Our Journey of Friendship and Service," sought to uplift, acknowledge, and celebrate the contributions, hard work, and abiding friendships found in the Southern Area while continuing to serve communities. She established the first electronic newsletter, *Link Lines*, produced an e-mail directory, and supported cluster meetings in North Carolina, South Carolina, Florida, Louisiana, and Georgia.

Anderson also established specific guidelines for conflict resolution in chapters and conducted Conflict Resolution Workshops, and she continued Area support of "Linkages To Life." She presided at the first stand-alone Southern Area Leadership Conference, hosted by the Bold City (FL) and Jacksonville (FL) Chapters, and ensured the Southern Area was in a positive financial position. Anderson also presided at the 37th Southern Area Conference, hosted by the first chapter established outside the continental United States, and donated funds to support programming and training to the Links Safe House for Females in Crisis in Nassau, Bahamas.

Margaret Thompson Johnson, 16th Area director (2003–2007), declared The Links superior:

The Legacy of The Links, Incorporated is second to none. This inheritance is shared by all Link sisters everywhere. Our legacy is a phenomenal gift as well as an awesome responsibility. We must always be focused upon what we are, who we are, what we have done and what we can do to better serve. Let us pledge to work together in full alignment with our national officers to ensure that our emerging legacy remains strong and bright.

Johnson instituted the first area-wide scholarship endowment fund targeting the 51 historically Black colleges and universities (HBCU) located in the Southern Area, leading with a $10,000 check to each of the four HBCUs in Florida. She also spearheaded the Links' Day at the State Capitol event and the *Links to Health* newsletter. In the wake of Hurricane Katrina, she led the Area's response efforts.

Under the banner "Linking Our Actions Today with our Dreams for Tomorrow," 17th Area Director Mary F. Currie (2007–2011) encouraged chapters "to promote and engage in educational, civic, and health activities in order to enrich the lives of the underserved as we work together towards achieving common goals." To that end, she developed the focus program "Prevention of Childhood Obesity" and the Commission on Childhood Obesity. She secured grants totaling $500,000 from GE Healthcare, Corporation of the Midsouth, Blue Cross/ Blue Shield, Safeway, and the Kellogg Foundation. "Childhood Obesity" morphed into a National initiative.

Eighteenth Area Director Eneid A. Francis (2011–2015) energized the Area with the theme "Effecting Change Through the Power of Friendship and Service." She concentrated her administration on enhancing member relations and offering life-changing service to Southern Area communities. Francis introduced the STEM-focused program "Mentoring with a Twist." This was done by using an art-integrated approach to STEM learning. Further, she introduced *Advantage*, the Southern Area e-zine, SOLACE, a program to provide support to Links in crisis, and Green Pages, a resource guide.

Sylvia Perry, Bold City (FL) Chapter, Southern Area director

The 19th Area director, Anne Turner Herriott, was creative, inclusive, and empathetic. During her administration, three successful initiatives were executed. "Southern Area Loves HBCUs," provided $55,000 in scholarships and grants for individual students and HBCUs. "One Mission, One Love" addressed humanitarian needs with international mission work. Herriott also secured funding to encourage "training for a healthy lifestyle," and chapters with International Trends and Services programs received $8,500 in incentive funding.

Herriott prioritized internal development within the Area, organizing the leadership team and chapter presidents to embrace a platform of accountability, accessibility, and alignment to improve interactions at all levels. To enhance communications and support, she appointed chairs for Mind, Body and Spirit and Disaster Planning and Relief.

Elected in May at the 45th (2019) Southern Area Conference, 20th Southern Area Director Sylvia Perry, Bold City (FL) Chapter, has begun work that will continue the outstanding service of her 19 predecessors. Perry had served as Area vice director and Area secretary prior to her ascension, so she understood well the expectations.

National recognition of the Southern Area's success in programming led to the adoption of Linkages to Life, Childhood Obesity, and Classics through the Ages as National initiatives. Linkages to Life became one of The Links' most renowned signature programs, the "Prevention of Childhood Obesity" and the Commission on Childhood Obesity were fodder for the National initiative on Childhood Obesity, and Classics through the Ages has remained a classic.

The Southern Area was equally adept in operations and special events with 5th Southern Area Director Maude K. Reid establishing the first protocol procedures, developing criteria for qualifications for Area officers, and crafting election procedures that were all adopted as National models. The White Rose Banquet, one of the most memorable Assembly events, originated in the Southern Area during the administration of 7th Southern Area Director Julia Brogdon Purnell.

Of the 17 National Presidents, five were elected while residing in the Southern Area: 3rd National President (Margaret) Pauline Weeden Fletcher Maloney, Lynchburg (VA) Chapter, the first president elected from the Southern Area; 5th National President Helen Gray Edmonds, Durham (NC) Chapter; 7th National President Julia Brogdon Purnell, Baton Rouge (LA) Chapter; 9th National President Regina Jollivette Frazier Miami (FL) Chapter; and 11th National President Patricia Russell-McCloud, Dogwood City (GA) Chapter. (Because Virginia was transferred from the Southern Area to the Eastern Area in 1965, Maloney is also claimed by the Eastern Area.)

Other Southern Area Links who held National positions included Regina Jollivette Frazier, Greater Miami (FL) Chapter, National vice president and member-at-large, and Bernice McLendon, Atlanta (GA) Chapter, National vice president. Delores Albury, Pensacola (FL) Chapter, and Josephine Davis, Fort Valley (GA) Chapter, served as recording secretary, and Nannie Inborden, Raleigh (NC) Chapter, was National corresponding secretary.

National treasurers were Clinita Ford, Tallahassee (FL) Chapter, Minnie Gaston, Birmingham (AL) Chapter, and Katherine E. Wilson, Bold City (FL) Chapter. Tyna D. Davis, Montgomery (AL) Chapter, and Ernestine Sapp, Tuskegee (AL) Chapter, served as National parliamentarian; Elreta Alexander (Ralston), Greensboro (NC) Chapter, was legal advisor; and Emma Clement Walker, Birmingham (AL) Chapter, and Thelma Perkins, Baton Rouge (LA) Chapter, served as Public Information officers.

Link Delores Bolden Stamps, Jackson (MS) Chapter, served as co-director, National Programs. Facet chairs included Jewell T. Thompson, Baton Rouge (LA) Chapter, The Arts; Francis Marsh Ellis, Baton Rouge (LA) Chapter, The Arts; Marie Hoard Metz, Charleston (SC) Chapter, National Trends and Services; Leila Potts Campbell, Charleston (SC) Chapter, Services to Youth; Dolly Desselle Adams, Atlanta (GA) Chapter, International Trends and Services; and Juel Shannon Smith, Tampa (FL) Chapter, International Trends and Services.

Operations chairs included former Area directors Bernice Martin, Southern West Virginia Chapter, and Nancy Shade Anderson, Greenville (SC) Chapter, Chapter Establishment officers; and Margaret Thompson Johnson Jacksonville (FL) Chapter, Human Resources chair; along with Chairs Earnestine Green McNealey, Tuscaloosa (AL) Chapter, Archives and History; Betty Bradley Smith, Orlando (FL) Chapter, Awards and Recognition; Bunnie Jackson-Ransom, Azalea City (GA) Chapter, Communications and Public Relations; and Eneid Francis, National Assembly Committee co-chair.

Members of the 2018–2020 National Executive Council from the Southern Area are Tyna D. Davis, Montgomery (AL) Chapter, National parliamentarian, and Sylvia Carter Perry, Bold City (FL) Chapter, Southern Area director. Committee chairs include Raynetta C. Waters, Asheville (NC) Chapter, Nominating; Earnestine Green McNealey, Columbia (SC) Chapter, Archives and History; Bridget W. Chisholm, Greensboro (NC) Chapter, Economic Empowerment; Cynthia Hightower-Jenkins, Shreveport (LA) Chapter, Rituals; Sharon

Dixon Gentry, Music City (TN), Technology; Karen M. Dyer, Greensboro (NC) Chapter, Organizational Effectiveness/Leadership Development co-chair; and the most recent appointee, 19th Southern Area Director Anne T. Herriott, Greater Miami (FL) Chapter, Chapter Establishment.

Of the 288 chapters in Linkdom, the Southern Area has the largest number with 80, and its membership of 4,403 members is second, generating more than $880,000 in revenue. During 2017–2018, the membership completed 310,633 documented hours of service. Ultimately, evidence shows that the Southern Area's role in helping to shape the development and character of The Links, Incorporated has been essential. The number of National Presidents and other Executive Council members, the quantity and quality of initiatives introduced and promulgated, and the number of members and chapters demonstrate the essential role the Area has played in the organization's overall development, progress, and culture. As Julia Brogdon Purnell declared, "Southern Area Leads!"

~ *Nancy Anderson*

SOUTHERN AREA DIRECTORS

Area	Director	Chapter	Tenure
#1	Bernice Martin	Southern West Virginia	1955–1957
#2	Georgia Schanek	Orlando (FL)	1957–1958
#3	Esmeralda Hawkins	Wilson-Rocky Mount-Tarboro (NC)	1958–1961
#4	Linda Riddick	Orlando (FL)	1961–1965
#5	Maude Reid	Miami (Fl)	1965–1969
#6	Gladys Woods	Greensboro (NC)	1969–1973
#7	Julia Brogdon Purnell	Baton Rouge (LA)	1973–1978
#8	Juanita Johnson	Tallahassee (FL)	1978–1981
#9	Regina Jollivette Frazier	Miami (FL)	1981–1984
#10	Martha Boone	Wilmington (NC)	1984–1985
#11	Carolyn Washington	Vicksburg (MS)	1985–1987
#12	Barbara Moore	Durham (NC)	1987–1991
#13	Katie Bell	Montgomery (AL)	1991–1995
#14	Joyce Dixon	Brevard County (FL)	1995–1999
#15	Nancy Shade Anderson	Greenville (SC)	1999–2003
#16	Margaret Thompson Johnson	Jacksonville (FL)	2003–2007
#17	Mary F. Currie	Atlanta (GA)	2007–2011
#18	Eneid A. Francis	Pontchartrain (LA)	2011–2015
#19	Anne Turner Herriott	Greater Miami (FL)	2015–2019
#20	Sylvia Carter Perry	Bold City (FL)	2019–

Conference #	Year	Location
1	1955	Charleston, SC
2	1956	Rocky Mount, NC
3	1957	Houston, TX
4	1958	Orlando, FL
5	1959	Columbia, SC
6	1960	Savannah, GA
7	1961	Raleigh, NC
8	1962	St. Petersburg-Tampa FL
9	1963	Birmingham, AL
10	1964	Fayetteville, NC
11	1965	Greenville, SC
12	1966	New Orleans, LA
13	1967	Wilmington, NC
14	1968	Tallahassee, FL
15	1969	Charlotte, NC
16	1970	Greensboro, NC
19	1971	Augusta, GA
20	1972	Montgomery, AL
21	1973	Jackson, MS
22	1974	Washington, DC
23	1975	Durham, NC
24	1977	Brunswick, GA
25	1979	Hilton Head, SC
26	1981	Orlando, FL
27	1983	Columbia, GA
28	1985	Daytona Beach, FL
29	1987	Jacksonville, FL
30	1989	Ft. Lauder Ville, FL
31	1991	Charleston, SC
32	1993	Winston-Salem, NC
33	1995	Baton-Rouge, LA
34	1997	Jackson, MS
35	1999	Charlotte, NC
36	2001	Birmingham, AL
37	2003	Nassau, Bahamas
38	2005	Orlando, FL
39	2007	Mobile, AL
40	2009	Jacksonville, FL
41	2011	New Orleans, LA
42	2013	Miami, FL
43	2015	Birmingham, AL
44	2017	Atlanta, GA
45	2019	Orlando, FL

* The numbering jumped from 16 to 19, but there are no missing years.

SOUTHERN AREA CHAPTERS

Aiken (SC)	Aiken	SC
Albany (GA)	Albany	GA
Alexandria (LA)	Alexandria	LA
Altamonte Springs (FL)	Lake Mary	FL
Asheville (NC)	Asheville	NC
Athens (GA)	Stone Mountain	GA
Atlanta (GA)	Sandy Springs	GA
Augusta (GA)	Augusta	GA
Azalea City (GA)	Mableton	GA
Baton Rouge (LA)	Baton Rouge	LA
Birmingham (AL)	Birmingham	AL
Bold City (FL)	Jacksonville	FL
Bradenton/Sarasota (FL)	Sarasota	FL
Brevard County (FL)	Palm Bay	FL
Brunswick (GA)	Waverly	GA
Buckhead-Cascade City (GA)	Atlanta	GA
Camellia Rose (GA)	Atlanta	GA
Charleston (SC)	North Charleston	SC
Charlotte (NC)	Charlotte	NC
Columbia (SC)	Columbia	SC
Columbus (GA)	Columbus	GA
Crescent City (LA)	New Orleans	LA
Crown Jewels (NC)	Charlotte	NC
Dade County (FL)	Miami	FL
Daytona Beach (FL)	Daytona Beach	FL
Dogwood City (GA)	Atlanta	GA
Durham (NC)	Durham	NC
Elizabeth City (NC)	Elizabeth City	NC
Fayetteville (NC)	Fayetteville	NC
Fort Lauderdale (FL)	Lauderhill	FL
Fort Valley (GA)	Warner Robins	GA
Gainesville (FL)	Gainesville	FL
Golden Crest (MS)	Columbus	MS
Greater Huntsville (AL)	Huntsville	AL
Greater Miami (FL)	Miami	FL
Greater Mobile (AL)	Mobile	AL
Greensboro (NC)	Tarboro	NC
Greenville (SC)	Greer	SC
Gulf Coast (MS)	Ocean Springs	MS
Hilton Head (SC)	Hilton Head Island	SC
Jackson (MS)	Jackson	MS
Jacksonville (FL)	Jacksonville	FL

La Capitale (LA)	Port Allen	LA
LaGrange (GA)	Opelika	AL
Lake Gaston Area (NC)	Warrenton	NC
LeFleur's Bluff (MS)	Madison	MS
Macon (GA)	Macon	GA
Magic City (AL)	Birmingham	AL
Magnolia (GA)	College Park	GA
Miami-Biscayne Bay (FL)	Miami	FL
Mississippi Delta (MS)	Clarksdale	MS
Mississippi Roses (MS)	Byhalia	MS
Monroe-Grambling (LA)	Monroe	LA
Montgomery (AL)	Montgomery	AL
Nassau, Bahamas	Nassau	Bahamas
Natchez (MS)	Monticello	MS
New Orleans (LA)	New Orleans	LA
North Broward County (FL)	Pompano Beach	FL
Orangeburg (SC)	Orangeburg	SC
Orlando (FL)	Orlando	FL
Pensacola (FL)	Shalimar	FL
Piedmont (NC)	Hickory	NC
Pontchartrain (LA)	New Orleans	LA
Raleigh (NC)	Raleigh	NC
Savannah (GA)	Savannah	GA
Selma (AL)	Selma	AL
Shreveport (LA)	Shreveport	LA
Spartanburg (SC)	Spartanburg	SC
St. Petersburg (FL)	St. Petersburg	FL
Tallahassee (FL)	Tallahassee	FL
Tampa (FL)	Riverview	FL
Treasure Coast (FL)	Jensen Beach	FL
Triangle Park (NC)	Durham	NC
Tri-County (AL)	Bessemer	AL
Tuscaloosa (AL)	Eutaw	AL
Tuskegee (AL)	Tuskegee	AL
West Palm Beach (FL)	Lake Worth	FL
Wilmington (NC)	Leland	NC
Wilson-Rocky Mount-Tarboro (NC)	Nashville	NC
Winston-Salem (NC)	High Point	NC

Chapters listed alphabetically by city; data provided by National Headquarters.

CHAPTER 12
THE WESTERN AREA:
Indispensable

The phrase "from sea to shining sea" became a reality when three California chapters—Los Angeles, Oakland Bay Area, and San Francisco—were established in 1950. The chain of friends now stretched across the continental United States from the Atlantic to the Pacific. One might ask the question, "Why California?" To answer this question, there is a need to explore the population and social climate of the state, as well as the growth and spread of the organization outward from Philadelphia.

In the Second Great Migration, starting in 1940, approximately five million people moved to the North and the West. California had the fifth-largest population in this decade, with New York, Pennsylvania, Illinois, and Ohio being the only states with larger populations. Approximately 132 million people lived in California; 1.8 percent were African American. Most Black California families came to the state from the south seeking better jobs and education. In cities such as Richmond and Oakland, African Americans migrated in massive numbers to work in the shipyards and other wartime industries.

"It was in these communities that physicians, dentists (many of whom attended Meharry or Howard Medical Schools) and other professionals established their offices to serve the growing African-American populations." Relationships formed at educational and professional institutions in the East and the South continued as graduates moved to the West Coast. The Western Area's creation—timing, milieu, and determination to succeed—fostered Linkdom. Relationships played a key role in the creation and growth of the Western Area—relationships that began years before, maintained across time and space.

The major groups included college sororities, business and professional associates, historically Black colleges and universities, and other institutions of higher learning, organizations such as Jack and Jill of America, Inc., Urban League, NAACP, and auxiliaries of the National Medical and Dental Associations. The profession and prestige of their husbands in the community was also a major consideration for membership.

In September of 1950, the Western Area became a part of this growing organization with the chartering of three chapters. Marjorie McPherson, a resident of Los Angeles, was the force behind the Los Angeles Chapter, September 16, 1950. Installed as the 23rd chapter of The Links, Incorporated and the first chapter to be installed on the West Coast, the group consisted of 18 civic-minded women. Vada Sommerville was elected as the chapter's first president.

The second and third chapters of the Western Area, the Oakland Bay Area (CA) Chapter and the San Francisco (CA) Chapter, had been chartered on September 23, 1950, the only time in the history of The Links, Incorporated that two chapters were chartered on the same date and same time and in the same hotel. Loraine Cady Rickmond, organizer and first president of the Oakland Bay Area Chapter, was also the first Western Area director. Hortense Thomas, organizer and first president of the San Francisco (CA) Chapter, was the wife of a physician and was known in San Francisco for her long-term volunteer work with children having special needs.

Prompted by an invitation in the form of a handwritten letter from Loraine Rickmond to Marjorie Patterson, the Sacramento (CA) Chapter became the fourth chapter on March 15, 1952. The state of California produced 21 more chapters between 1957 and 2010.

The state of Arizona had a lower population than its neighbor California and even fewer African Americans, but on March 17, 1952, the Phoenix (AZ) Chapter became the fifth chapter in the Western Area and the first chapter established outside California. Co-Founder Margaret Rosell Hawkins had asked Anna Julian to start a second chapter in Arizona. In the geographical realignment of 1953, the 5th Assembly approved the transfer of the Denver (CO) Chapter from the Central Area to the Western Area, adding the sixth chapter and the third state to the Western Area. One additional chapter, Colorado Springs, was established in 2015.

Delegates from the six chapters—Los Angeles, Oakland Bay, San Francisco, Sacramento, Phoenix, and Denver—came together for their first Area Conference in Los Angeles in April 1954. Loraine Rickmond, the newly appointed Area chairman, presided. Utilizing the theme "Communications,"

Rickmond designed an agenda that included formulating procedures and protocols for communication among chapters, between chapters and Area officers, means of financing chapter and Area operations, chapter geographical boundaries, and minimum chapter membership.

Recognizing the disadvantage of the small size of the Area, delegates expressed interest in expansion to equalize its voting strength. To that end, Chapter Membership Committee Chair Sydnetta Smith of the Los Angeles Chapter proposed consideration of establishing clubs in Texas to join the Western Area. The recommendation also included four additional cities for consideration—Tucson, Arizona, Tacoma, Washington, and Santa Barbara and San Diego, California. The uneven growth of the organization was also a National concern. At the 8th (1956) Assembly in Denver, Colorado, Pauline Weeden Maloney was appointed chair of a committee to study the problem of balancing the number of chapters in the Areas.

In the 1950s and 1960s, the African American community of Seattle, Washington, was segregated into a small area known as the Central District. During that time, African Americans were victimized by racial and social injustice in various ways,

Western Area Conference, Texas style

and employment and educational opportunities were limited. The Greater Seattle (WA) Chapter became the seventh chapter on December 9, 1955, and the newly created Area received a fourth state.

The process started with local Seattle educator Josephine Stokes, who had a friend in the San Francisco Chapter. Josephine mentioned the idea to her next-door neighbor Sarai Green. The two contacted friends and neighbors who could help them establish a chapter—friends who lived generally within twelve blocks of each other in Seattle's Central District, the historically African American community. The state of Washington produced three additional chapters: Tacoma, Spokane, and Tri-Cities.

The percentage of Blacks as a part of Oregon's total population was consistently small, totaling less than 1 percent as late as 1960. In the 1960s, Portland and many other communities in the country were still struggling to desegregate schools in a segregated city—a legacy of the housing restrictions placed on Blacks. It was in this environment that Portland resident Kathryn Bogle was approached by Thelma Toms of San Francisco in 1951 and again by Loraine Rickmond of the Oakland Bay Chapter in 1953 to start a Links chapter in Portland. On November 9, 1957, a group of 10 women became the Portland (OR) Chapter, the ninth chapter in the Area and the first in the state, which also increased the number of states in the Area to five.

The total population of Texas was more than seven million in the 1950s, of which 12.6 percent were African American. The Houston (TX) Chapter was chartered in the Southern Area on March 6, 1951. Texas was transferred to the Western Area during the 1955 realignment. The Dallas (TX) Chapter, organized by Fannie Smith, became the second chapter in the state on November 9, 1957, and the Fort Worth (TX) Chapter, pushed by Viola Borders (who was encouraged by an East Coast friend), was chartered December 5, 1959.

At the same time, Ethelyn Maynard Burnett and Marie Scott Platte were contacted by Co-Founder Sarah Strickland Scott, their cousin and niece, respectively, who encouraged them to put together a charter

group. When Burnett and Platte began calling their friends, they discovered that they were compiling a list of names for the same organization. This list became the list of "10 friends" who were inducted into the third chapter established in the state. Nineteen more chapters were subsequently established in Texas.

By the end of the first decade, the path of chapter establishment had moved from California in 1950 through Arizona, Colorado, Washington, Oregon, and Texas and accounted for 12 chapters in the newly formed Western Area.

THE SECOND DECADE AND BEYOND

The 1960s saw an increase of 10 chapters in four of the six populated states—California, Arizona, Washington, and Texas. Links with relationships to women in other cities made connections and received support and guidance. The early chapters began to sponsor new chapters.

The 1970s heralded the entrance of Nevada, the seventh state. Thelma Toms Morlock was instrumental in the birth of the Las Vegas (NV) Chapter on May 27, 1976. Morlock felt that there should be a chapter of The Links in Las Vegas. Many members of the interest group had come to Las Vegas from larger cities with established Links chapters, so they were familiar with the purpose and programs of The Links. Toms worked diligently to secure the number of women necessary to form a chapter. Lois Ice, who had seen The Links in action in Detroit, Michigan, joined forces with Toms. In May 1976, the chapter was established with 20 charter members. Las Vegas (NV) remains the lone chapter in the state.

Because of the unregulated rapid growth nationwide, the 18th (1972) Assembly vested the authority and responsibility for creating chapters with National, and National President Helen Edmonds named Anna Julian as the first Chapter Establishment officer. Julian continued a demographics study that she had begun as National Membership chair and set up guidelines and processes to promote regulated growth. To spur colonization in the Western Area and avoid further concentration of chapters in the

Eastern and Southern Areas, the Executive Council limited the establishment of new chapters to the Western Area during 1977 and 1978. The Bakersfield (CA), Fresno (CA), El Paso (TX), and Spokane (WA) Chapters were established.

The 1980s brought Hawaii and New Mexico. The Hawaii (HI) Chapter, the first chapter established outside the continental United States, was initiated by a letter from National President Julia Brogdon Purnell. Purnell encouraged Donnyss Cotton Rucker and Otharea Pitts to explore the possibility of a chapter in the state, which was located in the middle of the Pacific Ocean and had an African American population of less than 3 percent of the total population. With members from at least two of the islands, the chapter was chartered on January 11, 1986, and it is the sole chapter.

Former Western Area leaders

The Albuquerque (NM) Chapter, established on June 10, 1989, was organized by Charlotte K. Mock, an educator, a writer, a poet, a leader, and an organizer who wanted to start the first chapter of The Links, Incorporated in the state of New Mexico; it has remained the only chapter in the state.

Anchorage (AK), the lone chapter established between 2001 and 2010, was established in the 10th state because of the persistence and tenacity of Francina Thomas, formerly of Pomona, California. Thomas was determined to find 25 African American professional women with roots and the financial means to support a Links chapter in Alaska, where African Americans constituted only 8 percent the overall population of 300,000. She found 26, and the Alaska Chapter was chartered on May 3, 2001.

Today, the Western Area covers 14 states, is populated in 10 of those states, spreads over five time zones, includes 60 of 288 chapters, and has 3,066 of the 15,615 (19.6 percent) members. Of the 60 chapters, more than half (33, or 55 percent) are considered small chapters with less than 40 members. However, these chapters are extremely important because, in many instances, they represent the only voice for people of color; the only organization that will bring attention to and address the critical needs, community issues related to education, the welfare of children and youth, social injustice, and civil rights; and the only avenue by which cultural enrichment is offered to very small underserved populations.

PROGRAMMING – THE WEST AT ITS BEST

The Western Area's progressive programs have employed innovative and aggressive approaches to programming. Community service programs orchestrated by chapters have been guided by two mandates: the National goals and local community needs. Chapters, wherever located, found ways to resist the negative effects of de facto and de jure segregation, addressing such causes as education, the welfare of children and youth, civil rights, social injustice, and cultural enrichment through their community service programs. They developed a wide array of activities that provided opportunity, exposure, and access to disadvantaged people of color, particularly African American children and youth.

As each state entered the organization, the early chapters developed programs that addressed not only the focus of the National leadership but the needs of their respective communities. In California, the Los Angeles Chapter, just two years after its chartering, unveiled the legendary "Cotillion," a fundraiser, which evolved from a minuet performed at a dinner dance, to a summer-long Leadership Institute with a mandatory 75 community service hours per debutante and participation in structured workshops on timely topics that included legal savvy, financial planning, essay writing, navigating social media, and non-traditional careers. The program served as a model for chapters throughout Linkdom.

Oakland Bay, Phoenix, Houston, Tucson, and Orange County Chapters adopted the Cotillion as their hybrid fundraiser/community service program. Angel City, Sacramento, and San Diego Chapters implemented a similar program, the "Achievers Program/Beautillion," a five-umbrella program designed to provide tools, mentors, and long-term relationships to prepare young African American men for college and life.

Other California chapters partnered with community organizations to address a critical need. The Beverly Hills West Chapter used designated space to design, equip, and purchase books to establish the Mandell Library at the Boys and Girls Club in Venice. When the library at Thurgood Marshall Elementary School was dismantled to accommodate an overflow of students, the Eden Rose Chapter partnered with the Oakland Unified School District to re-establish the library and maximize use of the facility by students, parents, and community patrons. Through its award-winning program, "Links to Student Success Saturday School," the Pasadena-Altadena Chapter provided enrichment and tutoring for grades K–4, while the Inglewood-Pacific Chapter enabled success links for middle school girls via "Up the Emerald Staircase."

In Arizona, the Phoenix Chapter has won recognition for its leadership in the Coalition of Blacks Against Breast Cancer (CBBC), an integrated program

Lorna C. Hankins, Western Area director

that provides information and support for Black breast cancer survivors and educates the community about breast cancer prevention. CBBC is a collaborative effort with the Mayo Clinic and community organizations. Sickle cell screening for elementary school students was the early program focus for the Tucson Chapter.

The state of Colorado has focused on its youth. The Denver Chapter recognizes young boys and girls in middle and high school during its annual "Tribute to Black Youth" luncheon, the culmination of a year-long program that provides learning experiences, civic engagement, the arts, and public service. The chapter also raised $50,000 for the establishment of the Blair-Caldwell African American Research Library, which serves as a repository for African-American historical documents and artifacts from the West, one of five such libraries in the United States. One feature of the library is The Links Community Room, a multi-purpose meeting space for community-led activities. Monthly, the library logs more than 16,000 visitors, and The Links Community Room hosts some 100 events.

The Greater Seattle (WA) Chapter established the Martin Luther King, Jr. Scholarship at the Shoreline Community College in response to racial confrontations and requests for job training and open housing to improve economic and social opportunities for Black residents. In partnership with the Seattle Public Schools and the African American Academy, the chapter also led the organization of Friends of the African American Academy (FOAAA), a clearing house for community-based groups whose members volunteered at the school.

The Portland (OR) Chapter has partnered with various agencies to deliver services. Volunteer power is available to help with an array of services that include clothes for the Rafael House for Women, domestic violence assistance, voter registration and education, and anti-sex trafficking training. The Health Literacy card, produced with the African American AIDS Awareness Action Alliance, offers vital information about their health status.

The first three Texas chapters were among the first to support the NAACP life membership campaign. The Houston and Fort Worth Chapters also addressed health disparities among persons of African descent and supported medical facilities that catered to indigents in Houston's Fifth Ward. Assistance to children dealing with orthopedic challenges was one of its first projects, and the chapter also produced the documentary film *The History of African American Life in Houston during the Early 1900's*, which focuses on the development of education and religious, social, and business institutions in the community.

The Dallas Chapter partnered with the American Cancer Society to provide breast cancer screening for African American and other women of color, along with cancer awareness sessions, where Black physicians (Connecting Links) handled the Q & A portion. A partnership with the Dallas School District also provided books for children in the elementary schools through the Reading is Fundamental (RIF) program. The chapter also exposed African American children and youth to the symphony,

gifted the Dallas Museum of Art with a Jean Lacey Painting, and provided continuous support through membership, donations, and docent service to the Dallas African American Museum.

The Fort Worth Chapter invested $45,000 to develop and equip the Stop Six Community Health Center Dental Clinic. The chapter was chosen to pilot Links to Success: Children Achieving Excellence, which became a National signature program. The chapter also supported the arts, particularly the Jubilee Theatre, one of the premier African American theaters in the Southwest, and the Dallas African American Museum.

Two award-winning Texas chapters were among the first to implement the STEM initiative: The "STEM-U-lation: Left Brain–Right Brain" program for high school students in the Houston area (Missouri City Chapter) and SoSMAART (Set on Science, Mathematics, Aviation, Art, Reading and Technology) for girls of color in grades 4–8 (Trinity Chapter).

The Las Vegas (NV) Chapter fostered student academic achievement and increased awareness of the African American heritage and culture through its award-winning Black History Jeopardy Bowl. Students researched African American history and other current events during an after-school program with the Las Vegas Public Schools. The final competition round, held annually during Black History Month, determines the winning team and school. The program was a featured workshop of the 38th Western Area Conference in San Diego.

The Hawaii Chapter sought early to highlight and enhance the positive influence of African American citizens and to encourage high academic standards in students of color. During the annual Achievers' Awards Banquet, African American leaders have been recognized and scholarships have been awarded to deserving high school graduates. The chapter has also implemented a summer program at Central Middle School, a low-performing school serving many immigrant students in downtown Honolulu.

The Albuquerque Chapter secured funds to clean, repair, and bronze *Tender Mercies*, a soapstone statue at the Carrie Tingley Children's Hospital that was sculpted by an African American artist. Children hospitalized at Tingley helped to restore the sculpture, which depicts a mother and son following an acute illness. The chapter has also offered personal growth and development counseling, support for creative skills enhancement, development of positive communication skills, and knowledge of community and national affairs for "Women in Prison."

The Anchorage (AK) Chapter used its signature Umbrella Program, "Promise Linked," to help create a safe community. Program features include education on the value of healthy food choices and daily exercise and anti-bullying sessions that explore cyber-bullying and the dangers associated with the inappropriate use of social networks. The Promise Linked mentoring sessions at Tyson Elementary, Mt. View Elementary, and New Hope Baptist Church deliver service to approximately 100 students.

The Dallas and Golden Triangle Chapters have collaborated with Reading Is Fundamental and local school districts to make reading a fun and beneficial part of everyday life. Corporations such as Chevron, Exxon, Kellogg Foundation, FedEx, and governmental entities that include the Texas Legislature have funded selected pilot programs such as Project LEAD: High Expectations, STEM, Children Achieving Excellence, Childhood Obesity, etc.

One unique hybrid venture was the Dallas Black Dance Theatre California Residency, a collaboration between Foothill College, the Dallas Black Dance Theatre, and the Peninsula Bay and San Jose Chapters. The program included a master class for 50 Foothill College and community dance students and a midday mini performance for 1,000 area middle school children. Its popularity spawned DBDT appearances for several chapters—Golden Triangle (TX), El Paso (TX), San Antonio (TX), Fresno (CA), and Monterey Bay (CA)—from 1989 to 2015. The group also performed for the 34th and 37th Area Conferences.

LEADING FROM THE WEST

Proficiency in program, governance, operations, and membership is a key definer of an Area director's leadership. One of the Area director's primary duties is to produce the Area Conference. In concert with established policy, the Western Area convened annually until 1975, when a biennial rotation with the National Assembly began.

The first conference was held in Los Angeles in 1954 during the administration of Loraine Rickmond. The 12th (1960) Assembly prescribed that Area Conferences be held at the site of the National Assembly two days before the National Meeting. This happened only three times in the Western Area. In 1964, the 11th Western Area Conference in Nassau, Bahamas, prior to the 14th Assembly; 1968, the 15th Western Conference in Berkeley, California, in advance of the 16th Assembly; and in 1974, the 21st Western Area Conference in Washington, DC, before the 19th Assembly.

Western Area directors have also initiated or enhanced programs, protocols, and policies that have produced lasting legacies.

Loraine Cady Rickmond
First Western Area Director (1954–1956)

Rickmond played a central role in the growth of the Western Area when she organized the Oakland Bay Chapter and served as its first president. She was appointed as the Western Area chairman in 1951, and subsequently elected as the first director in 1954. Using the theme "Communications, Horizons: The Role of Links In Social Progress," Rickmond created an atmosphere of open communication between and among chapters and members, moving the Western Area toward greater loyalty and true friendship. She emphasized the importance of open and frequent communication between and among members, chapters, and officers, and initiated protocols for Area communication. Rickmond also recruited women to charter chapters in the newly formed Western Area. Rickmond also provided a firm foundation for the continued growth of the newly established Western Area.

Ursula Murrell
Second Western Area Director (1956–1960)

Murrell was a charter member and one of 19 delegates of the Los Angeles (CA) Chapter, host chapter for the first Western Area Conference. Her theme, "Making Ready Social Patterns For Complete Integration; Educating for Democracy," reflected the National theme, "Educating for Democracy." She embraced the idea of raising awareness of the needs of under-privileged youth and providing opportunities for them through the implementation of the "Search for Talented Youth" initiative, and she encouraged chapters to obtain life memberships with the NAACP in support of the civil rights movement.

Esther Garrett Nelson
Third Western Area Director (1960–1964)

Nelson was inducted into the Denver (CO) Chapter. As the third Western Area director, she streamlined and standardized the business practices of the Area, thereby creating more opportunities for the mission of service to the community. She fostered chapter and Area accountability and efficiency through the development of written report forms, initiated the Area newsletter, developed and distributed pre-conference information (a first), and she strengthened the elections process through the appointment of an Elections Committee.

Christine Meade
Fourth Western Area Director (1964–1968)

Her theme, "Implementing the Challenge of The Great Society," signaled her belief in the importance of building strong programming through exemplary work. She restructured the approach for evaluating and recognizing outstanding achievement and max-imized the value of service by appointing an Awards Committee to select and recognize the best chapter programs. She worked with chapters to build strong fundraising activities to fund programs that could have dramatic effects on youth development.

At Area Conferences, she began the practice of honoring local outstanding citizens and presenting awards to local talent in fine arts, performing arts, and Services to Youth. She also cemented the practice of extending hospitality to Connecting Links at Area Conferences. Because of her desire for exemplary service programming, she worked with chapters to build strong fundraising activities to enable the creation of programs that could have dramatic effects on youth development.

Vera A. Codwell
Fifth Western Area Director (1968–1972)

Codwell was a charter member of the Houston (TX) Chapter, the Area's flagship chapter. Using her theme, "Outward Reach—Upward Thrust: Effective Involvement Now," she led the charge to educate, inform, and provide support for sickle cell anemia throughout the Area and to create national interest in the Sickle Cell Research Project. Codwell added the Sunday devotional service to the Area Conference agenda and established the Area Contingency Fund designed to ensure that Area Conferences were finan-cially independent; she also discouraged the use of funds from the annual Area allotment slated for operations.

Julia B. Smith
Sixth Western Area Director (1972–1977)

A member of the Oakland Bay Chapter, Julia B. Smith was elected in 1972. Her theme, "Reach Out … Break Through: Opportunity of Excellence," focused on enhancing programs by studying the needs of communities and networking with oth-ers with similar missions. She initiated two major actions that changed the landscape of communication and programming in the organization: arranging chapters in close proximity into clusters to improve communication and networking between and among members and chapters, and instituting the umbrella program concept to reduce the number of one-shot activities. Smith also developed Membership and Program Facet booklets, refined the Area newsletter, and archived the Area Conference minutes.

Recounting a memory of her time as Area director during "A Legacy Moment" at the 37th (2005) Western Area Conference in Beverly Hills,

California, Smith informed the more than 800 delegates gathered in the first plenary session that she had joined The Links, Incorporated in 1950 and attended all Area conferences held between 1954 and 2005.

Marion Schultz Sutherland
Seventh Western Area Director (1977–1881)

Sutherland, a member of the Greater Seattle Chapter, chose the theme "Forward in Friendship: Improving the Quality of Life by Linking Leadership and Service to Meet the Challenge of Community and National, to keep the Western Area Viable and Focused on Building on the Successes of the Past." She compiled three publications on operations and the history of the Western Area—a fundraising booklet, a cluster handbook, and a historical facts booklet.

Sutherland improved the distribution and frequency of the Area newsletter, emphasized the need for the presence of goals, objectives, and evaluation in program planning and implementation, promoted the utilization of the cluster concept, and initiated the formal recognition of 25-year membership status with the issuance of a certificate at Area Conferences. She is also credited with instituting the practice of Area directors attending Area Conferences. To ensure that her Area Conferences were financially independent, Sutherland developed partnerships with the Seattle Seahawks.

Bobbie Reynolds Whitehead
Eighth Western Area Director (1981–1983)

Whitehead used her theme, "Making History – Providing Hope," to raise the level of organizational awareness and strengthen the ability of chapters to bring out the best in every single member through the development of a better accountability system. To that end, she restructured the Area newsletter to emphasize organizational information that was distributed to chapters quarterly and produced and distributed at Western Connections Journal twice per year. Whitehead was recognized and applauded for her leadership and skills when faced with the task of

dividing the Harbor Area (CA) Chapter and subsequently creating the Palos Verdes (CA) Chapter.

Doris Jewel McCarroll-Pelkey
Ninth Western Area Director (1983–1987)

McCarroll-Pelkey's theme, "Growth with Knowledge," allowed her to emphasize the importance of linking the past and future together and ensuring that The Links remained a viable asset in improving the quality of life for people of color. She reactivated clusters throughout the Area, developed informative workshops for cluster meetings, and promoted networking and programming within clusters. She published the quarterly Western Area newsletter, *The Communicator*, with copies distributed to every member. She participated in the historic dedication of the National Headquarters. In "Legacy Moment" remarks at the 37th (2005) Western Area Conference in Beverly Hills, California, McCarroll-Pelkey, who had recently celebrated her 90th birthday, said she always planned a meeting/workshop for chapter presidents during an Area Conference or National Assembly because Links "do a better job when we share and gain knowledge about taking care of Links business."

Edwina Gray Higgins
Tenth Western Area Director (1987–1991)

Higgins chose as her theme, "Collectively and Proactively Facing the Challenge of the 21st Century." She showcased the effectiveness, progression, and benefits of chapters working together, resulting in better communication and a stronger bond of sisterhood, published twelve editions of the Area newsletter, *The Wavelength*, secured approval for a $1,000 community service award to be presented at each Area Conference to a worthy organization in the host city, and reactivated Texas and Southern California Clusters. Higgins was recognized for her leadership when the Western Area contributed the largest amount of money to the Sarah Scott Memorial Fund. In recognition of the role Higgins played in the success of the Alley Theatre, the theatre emblazoned a chair with "Houston (TX) Chapter, The Links, Incorporated."

Thelma J. Rice
Eleventh Western Area Director (1991–1995)

Rice was an organizer and charter member of the Inglewood Pacific (CA) Chapter and served as the first president. She used her theme, "Promoting, Principles, Purpose" to foster communication, promote cooperation, and encourage mutual respect and trust among members. She published the *Booklet of Western Area Chapters – Locations & Maps* in 1990 and the first *Western Area Handbook* that included listings of Area bylaws, chapter and Area officers, and program coordinators (1991).

Under Rice's administration, the name of the Area newsletter, *The Chain*, was made permanent through the adoption of a resolution authored by Delores Smith, Western Area journalist. Eight issues were distributed to individual members. The first $1,000 Community Service Award, approved at the 30th Area Conference, was presented. Rice also initiated the Emerging Professional, Golden West, Community Service, and Meritorious Service Awards, and she raised funds to underwrite the distribution of tennis shoes in Christmas in April for the Western Area.

Barbara Lord Watkins
Twelfth Western Area Director (1995–1999)

Watkins's theme, "Connected in Friendship, Called to Service, Committed to Purpose," was perfect for the importance she placed on communication, membership, programs, services, and governance, with an emphasis on working harder, smarter, and leading the way with purpose and resolution to uphold the traditions, values, and high ideals of service to the African American community. She piloted National's Program Report Form and on-line registration, developed templates to help chapter officers become more efficient in managing the chapter's business, and incorporated digital media (discs, PowerPoint presentations, etc.) to present information.

Watkins published three documents: *Conference Standing Committee Manual*, "Program Report Form," and the *Western Area Archives Brief, 1975–77*. She also continued the Meritorious Service Award, funded the Western Area "Education across the Miles" school in Africa, and designated the Dallas African American Museum as the repository for the Western Area Archives. Continuing to ensure the financial independence of the Area Conference, Watkins forged sponsorships and partnerships with corporations and businesses that included General Mills, Exxon, IBM, J. C. Penney Company, Inc., Shell Oil Company, AT&T, American Airlines, and Anheuser-Bush Companies.

Norma Jean Tucker
Thirteenth Western Area Director (1999–2003)

Tucker's theme, "An Era of Excellence," stressed excellence in programming, chapter operations, collaboration, and most of all, sisterly relations. She produced and distributed the "Three Minutes" bulletin, a communications tool designed to be read in three minutes, to chapter presidents and quarterly issues of the Area newsletter, *The Chain*, to every Western Area Link. Tucker participated in the chartering of the South Africa Chapter, promoted the purchase of 10 schools by Western Area chapters, and she witnessed the induction of honorary member Rosa Parks.

Jasmine Dartez, Oakland Bay Area Chapter president, remembered Tucker as a firm believer of mentoring who was always teaching. "She loved 'The Road Not Taken' (Frost) and quoted it often. She was a leader extraordinaire and followed protocol and demanded that of others."

Sandra Dorsey Malone
Fourteenth Western Area Director (2003–2007)

"One Goal, One Passion … Making a Difference" was Malone's theme. She promoted the mission of the Area and the National organization through quality programming and more efficient and effective chapter operations, while emphasizing the value of friendship. With the help of a 25-member Executive Committee representing each of the 10 states in the Area, Malone conducted workshops on Chapter-National alignment and accountability with elected officers of the 54 Western Area chapters. It was preceded by a two-day Area Officer Orientation, conducted by National President Gladys Gary Vaughn.

Chapter bylaws were completed with a custom template, later adopted as the National standard. New initiatives included the launch of the Leadership Summit, a two-day capacity-building event for chapter officers, and Project ALERT, a train-the-trainer Alzheimer's disease awareness program in partnership with the University of Texas Southwestern Medical School. The Western Area also approved two resolutions that were also endorsed at the National level: to bestow the Congressional Medal of Honor to Dorie Miller, US Navy, and to decry the negative portrayal of Black women by the hip-hop music industry.

Malone also established the Western Area HBCU Scholarship Endowment Fund and disbursed $123,620 to the eight HBCU institutions physically located in the Western Area, and she added the Legacy Moment to the Conference Agenda. To shore up Conference finances, Malone introduced three fundraisers designed specifically for Links—the Area Conference VIP Registration for the 37th and 38th Western Area Conferences, and the sale of branded prints and two books, *Linkspirations for the Soul* and *Healthier Food for the Soul*. Malone secured sponsorships and partnerships from corporations and agencies that included AXA Financial, General Motors, Gilbreath Communications, Inc., Busch, Inc., and the University of Texas Southwestern Medical School.

Barbra Ruffin-Boston
Fifteenth Western Area (2007–2011)

Ruffin-Boston's theme, "Remembering the Pledge … Delivering the Promise," represented the foundation of the journey in Links and served as a reminder of the need for a strategic focus and mindfulness toward excellence to "deliver the promise." Her goals focused on implementing Area operations and

program functions that aligned with the vision and programs of The Links, Incorporated. She continued to support Project ALERT (Alzheimer's Link to Education Research and Treatment), the Cardiovascular Partnership with the University of California, Davis, actions against negative images of African American women in the hip-hop industry, and historically Black colleges and universities in the Western Area. Ruffin-Boston also led a 25-member Western Area Executive Committee, which provided training on delivering and sustaining transformational programs.

While providing administrative oversight for 2,000 members in 55 chapters in the 10 states, Ruffin-Boston launched new initiatives that included the Western Area's science, technology, engineering, and mathematics (STEM) program, and "The Heart of the Matter," a central framework that focused on prevention and health risk factors for people of African descent. She also developed the "Obesity Service Delivery Model" that encouraged healthy eating, exercise, and weight loss, and she published *60 Years of the Western Area Chapters' Accomplishments, Commitments, Interests and Ideas*, an update of the original *Western Area Historical Facts, 1954–1995*. She also awarded $100,000 to HBCUs supported by the Western Area, and secured support for Area Conferences via special fundraising efforts, vendors, sponsors, and partners that included BP America, ExxonMobil, Shell Oil, Continental Airlines, and American Airlines International.

Constance Fitzpatrick Smith
Sixteenth Western Area Director (2011–2015)

Smith believed that her theme, "Seize the Moment……. Strengthen the chain!" should remind every Link that anytime is the right time to incorporate the goal of promoting and delivering "Friendship and Service." She also stressed Alignment, Balance, and Civility.

- Alignment – Understanding the National Documents increases the members' knowledge of the culture and expectations of the organization.

- Balance – Active erudite women of Linkdom must be ever cognizant of the necessity to balance the challenges of family, career, and civic engagement.
- Civility – Being Sisterly is paramount in all actions.

Smith communicated regularly with the membership via the *Western Area Times*, a monthly newsletter, and telephone conferences; and she scheduled conference workshops to help chapters embrace new initiatives such as STEAM, Human Trafficking, Mental Health, and HIV/AIDS. She launched the Area Director's Award, honoring Carlotta LaNier, Denver (CO) Chapter, one of the brave Little Rock Nine; and she witnessed the induction of Honorary Members Ellen Johnson Sirleaf, president of Liberia, and Dr. Condoleezza Rice, former secretary of state. Smith contributed $95,805 to the HBCU Scholarship Endowment initiative and awarded $137,730 for program implementation across the Western Area.

Roxann Thomas Chargois
Seventeenth Western Area Director (2015–2019)

Under the theme **"A Mind for Business and a Heart for Service,"** Chargois ensured that her Executive Committee included at least one representative from each of the 10 states, from chapters large and small. She implemented a comprehensive and aggressive training schedule for all chapter officers and committee chairs through the concept of "Learners Becoming Leaders," increasing the administrative skill level within chapters through targeted training to increase the efficiency of chapter operations. Existing programming was enhanced and new initiatives were developed to address disparities and social injustice, including: a groundbreaking mental health retreat in the wake of community tragedies and natural disasters in the Western Area; HIV; a Black Lives Matter resolution endorsed by all Western Area chapters; and programs to bridge the STEM gap between Black children and other racial/ethnic groups.

Chargois's 2017 and 2018 mission trips to Haiti—"2,000 Boots on the Ground"—gave Western Area members the opportunity to go on a mission trip and to help finance much-needed water wells. A second new initiative, the "59 for the Future," a visionary, innovative concept in Links programming, equipped academically advanced high school girls to address issues relevant to the local and global communities. Students participated in research, strategic thinking, writing, and oral exercises. Her support of the Western Area HBCU Scholarship Endowment included reconstituting the committee and adding a new HBCU school, Charles Drew University, and contributing to the Area's endowment fund, which now totals more than $575,000.

Lorna C. Hankins
Eighteenth Western Area Director (2019–)

Recently elected, Lorna Hankins, Gulf Coast Apollo (TX) Chapter, has received the charge to exemplify leadership that will further enhance the noble imprints left by the 17 Area directors who preceded her. Synthesis, progressive programs, and membership cultivation have made the last Area colonized indispensable to Linkdom.

~ *Sandra Dorsey Malone*

WESTERN AREA DIRECTORS

Area	Director	Chapter	Tenure Dates
#1	Loraine Rickmond	Oakland Bay Area (CA)	1954–1956
#2	Ursula Murrell	Los Angeles (CA)	1956_1960
#3	Esther Garrett Nelson	Denver (CO)	1960–1964
#4	Christine Meade	Seattle (WA)	1964–1968
#5	Vera A. Codwell	Houston (TX)	1968–1972
#6	Julia B. Smith	Oakland (CA)	1972–1977
#7	Marion S. Sutherland	Seattle (WA)	1977–1981
#8	Bobbie Whitehead	Seattle (WA)	1981–1983
#9	Doris Jewell Mc Carroll	Pasadena-Altadena (CA)	1983–1987
#10	Edwina G. Higgins	Houston (TX)	1987–1991
#11	Thelma J. Rice	Inglewood-Pacific (CA)	1991–1995
#12	Barbara Lord Watkins	Dallas (TX)	1995–1999
#13	Norma Jean Tucker	Alameda Contra Costa (CA)	1999–2003
#14	Sandra Dorsey Malone	Dallas (TX)	2003–2007
#15	Barbra Ruffin-Boston	San Francisco (CA)	2007–2011
#16	Constance Fitzpatrick Smith	Stockton (CA)	2011–2015
#17	Roxann Thomas Chargois	Missouri City (TX)	2015–2019
#18	Lorna C. Hankins	Gulf Coast Apollo (TX)	2019–

Alameda Contra Costa (CA)	Union City	CA
Albuquerque (NM)	Rio Rancho	NM
Anchorage (AK)	Anchorage	AK
Angel City (CA)	Inglewood	CA
Austin (TX)	Austin	TX
Bakersfield (CA)	Bakersfield	CA
Beverly Hills West (CA)	Los Angeles	CA
Channel Islands (CA)	Westlake Village	CA
Claremont Area (CA)	Corona	CA
Colorado Springs (CO)	Colorado Springs	CO
Dallas (TX)	Lancaster	TX
Denver (CO)	Denver	CO
East Texas (TX)	Tyler	TX
Eden Rose (CA)	Union City	CA
El Paso (TX)	Canutillo	TX
Fort Bend County (TX)	Sugar Land	TX
Fort Worth (TX)	Southlake	TX
Fresno (CA)	Clovis	CA
Golden Triangle (TX)	Port Arthur	TX
Greater Denton County (TX)	Irving	TX
Greater Pearland Area (TX)	Houston	TX
Greater Seattle (WA)	Seattle	WA
Gulf Coast Apollo (TX)	Seabrook	TX
Harbor Area (CA)	Long Beach	CA
Hawaii (HI)	Mililani	HI
Houston (TX)	Houston	TX
Inglewood-Pacific (CA)	Los Angeles	CA
Katy-Richmond Area (TX)	Richmond	TX
Las Vegas (NV)	Las Vegas	NV
Lone Star (TX)	Round Rock	TX
Los Angeles (CA)	Los Angeles	CA
Mid-Cities (TX)	Coppell	TX
Missouri City (TX)	Katy	TX
Monterey Bay (CA)	Salinas	CA
Oakland Bay Area (CA)	Danville	CA
Orange County (CA)	Lakewood	CA
Palos Verdes (CA)	Harbor City	CA
Pasadena-Altadena (CA)	Tujunga	CA
Peninsula Bay (CA)	South San Francisco	CA
Phoenix (AZ)	Mesa	AZ
Plano North Metroplex (TX)	Plano	TX
Port City (TX)	Houston	TX

Portland (OR)	Portland	OR
Sacramento (CA)	Sacramento	CA
San Antonio (TX)	San Antonio	TX
San Bernardino Valley (CA)	San Bernardino	CA
San Diego (CA)	La Mesa	CA
San Fernando Valley (CA)	Northridge	CA
San Francisco (CA)	Oakland	CA
San Jose (CA)	San Jose	CA
Solano County (CA)	Vallejo	CA
Spokane (WA)	Spokane Valley	WA
Stockton (CA)	Stockton	CA
Tacoma (WA)	Tacoma	WA
Texas Spring Cypress (TX)	Houston	TX
Town Lake (TX)	Austin	TX
Tri-Cities (WA)	Pasco	WA
Trinity (TX)	Dallas	TX
Tucson (AZ)	Tucson	AZ
Waco Central Texas (TX)	McGregor	TX

Listing provided by Headquarters.

Western Area Director Lorna Hankins (foreground) and other officers were elected at the 2019 Western Area Conference in June.

PART VI

Interconnectivity

Infrastructure

We will find a building, which reflects The Links' image in style and taste, which is within our means, and which will be large enough to serve our needs for the next 20 years.

~ 8TH NATIONAL PRESIDENT DOLLY DESSELLE ADAMS,
ADDRESSING THE 24TH (1984) ASSEMBLY

Links National Headquarters, 1200 Massachusetts Avenue, Washington (DC)

CHAPTER 13
THE NATIONAL
Headquarters

Where was I going to come up with that kind of money in two weeks?

~ 14TH NATIONAL PRESIDENT GWENDOLYN BYRD LEE

November 16, 1985: National President Dolly Desselle Adams cuts the ribbon on the newly purchased and renovated National Headquarters.

*I*n the spring of 2007, 14th National President Gwendolyn Lee was attending the Central Area Conference when she received an unexpected call from Headquarters. "The gentleman next door needed to speak with me," Lee said. Her first reaction was, "Who is this guy?" "It's about what?" Once the staff provided additional details, Lee returned the call, and she received an offer she didn't want to refuse.

The gentleman next door had called to honor a commitment he had made to 8th National President Dolly Desselle Adams 23 years earlier when The Links bought 1200 Massachusetts Avenue. He had decided to sell 1204 Massachusetts Avenue, the adjacent building; and as promised, he was giving The Links the right of first refusal.

How providential, Lee thought. Space, again, had become a concern; her Building and Properties Committee was exploring options to accommodate the concomitant service needs and increased staff wrought by a membership that had more than doubled. There was just one caveat. Lee had only two weeks to close the deal; she needed a deposit.

"Where was I going to come up with that kind of money in two weeks?" True to her theme, she seized the opportunity: "Members in this organization are phenomenal, phenomenal," she said. "I picked up the phone, I emailed, and I put it out there; and they responded," Lee said.

But that was just the beginning. To proceed, she needed the approval of the Assembly, and she needed "more money!" She launched a full-fledged information campaign to get members to back a plan that would transform 1200 Massachusetts into a $20 million property. Lee and her team continued the crusade with an open session at the 36th (2008) Assembly, where they presented the master plan, complete with architectural schematics and additional details from Queen Gladden, Seattle (WA) Chapter, chair of the Building and Properties Committee.

Lee then had an open mic, letting members ask anything they wanted to know about buying 1204 Massachusetts Avenue and combining it with The Links headquarters at 1200 Massachusetts Avenue. "I told my team we weren't going anywhere until everybody who wanted to speak had talked," Lee said. Her patience was rewarded when the Assembly overwhelmingly ratified the purchase of 1204 Massachusetts Avenue, and approved a funding package—including a $600 per-member assessment—for the renovation, restoration, and renewal effort.

Initially, the construction and renovation moved right along, but some things like those "dastardly permits" got in the way. "I've never had anything this horrific or horrendous in my life," Lee said.

> *The building is located in the Shaw Historic District, so some of the original things had to remain … Then we had to do reconstruction. Unfortunately, that meant in many ways, we had to demolish part of the first building … to make the two buildings equal in size. So we had to put stairs to lead up to the next area … And, then you go down town and you have to get the permits in Washington, DC.*

Lee had been trying to secure permits forever before a power Link asked, "What permits do you need?" Then, it was "boom, boom, boom; no problem," Lee said.

The pace was also slowed by Lee's desire to secure LEED certification for the building.

> *I don't know if everybody knows this, but we have gold designation, and we are very proud of that. That's what took up a lot of time. But I said, "If we're going to do this, let's do it right."… We have a rooftop and space for a rooftop garden. We also have a little courtyard … because we wanted to have some open space.*

Obtained under the US Green Building Council's program for Leadership in Energy and Environmental Design (LEED), the gold certification was another first for Links. The Links became the first African American organization to commission a LEED Gold-certified headquarters building, meaning architects R. McGhee & Associates had to integrate 1200 and 1204, while retaining historic exterior and interior elements from two different eras and modernizing systems to be environmentally green.

The work was intricate. "Some of the green design elements included light fixtures equipped with LED and fluorescent lighting, along with a high efficiency mechanical system to reduce electrical demand; roofing material with high reflective qualities to reduce heat and a green-planted areas to supplement thermal insulation while reducing storm water runoff." The Links were also required to use recycled products or those from renewable sources such as steel beams with high recycled content and bamboo flooring.

When Lee's tenure in office ended in 2010, the project was well underway, but lots of work remained. The staff relocated to temporary quarters one year earlier so that the demolition could begin, and it would be April of 2011 before the building was cleared for occupancy. However, 15th National President Margot James Copeland, Lee's successor, was thrilled "to have the opportunity to put my thumbprint on the property, too."

Explaining the load handled by her team, Copeland said:

> *Although much of the concept and design work had been done for the expansion, the construction had to be completed; so, my administration just picked up, almost picked up the hammer and the nails and the tools, and we completed it.*

Since the construction had extended into 2011, Copeland decided to schedule the ribbon cutting in concert with the 65th anniversary celebration of The Links' founding. The Big Reveal for the 9,356-square-foot, $6.5 million wonder on November 10 kicked off three days of festivities.

More than 500 keepsake bookmarks bore the imprint "We celebrate this Open House to honor our history …"

On hand to help Copeland greet the more than 500 Links, Connecting Links, Heir-O-Links, and friends were two key history makers, Lee and Adams. A quarter of a century had passed since Adams presided over the first dedication for 1200 Massachusetts Avenue NW, which she purchased in 1984, and transformed into a headquarters of the first order.

"We bought the house, paid for it, had it renovated and redone, moved in, and furnished it," she said. The significance of the purchase loomed larger as the years went by. Adams ranked the acquisition as one of the two greatest accomplishments during her tenure, but the building got the nod as the most unforgettable. "Dedicating the building was my most memorable moment," she said.

Establishing The Links' first permanent headquarters was not part of Adams's platform when she ran for election at the 23rd (1982) Assembly; it was a directive. "Julia Purnell's Assembly instructed that the new person coming in buy a house with all deliberate speed," which was fine with Adams. But, the "enormous mandate" had not come with capital. "They left that to me, too." Adams said. At the next biennial meeting, the 24th (1984) Assembly endorsed Adams's funding proposal to cover the purchase and establish a Capital Improvement Fund, a $100 per-member assessment, a set-aside of $100,000 from the unrestricted fund balance, as of April 30, 1984, and $50,000 per year for a three-year period beginning FY 1984–1985.

To preclude assumptions that the purchase would occur overnight, Adams made it clear that a site was still pending. Then, she promised, "We will find a building which reflects The Links' image in style and taste, which is within our means, and which will be large enough to serve our needs for the next 20 years." In less than three months, Adams had a contender.

On August 27, 1984, the Executive Council met in open session to view a 5,552-square-foot, three-story stately structure with a basement at 1200 Massachusetts Avenue NW. Armed with the Council's affirmative vote, Adams set the closing date for August 30, 1984. "So, I did not get it done probably until about 1985; it was a process," Adams said.

At the core of her success were her approach and support staff. Adams split responsibilities among three subcommittees, with Lynnette Taylor, Juanita Shell, and Dorothy Orr chairing site selection, special individual donors, and corporate and foundation relations, respectively; and she moved Mary Douglass from associate director into the director position. "I don't know all the stuff that girl did," Adams said. Former National Presidents Purnell and Ellison and "my vice president Regina Frazier" offered their assistance and counsel.

In keeping with The Links' policy of supporting African American businesses, Adams employed a number of Black professionals, including Links. Laura Brown, Arlington (VA) Chapter, was the realtor, and Adams used a black insurance broker and title agency. However, "had it not been for a whole bunch of Connecting Links," the process would have been even more difficult and more costly, Adams said.

The Connecting Links helped to refurbish the building, and Adams got pro bono services from Howard Law School faculty like Dean Wiley Branton. "We paid no lawyers," Adams said. Even "Vernon Jordan was my lawyer for free. I had friends like that, and I guess I didn't have sense enough to ask them if I owed them, and they never billed me," she chuckled.

Adams also got professional advice and assistance from "John Chase, who I had known when we lived in Houston, Texas, and John Adams, my husband." Chase, the first African American licensed to practice architecture in the state of Texas, was her unpaid project consultant. "I called John; I said, John, I don't know anything about what I'm doing; and he said, okay." He followed up by getting a Black architect he knew to coordinate "the inspection, determine what needed to be done, and do the renovations." But, Adams added, "We paid him, and we paid for the renovations."

Bishop John Hurst Adams really saved the day, providing the $10,000 Adams needed to reach her target. "At the very last minute when we realized we were $10,000 short, I went in crying, and he loaned it to us; but he never got paid back because I was not authorized to get the loan in the first place, and there was no place to go to get his investment back. Those were the kinds of people who really helped me through it," Adams said.

The dedication on November 16, 1985, ended a chapter in the enduring and rich legend of the National Headquarters, but other National Presidents had authored the prologue, penning the first entry in 1951. "The only recommendation I would like to make is that the next president be assigned a part-time paid secretary," 1st National President Sarah Strickland Scott told the 3rd Assembly in a lamentation on the quandary of trying to respond to the needs of an infant organization with no staff support.

"It was absolutely physically impossible for me to attend promptly to the mass of correspondence that flooded me as the year went on, and we grew like a snowball," Scott said. Handling a few chapters had been challenging enough, but the number of chapters had almost tripled, Scott lamented:

> When it was difficult to manage the correspondence of 18 chapters, you can well imagine what the personal correspondence of 42 chapters plus 16 members of the Executive Council involved. There has never been a week when there has been less than twenty-five letters to be personally answered. These were aside from the routine correspondence that our National Secretary handled, which likewise has been very busy.

While Scott put a National Headquarters on the agenda, 13 years passed before any kind of definitive action was taken. At the 14th (1964) Assembly, delegates backed 4th National President Vivian Beamon's push for administrative support and centralization of Links records. Beamon named a Centralization Committee to design and implement the process. The rudimentary challenge for Pauline Weeden, chair, was to find a "staff assistant who had an administrative background and was also skilled in the day-to-day operations of business machines," and she launched the search August 7, 1964, with an advertisement:

> The position holds a real challenge to a member who is interested in bringing about the greatest efficiency and best possible communication among our Link Chapters. A minimum of ten hours per week will be required, with a schedule of specific times to be worked out to the convenience of the employee and the committee chairman. Salary for the beginning two-year period has been budgeted at $100 per month plus taxes. Equipment such as a typewriter, files, duplicating machine, etc., will be purchased by the committee if needed.

Weeden found a fit in Susie Robinson Verdell, a stenographic supervisor at Virginia State University in Petersburg. In a *Link to Link* column (May 1966), Verdell updated the membership on the progress she had made during the first year and expressed delight that she had been selected to begin the transition to a professional staff, a milestone in Linkdom. "Your new executive secretary wishes to acknowledge with great humility the honor of being named your first Executive Secretary."

In 1968, Mildred Henderson of Wilberforce, Ohio, succeeded Verdell. Both Henderson and Verdell, however, were part-time employees. While their assistance provided some amelioration, it was limited. Operations were not centralized, and execution was dependent on third parties. As she prepared to leave office following her eight-year reign, Beamon voiced concern about the precarious nature of the administrative support in her address to the 17th (1970) Assembly:

> At present our headquarters reside in the residence of the president. The administrative assistant to the president has been elsewhere, principally on college campuses where materials are at a low cost and equipment available without cost to the organization. The quality of performance of each officer is to a large extent due to the use of a paid office not under Links employment or the skills and expertise of friends of the office holder used as gratis.

With that prelude, Beamon called upon the Assembly to revisit the issue. "I, therefore, recommend that the Executive Council be empowered to study the problem," she said. The Assembly endorsed the recommendation, and upon assuming office at the close of the 17th (1970) Assembly, 5th National President Helen

Gray Edmonds immediately began to explore options with her Executive Council. The Council approved an upgrade from an administrative assistant to a full-time secretary, and Edmonds was authorized to secure office space in her hometown. Such would have alleviated two of the bottlenecks of the previous arrangement.

Nevertheless, Edmonds believed that the plan, as structured, would place an excessive financial burden on the organization. The practice of staffing an office in the hometown of each president particularly alarmed her. Therefore, she chose not to activate the services, but she left no doubt that action on a headquarters and staff was still sorely needed. Addressing the 18th (1972) delegation, Edmonds exclaimed:

> *May I remind you that though I use the term*
> National Office, *we have no National Office.*
> *We have no secretary. We have not one file, nor*
> *one typewriter. Link Rebecca Edmonds serves as*
> *administrative assistant out of the goodness of her*
> *heart and receives no salary.*

Adding fodder to her argument, Edmonds pointed to two "clear and dangerous" repercussions. The absence of a national headquarters had precluded the issuance of a mailing permit and delayed the application for tax-exempt status. In response to the declarations, the Executive Council in March 1973 approved the creation of a Centralization Committee to conduct a cost analysis for establishing and staffing a central office. Rather than appoint a new group, however, Edmonds assigned the tasks to her National Advisory Committee under the leadership of Ursula Murrell of the Los Angeles (CA) Chapter.

At the 19th (1974) Assembly, Murrell presented the definitive proposal crafted by the committee. The Assembly not only endorsed the plan, but it also authorized Murrell to sign a two-year lease on "office space available in a most desirable area, 16th and P Streets, NW, Washington, DC;" a 250-square-foot rental for $224.16. The Links would finally have an address at 1424 16th Street NW. Hailing the accomplishment, Edmonds noted the next administration needed only "to move in."

The task of transforming the space into central operations fell to 6th National President Pauline Allen Ellison. With a budget of $1.50 per capita from the dues of each of the 3,164 members and a special allowance of $4,000 for furniture and file cabinets, Ellison was charged to use the two-year trial period to staff, equip, and furnish the office for the multitude of functions delineated by the National Advisory Committee.

The order was a tall one, as outlined by Murrell in her report to the 20th (1976) Assembly. The committee envisioned that the office would:

- Serve as a specific location where all functions of the organization could be centralized and administered.
- Add strength, increase efficiency and solidify the organization's image as a national organization.
- Be a public relations facility.
- Serve all National officers and committees.
- Serve as a storage area for all past records from offices.
- Be a clearinghouse and distribution center for all National materials, to be supplied to other agencies, organizations, or groups.
- House copies of the works of Links members in literature, art, etc.
- Provide space for office personnel.
- Conduct all facets of business relating to the National Program of Links, Incorporated.
- Hold any meeting, council or committee, that the president may deem necessary.
- Reproduce National Assembly minutes.
- Enable flow of all standard forms.

The 20th (1976) Assembly's decision to continue the operation signaled that Ellison had made progress toward achieving the objectives. She credited her choice of Catherine Dickerson Tate, a retired budget analyst from Arlington, Virginia, as the first director. Noting that Tate was salaried for only four hours a day, but worked in excess of 50, for the accomplishments. "She performed Herculean tasks," Ellison said.

Reporting to the 21st Assembly two years later, Ellison reviewed the directive she had received from the 19th (1974) Assembly: "My challenge was to establish, equip, maintain and staff the National Headquarters and to affect the transition and centralization of records." Ellison, Tate, and a part-time secretary were assisted by local Links who volunteered their services. Additionally, chapters and individual Links donated supplies, books, and more.

Enumerating some of the problems, Ellison said, "Quite candidly, it appeared that we would remove one stumbling block only to find another blocking our path." Tate resigned in 1976 for personal reasons, but with the aid of interim director Anne Cooke Reid and a Transition and Personnel Committee under the leadership of Dorothy Harrison, Ellison had persevered.

Declaring victory, she declared:

> Your president is pleased to report that 1978 represents a milestone and a turning point for The Links, Inc. We have removed records from parlors, dressing rooms and bedrooms into a true business office—from an operation, which was disparate to one, which is centrifugal. National Headquarters is more than just an address at 1424 16th Street, NW, Washington, DC. It now represents the steps from amateurism to professionalism—a whole new plateau in organizational management.

Endorsing the strides, the National Advisory Committee called for kudos to Ellison's leadership and the "great personal expense" she incurred to establish the office. On the recommendation of Chair Ruth McCants, the Assembly also renewed the lease—which at $440 had almost doubled—for a maximum of three years; and they added provisions to improve the appearance and working efficiency of the office with paint, carpet, and moveable partitions at a total cost not to exceed $750. The Assembly further prescribed that a storage facility be utilized for records over five years old.

Recommendations by the Transition and Personnel Committee complemented the National Advisory Committee's report. Dorothy Harrison, chair, presented the name of Nan Delany Johnson, a former Detroit Public School administrator and charter member and organizer for the Rocky Mount-Tarboro (NC)

Chapter, to fill the director slot. The Assembly endorsed Johnson's hiring, approved a bookkeeper/secretary and a part-time clerk typist, and authorized contractual services for financial management.

Even more changes in operations lay ahead. Julia Brogdon Purnell, elected as the 7th National President, heeded her predecessor's assessment that both larger quarters and more staff were needed to meet the needs of The Links' increasing membership. Rather than renew the lease that was ending August 31, 1978, Purnell and Johnson began a search for a more appropriate space. They found a suite that met their needs just four blocks from the White House; 1522 K Street NW became the new address for The Links, Incorporated.

Two years later, Purnell leased additional space for activity tied to the 22nd Assembly. Coupled with increasing rental costs, and membership growth that would require even more space, she questioned the value of continuing to lease space; so, she appointed a Housing

July 2008: National President Gwendolyn Lee at 36th (2008) Assembly, where she secured a package to fund the purchase of 1204 Massachusetts Avenue and begin the construction and renovation required to merge 1200 and 1204.

National President Margot James Copeland cutting the ribbon on the newly renovated National Headquarters.

Committee (Zola Boone, chair) to determine whether it was time for The Links to purchase a place of its own.

The committee compiled a questionnaire to determine whether chapters would support a purchase. The survey included data for previous rental periods, as well as projections for the future. Reporting to the 23rd (1982) Assembly, Housing Chair Zola Boone and Finance Committee Chair Leatrice Pride reported members' willingness to back a purchase. As a result, the Assembly directed the incoming administration to proceed "with all deliberate speed" in identifying, financing, and purchasing a building. The directive was honored with the purchase of 1200 Massachusetts Avenue in 1984 and valued at $1.2 million when renovations were completed in 1985. The 2007 acquisition, unification, and renovation of 1204 Massachusetts transformed the stately building into a $6.2 million wonder.

With the primary focus on the physical structure, the *raison d'etre* for the National Headquarters took a back seat. From the outset, the headquarters' purpose was interconnectivity—a central hub, staffed by professionals who as the membership grew, its operations and programs became more complex. Staffing needs, once satisfied with basic administrative skills, required something more. National President after National President sought a staff executive who could inject exemplary management principles and practices into operations and create a culture where excellence was the staff's signature.

Solutions have focused on skills, the nature of the employment, and the employee's ability to perform. Concerned about the staff's unfamiliarity with contemporary processes and technology, 11th National President Patricia Russell-McCloud employed changes "to bring Headquarters operations into the 21st century." 13th National President Gladys Gary Vaughn believed "a viable executive directorship position (permanency as opposed to acting and interim)" would have improved operations during her tenure; and 16th National President Glenda Newell-Harris "hired director-level leadership in communications, programming, membership, technology and fund development" who could deliver exceptional service.

Reiterating that "the National Headquarters exists to support us, chapter concerns, Area issues, and individual Links matters," 17th National President Kimberly Jeffries Leonard made "stabilizing the National Headquarters" to a priority for her administration. As she searched for a permanent director, Leonard brought in a "seasoned" interim director to "streamline workloads for increased effectiveness that will ensure that our membership has the precise tools needed to be productive."

Leonard's goal is consistent with Adams's message in the 1986 celebration program, which aptly summarized the role of The Links' National Headquarters: "To facilitate the coordination and support essential for strengthening programs … [so that this] house will serve as a national Community Center from which people, projects, and programs are developed and empowered."

~ *Earnestine Green McNealey, PhD*

Former National Presidents join National President Kimberly Leonard in a ceremony for the newly restored oil paintings of Co-Founders Margaret R. Hawkins (right) and Sarah S. Scott (left). The portraits grace the entrance of the National Headquarters.

NATIONAL HEADQUARTERS ADMINISTRATORS	TITLE	TENURE	CHAPTER
Susie Robinson Verdell	Executive Secretary	1966–1968	Petersburg (VA)
Mildred Henderson	Administrative Assistant to the National President	1968–1970	Wilberforce (OH)
Rebecca Edmonds *(No compensation)*	Administrative Assistant to the National President & Assembly Coordinator	1970–1974	Durham (NC)
Catherine Dickerson Tate *(First to serve from Headquarters site)*	Director	1974–1976	Arlington (VA)
Anne Reid Cooke	Interim Director	1977–1978	Washington (DC)
Nan Delaney Johnson	Director	1978–1982	Annapolis (MD)
Mary P. Douglass	Chief Administrative Officer	1982–1996	Prince George's County (MD)
Bonnie Mann	Executive Director	1997–1998	Non-Link
Ethel C. S. Bothuel	Executive Director	1998–2000	Non-Link
Eleanor M. Harris, EdD	Interim Executive Director	2000–2002	Annapolis (MD)
Loretha F. Davis	Interim Executive Director	2002–2004	
Mary E. Clark	Acting Executive Director	2004–2005	Reston (VA)
Janet Baker Walker, JD	Executive Director	2005–2007	Capital City (DC)
Kristie Patton Foster	Executive Director Chief Administrative Officer of the Links, Inc. and the Links Foundation, Inc.	2007–2010	Affiliate Member*
Eris Sims	Executive Director	2010–2016	Affiliate Member*
Madeline Y. Lawson	Interim Executive Director Executive Director	2016–2018	Capital City (DC)
Gwendolyn E. Boyd, DMin	Interim Executive Director	2018–2019	Capital City (DC)
Kristie Patton Foster	Executive Director	2019–	Affiliate Member*

Kristie Foster has returned as executive director of The Links and The Links Foundation. Foster assumed command of the office as chief administrative officer; the position was later changed to executive director.

Consistent with policy that permanent chief staff executives become affiliates during their tenure.

Listing compiled from Assembly minutes, Links website www.linksinc.org

NATIONAL HEADQUARTERS TIMELINE

1964 The 14th Assembly approves President Vivian Beamon's recommendation for administrative support.

Beamon appoints Centralization Committee (Pauline Weeden, chair) to design and implement the process.

1965 Susie Robinson Verdell, Petersburg (VA) Chapter, becomes first "executive secretary."

1968 Mildred Henderson, Wilberforce (OH) Chapter, succeeds Robinson as executive secretary.

1970 President Vivian Beamon sounds alarm on using recruits "not under Links employment," described as friends of the office holder or office staff principally on college campuses.

Beamon recommends that the "Executive Council be empowered to study the problem."
The 17th Assembly approves the request.

1972 President Helen Gray Edmonds advises the 18th Assembly that the plan presented by the Executive Council would have placed an excessive financial burden on the organization; so, she rejected it.

Edmonds had utilized unpaid services of her daughter (Link Rebecca Edmonds); a central office with professional staff was still needed.

1973 The Executive Council approves the creation of a Centralization Committee to conduct a cost analysis for establishing and staffing a central office.

Edmonds assigns task to her National Advisory Committee (NAC) under the leadership of Ursula Murrell, Los Angeles (CA) Chapter.

1974 The 19th Assembly endorses the Advisory Committee's plan and authorizes Murrell to sign a two-year lease for the property, located at 16th and P Streets NW, Washington, DC.

President Edmonds notes, "The next administration only needs to move in."

Incoming President Pauline Ellison is directed to use the two-year trial period to staff, equip, and furnish the office.

The Executive Council approves Ellison's recommendation to employ Catherine Dickerson Tate as the first "director."

1976 President Ellison appoints Committee on Transition and Personnel under the leadership of Dorothy Harrison.

Anne Cooke Reid becomes interim director.

The 20th Assembly approves the National Advisory Committee's recommendation to continue the lease.

1978 President Ellison calls 1978 a "milestone and turning point" for Links, "a whole new plateau in organizational management."

The Assembly endorses hiring Nan Delany Johnson as director; approves a bookkeeper/secretary and a part-time clerk typist; and authorizes contractual services for financial management.

7th National (and newly elected) President Julia Brogdon Purnell and Johnson seek larger quarters, eventually leasing 1522 K Street NW.

	The 23rd Assembly approves recommendation to purchase and staff a headquarters "with all deliberate speed."
1980	Forced to acquire additional space for activity tied to the tied to the 22nd Assembly, increasing rental costs, and membership growth that would require even more space, President Julia Purnell appoints a Housing Committee (Zola Boone, chair) to determine whether the organization should continue to lease space or purchase a place of its own.
	Boone sends membership a survey (includes data for previous rental periods, as well as projections for the future).
1982	Purnell's administration recommends that The Links purchase a place of its own with all deliberate speed.
	The Assembly directs incoming National President Dolly Desselle Adams to proceed "with all deliberate speed" in identifying, financing, and purchasing a building.
	President Adams appoints three sub-committees and moves Mary Douglass from the associate director position to the director position.
1984	The 24th Assembly approves a $100 one-time assessment to "ensure the upkeep of the building without the necessity of further taxation."
	President Adams tells the 24th Assembly, "We will find a building which reflects The Links' image in style and taste, which is within our means, and which will be large enough to serve our needs for the next 20 years."
	The Executive Council endorses the committee's choice, a 5,552-square-foot, three-story stately structure with a basement at 1200 Massachusetts Avenue, NW.
1985	Adams presides over the dedication of the first permanent Headquarters, a $1 million stately edifice, on November 16.
2007	14th National President Gwendolyn B. Lee is notified that the building next to Headquarters will be sold; she is offered the property, consistent with a gentleman's agreement extended when The Links purchased 12000 Massachusetts NW.
	Lee generates funds for a down payment and accepts the offer.
2008	The 31st Assembly approves Lee's Building Committee's expansion and renovation proposal, which includes a $600 per member assessment.
4/2009–8/2011	Headquarters moves to temporary location, sharing quarters with the Greater Washington (DC) Urban League.
11/11/2011	Copeland holds Ribbon Cutting and Open House as part of Links 65th anniversary celebration.
2/2/2019	Restored portraits of Co-Founders dedicated.

PART VII

Transformative
Programs

Strong Communities

I SHALL EARNESTLY ENDEAVOR TO DO MY SHARE TOWARD SERVING MY COMMUNITY ... TO THE BEST OF MY ABILITY.

Your fulfillment of the dream that Margaret Rosell Hawkins and I cherished in 1946 has more than satisfied our highest expectations. Thousands have found a better life because of our collective efforts.

~ Sarah Strickland Scott
First National President

This aim was, and is, three-fold: to do some good to help less fortunate citizens, to raise the cultural level of our race, and to enjoy the social company of our friends.

~ Margaret Josephine Rosell Hawkins
Second National President

Our past has given us great cause for pride, but this must not make us unmindful of the challenges of the '60s. Let us continue to move ahead with wisdom and vigor and accept the opportunity for service that is uniquely ours.

~ Pauline Weeden (Maloney)
Third National President

We move in 1970 from a decade of involvement to a decade of commitment—our sacred pledge to achieve the long-range goals of humanity, social justice and equality for all people; and, the firm determination that each link member and each Links chapter are the vehicles for this accomplishment.

~ Vivian J. Beamon
Fourth National President

We do big things; we do them in a big way, and we do them well.

~ Helen Gray Edmonds, PhD
Fifth National President

Our practical day-to-day demonstrations [show] that social responsibility is our theme, and service to humanity is our watchword.

~ Pauline Ellison, LHD
Sixth National President

The Links shall forever be a force for good, a force for justice, a force for equality ... improving the quality of life in our America.

~ Julia Brogdon Purnell, LHD
Seventh National President

It is evident that Links chapters are reflecting growth, maturity, and seriousness of purpose as they design and implement their local programs. Not only are chapters finding their own projects, but, increasingly, outside foundations are so impressed with the project that they are being underwritten for further implementation ... this is a development which signals the recognition of Links as an organization of intelligent, committed women, willing and able to do a job and do it well.

~ Dolly Desselle Adams, PhD
Eighth National President

Ready to Serve – Links awaiting their assignment in aftermath of Katrina

We shall move forward in one accord to preserve our colleges, take the offense in any initiatives to ensure our rights, arrest the spread of drug addiction in our community, and ensure the survival of our families.

~ *Regina Jollivette Frazier*
Ninth National President

No one who is interested in the life and times of African Americans should have to wonder, who are, or what is, The Links? We know who we are, and others should be made aware of our outstanding accomplishments.

~ *Marion Sutherland*
Tenth National President

We are women linked in a chain of friendship to give service to humankind. We will be better for it; but, more importantly, so will those we serve!

~ *Patricia Russell-McCloud, JD*
Eleventh National President

The Links, Incorporated has become synonymous with effective programming.

~ *Barbara Dixon Simpkins, EdD*
Twelfth National President

The Links, Incorporated is, indeed, the entity where new triumphs for communities of color will be dreamed, incubated, planned, and unfolded.

~ *Gladys Gary Vaughn, PhD*
Thirteenth National President

When women make a conscious decision to accept invitations to become members in our chapters, they accept not because of what we wear or who we think we are. They accept because of our enthusiasm for what we do. We are living in perilous times, but we must remain steadfast in our enthusiasm for service.

~ *Gwendolyn Byrd Lee, PhD*
Fourteenth National President

With Links' Hands

What started as a national talent search for academically talented and gifted youth has since grown in to five robust facets, replete with over 20 programs and numerous national partnerships and collaborations. National programming of The Links, Incorporated has developed into a standard by which all community programming should be measured.

~ *Margot James Copeland*
Fifteenth National President

Area by Area, chapter by chapter, member by member, The Links' impact has been felt and communities are stronger and healthier as a result of our service.

~ *Glenda Newell-Harris, MD*
Sixteenth National President

Times have changed, but our fight remains the same. We are charged with uplifting our communities.

~ *Kimberly Jeffries Leonard, PhD*
Seventeenth National President

CHAPTER 14
POWER CHANNELS
The Facets

*The Links, Incorporated is the greatest movement of Negro
women with the greatest potential to help advance social change
and governmental reform in our nation today.*

~ THE LINKS JOURNAL, JUNE 1970

*A*s it was when it was conceived in 1946, so it was in 1940; and so it is four decades and nine years later. The Links has been a formidable force for empowering purposeful lives and strong communities. In chapters, Areas, the nation, and beyond the borders, The Links has "used transformational programs to enrich, sustain, and ensure the identities, culture and economic survival of African Americans and persons of African descent." The Links has "done big things in a big way, and done them well," always cognizant that there is more work to be done and committed to improving the way the work is done.

Transformative programming has powered unparalleled success across initiatives. Not content with static and safe approaches, The Links continuously "has sharpened its focus and expanded its program dimensions," as dictated by the exigency, the population served, community dynamics, and available resources. To maximize the quantity of initiatives, the scope of the outreach, and the diffusion level, The Links has also collaborated with federal, state, and local agencies, community groups, and advocacy organizations, as well as securing corporate sponsorships.

Program success has also been driven by a continual passion to raise the bar. The Links' programming has been informed and enhanced by constant examination of its delivery methods and service channels. In 2000, The Links advanced its efforts to deter one-and-done activities masquerading as programs by redefining the appellation; Links defined a program as "a comprehensive approach to solving a problem in a local, national or global community." The approach was refined even more with the introduction of The Links Service Delivery Model (LSDM) in 2006.

The LSDM strengthened programming by actively involving chapters in planning impactful programs. Before providing a service, Links chapters determine the community-level impact (change) to be created and the outcomes or behaviors recipients will manifest/achieve before they plot the programs, strategies, or services needed to achieve the outcomes. Their plan is then assessed for viability—resources needed to execute the program and identification of factors that could impinge on the plan's success. An evidence-based evaluation is then used to determine the program's effectiveness, its actual impact, as opposed to its perceived benefits. To complement the LSDM, The Links developed on-line chapter report processes that included an integrated data collection and chapter report form.

Another boost to programming excellence was the assessment variables inherent in the LSDM. The

Links had always recognized exceptional programs, but in 2002, chapters began to realize how the LSDM made the selection process more objective. That became even more important in 2002 when The Links began attaching cash awards to select categories of winning programs; and in 2010, for the first time, cash came with first, second, and third place awards for National programs. First place winners received up to $5,000 to reinvest in their program.

Links programming was prescribed from the outset, and through the ages, programming has targeted critical, continuing, and emerging issues in African American communities under three foundational rubrics: educational, cultural, and civic engagement. This trilogy has been fueled through program channels known as facets. Services to Youth, instituted in 1958, was the lone facet in the service crown, but as exigencies changed, more focused attention led to the creation of National Trends and Services (NTS) in 1964 and The Arts in 1966. International Trends and Services, spun from National Trends and Services in 1970 as an ad hoc committee, became a facet in 1978. Health and Human Services, the fifth facet in the service crown, found independence from NTS in 2010.

Additional programming grids enabled a sharpened focus on emerging and current issues in addition to dire needs within the global Black community. The programs, classified as Signature/National programs have propelled collaborative efforts with other organizations, agencies, corporations, and advocacy groups. Signature/National programs have also transcended administrations, enabling (and requiring) chapters to create on-going initiatives.

THE FIRST NATIONAL INITIATIVE

While the LSDM and other program upgrades have generated excellence in chapter, Area, and National programs, Links programming has always been noteworthy. The Links' first National project was a milestone response to a national call from the nation's oldest civil rights organization to "Invest in Freedom." The Links pledged full participation by its chapters in the National Association for the Advancement of Colored People (NAACP) "Life

LINKS-STEMREADY, Birmingham (AL)

Membership" campaign during the 4th National Assembly in 1952.

The Links honored its commitment during the 6th Assembly in 1954, with Daisy Lampkin, Pittsburgh (PA) Chapter, presenting a $26,850 check to Roy Wilkins, administrator, and Thurgood Marshall, legal counsel. An article in the August–September 1954 *The Crisis* magazine hailed the payment as "the largest single gift to the NAACP." The Los Angeles (CA) Chapter was the first of the 55 chapters to purchase a life membership during the prescribed two-year period, answering the call just three months following the Assembly's action; and by 1960, the amount had reached $36,000, with 72 Links chapters contributing.

The Links' first National President, Sarah Strickland Scott, had appointed Lampkin, a charter member of the Pittsburgh Chapter, as chair of a special committee to develop a National Program. In response to the many social issues facing African Americans, Lampkin's committee had recommended that each chapter purchase the NAACP life membership. When the check was presented in 1954, Margaret Hawkins was at the helm.

Second National President Margaret Rosell Hawkins continued the NAACP effort, with Leola Nixon of the Orlando (FL) Chapter serving as National Program chair. Nixon, who had been a member of the NAACP project group, encouraged chapters to fulfill their constitutional requirement by submitting a summary of the chapter's program activities. She compiled the reports into the first release of a Chapter Program handbook. As Nixon summarized in the preface of the 1957 booklet, "It is the purpose of this booklet to record achievements of LINKS by giving detailed accomplishments to animate and to enable its readers to form a definite conception of the serviceable and worthwhile women connected with the organization."

Further championing the booklet's utility, Nixon wrote:

> *These reports will provide background and theory for definite, practicable, and workable evidence to use yearly in planning chapter work … The individual and collective needs of LINKS and LINKS CHAPTERS can be widened, their thinking can be stimulated, and their yearly projects can become a bit of creative artistry.*

Nixon's Program report book was so successful that the publication became a standard for the organization. It continued to serve as an effective instrument for exchanging ideas, providing inspiration for addressing issues, and recognizing exemplary efforts. Although the methodology has changed, The Links retained the practice of sharing Best Practices of Chapters by featuring the programs in print and using them as models for workshop sessions.

Programming under Hawkins also included educational programs. Chapters were encouraged to offer scholarships, provide guidance and counseling for students, and render public service in their communities. Hawkins also declared "National Links Week," during which chapters showcased their programs during the first week in November.

The end of Hawkins's tenure marked the end of free-form programming, as The Links moved toward the formalization of common programs in defined frameworks. Over time, five facets and ancillary Signature, Linkages, and National programs were created.

~ *Earnestine Green McNealey, PhD*

~ *Mary P. Douglass*

SERVICES TO YOUTH (1958)

Third National President Pauline Weeden's desire to infuse Linkdom with distinctive programming engendered The Links' first program facet. Many members took pride in the fact that The Links had coalesced to purchase NAACP life memberships as its first National project, but Weeden, understanding the rich talent and resources in Linkdom, wanted The Links to develop its own program. Weeden charged a small committee to work with her senior officers to explore the idea of a collective effort. Bernice Munce, who would lead the effort, suggested "Education for Democracy" as a comprehensive theme around which the desired National Program could be developed.

It was a research program, with each chapter responding to the needs of its own community. The four-year action-research program encouraged chapters to aid students in their community in a manner consistent with its resources—providing scholarships, financial aid, cultural enrichment, tutoring, social interaction, and more. Munce was appointed director from 1958 to 1970 and was given the title "Initiator of Link Programs for Services to Youth." Services to Youth debuted as a national talent search for academically talented and gifted youths at the 10th (1958) Assembly, and by 1962, 2,000 unknowns had been discovered.

While the initial goal was noble, the need to broaden the offerings was recognized by the 13th (1962) Assembly. Subsequently, under the leadership

Links-NSBE Jr. Chapter, Port-City (TX)

of 4th National President Vivian Beamon (1962–1970), the focus for "Education for Democracy" was expanded to include educationally disadvantaged and culturally deprived youth. This approach also answered the clarion call by President Dwight Eisenhower's (February 1957) conference on minority resources to train all youth:

> *Successful participation in a Democracy demands that citizens reach their highest educational potential not only for the purpose of being informed citizens, but that they may acquire special learnings and special techniques in those areas where they can become real contributing as well as real participating members of our social and economic order.*

Academic readiness became an integral part of the design for youth progress. The 16th (1968) Assembly (Beamon) resolved to help Black youth attain the highest educational goals their talent demanded. The Links also "aided the strongest organization in the land in seeking to understand the problems of the inner cities, donating $100,000 to the National Urban League for its 'Forward Thrust' program."

Over the years, services spread to other aspects that included career development, which became a focal point. Chapters worked to ensure that all programs and projects were interrelated and instrumental toward productive and rewarding skills, careers, and lifestyles. By vote of the 20th (1976) Assembly, Ellison's theme, "Meeting Community Needs by Focusing on Careers," was approved as a subtitle to the general theme, "National Focus on Career Development."

The 1964 push toward educational attainment was crystallized when the 21st (1980) Assembly (#7 Julia Brogdon Purnell) awarded $10,000 to the National Merit Scholarship Corporation (NMSC) to establish scholarships for minority high achievers. Each year in March, NMSC selected six top high school minority achievers (one from each Area), as judged by their scores on the SAT/ACT and other criteria, for a one-time non-renewable award of $2,000. Awards

National President Glenda Newell-Harris (left) and Links officials serving at the 41st (2018) Assembly in Indianapolis.

were made to four Areas, a fifth went to a high school abroad, and a sixth to a gifted student artist.

With youth indifference and violence in epidemic proportions in the 1970s, Purnell also added prevention and treatment of juvenile delinquency in girls as a dimension. By the 21st Assembly, The Links, in partnership with the YMCA National Board – Juvenile Justice Project, had initiated two model projects. "Link Wings and Fly" and "Links: A Chain to Change" offered counseling and tutoring services for high-risk young women. The efforts were supported by a $101,205 grant from the Office of Juvenile Justice and Delinquency Prevention.

In 1982, drug and alcohol abuse cried for attention, and The Links sought means for education and prevention. A 1985 grant (Adams) from the National Institute of Drug Abuse funded developmental training sessions for Links National leaders, who, in turn, conducted a series of workshops on drug abuse and prevention at the chapter, Area, and National levels. Project LEAD (Links Erase Alcohol and Drug Abuse) subsequently became a National Umbrella Program

that targeted varied factors intertwined with drug and alcohol abuse, including teenage pregnancy, juvenile crime and delinquency, mental and emotional illnesses/disorders, breakdown of the family, unemployment, and education.

Aware of the critical role that self-esteem and hope played in helping youth make the right choices, The Links also provided opportunities for nurturing and strengthening positive values under Youth Eighties Survival – A Family Affair, and the Executive Council (Frazier) established a Self-Esteem Task Force in 1988. A major activity of the task force was partnering with the Library of Congress in its 1991 (#10 Marion Schultz Sutherland) literacy campaign. In 1993, Sutherland also began a collaborative effort with Youth Service America to sponsor annual public awareness and education campaigns designed to broaden national, regional, and local recognition of the power of organized youth, and she launched Operation SEED (Self-Esteem Enrichment Day).

Links "Leader Path to College," High Point (NC) Chapter

Two programs under 11th National President Patricia Russell-McCloud turned attention toward health and identified a range of factors that impacted the quality of life for youth. Project Walking Fete: Make Health a Habit promoted moderate physical activity in African Americans, and Links to Success: Children Achieving Excellence (LSCAE) was approved as The Links' first Signature Program. Implementation fell to 12th National President Barbara Dixon Simpkins, who had co-authored the proposal. LSCAE provided mentoring and nurturing services that addressed a range of needs impacting a child's ability to learn. The program's impact was exceptional; 13th National President Gladys Gary Vaughn, also a

TOP: Distributing Back to School supplies at 41st Assembly

BOTTOM: Dedication and ribbon-cutting for newly completed exercise fitness trail at Burton Pack Elementary School, Columbia (SC) Chapter

co-author of LSCAE, made it a centerpiece of The Links Care (TLC) programming model.

Fourteenth National President Gwendolyn B. Lee hosted a public forum to discuss reauthorization of the federal No Child Left Behind Act; 15th National President Margot James Copeland established the STEM education and career readiness initiative that integrated science, technology, engineering, and math educational programming from kindergarten to college; and 16th National President Glenda Newell-Harris partnered with the National Society of Black Engineers (NSBE) to increase access to STEM.

~ *Mary P. Douglass*
~ *Earnestine Green McNealey, PhD*

NATIONAL TRENDS AND SERVICES (1964)

The fight for civil and human rights moved to the center ring during the 1960s. On the heels of the 1957 Civil Rights Act, four students sat down at a counter in Greensboro, North Carolina, on February 1, 1960, and demanded to be served. Freedom Riders traveled to the South to test a ban on segregation in interstate bus terminals, only to have their bus firebombed in Anniston, Alabama, on May 20, 1961. Negro activists, crying, "Now is the time," demanded integration with protest after protest—from wade-ins in at public beaches to kneel-ins in whites-only churches.

As America received notice that the burgeoning conditions would no longer be ignored, many were content to leave the resolution to stalwart organizations such as the National Association for the Advancement of Colored People, the Congress of Racial Equality, Southern Christian Leadership Conference, and the Student Non-Violent Coordinating Committee. But Links chapters across the nation tagged in to take their place in the arena. Their actions, which garnered recognition and commendations, prompted National Links leaders to consider ways to incorporate the approaches into Links programming.

Fourth National President Vivian Jones Beamon subsequently commissioned renowned historian and government-savvy Helen Gray Edmonds, Durham (NC) Chapter, to develop a position paper on a unifying theme and parameters to focus and guide

Engaging youth

Links' involvement. At the 13th (1962) Assembly, delegates added National Trends and Services to the National Program, and the 14th Assembly officially adopted the program in 1964.

Designed to provide "services for the total good," the facet facilitated greater understanding of and participation in national concerns. Currency, as embodied in trends, was the key for program implementation. Programming was deemed effective, only to the extent that it addressed current issues and developments. In 1964, realizing the increasing role and interconnectedness of global issues, the 14th (1964) Assembly endorsed adding international trends as a focal point.

At home and abroad, Links "healed the world and made it a better place for the entire human race." After a ten-year run, however, the scope of international activities demonstrated the need for a solo run. As a result, the 18th (1972) Assembly (#5, Edmonds) approved International Trends and Services as an ad hoc facet, thereby leaving National Trends and Services with its original name.

Over the years, the program emphasis has been modified, but the overall goal of creating and supporting environments to empower African American families has remained constant. Links programming has engendered economic independence, academic achievement, civic engagement, and healthier communities. Standouts include the following:

- Project Discovery (#8 Adams) – Offered training to prepare middle-aged, middle-income minority women to enter the job market or upgrade their skills. The work (1983–1985) was supported by a grant of $100,00 from the Department of Labor, Women's Bureau.

- Fulfilling the Dream (#9 Frazier) – Encouraged wellness (mind, body, and spirit) of the Black family. To achieve maximum impact, partnerships were formed with national agencies, including the National Cancer Institute (NCI).

- The Walk for Health and Hunger (#11 Russell-McCloud) – Held annually in September since 1995, the walk encourages African American families to "Make Health a Habit." The first walk promoted physical activities, and in 1996, health screenings were added.

- The African American Family Summit (#11 Russell-McCloud) – Convened March 20–22, 1998, to examine the status and needs of African American families and explored strategies that could help minorities to become more self-sufficient, proactive citizens.

- Linkages to Life (#12 Simpkins) – Initiated in 2001 to increase the number of minority organ donors. Of the 90,000 people currently waiting for lifesaving organ transplants, more than 27 percent of people waiting are African American, but only about 12 percent of donors are Black.

During 14th National President Gwendolyn B. Lee's term (2006–2010), The Links worked to eliminate economic and social inequalities in the areas of education, income, health, and employment. The "Heart Truth Campaign" was adopted by the 36th (2008) Assembly as a Signature Program. The Links also targeted childhood obesity as a means of helping children to grow into healthy adults and pushed justice and equality initiatives that included reauthorization of the Fannie Lou Hamer, Rosa Parks, and Coretta Scott King Voting Rights Act.

Fifteenth National President Margot James Copeland established programs to support historically Black colleges and universities (HBCU Initiative) and to help minority students navigate community college (Achieving the Dream Initiative), and she hosted a forum on "Violence in America – Its Impact on Our Children, Our Community."

Sixteenth National President Glenda Newell-Harris focused on eliminating disparities and inequality through financial literacy and anti-bullying efforts. She also instituted two new initiatives—Black Lives Matter: Linking Knowledge to Action, and Human Trafficking: Linked Voices Against Violence.

~ *Earnestine Green McNealey, PhD*

~ *Mary P. Douglass*

THE ARTS (1966)

The Arts are in the DNA of The Links. Links visionary Margaret Rosell Hawkins possessed innate artistic talents, as reflected in the Philadelphia Public Schools awarding her a four-year scholarship to the Philadelphia School of Design for Women (later known as Moore College of Art and Design). She received a bachelor's degree in fine arts in 1931, became an art teacher in the Camden, New Jersey schools, and practiced her craft at a level so superb that her work graced the walls of her church.

Although The Arts, the third of The Links' five facets, was established three years after Hawkins passed, many credit her as the spark; so, perhaps the genes notion is not that far-fetched. The facet was actually introduced at The Links' 14th (1964) Assembly, the first meeting following Hawkins's death in 1963; so, the timing for a facet in her honor would have been perfect, but the Assembly paid homage to her by establishing the Margaret Hawkins Memorial Trust Fund. Furthermore, while The Arts facet was introduced at the 14th Assembly, it was not endorsed until the 15th Assembly.

Fourth National President Vivian J. Beamon was actually the driving force. Encouraging more commitment from members in her 1970 Call to the Assembly, Beamon included a reminder of why the facet had emerged: "When the talents of youth found little

outlet for their creative expression, and when every testing device in the American educational system revealed that our youth were deficient in the creative and performing arts, Links moved to the program emphasis of Freedom and the Fine Arts. The primary purpose was to help young and old to release their God-given secret power to create, to portray, and to appreciate." Margaret Hough, Cincinnati (OH) Chapter, was the first National director.

Over the years, The Links has continued to propel The Arts singularly and in partnership with local museums, symphonies, arts councils, educational institutions, and corporations. Special performances by students and professionals, as well as Master Classes provide innovative opportunities for constructive—and instructive—interactions to occur. The spoken word with original poetry, classical and modern dance, jazz and classical music, vocal and instrumental music, and more have thrived in concert with traveling exhibits. The Virgin Arts series, initiated by 12th National President Barbara Dixon Simpkins, was designed to showcase the talents of novice young artists who could then sell their work.

Consistent with her expansive view of the clout and capacity within Links, 11th National President Patricia Russell-McCloud launched "The Living Legends: Wade in the Water," a traveling exhibit of Negro spirituals that reflected the various genres of music throughout the African American experience. The exhibit highlighted many of the voices in the African diaspora and featured acclaimed vocalist

Southern Area Links assembling "New Mommy" kits during 2017 Area meeting in Atlanta.

William Warfield. The Smithsonian Institute served as curator for the exhibit, marking the first collaborative effort between The Links, Incorporated and a renowned national museum.

The Ritz Chamber Players were the nation's first chamber music ensemble comprised solely of musicians spanning the African diaspora. From 2002 to 2006, 13th National President Gladys Gary Vaughn sponsored the remarkable ensemble in performances that introduced audiences to classical music and promoted Black artists. The ensemble performed broadly within the organization at all levels and at public schools. Links also feted the group in a special 2006 Mother's Day performance in Jazz at Lincoln Center and the Metropolitan Museum of Art.

One touring exhibition was six years in development. "Forever Free: Art by African-American Women, 1862–1980" was a historical exhibition of 118 works by 49 artists. Resistance by the network of museums in the country and naysayers regarding a "black show" was formidable, but the entrenched racism and sexism were eventually surmounted. The Links provided enthusiastic support and encouragement from its inception, along with essential seed money. With the guidance of established artist and scholar David C. Driskell, "Forever Free" came to fruition.

In the visual arts, 8th National President Dolly Desselle Adams made a "major acquisition" with the purchase of a sculpture by world-renowned artist Elizabeth Catlett for the National Headquarters. The sculpture was placed in memory of Margaret Hawkins. 11th National President Patricia Russell-McCloud also commissioned Catlett to sculpt a lithograph to commemorate The Links' 50th anniversary. Catlett's 1996 bronze sculpture depicts three generations of women with their arms intertwined as in The Links' chain of friendship. Posters were reproduced from the lithograph.

By design, Links have captured programmatic ideas with the potential to transform lives via designated Signature Programs. "Classics through the Ages," the first Signature Program for The Arts, was adopted at the 36th (2008) National Assembly. Designed to increase interest, knowledge, and

Kids in Jamaica mastering CPR

participation of primarily African American youth in the classical arts, the program has helped students learn to appreciate classical music, gain confidence and competency, and opened pathways to successful careers.

The National Poster Art Contest was created in 1995 in conjunction with The Links, Incorporated's National Walk-a-Thon. The Poster Art Contest, initiated during 11th National President Patricia Russell-McCloud's tenure, regained its vibrancy under 13th National President Glady Gary Vaughn, and the 16th National President gave it another boost by opening the competition to "our greater communities and supporters to participate." The initial effort, chaired by National Arts Director Marcia D. White, enlisted 144 chapters and engaged 6,000 students. The exhibition, designed by K. Joy Peters, was held at the 35th (2006) National Assembly in Philadelphia. Sixteenth National President Glenda Newell-Harris gave it another boost when she opened the competition to community supporters.

Recognition of The Links, Incorporated, alongside best-selling author Walter Mosley at the New York Historical Society in 2007, during the administration of 14th National President Gwendolyn Lee beautifully attested to the stellar artistic legacy The Links had built. Over the years, The Links honored many African American artists, including Gwendolyn Brooks, Jacob Lawrence, Cicely Tyson,

Brock Peters, Leontyne Price, Alice Walker, and Katherine Dunham.

New arts initiatives also energized programming. The Link Sisters in Cinema Committee, chaired by Lisa Simmons, facilitated the screening of films produced by Links at the 2008 Roxbury Film Festival, the largest festival in New England dedicated to films celebrating people of color. In March 2008, The Links National Black Writers Conference Liaison Committee, chaired by Link Phyllis Rice, sponsored a young adult authors panel at the Ninth National Black Writers Conference, the largest domestic gathering of its kind clearly focused on literary excellence in the Black diaspora. National President Kimberly Jeffries Leonard's partnership with the March on Washington Film Festival will be educational, and also offer film internships for youth.

The Links has remained true to its founding values, as it has forged new partnerships and strengthened our programs with straightforward guidelines that made Arts Integration a familiar feature of Umbrella Programming. Combining program facets resulted in benefits to all involved—the chapters and community alike, and the efficacy of this approach is evident in the quality of the chapter programs.

~ Alpha Coles Blackburn
~ Marcia Denise White

INTERNATIONAL TRENDS AND SERVICES (1978)

A call for help from Will Mercer Cook, US ambassador to the Republic of the Niger, ignited The Links' foray into international relations. Cook sought financial assistance to transport prescription drugs donated by American pharmaceutical companies to Niger. Under the leadership of 3rd National President Pauline Fletcher Weeden Maloney (1957–1962), The Links responded with a $500 donation. The aid expanded The Links' concern for human rights beyond the nation's borders, and it set the stage for even greater strides.

Fourth National President Vivian Jones Beamon led the 13th (1962) Assembly in approving support for the Peace Corps. Later that year, The Links was one of four women's groups invited to participate in the American Leadership Conference on Africa. The pace further quickened, with The Links participating in several state and national meetings of the International Women's Year, and in 1973, 6th National President Pauline A. Ellison added an International Women's Year (IWY) Committee, headed by Etta Moten Barnett. With the scope of international activities burgeoning, ITS, originally included with the National and International Trends and Services facet and approved as an ad hoc committee in 1970, became a facet in 1978 (Ellison) by vote of the 21st Assembly.

Links in Liberia, where The Links adopted four schools

#13 Gladys Gary Vaughn (tan raincoat) leading a mission trip to schools Links adopted as part of Education across the Miles.

Incoming National President Julia Brogdon Purnell (1978–1982) tapped Dolly Desselle Adams as ITS director. Adams focused her attention on primary ITS components, including observance of the United Nations and Human Rights Day, Great Issues, and the International Year of the Child. The Links provided financial support to the African Water Wells project and International Drinking Waste Supply and Sanitation (1981–1990), and also sent delegations to the first National Women's Year Conference in Mexico City in 1979 and subsequent conferences held in concert with the International Women's Decade.

At the 25th (1986) Assembly, Adams became National President, and she selected Gwendolyn H. Welters to lead the charge. The Links was on the A-list of organizations invited to play key roles in international projects, and Welters traveled to Zimbabwe as a member of the Women's Planning Team assembled by the African American Institute (AAI) to explore the possibility of building a relationship with women leaders. The Links also partnered with Africare, a leading non-profit program, to support construction of water wells in southern Zimbabwe, subsequently providing water to approximately 4,000 families. In May 1985, The Links also

achieved United Nations status as a non-governmental organization (NGO).

Ninth National President Regina Jollivette Frazier (1986–1990) continued to build on the strength and strong momentum of expansion on the world stage by establishing international chapters in Frankfurt, Germany, and Nassau, Bahamas. She named Freddie Lucas as ITS National director, and they synchronized the 1986–88 biennium celebration of "The Black Family" with ITS programs.

Tenth National President Marion Schultz Sutherland continued the project and other initiatives with Freddye A. Prophet as ITS National director. The Links-Africare initiatives resulted in contributions of over $75,000, which funded the Women's Finance Trust in Zambia and provided clothing for people in Mozambique and other countries in Southern Africa. The Links' participation in the Fourth World Conference on Women in Beijing in 1995 was facilitated by Betty Shabazz, appointed as ITS National director for the 1994–96 biennium by 11th National President Patricia Russell-McCloud.

In 1996, Russell-McCloud named Juel Shannon Smith as the ITS National director, and 12th National President Barbara Dixon Simpkins (1998–2002) continued Smith's tenure. Several ITS projects were put into place over the six-year period. Links chapters collaborated with religious, professional, and community-based organizations to collect new dolls for distribution to children in Links-funded South African schools as part of The Links "Black Dolls Project." The Links also created quick-response, self-contained mobiles designed to allow the teacher to set up a classroom anywhere in Rwanda and Liberia for up to 80 children. Additionally, The Links' Uganda Tour of Light, in partnership with the Daughters of Charity Orphanage of Kampala, gave birth to an award-winning dance troupe of 20 Ugandan children orphaned by AIDS and raised $500,000 for the orphanage.

Because of the need for more classroom space, The Links joined the effort to purchase Container Schools in Capetown. In association with the African American Institute (AAI), The Links also supported a Mentoring African Women program that catered to African women pursuing degrees in America and joined in the annual observance of Day of the African Child, a day the Organization of African Unity (OAU) began commemorating in 1990 in memory of Black South African school children who were killed in a massacre.

In 1998, Links involvement added a monumental dimension, Education across the Miles, a cooperative venture to build schools in Africa, anchored by the International Foundation for Education and Self Help (IFESH). Thirteenth National President Gladys Gary Vaughn (2002–2006) appointed Joyce Black as director and authorized a new memorandum of understanding between IFESH and The Links. Sixty-four schools were built as part of the initiative.

ITS thrived as The Global Trilogy—International Trends and Services, the United Nations, and the international Signature Program, Education across the Miles. The approach incorporated traditional programs and added initiatives. Appointed in 2006 by 14th National President Gwendolyn Lee, Kamala Buckner, ITS National director, expanded the global platform with programs that included the Foreign Service Empowerment Program for Youth Career Development, which introduced minority youth to career options in international business and the Foreign Service.

Creator of Linkages to Life, former Southern Area Director Joyce Dixon

Fifteenth National President Margot James Copeland expanded The Links' presence with Sharon Richardson as ITS director. The focus shifted to Liberia, where The Links adopted four Liberian schools: Ann Sandell, Todee Mission School, AME University, and School for the Blind. To develop Links Libraries at the schools, The Links provided 22,000 text and library books through "Books for Africa" and trained 20 Liberian teachers in the areas of lesson planning, reading comprehension, and classroom management. In partnership with Africare, The Links also funded construction of two Links Maternal Waiting Homes and packaged and distributed 1,100 "Maama Kits" to six Maternal Waiting homes. Domestic ITS programs included Links' ongoing collaboration with the United Nations.

During the administration of 16th National President Glenda Newell-Harris, The Links traversed Jamaica. Newell-Harris used a "boots-on-the-ground" approach to support school-aged children at Watford Hills, St. Mary's, and Mt. Zion primary schools, Montego Bay, Jamaica. The Links offered instruction, provided books and supplies, and taught students how to administer CPR.

~Juel Shannon Smith, PhD

HEALTH AND HUMAN SERVICES (HHS) (2010)

As the first physician to head The Links, 16th National President Glenda Newell-Harris was licensed to issue a prescription, and the four-year-old Health and Human Services facet was the ideal script for supporting good health and eliminating health disparities in communities of color through focused treatment and advocacy, the goals of Health and Human Services, established by vote of the 37th (2010) Assembly.

Forty-plus years had passed since the Assembly had approved a new facet, so the vote was significant. The campaign was orchestrated by 14th National President Gwendolyn Lee, with National Program Chair Alma Dodd and National Trends and Services Chair Kimberly Jeffries Leonard directing. The move followed the trio's 36th Assembly's endorsement of "HeartLinks" as a Signature Program.

The case for a dedicated facet was strong. Race was still a significant factor in determining whether an individual received care, whether an individual received high-quality care, and in determining health outcomes. For some measures being tracked, gaps in care were getting larger rather than smaller. The Links had programs that were making a difference, but for optimal impact, laser focus was required.

The Health and Human Services facet was needed to promote and facilitate programs that "supported the maintenance of good health and the elimination of health disparities in communities of color

Bernice Munce, first facet director

through education, health advocacy and the optimal use of health resources," as expressed by the committee that operationalized the facet under 15th National President Margot James Copeland, National Program chair and the first Health and Human Services chair, Monica Parker, MD.

Under the theme, The Links Incorporated, "Change Agents for Wellness—Making Women's Health a Priority," the committee set four goals:

1. Links and the communities we serve will become better informed about good nutrition;
2. Links and the communities we serve will become better informed about the benefits of physical activity;
3. We will encourage African Americans' participation in clinical trials and health disparities research; and
4. We will partner with select organizations whose missions align with The Links, Incorporated, to create a comprehensive road-map and strategy for chronic disease disparity elimination.

HHS began its work by surveying chapters on the nature of their health programming. Based on the responses from 208 chapters, the committee charted its work. Noteworthy outcomes included the following:

- Launched the National Childhood Obesity Initiative across all of Linkdom.
- Obtained $10,000 HeartLinks grant through the Coca Cola Foundation "Capture the Flag" contest. The award funded $500 grants to 20 chapters for cardiovascular disease programming with the HeartLinks curriculum.
- Partnered with Susan G. Komen to offer roundtables on the high incidence of breast cancer in women in Nassau, Bahamas. The Links also donated $25,000 to St. Margaret's Hospital to fund mammograms for women.
- Secured $500,000 Childhood Obesity grant from GE Healthcare, Corporation of the Midsouth, Blue Cross/ Blue Shield, Safeway, and the Kellogg Foundation to fund chapter childhood obesity programs. More than 100

chapters participated. Funds also supported the launch of a national website, "Can you Imagine Me," with Community Voices of Morehouse School of Medicine and the publication of a legislative brief and program document.

■ Marked Oral Health's approval as a National Program by the 39th Assembly by conducting oral health screenings for 200 children at an Orlando (FL) community health center in collaboration with Colgate-Palmolive and the National Dental Association.

Newell-Harris placed special emphasis on members being healthy. "Keep your appointments, stay healthy was a resounding message to all." Each member also received a "Personal Health Passport." More than 50 chapters brought 9.8 million Bright Smiles, Bright Futures to kids through The Links-Colgate-Palmolive partnership; four chapters received grants for their Hep C Awareness Program (Bristol Meyers grant award); and a Mental Health Toolkit was developed.

~ Earnestine Green McNealey, PhD

Advocate for Community Service at Area Conferences and Assemblies, former Central Area Director Joahn Brown Nash

LINKS LARGESSE: INITIATIVES THROUGH THE YEARS

AARP Links Academy
In concert with AARP, "the nation's largest nonprofit, nonpartisan organization dedicated to empowering Americans 50 and older to choose how they live as they age," provided tools and resources to support African American women who are either preparing for life as they age or are currently dealing with the aging process. The program includes components for preventative measures during each specific life stage and provides health, wellness, and financial support and services to the 50-plus community.

Achieving the Dream, Incorporated (ADI)
Community College Initiative
Partnered with ADI to help more minority and low-income students attend community colleges, improve their learning outcomes, and help them graduate. Sustainable program models were piloted at five sites, and a manual was developed to assist other Links chapters in implementing the model.

Africare
Funded water wells and the Africare House with donations that exceeded $13,000 in 1984; supported development efforts via information campaigns and grants totaling $88,000 in 2012 and 2013—$75,000 funded the Women's Finance Trust in Zimbabwe and provided clothing for people in Mozambique and other countries in Southern Africa. "Moments of Global Awareness" and "Moments of Global Action" also called chapters' attention to crises that included Somalia (2011). The first $46,000 supported the distribution of 1,100 kits to mothers in six maternity waiting homes in Bong County (December 2012) and construction of the first Links home, which opened in Bong County near the Phebe Hospital on February 8, 2013. Within the first year of operation, 125 safe deliveries were made. An additional $42,000 (March 2, 2013) funded a second maternity waiting home near the Maama Clinic in the Maama District of Bong County, Liberia (June 2014).

Western Area hosting Junteenth Celebration

Affordable Housing

Habitat for Humanity

Collaborated with Habitat for Humanity to assist those living without decent and affordable housing in the United States. The Links worked through the organization's local affiliates to volunteer and raise awareness. Also donated $50,000 to spur HH ongoing relief efforts for Haiti following the devastating 2010 earthquake.

Black Lives Matter: Linking Knowledge to Action

Instituted a comprehensive program to develop solutions, provide education, and create awareness of the challenges affecting African American youth and young adults relative to police action and the criminal justice system.

Black Arts National Diaspora (BAND)

An after-school program to stimulate and develop the creative and intellectual potential of students who might be challenged by traditional school curricula. The program addressed the lack of interest in school and low, basic skill levels, which often resulted in increasing involvement in drugs, petty crimes and vandalism.

Boots on the Ground Jamaica Trips

Volunteers: 300

- Service hours: Over 5,000 by members of The Links, Incorporated
- Over $1 million in economic support and impact

- Over $550,000 in-kind donations and monetary support
- CPR Training: Students and parents
- Dental Screening: Over 1,200 youth dental screenings
- Nutrition Education: Over 1,200 youth and parents provided with nutrition education
- STEM Education: More than 1,200 Kindle Fires donated

Consultations I, II, III, and IV

Lilly Endowment

Four Consultations of Black Women's Organizational leadership. This coalition of 15 of the largest Black women's organizations in America was supported by grants totaling $120,000 from the Lilly Endowment of Indianapolis. We are indebted to Link Jacqui Burton-McCullough, Program officer and a member of the Indianapolis Chapter, for her constant and continuing support of this program. At Consultation IV, the organization became autonomous and elected its own president, 8th National President Dr. Dolly Desselle Adams.

National Childhood Obesity (CO) Initiative (2012)

Secured $500,000 grant from GE Healthcare, Corporation of the Midsouth, Blue Cross/ Blue Shield, Safeway, and the Kellogg Foundation to develop programs to reduce obesity in children. More than 100 Links chapters conducted activities, a legislative brief and program document were published, and a national website, "Can You Imagine Me," was launched in concert with Community Voices of the Morehouse School of Medicine.

The National Poster Art Contest was created in 1995 in conjunction with The Links, Incorporated's National Walk-a-Thon. Entries are centered around

Pumps on the Hill – National President Glenda Newell Harris (third from the right) and Links in Congress

a healthy, energetic, active lifestyle. Entries, which are submitted through chapters, are selected by a National panel of judges. Winning works are displayed at the National Assembly.

Project Discovery

A pilot project funded by the Department of Labor, Women's Bureau, was expanded to eight chapters. Grants totaling $100,000 supported the nine projects. Six of the eight chapters implemented additional seminars from their own funds. These projects are ongoing, with the Department of Labor seeking to co-sponsor further projects/programs with The Links, Incorporated.

Schools, Cape Town

Purchased quick-response, self-contained mobiles to enable teachers to set up classrooms for up to 80 children anywhere in Rwanda and Liberia. In concert with the African American Institute, also established a mentoring program for African women pursuing degrees in America.

Trash Talking: It's No Joke!

Empowered youth with the tools and skills to address bullying in all forms; Children learned to avoid victimization, deter offender behavior, and promote disclosure of abuse. The program was piloted by eight chapters: Alameda Contra Costa (CA), Bradenton/Sarasota (FL), Gainesville (FL), Greenville (SC), Louisville (KY), New Orleans (LA), Omaha (NE), and Philadelphia (PA). All chapters also received access to a tool kit with educational and training components that stressed the legal and ethical issues for youth and adults, as well as pre- and post-evaluations and an anti-bullying contract and pledge.

Signature Arts Program: Classics through the Ages

The Signature Program of The Arts facet, Classics through the Ages, increases the interest, knowledge, and participation of African American youth in the classical arts. This exciting initiative seeks to afford exemplary student artists opportunities to hone their talents and skills and earn recognition and support for

A Links Catlett

their educational and career pursuits. Using an innovative dual mentoring program, chapters, in conjunction with artistic partners, mentor promising student artists, who in turn mentor their peers. A key to the program's success has been the development of artistic and community partnerships, which optimize the impact for promising students in a selected arts discipline (e.g., visual arts, performing arts, or humanities).

Education across the Miles

International Foundation for Education and Self-Help (IFESH)
Collaborated with IFESH to fund the construction of schools in South Africa. Released detailed report on the 62 schools that had been built by 2010.

Forward Thrust

National Urban League
Contributed $100,000 to the National Urban League to address disillusionment and despair in inner-city youth and help them develop employable skills.

Equation for Excellence

Improved the consistency and quality of volunteer and mentoring interventions, student learning outcomes, and subsequent matriculation into higher education institutions; also encouraged student-family financial literacy.

HeartLinks

The Heart Truth, National Heart, Lung & Blood Institute (NHLBI); and the Office of Women's Health, University of California-Davis

Raised the defense against heart disease, the number one killer of African American women. The program subsumed existing heart disease prevention efforts, including the Walk for Healthy Living, Linkages to Life, childhood obesity, and cardiovascular programming. Through events like the Red Dress campaign, created by NHLBI's Heart Truth, and World Heart Day, a global effort to raise awareness of heart disease, The Links increased women's awareness of heart disease and its dangers. In collaboration with the Office of Women's Health, University of California-Davis, The Links also offered an educational series on identifying, preventing, and treating cardiovascular disease; and UC-Davis funded an intervention program based on community-based cardiovascular disease.

International Women's Decade

During the summer of 1985, 8th National President Dolly Adams and Etta Moten Barnett led a Links delegation of 150 on a historic trip to Nairobi, Kenya, where they participated in events that marked the end of the International Decade of Women.

Legislative Issues, Public Affairs, and Disaster Relief

Congressional Black Caucus, the NAACP, and League of Women Voters

Pushed advocacy agenda; developed a GOTV (Get Out The Vote) Toolkit to register, mobilize, and empower voters to make informed decisions through education and advocacy; and held public-issues forums on topics that included closing the achievement gap and community violence. Position papers also addressed gun safety.

The LIFE Program (International, Foreign Affairs, and Business Empowerment for Youth)

Successfully launched LIFE on Howard University's campus in the summer of 2008. Recruited and encouraged minority high school students in grades 9–10 to study international affairs, explore international career possibilities in foreign affairs and

Tenth annual Black Writers Conference. Seated, left to right: Sonya Sanchez, Toni Morrison, Kamau Brathwaite, and Amiri Baraka. Standing, left to right: Susan Taylor, Marsha White, Brenda Green, and Cornell West.

Black Dolls project, Southern Area support

business, and close the race and gender gap in the pool of those qualified for international positions

The Links Black Doll Project

Collected new dolls for distribution to children in South African schools built by The Links.

Linking with Haiti

In August 2011, donated $50,000 to support Habitat for Humanity's ongoing relief efforts in Haiti. In 2011, the NGO Committee launched a program initiative, adopted from the Brooklyn (NY) Chapter, titled "Linking with Haiti: Survival Kits for the Women and Girls of Haiti." Links chapters identified US and international agencies with whom to partner in order to collect, ship, and distribute these kits in Haiti. As of 2013, Links chapters nationwide had donated over 16,000 Survival Kits, including Survival Kits assembled *en masse* by Links at the 38th (2012) National Assembly in Orlando, Florida.

Linking With Liberia

Transitioned the Education across the Miles signature program from South Africa to Liberia, a West African country, where the illiteracy rate exceeds 60 percent. Assisted in the education of 4,500 students at four adopted schools: The Ann Sandell Independent School, The School for the Blind, Todee Presbyterian Mission School, and the African Methodist Episcopal

University. Also, provided 22,000 text and library books through "Books for Africa" to develop Links Libraries at the schools, and trained 20 Liberian teachers in the areas of lesson planning, reading comprehension, and classroom management. In the "Train the Trainer" model, the Liberian teachers trained other teachers at their respective institutions.

Linkages to Life (subsumed under Heart Links, now part of HHS)

"Linkages to Life," a program rooted in the Southern Area to educate African Americans about the importance of becoming an organ donor, was endorsed at the 32nd Assembly in 2000 and became a National Signature Program.

Links to Success: Children Achieving Excellence (now part of National Mentoring)

Revamped and revitalized original Links to Success program. Links mentored and helped to close the achievement gap for K–3rd-grade minority students; also partnered with national organizations to promote early childhood literacy, teach critical thinking tactics, introduce STEM education and career readiness programs, prevent early childhood obesity, and promote a healthy lifestyle, as well as expand education and career awareness.

LINKS-NSBE Jr. Chapters

National Society of Black Engineers (NSBE)
Promoted and facilitated STEM education and career readiness for underrepresented minority students through the establishment of LINKS-NSBE Jr. chapters. The Links established 70 chapters in 24 states by the end of 2018, and at least five additional chapters will be chartered in concert with the new Memorandum of Understanding (MOU), which extends the partnership through 2021. The alliance enables chapters to tap into the technical and career resources of the larger NSBE network and to create positive peer interactions for students via NSBE Jr. conferences, as well as access age-appropriate STEM programming for grades 3–12, NSBE scholarships, and resources tailored to help prepare high school students for STEM majors in college.

General Motors also donated a $35,000 STEM grant to provide a matching $300 grant to any Links chapter that donated a minimum of $300 to start a new LINKS-NSBE Jr. chapter or support an existing one.

March of Dimes

Provided support for Black mothers and Black babies.

March on Washington Film Festival

A partnership that will provide film internships for African American youth.

Mayo Clinic Partnership

A community-engagement and education initiative to reduce health disparities through educational and research initiatives in communities served by Links chapters. Attention is directed to preventing diseases that that disproportionately plague African American communities, including cardiovascular diseases, cancer, and obesity. An effort is also made to register organ-transplant donors. Completed PSA advocating that African Americans and other people of color participate in clinical health disparities research, featuring Dr. Vivian Pinn, first director of the Office of Research in Women's Health at the National Institutes of Health.

Million Dollar Grants

Presenting a check for $132,000 at the 18th (1972) Assembly in New Orleans to UNCF, 5th National President Helen Gray Edmonds said the award was being made to UNCF "in recognition of the absolute importance of higher education to Black people at this time in history." UNCF characterized the amount as "the highest ever donation presented by a Black organization."

#1 – United Negro College Fund, 24th Assembly (1984)
Chapters heeded the call on the local level and also responded nationally, sending in a record $100,000-plus for Grants-in-Aid. Edmonds maximized the impact and imprint by setting a record half-million-dollar goal for the United Negro College Fund (UNCF). The 19th (1974) Assembly voted to continue the effort, and by 1984 (Dolly Desselle Adams), the effort had blossomed into the first of The Links' million-dollar campaigns. Grants awarded in installments to non-profits that have made African American lives and communities a priority.

Initially, the time period to complete the grant payment was 20 years, but the duration was reduced to eighth years in 2006.

#2 – National Association for the Advancement of Colored People Legal Defense Fund, 34th Assembly (2004)
"The search for first class citizenship social justice, and the right to be dissipated the American mainstream virgin into the greatest civil rights crusade, led by the strongest legal arm of our time, the NAACP Legal Defense Fund."

#3 – The National Civil Rights Museum (2014)
To establish The Links Educational and Cultural Center that will provide resources for teachers, students, scholars, and grassroots citizens to address the pervasive lack of general awareness among young people about the American civil rights movement and how the movement impacts and influences human rights struggles of today.

#4 – Smithsonian National Museum of African American History and Culture

To help fund the construction of "the only national museum devoted exclusively to the documentation of African American life, history, and culture." It was established by an act of Congress in 2003, following decades of efforts to promote and highlight the contributions of African Americans. To date, the museum has collected more than 36,000 artifacts and nearly 100,000 individuals have become members. The museum opened to the public on September 24, 2016, as the 19th and newest museum of the Smithsonian Institution.

#5 – St. Jude Children's Hospital

To support the expansion of three St. Jude clinical efforts, including studies designed to increase knowledge of cognitive deficits in children with

Co-Founder Award Recipient Judith Jamison with former National Arts Directors Alpha Blackburn, Marcia White, and Lillie Fontenot

sickle cell disease, the development of a community health worker education program to counsel parents of infants with sickle cell disease in Nigeria, and an age-appropriate mobile app to help sickle cell patients develop adequate self-care and disease literacy.

Model United Nations

Model United Nations and the United Nations Youth Educational Conference Series
Linking with Haiti: Survival Kits for the Women and Girls of Haiti

Sponsored participation by 200 youth in educationally enriching and rewarding experiences through the United Nations Youth Programs. Topics included the "Transatlantic Slave Trade," and American students interacted by SKYPE with students from other countries, as well as those from Links chapters in America. Also sponsored Linking with Haiti: Survival Kits for the Women and Girls of Haiti, which resulted in the donation of 16,000 survival kits. Chapters partnered with US and international agencies to collect, ship, and distribute the kits.

NAACP Life Membership Project

National Association for the Advancement of Colored People (NAACP)

Purchased a life membership in the National Association for the Advancement of Colored People (NAACP) to promote social responsibility for all members. The action was approved during the 4th (1952) Assembly in San Francisco (CA) and was submitted to individual chapters for adoption. The first grant, a $28,000 payment, was presented at the 6th Assembly.

National Achievement Scholarship Program

Merit Scholars

Employed mechanism for financial support of National Merit Scholarship Program for Black Students as a means of helping Black youth attain the highest educational goals that their talent demanded. The compensatory competitive scholarship effort entrusted grants to the National Merit Scholarship Corporation (NMSC) for distribution to promising Black students, as defined by their scores on the

Scholastic Aptitude Test. The 23rd (1982) Assembly approved $12,000 to fund six one-time, non-renewable awards of $1,000 in 1983 and 1984. The 24th (1984) Assembly increased the award amount to $2,000. The awards, set in motion with a resolution from the 16th (1968) Assembly, continue today via scheduled payments to NMSC from the Grants-in-Aid program.

National Association for the Advancement of Colored People Legal Defense Fund (LDF)

Approved a $100 per-member tax to support NAACP Legal Defense Fund at the 8th (1956) Assembly. A $75,000 grant was proposed at the 14th Assembly, and the amount was increased by $25,000 at the 15th (1966) Assembly.

The National Breast Health Initiative

Educated The Links membership and the communities it serves about the importance of knowing one's family history and the risk factors for breast cancer. The goal encompasses advocacy and personal health record retention to ensure proper healthcare maintenance. Mentoring, encouragement, and a safe haven are also foci.

National Disaster Relief

Contributed $38,000 to the national disaster relief fund and Habitat for Humanity to support responses to crises (2010). The fund was re-established in 2017 to respond to the devastating hurricanes that swept through the Southern and Western regions of the United States. The LinksFoundation, Incorporated donated $25,000 to each of these areas. The $50,000 donation provided Links members and the general community the support they needed to help get back on their feet. The checks were presented at the Open House at National Headquarters in September 2017.

National Mentoring Initiative

Provided intervention and services to children who are growing up without the guidance and support of a caring, responsible adult. Research shows that mentoring decreases the likelihood that young people will engage in harmful behaviors, while improving the chances that they will attend school regularly, improve academically, increase self-esteem, and engage in healthier lifestyles.

Mentoring is a structured and trusting relationship that brings young people together with caring adults who offer guidance, motivation, support, and encouragement aimed at developing the skill set necessary for a successful and productive lifestyle.

Mentoring is strategically integrated into all Services to Youth programs and initiatives. Chapter members mentor, recruit, register, and support mentors in their communities. The National Mentoring Initiative also supports the Young Achievers, Project LEAD: High Expectations, and Links to Success: Children Achieving Excellence programs.

National Caucus and Center on Black Aging (NCBA), 1992

Joined forces with NCBA, "advocates for health, employment, and housing for African American aging and elderly and other low-income minority seniors." Focused on the well-being of the elderly and caregivers of the elderly. Links program leaders attended a series of NCBA workshops in eight cities and subsequently worked with chapters in structuring and implementing activities that addressed the respective needs in their communities.

National HBCU (Historically Black Colleges and Universities) Initiative

Supported excellence and sustainability at HBCUs through varied initiatives that included direct grants and the establishment of Links HBCU Endowments and Links Scholars, along with college fairs, STEM partnerships, and mentoring.

Oral Health

Colgate Bright Smiles, Bright Futures, and National Dental Association

Provided oral health screenings for 200 children via mobile dental clinics and health clinics.

Million-dollar grant to the Civil Rights Museum

Project LEAD: High Expectations

Links Erase Alcohol and Drug Abuse

Originally developed to focus on alcohol and drug abuse (1985), the title was expanded to include High Expectations, and the program also widened its mission to include educational and collaborative outreach programs for high-risk African American youth.

Project LEAD – High Expectations (now part of National Mentoring)

Links Educate, Accommodate and Develop with High Expectations

Recast original Project LEAD to reflect the sum of elements that help children in grades 4–8 achieve.

Traditional literacy topics were expanded to include career awareness, health and fitness, emotional health, mentoring, and financial literacy as a means of closing the academic achievement gap of middle school students; promoted college readiness and empowered youth to become leaders in violence prevention.

Project Walking Fete: Make Health a Habit/ Walk for Healthy Living

Centers for Disease Control and Prevention

Joined eight other national organizations in launching Project Walking Fete: Make Health A Habit, the country's first national physical activity initiative (1995). Initial funding came from the Centers for Disease Control and

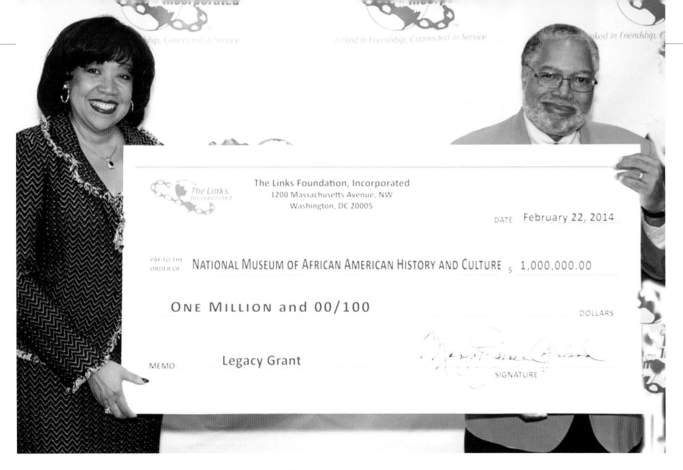

Million-dollar grant to the Smithsonian Museum of African American History and Culture

Prevention. The Links not only embraced the opportunity to promote walking as a healthy pastime for improving health, but also recast it as an annual Walk for Healthy Living, and subsequently assigned "signature" status to it. The 2019 rendition was held on August 23.

Ritz Chamber Players

Named Black chamber group as the Signature Arts Program; also sponsored a series of performances that included Jazz at Lincoln Center in New York, the Metropolitan Museum of Art, Links Area Conferences, and public schools in New York, along with workshop sessions at two public schools in New York.

Safe Motherhood Initiative, the MAAMA Kits Project

World Health Organization and the Uganda Ministry of Health
Funded the Safe Motherhood Initiative, the MAAMA Kits Project with a gift of $100,000-plus to the World Health Organization and to the Uganda Ministry of Health. Sterile gloves, soap, cotton, wool, and razor blades were among the instruments that improved safety and cleanliness for women during the birth process. The program later shifted to Liberia, where it was customized to focus on the most pressing needs of women and

children in Liberia, which has one of the highest maternal and infant mortality rates in Sub-Saharan Africa.

National STEM

Enhanced STEM with educational and career readiness initiatives that are closing the STEM education gap, assisting students in grades K–16, and preparing students for entry in four-year college STEM programs. By preparing and encouraging students to attend colleges and universities with STEM related programs, The Links, Incorporated equips students of color with the skills to compete and excel in a global workforce that increasingly relies on individuals with STEM-related proficiencies. The Links, Incorporated aims to identify and align with select STEM-related organizations to prepare youth for STEM-related careers.

STEM-U-Lation: Left Brain–Right Brain

A $250,000 two-year renewable grant from Chevron in 2012; $75,000 from AT&T in 2013; and program resources from NASA and Achieving the Dream.

Became first African American women's organization to establish a STEM National Program Model—STEM-U-Lation: Left Brain–Right Brain.

Funded chapter programming to close the STEM education gap by implementing or enhancing current program curriculum with an emphasis on STEM disciplines, engineering, and energy-industry career readiness. In the first year of the STEM initiative, more than 38 chapters implemented STEM programs that served more than 5,000 youth, and 60 chapters established mentoring programs. Along with STEM educational programming for K–16 and mentoring, the program also provided enhanced STEM-related career opportunities for minorities, and codified educational partnerships with the NASA STEM curriculum, which utilizes experiential learning for students through practical application and exposure to careers in related communication, science, technology, engineering, and mathematics fields for grades 6–12.

Over an eight-year period, donated $500,000 to boost the African American outreach initiative Circle of Promise, which supports media and a grassroots campaign that dispels the myths associated with breast cancer by understanding truths and encouraging action. The campaign included online surveys designed to ascertain African American women's "truth versus myth" perceptions; online and offline resources to assist 63,000 Komen Ambassadors who educate the public and raise money for Circle of Promise; and the distribution of materials developed in support of the Circle of Promise activities.

Turning STEM into STEAM

Chapters of The Links, Incorporated are integrating art into their STEM programming, turning STEM into STEAM. By bringing art into the educational mix, students are learning to think beyond the borders of STEM and expand their scholastic experience. The Links believes that spending time creating is equally as important to spending time measuring.

Uganda Tour of Light
Daughters of Charity Orphanage of Kampala

The Links' Uganda Tour of Light, in partnership with the Daughters of Charity Orphanage of Kamala, gave birth to an award-winning dance troupe of 20 Ugandan children orphaned by AIDS, raising $500,000 for the orphanage.

UNICEF/USA–Schools in Africa, HBCUs

Funded Schools in Africa and international experiences for HBCU graduates.

United Negro College Fund (UNCF)

Million-Dollar Grantee

At the 18th (1972) Assembly, UNCF received $132,000 of what subsequently became the first million-dollar grant "in recognition of the absolute importance of higher education to Black people at this time in history." The final installment of the grant was made at the 24th (1984) Assembly.

United States Department of Justice/YWCA

Black Women's Juvenile Justice Delinquency Prevention Program, LEAA.

In concert with the National Board of the Young Women's Christian Association, The Links provided services to address delinquency in girls ages 11 to 17.

Wallet Wise

Used the Ally Financial Model to provide financial literacy instruction in 34 target markets and hosted 64 Smart Edge workshops, where participants learned the rudiments of establishing good credit, managing a budget, and evaluating finance and insurance options.

Women's Issues and Economic Empowerment

Collaborated with other organizations to develop a national platform on relevant women's issues. Committee focuses on the education and empowerment of women. The committee collaborates with other organizations to develop a national platform on relevant women's issues.

Young Achievers

Under the rubric "Developing the Whole Child," The Links developed mentoring programs for students in grades 9–12. High school academic achievement gaps were closed, STEM-related career awareness programs were implemented, and HBCUs were touted as viable options for higher education. Participants were also introduced to financial literacy, and some received scholarships to attend college.

Of Note: Legacy Awards were given for sustained, high-level programs that had been in operation for five years, had exhibited a progressive expansion of services that addressed the original problem, and had been recognized for excellence at the Area or National level.

Signature Program honorees received monetary awards for the first time during the 37th (2010) Assembly.

Program Awards – 37th (2010) Assembly

NATIONAL TRENDS AND SERVICES

Best Practice Awards	Arlington (VA), Birmingham (AL), Buckhead-Cascade (GA), Fairfield County (CT), Fresno (CA), Greater Kansas City (KS), Greensboro (NC), Jackson (TN), Lake Shore (IL), Missouri City (TX), Prince George's County (MD), Portland (OR), Sacramento (CA), Shelby County (TN), and Washington (DC) Chapters

SIGNATURE PROGRAMS

Linkages to Life	Greater Kansas City Chapter, "Links to Healthy Lifestyle Choices, the Gift of Life"
Walk for Health and Hunger	Jackson (TN) Chapter
Heart Links	Arlington (VA) Chapter for its educational outreach program that has served over 650 people
Heart Health Prevention A Better Life	
1st	Lake Shore (IL) and Shelby County (TN) Chapters
2nd	Fairfield County (CT) Chapter for "Link to Health"
3rd	Buckhead-Cascade (GA) Chapter
Legacy Award	Portland (OR) Chapter for its program on HIV-AIDS
Co-Founders Award	Malaak Compton Rock, founder, The Angelrock Project, an on-line e-village that promotes volunteerism, social responsibility, and sustainable change. Includes information on how to volunteer, advice on making monetary or in-kind donations, links to life-changing non-profit organizations, and recommendations for fair trade companies whose products sustain third-world artisans.

SERVICES TO YOUTH

Best Practice Awards

1st	Essex County (NJ) Chapter for "Roadmap to College"
2nd	Greensboro (NC) Chapter for "Bennett/Middle College" program
3rd	Chattanooga (TN) Chapter for its Links Academy

Legacy Award — Angel City (CA) Chapter for its 25-Year-Old Achievers Program

Signature Program — Fairfield County (CT) Chapter for its three-year program, "Children Achieving Excellence"

Co-Founders Award — Dr. Beverly Tatum, 9th President, Spelman College
Created Center for Leadership and Civic Engagement; established annual Women of Color Leadership Conference; expanded curriculum to include Chinese language with a gift of $17 million.

INTERNATIONAL TRENDS AND SERVICES

Best Practice — Inglewood-Pacific (CA) Chapter, for its Darfur initiative, which reduced the impact of rape, mutilation, and murder on women. Solar stoves precluded women being attacked as they searched for wood to build fires for cooking, and the chapter donated $13,000-plus to renovate a maternity clinic.

River City (TN) Chapter for creating a cultural exchange and partnership with the African community in Memphis.

Westchester (NY) Chapter for its collaborative program on international travel etiquette with the City University of New York and Mercy College.

Signature Program — Bucks County (PA) Chapter for creating a "Village in Motion," an Exchange Program that provided medical support, clothing, and scholarships for people in the Kuntu Village, Ghana, West Africa.

Legacy Award — Renaissance (MI) Chapter for expanding educational opportunities for students in Haiti. Students initially met on the beach with one teacher, but support from the chapter enabled 250 to study in a new, three-room school.

Co-Founders Award — Susan Rice, ambassador to the United Nations
Janet Nkubana, leader of the Rwanda women's cooperative

THE ARTS

Best Practice	Brooklyn (NY), Capital City (DC), Long Island (NY), Azalea City (GA), Brunswick (GA), North Broward County (FL), Lake Shore (IL), River City (TN), South Suburban Chicago (IL), Albuquerque (NM), Houston (TX), and Las Vegas (NV) Chapters
Top Three Classics through the Ages	Long Island (NY), Missouri City (TX), and North Jersey (NJ) Chapters

Facet Awards

1st	South Suburban, Chicago (IL) Chapter for annually exposing 150 people to cultural enrichment programs
2nd	Houston (TX) Chapter for "Artspiration," which annually served 400 people and inspired them to seek careers in diverse fields of endeavor
3rd	Brunswick (GA) Chapter for expanding cultural arts in the Golden Isles community
Signature Award	Missouri City (TX) Chapter for "Classics through the Ages: Sustaining Arts Smart Through the Ensemble Theater"
Legacy Award	Long Island (NY) Chapter for sustaining its "Links Care" chapter program over a ten-year period. The program has garnered multiple awards for efforts with autistic, gifted, and other diverse students.

UMBRELLA AWARDS

1st	Missouri City (TX) Chapter for partnering with the Choice Foundation, E-STEM Academy, Ryan Middle School, Texas universities, and the Ensemble Theater for "STEMulation," which fostered deep knowledge and strong passion for science, technology, engineering, and math.
2nd	Windy City (IL) Chapter for its multifaceted program to increase awareness of risk factors associated with cardiovascular disease; extended the program to the Mufu School near Durban, South Africa.
3rd	Wilmington (DE) Chapter for partnering with Kappa Alpha Psi fraternity to implement the Achievers program, a comprehensive initiative designed to assist young African American males in developing self-confidence, self-respect, and self-pride.
Legacy Award	Detroit (MI) Chapter for "Linking Adolescent Students to Success," which enriched the lives of underprivileged young women by providing opportunities that fostered positive self-esteem.

Program Awards – 39th (2014) Assembly

UMBRELLA PROGRAMMING

1st	Bakersfield (CA) and Jacksonville (FL) Chapters
2nd	Louisville (KY) Chapter
3rd	Commonwealth (VA) Chapter
Legacy	Atlanta (GA) and Trinity (TX) Chapter

NATIONAL TRENDS AND SERVICES

1st	Texas Spring Cypress (TX) Chapter
2nd	Newport News (VA) Chapter
3rd	Shelby County (TN) Chapter
Legacy Award	Palos Verdes (CA) Chapter

SERVICES TO YOUTH

1st	South Suburban Chicago (IL) Chapter
2nd	Wilmington (DE) Chapter
3rd	Shelby County (TN) Chapter
Legacy Award	Plano North Metroplex (TX) Chapter

INTERNATIONAL TRENDS AND SERVICES

1st	Birmingham (AL) Chapter
2nd	Twin Rivers (OH) Chapter
3rd	Brooklyn (NY) Chapter
Legacy Award	Windy City (IL) Chapter

THE ARTS

1st	Orlando (FL) Chapter
2nd	South Suburban Chicago (IL) Chapter
3rd	Harbor Area (CA) Chapter
Legacy Award	Penn Towne (PA) Chapter

HEALTH AND HUMAN SERVICES

1st	Sacramento (CA) Chapter
2nd	Fort Valley (GA) Chapter
3rd	Greater New York (NY) Chapter
Legacy Award	Portland (OR) Chapter

NATIONAL POSTER ART CONTEST

Eastern	Bucks County (PA) Chapter, Wanda Vadenia, age 16
Southern	North Broward County (FL) Chapter, Amira Rasheed, age 14
Central	Fort Wayne (IN) Chapter, Colin Shaw, age 10
Western	Bakersfield (CA) Chapter, Manuela, age 8

Program Awards – 40th (2016) Assembly

UMBRELLA PROGRAMMING

1st	Young LITES Program, Mississippi Delta (MS) Chapter
2nd	STEM-U-Lation: Left Brain–Right Brain, Harbor City (MD) Chapter
3rd	Project LEAD Expectation, Denver (CO) Chapter
Legacy, 1st Place	Mt. Zion All Age School, Montgomery County (PA) Chapter
Legacy, 2nd Place	DIA Program, Detroit (MI) Chapter

NATIONAL TRENDS AND SERVICES

1st	Becoming Sound & Savvy, Sister to Sister, Ally Wallet Wise, Gulf Coast Apollo (TX) Chapter
2nd	I Am a Voter, River City (TN) Chapter
3rd	Successful Aging Initiative, Greater Huntsville (AL) Chapter
Legacy Award	Institute for Women's Empowerment, Shelby County (TN) Chapter

Integrated Awards

1st	Healthy Families, Changing Our Lifestyles, Durham (NC) Chapter
2nd	Empowering African Americans and People of Color, Trinity (TX) Chapter
3rd	Combating Bullying at King Elementary, South Suburban Chicago (IL) Chapter

SERVICES TO YOUTH

Best Practice Awards

1st	What's Up Doc, Prince George's County (MD) Chapter
2nd	Mad Science & First LEGO League Mentoring, Arlington (VA) Chapter
3rd	STEM Educational Initiative, Town Lake (TX) Chapter
Legacy Award	Washington Eagles Soar and Explore, Turning STEM into STEAM, South Suburban Chicago (IL) Chapter
Integrated Award	STEM Inspired Genius, San Diego (CA) Chapter

INTERNATIONAL TRENDS AND SERVICES

1st	Linking HEARTS, Windy City (IL) Chapter
2nd	World AIDS Day Getting to Zero, Inglewood Pacific (CA) Chapter
3rd	LIFE on Long Island and Beyond, Long Island (NY) Chapter
Legacy Award	Feed a Mind – Help a Nation, Twin Rivers (OH)
Integrated Award	Project Disaster Recovery: Linking with Haiti, Pontchartrain (LA) Chapter

THE ARTS

Best Practice Awards

1st	Links to Art, Missouri City (TX) Chapter
2nd	Artspiration, Houston (TX) Chapter
3rd	Classics through the Ages, Prince George's County (MD) Chapter
Legacy Award	Closing the Arts Enrichment Gap, South Suburban Chicago (IL) Chapter
Integrated	Links to Art, Palos Verdes (CA) Chapter
Integrated – Honorable Mention	Classics through the Ages, Baton Rouge (LA) Chapter

National Poster Art Contest Winners

1st	Miami-Biscayne Bay (FL) Chapter
2nd	Pasadena (CA) Chapter
3rd	Tampa (FL) Chapter

HEALTH AND HUMAN SERVICES

1st	Community Health Ambassador Initiative, Portsmouth (VA) Chapter
2nd	Increasing Breast Cancer Awareness, Kent Area (OH) Chapter
3rd	African American AIDS Awareness Action Alliance, Portland (OR) Chapter
Legacy Award	Eatin' Good in the Neighborhood, Orlando (FL) Chapter
Integrated	Food Deserts, Greater Hudson Valley (NY) Chapter

NATIONAL POSTER ARTS COMPETITION

Southern	Miami-Biscayne Bay (FL) Chapter
Western	Pasadena (CA) Chapter
Southern	Tampa (FL) Chapter

Program Awards —41st (2018) Assembly

NATIONAL TRENDS AND SERVICES

Single Facet Awards

1st	I Am A Voter, River City (TN) Chapter
2nd	Institute for Women's Empowerment, Annapolis (MD) Chapter
3rd	Piece Program, Stockton (CA) Chapter

Integrated Awards

1st	AARP, Are You Ready, Westchester (NY) Chapter
2nd	Sisterhood, Young Women Empowerment, Omaha (NE) Chapter
3rd	Empowering Women's Lives, Archway (MO) Chapter

Umbrella Awards

1st	Children's House of Champions, Azalea City (GA) Chapter
2nd	STEM Career Academy, Selma (AL) Chapter
3rd	Literacy and Mentoring Program, Los Angeles (CA) Chapter
Legacy Award	Black Diamond Leadership, Youngstown (OH) Chapter

SERVICES TO YOUTH

Single Facet Awards

Ist	Igniting STEAM Dreams in Adolescence, Fort Valley (GA) Chapter
2nd	The Links Academy 2018, Chattanooga (TN) Chapter
3rd	Building a Healthy Community and Tomorrow's Leaders, Chesapeake–Virginia Beach (VA) Chapter

Integrated Awards

Ist	2016–2018 Young Achievers Program, Westchester (NY) Chapter
2nd	Linking Girls to Success, the Marian Middle School LEAD Project, Archway (MO) Chapter
3rd	Linking Children to Success: Achieving Excellence Pre-K to 6th Grade, Azalea City (GA) Chapter
	STEM and Mentorship III, Niagara Falls (NY) Chapter

Umbrella Awards

Ist	Full TEAM Ahead Toward Legacy, Jackson County (MO) Chapter
2nd	Building STEAM 2016–18, the Greater Seattle (WA) Chapter
3rd	2018 Linking to the Future, Waterbury (CT) Chapter

Best Practice Awards

	Magic, Making A Positive Impact Together with Eden Rose, Eden Rose (CA) Chapter
	A Better Mind, A Better Life, Central Illinois (IL) Chapter
Legacy Award	Links Reaching New Heights Rising Stars, Pontchartrain (LA) Chapter

THE ARTS

Single Facet Awards

Ist	Linkages, Women of African Descent Film Festival, Brooklyn (NY) Chapter
2nd	Classic Ballet Focus, Lake Shore (IL) Chapter
3rd	Opera Academy, Fort Bend (TX) Chapter

Integrated Awards

Ist	Respect Yourself Symposium, Alameda Contra-Costa (CA) Chapter
2nd	Beauford Delaney from Knoxville (TN) Chapter

Umbrella Awards

Ist	Links to Arts, Palos Verdes (CA) Chapter
2nd	Promoting Learning through The Arts at Seaford Elementary School, Cream City (WI) Chapter
3rd	Rhythms for Life, Morris County (NJ) Chapter

Legacy Award	Links to Aspiration, Houston (TX) Chapter

NATIONAL POSTER ART CONTEST WINNERS

Category 1   We Stand Together Against Bullying, Jazmin Hernandez, Bakersfield (CA) Chapter

Category 2   My Vision, My Future, by Asada Jenkins, Atlantic City (NJ) Chapter

Category 3   Weight of the World, Maya Cole from the Westchester County (NY) Chapter

Category 4   United for a Healthy and Happy Future, Cheyenne Alburg, Central (NJ) Chapter

INTERNATIONAL TRENDS AND SERVICES

Single Facet Awards

1st   Ultrasound machine donation to Jamaica for the "Jamaica Signature Project," Milwaukee (WI) Chapter

2nd   Links International Business, Foreign Affairs and Empowerment, Washington (DC) Chapter

3rd   Expanding the Pursuit of Global Medical Education, Brunswick (GA) Chapter

Integrated Awards

1st   LIFE on Long Island and Beyond – An Integrated Concept, Long Island (NY) Chapter

2nd   LIFE Program, Westchester County (NY) Chapter

3rd   Linkages to Jamaica: Central Basic School, West Towns (IL) Chapter

Umbrella Awards

1st   Links to the Border (US/Mexico), Palos Verdes (CA) Chapter

2nd   Mt. Zion All Age School, Montgomery County (PA) Chapter

3rd   A Haitian Love Affair, Greater Miami (FL) Chapter

Legacy Award   Linking with Haiti: Project Boots on the Ground, Pontchartrain (LA) Chapter

HEALTH AND HUMAN SERVICES

Single Facet Awards

1st   SF Links Connect: Building Healthy Communities Together, San Francisco (CA) Chapter

2nd   Oral Health Project, Suffolk (VA) Chapter

3rd   Shades of Pink Breast Cancer Awareness Campaign, West Palm Beach (FL) Chapter

Integrated Awards

1st   Links2Hope – Closing the Mental Health Gap in the African American Community, Chicago (IL) Chapter

2nd   Mental Health Again – Red Dress Heart Health, Washington (DC) Chapter

3rd   Linking Families to Healthy Body, Minds and Practices, Lake Shore (IL) Chapter

Umbrella Awards

1st   Many Facets of Mental Health, Tacoma (WA) Chapter

2nd   Continuing to Lead and Empower Youth toward Healthy Minds, Bodies and Futures, New Haven (CT) Chapter

3rd   Small Steps to Better Health and Wellness, North Jersey (NJ) Chapter

Legacy Award   Linking Together Against Syndrome X, Treasure Coast (FL) Chapter

35th (2006) Assembly
Grants-in-Aid: $181,000

Awards are made each biennium to innovative programs that benefit communities of African descent. Distributions at the 2006 Assembly included:

$5,000 Awards to Local Programs in the Philadelphia Area
YWCA of Bucks County
Habitat for Humanity of Philadelphia County
Habitat for Humanity of New Castle County (DE)
The Marion Anderson Museum

$30,000 Award
National Merit Scholarship of Boston, Massachusetts
(Contributed each biennium)

$20,000 Awards
Virginia Historical Society, Richmond (VA)
"Documenting the African-American Experience in Virginia"
Recommended by the Richmond Chapter

Young Musicians Program
Music-based Youth Development and Educational Enrichment Program, Berkeley, CA
Alameda Contra-Costa (CA) Chapter and Oakland (CA) Chapter

$10,000 Awards
Buffalo Prenatal-Perinatal Network, Buffalo (NY)
"Baby and Me Cessation Program"
Recommended by the Buffalo Chapter

African-American Ethnic Academy, Madison (WI)
"Pre-school Child and Family Education Project"
Recommended by the Madison Metropolitan Chapter

Alternatives for Girls in Detroit (MI)
Shelter Services for homeless Girls and Boys
Recommended by the Renaissance (MI) Chapter

Huron Hospital of Cleveland, Cleveland, OH
"Lennon Diabetes Links Awareness Program"
Cleveland Chapter

Carolina Youth Center, Charleston, SC
"Life and Job Skills Development for Children who Are Aging out of the Foster Care System"
Charleston Chapter

Louisiana Art and Science Museum, Baton Rouge, LA
Howard Dina Pendel Exhibition
La Capitale Chapter

Girls, Incorporated, Wilmington (NC)
After-School and Summer Enrichment Program
Wilmington Chapter

Techcorp Texas, Houston
Technology Education Program Student-Run Help Desk-Houston Schools
Gulf Coast Apollo (TX) Chapter

$6,000
St. Thomas African Episcopal Church in Philadelphia
Special contribution in honor of Co-Founders Margaret Rosell Hawkins and Sarah Strickland Scott on the occasion of the 60th anniversary of The Links.

36th (2008) Assembly
Grants-in-Aid: $150,000

$20,000
The Community Boys & Girls Club of Wilmington (NC) to support the Media Links Project, including reading, writing, and web design.

The Goal, Incorporated to fund the pilot and replication of a group mentorship program for middle school girls in two schools in Atlanta (GA).

The Harlem (NY) Academy in support of a before- and after-school program for students in grades 1–4.

The National Center for Children and Families in Montgomery County (MD) in support of an emergency shelter serving homeless families, primarily mothers with children.

$15,000

The Augusta (GA) Partnership for Children, Incorporated to support a pregnant and parenting teen's program addressing prenatal health, infant health issues, and life skills.

The Fort Wayne African American Cancer Alliance to underwrite a case manager who will provide assistance to patients.

The South Suburban Pads in the Homewood and Chicago Heights (IL) area in support of the operation of a homeless healthcare network which provides services for over 1,200 homeless men, women, and children.

$10,000

The Black Child and Family Institute to support fine arts summer enrichment camp for low-income youth in Lansing (MI)

The Texas Association of Developing Colleges, Dallas, to support "Black Male Youth Accessing Higher Education with E's," a college readiness program that enrolls high school juniors from low income families.

37th (2010) Assembly
Grants-in-Aid: $225,129

$30,000

Big Brothers/Big Sisters of North Texas, Irving, to the mentoring program for African American men and youth.

$25,000

Niles Home for Children, Kansas City (MO), to a residential and day treatment foster care setting by improving the health and self-esteem of children ages 7–17. The program inspires youth to acquire healthy lifestyles through physical activity, community gardening, and "Fit for Reading" literacy component.

Focus Hope, Detroit (MI), to support the 37th National Assembly Community Outreach Project, The Links Family Learning Center.

$21,000

National Achievement Scholarship Program, Boston (MA), to fund minority scholarships.

$20,000

Big Brothers/Big Sisters of Central Ohio to increase the number of community-based mentoring relationships for children of prisoners in a five-county area.

Black Liberated Arts Center, Oklahoma City (OK), to use the arts as a tool for teaching reading, math, and writing, targeting 600 students in three elementary schools and one high school.

Ionia R. Whipper Home, Incorporated, Washington (DC), to provide supportive services to birth parents and surrogates of African American foster care female youth, ages 12–21, through a parenting education program and enhanced child visitation program.

$16,000

Facilitating Leadership in Youth, Washington (DC), to support the salary of the executive director to enable continued outreach to youth ages 7–18 in the Barry Farm Community of Southeast Washington, DC. Program includes one-on-one tutoring/mentoring, college preparedness, a youth leadership council, and educational advocacy.

$15,000

A Better Chance, New York (NY), to increase the recruitment of students from low-performing high schools and community-based organizations.

The literacy problem by Communities in Schools, Houston (TX), for Project MOVE, providing free dental care and oral health education to 450 K–5 economically disadvantaged children.

$10,000

The Witness Project, Bridgeport (CT), to support and increase outreach efforts to African American women by African American women who are themselves breast cancer survivors.

$5,000

Habitat for Humanity of Bucks County, Chalfont (PA), to involve youth in funding and building a home for a low-income family in Bucks County in Partnership with the Women Build Program, which empowers women to be self-sufficient in construction and providing networking opportunities.

$2,929

Young Audiences of Northeast Ohio (Cleveland), for a literacy program for fourth-grade students, blending creativity and discipline of the arts to raise student achievement in reading and writing.

Source: Assembly Minutes 2006, 2008, 2010

CHAPTER 15
TRANSFORMATIVE DRIVERS
Fueling Stations

*T*he 1980s award-winning TV series *Fame* opened with audition judge Lydia Grant sternly telling performing arts students: "You've got big dreams. You want fame. Well, fame costs. And right here is where you start paying … in sweat." In Linkdom, the big dream is service—transformative service. The dream was entrenched in Linkdom from the outset. Members invested sweat equity and dollars to make a difference in their communities, and change was evident. However, marked shifts have been powered by strategic moves, big bucks, and alliances.

GRANTS-IN-AID

Early Links programming was funded through member and chapter assessments and dues, which began when the 4th (1952) Assembly approved a $10 assessment for NAACP life memberships, the first National project. Periodic assessments gave way to annual Grants-in-Aid taxes, set at $25 by the 14th (1964) Assembly. By 1970, more than $100,00 had been donated to the NAACP, and a $100,000 commitment to the National Urban League had also been satisfied.

The Assembly, under the direction of 4th National President Vivian Beamon also adopted the United Negro College Fund and sickle cell as National projects, and by the 18th (1972) Assembly, 114 of 118 chapters had donated more than $64,000 for UNCF and $43,000 for sickle cell. Convinced that Links contributions should be sizable enough to make a statement about the organization's commitment, however, 5th National President Helen Gray Edmonds pushed a more strategic approach.

Delegates to the 18th (1972) Assembly made the United Negro College Fund the exclusive National project and approved a $50 per-capita assessment. The move paid off at the 19th (1974) Assembly, with Edmonds presenting a check for $132,000 to UNCF Director Christopher Edley. It was the largest single donation made by a Black organization, and the beginning of The Links' million-dollar awards.

Another tactic was the division of funds available from Grants-in-Aid. The 19th (1974) Assembly capped the distribution at 80 percent (of funds available for distribution) for the primary designee. Presented by Grants-in-Aid Chair Eugenia Long, Tyler (TX) Chapter, the stipulation reserved the remaining 20 percent for community grants, including a mandatory award to a recipient in the city hosting the Assembly. The action sparked Links' support of fledgling community initiatives and simultaneously maintained its eminence as an organization true to Edmonds's avowal, "We do big things, and we do them in big ways."

Subsequent awards, including $150,000 installments in 1976 and 1978 during the administration of 6th National President Pauline Ellison and $160,000 in 1980 with 7th National President Julia B. Purnell at the helm, were capped by the completion of the first million dollars at the 24th (1984) Assembly during the tenure of 8th National President Dolly Desselle Adams.

Seeking to maximize its dollars and outreach, The Links employed other carefully designed measures. During 2004, based on recommendations from the Finance Committee, the Executive Council approved a contractual arrangement with a fund manager to invest receipts for the National Assembly and prepaid membership dues. In the past, the funds had been dispersed in multiple accounts (to comply with FDIC limits) with a low return on the resources. The fund earned more than $20,000 in less than one year.

THE LINKS FOUNDATION

As early as 1968, The Links pondered ways to enable members to receive a tax exemption for their donations; but obtaining 501(c)(3) status took years of diligence. Initial action can be traced to a recommendation to change the organization's IRS designation from 501(c)(4) to 501(c)(3), presented at the November 1968 Executive Council meeting. In response, 4th National President Vivian J. Beamon sought counsel and, based on the advice, decided not to proceed with an application. Reporting to the 1970 Assembly, she wrote:

To effect this change, we contacted Dr. Davis of the Legal Defense Fund … Into our office came a three-page directive from top legal counsel giving us guidelines on setting up such a plan. A copy of the proposal was sent to each member of our Executive Council for study. The conclusion reached was as follows: To comply with demands, our constitution would have to be changed beyond our power—for these changes in effect would drastically change the purpose of our organization. To this end, it was agreed that we would proceed to operate as usual until further study and proposals could be made to the body.

The matter was reviewed again in 1974, when 6th National President Pauline Ellison (1974–1978) requested that Allie Weeden, The Links' general counsel (parliamentarian), prepare information on setting up a tax-exempt fund. In a June 23, 1974, memo, Weeden proposed that The Links set up a separate fund to be called the Link Fund.

In 1976, the Executive Council supported the recommendation and forwarded it to the 20th National Assembly for action. The recommendation read: "The Links, Inc., through the Finance Committee … set up a separate Link Fund as a 501(c)(3) organization to cover the national organization and all the Link chapters." The Assembly approved the action, and Ellison appointed a committee to study the procedures and prepare the necessary documents, including articles of incorporation, bylaws, and the Application for Recognition of Exemption under Section 501(c)(3). Key stipulations were that the fund would be sponsored by The Links and would be governed by a board of directors comprised of Links.

FIL 3 FEE $10.00
INDEXING FEE 2.00
$12.00

Articles of Incorporation

of

The Links Foundation, Inc.

To: The Recorder of Deeds, D.C.
     Washington, D.C.

We, the undersigned natural persons of the age of twenty-one years or more, acting as incorporators of a corporation, adopt the following Articles of Incorporation of such corporation pursuant to the District of Columbia Non-Profit Corporation Act, 29 D.C. Code §29-1001 et seq.:

FIRST: The name of the corporation is THE LINKS FOUNDATION, INC.

SECOND: The period of its duration is perpetual.

THIRD: The purposes for which the corporation is organized are as follows:

1. To design, support, and conduct charitable and educational activities useful to the individual and beneficial to the community within the meaning of Section 501(c)(3) of the Internal Revenue Code of 1954 (the "Code").

2. To provide services to youth, directed toward the upgrading of academic, artistic, and technical skills, and fighting juvenile delinquency.

3. To support and defend human and civil rights secured by law.

4. To provide charitable services to senior

FILED
DEC 20 1979

Foundation Articles of Incorporation

Reporting to the 21st National Assembly on July 5, 1978, Weeden voiced the committee's intention to move forward in establishing a 501(c)(3) organization mandated by the 20th (1976) Assembly, but she noted that the committee's efforts had been hampered. "Transition implementation has delayed getting the necessary financial data needed for submission of the application to IRS," she said.

In October 1978, newly elected National President Julia B. Purnell (1978–1982) directed Nan Johnson, director of The Links, Inc., to prepare an update on the status of the application for 501(c)(3) status. Johnson reported that she had contacted Weeden and others who might have information/documentation on transactions, but she was "unable to secure any documented facts" that any progress had been made. With approval from Purnell, Johnson secured "guidance" from the firm of Nathan and Mause.

In March 1979, Purnell, acting on recommendations from the attorneys, took the initial steps to obtain 501(c)(3) status. She named three Links to serve as incorporators, appointed an interim board of directors, and authorized the attorneys to take the lead in developing articles of incorporation for submission to the IRS. As incorporators, Purnell designated Janet Ballard, Richmond, Virginia, Beatrice Butler, Baltimore, Maryland, and Reba Gaston, Dayton, Ohio, and she tapped seven Links as members of the interim board: Mary Bell, Pearl Brackett, Ann Hutchinson, Samella Lewis, Arlene Rayford, Jacqueline Robinson, and Lizzie Willis.

The Foundation *Articles of Incorporation*, while built around the organization's *Articles of Incorporation of The Links, Incorporated*, also had to be structured to satisfy incorporation requirements in the District of Columbia. A draft was circulated to the Executive Council, former National Presidents, and chairmen of National standing committees of The Links, Incorporated, along with the Foundation's interim board of directors; and on July 23, the attorneys submitted the final copy of the *Articles of Incorporation* for each incorporator's signature.

Completing the *Bylaws* was the next step. In a telephone conference call on February 23, 1980, the interim Foundation board voted to adopt standard bylaws "used in the District of Columbia for this type of organization, and the collection data was sent to IRS." By March 7, 1980, The Links Foundation/Fund had received an advanced ruling granting 509(a)(1) and 170(b)(1)(A)(vi) designations through April 30, 1982, provided the submissions were in order. Notice of the probationary status was sent to all National officials of the Links, Incorporated and published in *Link to Link*, the National President's newsletter. Purnell also placed the item on the agenda for the 1980 Assembly, where delegates endorsed continuation of the process.

The next step for the interim board of directors was to present the *Bylaws* to the Assembly for approval. Ballard, in her position as National parliamentarian of The Links, Incorporated, presented and read the *Bylaws* to the Links Assembly on July 8, 1982. On July 9, 1982, convening as The Foundation, members adopted (315-7) the *Bylaws* "as presented and read on Thursday, July 8."

The meeting agenda also included the election of officers, spurring a modification in the holders of at-large seats. Along with the president, vice president, and secretary, whose offices and tenures in the Foundation corresponded to their elected position in The Links, Incorporated, the amendment designated the Area directors and treasurers—rather than Area directors and Area secretaries—to serve as at-large members until an election could be held in 1983 at the annual meeting. Purnell then declared, "We have the elected officers and members–at–large and the Board of Directors of the Links Foundation, Inc., thereby being ready to function."

Although 1982 has been historically listed as the year of creation, The Links Foundation apparently became a reality three years earlier. Documents show that the Corporation Division of the Government of the District of Columbia issued a certificate to The Links Foundation, Inc. on December 20, 1979, nine months following Purnell's directive to Johnson. One of four "purposes for which the corporation is organized" was "1. … to design, support, and conduct charitable and educational activities useful to the

Partnerships
President Kimberly Jeffries Leonard and NOBLE (National Organization of Black Law Enforcement Executives) President Vera Bumpers ink historic partnership.

individual and beneficial to the community within the meaning of Section 50l(c)(3) of the Internal Revenue Code of 1954 (the 'Code')."

Nonetheless, on July 9, the Foundation was entrusted to incoming National President Dolly Desselle Adams (1982–1986). A key change during Adams's tenure was membership requirements in the Foundation. Initially, membership was voluntary: "The Links Foundation strongly encourages the payment of One Dollar ($1.00) by all chapter members as dues to The Links Foundation."

Beginning in 1992, membership in the Foundation came in tandem with membership in The Links. The action originated with 10th National President Marion Sutherland, who sought to strengthen the connection between The Links and The Links Foundation. The 28th National Assembly approved a $30 per-member, per-year assessment to build an endowment fund to

support programs. The assessment, initially approved for a two-year period, has continued as a perennial source of individual member support, along with Assembly set asides and fundraisers, enabling The Links Foundation to issue grants of more than $25 million.

Fundraisers and special campaigns have also expanded The Links' ability to offer hope to individuals and organizations. To demonstrate "that we were serious, focused and intentional about contributing to our own Foundation," 11th National President Patricia Russell-McCloud initiated a members' campaign that netted $675,000 in 1996. Following suit, other presidents added millions. Fifteenth National President Margot James Copeland raised more than $600,000 during the 65th anniversary celebration and added more than $350,000 through special campaigns that included direct solicitation of new donors and a "$1,000 from 1,000" effort. With her "Vision

2020" and "1946 Society" campaigns, the 16th National President generated $2 million.

Additionally, turbo boosts through federal programs have enhanced and expanded programming. In 1982, the Office of Juvenile Justice and Delinquency Prevention awarded The Links its first six-figure grant, a $101,205 award to prevent and treat delinquency among girls ages 12–17. The largest sole-source grant came in 1987, when the Foundation received $938,000 to reduce substance abuse, adolescent pregnancy, and sexually transmitted diseases in high-risk youth. The project was funded by the Office of Substance Abuse and Mental Health Administration within the US Department of Health and Human Services.

Another driver has been corporate sponsorships. The largest multi-source grant was a 1998 $1 million award from Kellogg, UPS, and the Exxon Foundation to implement Links to Success: Children Achieving Excellence, one of The Links' most vaunted Signature Programs. A 2012 half-million grant from GE Healthcare, Corporation of the Midsouth, Blue Cross/Blue Shield, Safeway, and the Kellogg Foundation funded chapter childhood obesity programs. The Links' STEM-U-Lation: Left Brain–Right Brain was funded through a $250,000 two-year renewable grant from Chevron in 2012, along with $75,000 from AT&T in 2013, and program resources from NASA and Achieving the Dream.

Collaborative alliances have also helped to power and refuel The Links' mission of transforming communities. National partners engaged for 2018–2020 include AARP, Achieving the Dream Leader College, Africare, Ally, Colgate-Palmolive, NAACP, National Dental Association, National Society of Black Engineers, Partnership for a Healthier America, The Sullivan Alliance, and General Motors.

The super driver in Links' outreach has always been human capital. The Links has employed two generators to transform participation by its members into leadership and engagement. The Scott-Hawkins Leadership Institute targets members under 40 and the Links Leadership Academy is reserved for members 40 and above.

THE SCOTT-HAWKINS LEADERSHIP INSTITUTE (SHLI)

The Scott-Hawkins Leadership Institute (SHLI) was created to embolden young Links leaders to respond to emerging organizational and community needs. The two-year fellowship program was envisioned and institutionalized in by 13th National President Gladys Gary Vaughn to sustain the viability of The Links and to create leaders committed to service within the Black community.

Named in honor of Co-Founders Margaret Rosell Hawkins and Sarah Strickland Scott, SHLI emerged at the 34th (2004) Assembly. Links ages 25–39 (originally 21–45) who have held a chapter office are eligible to compete for admission. Candidates must also have demonstrated professional achievement and leadership capabilities, a commitment to community service and volunteerism, and behavior consistent with the Links Code of Ethics.

SHLI has fostered a sustained philosophy of lifelong leadership development intended to impact positive change within The Links, Incorporated, civic and social organizations, professional environments, and society. Fellows are expected to become leaders at all levels through guided learning, social engagement, self-reflection, and skill development and refinement.

Inaugural Dean Josephine Davis, Fort Valley (GA) Chapter, centered the curriculum on five principles: Spirituality, Leadership Development, Health and Wellness, Mentoring, and Civic Engagement. Class size has ranged from 39 to 60, with a low of 39 and a high of 58 graduates. SHLI received instant credibility with Vaughn's appointment of 7th National President and renowned educator Julia Brogdon Purnell as Dean Emeritus.

Jayne Baccus Khalifa, Minneapolis/St. Paul (MN) Chapter, was named dean, and Jan Collins-Eaglin, Ann Arbor (MI) Chapter, and Jennifer Brooks Giddings, Fort Worth (TX) Chapter, served as associate deans. The W. K. Kellogg Foundation and the Key Bank Foundation provided initial funding for the institute.

Fourteenth National President Gwendolyn B. Lee ensured that SHLI fellows continued to acquire a "solid orientation to the fundamentals of The Links, Inc." and further understand the opportunities and responsibilities associated with membership by placing the Institute under the National vice president and appointing Jayne Baccus Khalifa, Minneapolis/St. Paul (MN) Chapter. Khalifa (2006–2010) built on the five principles established by Davis and expanded the curriculum, continuing to make the program relevant to the changes in demand and expectations of leaders.

Within the first six years (2004–2010), the organization touched the lives of some 160 fellows. The curriculum for the first year included the Black Women's Club Movement, Health and Wellness, and Leadership Development. Three other leadership dimensions focused on organizational effectiveness, the role personal spirituality plays in decision making, and the importance of "community engagement" in delivering meaningful programs and sustained community service. Khalifa's administration also introduced the inaugural SHLI fall retreat.

Fifteenth National President Margot James Copeland named Jan Collins Eaglin, Claremont Area (CA) Chapter, dean, and Deborah Brittain, Arlington (VA) Chapter, associate dean, along with assistant deans Mildred Edwards, Wichita (KS) Chapter, and Valerie Kennedy-Miller, Metro-Manhattan (NY) Chapter. Deans expanded the curriculum into a learning continuum featuring an emphasis on leading

on different levels, and they hosted leadership training programs at Area conferences and the inaugural Leadership Summit in Houston, Texas.

Eaglin developed and initiated the graduation ritual and standardized the application, nomination, review, and acceptance process. She and her team also served Cohort V. By the summer of 2014, approximately 250 Links had participated and graduated from five cohorts with 39 additional fellows preparing to begin their fellowship experience.

Deborah Brittain, Arlington (VA) Chapter, was named dean (2014–2018) by 16th National President Glenda Newell-Harris. The curriculum for Cohorts VI and VII focused on principle-centered and strength-based leadership through the lens of personal, interpersonal, organizational, and community-based leadership competencies. Brittain's team of deans worked to establish a cohort mission and vision, and a formal capstone project process was also implemented. Soraya Moore Coley, alumna, Western Area, Lynn Wooten, Ann Arbor (MI) Chapter, and Alexia Hudson-Ward, Cleveland (OH) Chapter, served as associate deans.

By the summer of 2018, 396 fellows had been invited to participate in SHLI, and 340 (97 percent) had graduated. A survey administered at the 10-year mark did not provide definitive results of the program's effectiveness. However, the heights that SHLI fellows have reached in Linkdom document that some progress has been made. The 17th National President, Kimberly Jeffries Leonard, was a fellow

Scott-Hawkins Cohort VIII participants

of Cohort I. Leonard's career and volunteer trajectory within The Links and other organizations and communities exemplify the mission and vision of SHLI fully. Nine SHLI fellows have been elected/appointed to the 2018–2020 National Executive Council.

- National President, Kimberly Jeffries Leonard, Arlington (VA) Chapter, Cohort I
- National Secretary, Crystal Kendrick, Queen City (OH) Chapter, Cohort IV
- Eastern Area Director, Shuana Tucker Sims, Fairfield County (CT) Chapter, Cohort I
- Southern Area Director, Sylvia Perry, Bold City (FL) Chapter, Cohort IV
- National Nominating Committee Chair, Raynetta Waters, Asheville (NC) Chapter, Cohort IV
- National Communications Chair, Rozalynn Frazier, Metro-Manhattan (NY) Chapter, Cohort II
- National Chair of Economic Development, Bridget Chisholm, Greensboro (NC) Chapter Cohort I
- National Chief of Staff, Kristie Patton Foster, Mid-Cities (TX) Chapter, Cohort I
- Dean, SHLI, Mildred Edwards, Greater Kansas City (MO) Chapter, Cohort I

A number of former SHLI fellows and/or former deans were also selected to serve Cohort VIII: Associate Dean Kimberly Conliffe Stephens, Silver Spring (MD) Chapter (Cohort I), and Assistant Deans Michelle Lee Murrah, South Suburban Chicago (IL) Chapter (Cohort III), and Jennifer Giddings Brooks, Fort Worth (TX) Chapter (Cohort I).

Comparable to former cohorts, SHLI Cohort VIII is comprised of 47 diverse leaders, with expertise and talents just as diverse. Fifteen attorneys; a concert pianist; educators, human resources, public relations, and medical professionals; a museum curator; political strategists; operations, communications, non-profit, and community affairs executives; a banker; 19 DOLs; 18 married professionals; 18 mothers; and 28 single professionals comprise the membership.

Building on data gained in the ten-year SHLI Alumni Survey and the success of previous Cohorts, Edwards developed the current SHLI curriculum to further enhance leadership skills and organizational effectiveness intended to sustain The Links and other professional and community-based organizations targeting the African American community, while also building their attention to personal wellness, authenticity, and loving support of others.

The Cohort VIII fellowship curriculum features four parts: Leadership is an Inside Job, African-American Female Leaders Masters Series, Leading within The Links, Incorporated, and completion of a Capstone Project that highlights the fellow's plans to sustain the mission of The Links, Incorporated or other organizations.

~ Mildred A. Edwards, PhD

THE LINKS LEADERSHIP ACADEMY

In kinship with the Scott-Hawkins Leadership Institute, The Links Leadership Academy was created to provide continual leadership development for Links 40 and over. Some 345 Links completed the training, with 144 registrants for the inaugural sessions in 2014. In 2016 and 2018, 76 and 125 registrants, respectively, enrolled.

Fifteenth National President Margot Copeland tapped former Scott-Hawkins dean Jayne Kalifa to develop a program that would enable Links to serve effectively at the Chapter, Area, and National levels. The program falls under organizational effectiveness, whose mission is:

> *To provide interactive in-person and on-demand online training designed to enhance leadership skills at every level of The Links, Incorporated as we position ourselves individually and collectively to lead our organization. Strong character, knowledge of organizational governing documents, strategic leadership skill development, and effective communication skills are all required by elected, appointed, and general membership if we are to remain relevant, continue to attract new members, and provide programming that is truly transformational.*

SCOTT-HAWKINS LEADERSHIP INSTITUTE

Cohort & Year	Dean	Associate Deans	Assistant Deans	National President	Inducted National Assembly	#	Graduated National Assembly	#
I 2004– 2006	J. Davis	J. Baccus Khalifa J. Giddings Brooks	J. Collins Eaglin	13th – G. Gary Vaughn	2004 – 34th Atlanta, GA	46	2006 – 35th Philadelphia, PA	46
II 2006– 2008	J. Baccus Khalifa	J. Collins Eaglin	D. Brittain	14th – G. Lee	2006 – 35th Philadelphia, PA	60	2008 – 36th Seattle, WA	58
III 2008– 2010	J. Baccus Khalifa	J. Collins Eaglin	D. Brittain	14th – G. Lee	2008 – 36th Seattle, WA	52	2010 – 37th Detroit, MI	51
IV 2010– 2012	J. Collins Eaglin	D. Brittain	M. Edwards V. Kennedy Miller	15th – M. James Copeland	2010 – 37th Detroit, MI	53	2012 – 38th Orlando, FL	51
V 2012– 2014	J. Collins Eaglin	D. Brittain	M. Edwards V. Kennedy Miller	15th – M. James Copeland	2012 – 38th Orlando, FL	48	2014 – 39th National Harbor, MD	46
VI 2014– 2016	D. Brittain	S. Coley A. Hudson-Ward L. Wooten		16th – G. Newell-Harris	2014 – 39th National Harbor, MD	39	2016 – 40th Las Vegas, NV	39
VII 2016– 2018	D. Brittain	S. Coley A. Hudson-Ward L. Wooten		16th – G. Newell-Harris	2016 – 40th Las Vegas, NV	51	2018 – 41st Indianapolis, IN	48
VIII 2018– 2020	M. Edwards	K. Conliffe Stephens	E. Baccus M. Lee Murrah J. Giddings Brooks	17th – K. Jeffries Leonard	2018 – 41st Indianapolis, IN	47	2020 – 42nd New Orleans, LA	

PART VIII

Core Affinity
The Links Banner

*Friendship is an action verb. Friendship is
the essential pillar of our continued existence.*

~ KIMBERLY JEFFRIES LEONARD
NATIONAL PRESIDENT

The Lady Is a Link, Waco (TX) Chapter

CHAPTER 16
THE LADY IS A LINK

*From all those who accept the rare invitation to don the
mantle of The Links, Incorporated, much is expected.*
~ GLADYS GARY VAUGHN 13TH NATIONAL PRESIDENT

"As Links, we are the legacy keepers of a distinct and significant history," National President Kimberly Jeffries Leonard reminded members in the March 2019 issue of *Link to Link*. What readily distinguishes a Link is her embodiment of the consummate ideals of friendship and service brilliantly conceived and flawlessly personified by Co-Founders Margaret Rosell Hawkins and Sarah Strickland Scott. Consequently, "from all those who accept the rare invitation to don the mantle of The Links, Incorporated, much is expected."

By design, The Links will never be the largest women's organization. Through limits on the number of members in a chapter, unanimous votes, and a national capacity cap, The Links controls the makeup and size of its membership. From the outset, membership was comprised of nine well-heeled, socially prominent, highly educated, married women committed to collective engagement for the betterment of the Philadelphia community. Those characteristics became the mold, with social status serving as the controller.

"Membership in The Links, Incorporated is a privilege," as explicitly proclaimed in the *Bylaws*. While having a "90210-ish" zip code is no longer "the" gatekeeper, membership is still selective. Even

Becoming

302

daughters of Links, though exempted from a two-thirds vote requirement, must receive a majority endorsement for admission. Individuals invited to wear the Links symbol must declare a willingness to devote the necessary hours to implement programs and emulate The Links' ten core values: friendship, service, legacy, respect, family relationships, honesty/truth, confidentiality, integrity, courage, and responsibility/accountability. However, a litmus test of documented likeness ultimately determines whether an offer is ever extended.

As the first of the ten, friendship is paramount. The Links is a circle of friends. "Friendship is the essential pillar of our continued existence. It is an action verb," National President Kimberly L. Jeffries and her predecessors continually stressed. Accordingly, "women invited to join our ranks must have the capacity for friendship," 15th National President Margot James Copeland stressed. "Links are expected to exhibit and promote friendship, despite natural discord that sometimes accompany human interactions," Copeland said. Seventh National President Julia Brogdon Purnell stressed the entirety of being friends. "In the chaotic world today, true sisterhood is of utmost importance. … Friendship is empathy, it's sympathy, it's togetherness, it's tolerance," she counseled.

Friendship is intentional. Members come in with bonds that have been engendered through common ties, experiences, and values—Links are highly educated, family oriented, socially engaged, successful, influential, and affluent women. The Links nurtures those ties through formal rituals and scheduled events like Friendship Week. More importantly, the bonds are continually strengthened and renewed through relationships fortified by the embrace of service—not as a choice, but as a responsibility, an attitude that creates and delivers solutions that affirm, "We are our sister's keeper." Consequently, the makeup of the membership is critical.

The first formal data-driven profile of Links, a "Woman Power Study," was initiated during the administration of 4th National President Vivian Jones Beamon (1962–1970). National Vice President and Membership Chair Anna Roselle Johnson Julian, Chicago (IL) Chapter, conducted the survey between

TOP: Toasting

BOTTOM: Connecting

1962 and 1964. Noting the reliability, Julian assured the Assembly that she had "discussed materials and treatment of same" with Science Research Associates, a firm that graded all national merit examinations and developed research techniques, tests, and scoring devices for universities and corporations.

Findings presented to the 14th (1964) Assembly cast Links as mature, highly educated, married professionals who enjoyed social contact with others. Statistically significant (a sample of 57 percent was drawn from the responses by 889 {53 percent} of the 1,669 members), the study showed that 43 percent were over 50; 96 percent had completed high school, 76 percent held a college degree, and 35 percent held a master's degree; 78 percent were married, with another 12 percent widowed and 4 percent divorced; and 69 percent were employed, with 44 percent serving as educators. A 1966 report showed that most members were 51 to 65 years old, held college degrees, were educators, and lived with their husbands, who were typically doctors, lawyers, or businessmen.

Surveys conducted through the years have provided even stronger credence for each finding, save age, where there has been a slight shift toward a younger membership. Also, while educators still make up the largest segment, more Links can be found in non-traditional professions. A 1978 composite by Vivian Pinn, Boston (MA) Chapter, further showed that Links were sorority members, attended church regularly, and belonged to social groups.

Consistent with the trending, National Vice President and Membership Chair Marion Sutherland,

Seattle (WA) Chapter, told the 26th (1988) Assembly that the membership was getting younger, with a high of 12 percent under 30. Additionally, while educators still dominated, the numbers in business and commerce, as well as in the health sciences, had grown. Of the 387 new members, 35 percent were elementary, secondary, and higher education teachers, but 14 percent were business professionals, and 13 percent were doctors, dentists, and health science administrators.

A survey of the membership by the Woman Power Commission in 1998 showed that educators still reigned (51 percent). Numbers in other categories showed growth in non-traditional fields, including administrators (12 percent), medical professionals (4 percent), and business owners (3 percent). Chair

Inspiring

Bonding

Learning

Ann Taylor, Petersburg (VA) Chapter, noted, "There is support data to show who we are, what we do, and our area of expertise." Another key finding was that only 2 percent of members were homemakers. A decade later, results from a 2008 study illuminated the traits discerned in the 1998 report, as well as characteristics outlined in the initial 1964 report. The typical Link is over 50, highly educated, married, and employed.

The 15,870 women on the Links 2018–2019 roster shared other characteristics. A 2019 chapter survey with a 95 percent response showed a slight decline in the graying of Links, with most members in the 40 to 69 range (57 percent) and Links 50 to 59 dominating. The 57 percent for Links 40 to 69 was also consistent with a 2015 demographic that showed 59 percent of Links were 41 to 70 years of age. Both the 2015 and 2019 surveys cast Links 20 to 40 (8 percent) as the smallest group.

Because of the small number of members in the 20 to 40 demographic, a concerted effort was made to increase that demographic by 2 percent in program year 2015, by 3 percent in program year 2016, and by 4 percent in program year 2017. While there was not a continual increase, there was progress. Of the 3,249 members inducted during the four-year period, 1,345 (41 percent) were under 40. Recruiting members between the ages of 20 and 40 has remained a priority.

The 2019 survey was clustered in seven 10-year groupings; four groups fell within three percentage points, with the edge going to Links 50 to 59 (19.6 percent), closely followed by Links 60 to 69 (18.9 percent), Links 40 to 49 (18.49 percent), and Links 70 to 79 (16 percent). The slight amelioration can be traced to the focus on younger Links, but the general perception of The Links as a middle-aged (45 to 65) group is solid. The Links also has holding power. A whopping 77 percent of members have been Links for 4 to 15 years. Of that percentage, 35 percent of Links have been members for 16 years or more.

Members are expected to follow the rules. Among the requirements set out in the *Constitution and Bylaws* are one-in-five and 48-hour standards that have been beneficial. Attending an Area

Conference or National Assembly at least once during a five-year period encouraged members to interface beyond the chapter level and become more knowledgeable about programs and operations, while performing a minimum of 48 hours of service annually provided opportunities for members to address needs in their community. Links members contribute more than 500,000 documented service hours in their communities annually.

Other compliance rudiments such as attendance, residency, and fees are also detailed. However, The Links Code of Ethics more explicitly "articulates the Links way—its legacy, values, and the standards of conduct essential to perpetuating Linkdom." All Links are charged to exemplify the high ideals and values upon which the organization was founded. Ten tenets constitute the core set of values: friendship, service, legacy, respect, family relationships, honesty/truth, confidentiality, integrity, courage, and responsibility/accountability.

Links are achievers. The chapter survey revealed that 67 percent of members held at least 51 percent ownership in a business. Links are also classroom teachers, neighborhood preachers, attorneys, physicians, and dentists; they are in the halls of Congress, in state legislatures, and on State Supreme Courts; and they are mayors and members of county commissions, city councils, school boards, and national commissions.

Links are athletes, journalists, writers, foundation heads, corporate leaders, college presidents, association managers, convention bureau chiefs, and Wall Street financiers. They are fraternal members—AKAs, Deltas, Zetas, and Sigma Gamma Rhos; they are church goers—Baptists, Methodists, Catholics, Muslims, and Pentecostals; and they are social joiners—100 Black Women, Girl Friends, Carats, and Jack and Jill; they are mostly married mothers, grandmothers, and great grandmothers; and so much more.

Family is one of the core values, and Links have titles for their husbands and children, who are called Connecting Links and Heir-O-Links, respectively. Females who become candidates for membership are also known as daughters of Links or DOLs.

Platinum Medallion

A Platinum Welcome

PLATINUM LINKS

The Links counts among its special members 451 Links who were endowed with Platinum status during the 2014 (114), 2016 (179), and 2018 (158) Assemblies. A Platinum member "is an active or alumna member who has reached eighty (80) years of age or older and who has given at least thirty (30) years of service, or who has given at least fifty (50) years of active service or who, regardless of age, has given at least forty-five (45) years of active service and has served in an elected position in her chapter and/or an elected or appointed position on the Area or National level." Among the honorees were Jessie Jones, Rocky Mount-Wilson-Tarboro (NC) Chapter, who served as Southern Area archivist for 16 years; Jewell E. Larue, Indianapolis (IN) Chapter, who served as chapter recording secretary; and Marjorie Mims, Chicago (IL) Chapter, 11th Central Area director.

Platinum Member Jessie Jones

Platinum Member Jewell Larue

Platinum Member Marjorie Mims

POWER LINKS

A listing of Power Links would be endless, but the greats below are representative.

- Lybra Clemons, San Jose (CA) Chapter, global head of diversity and inclusion for PayPal, was named to the *Black Enterprise* Most Powerful Women in Corporate Diversity list.

- Gloria Roberts Boyland, Memphis (TN) Chapter, Corporate Vice President of Operations and Service Support, Fed Ex, Memphis.

- Cheri Lynn Beasley, JD, Triangle Park (NC) Chapter, first African American woman to serve as Chief Justice of the North Carolina Supreme Court.

- Alicia Boler-Davis, Oakland County (MI) Chapter, is General Motors Executive Vice President of Global Manufacturing.

- Paula Coates, Arlington (VA) Chapter, is the first African American female appointed to the American Academy of Pediatric Dentistry Board of Trustees.

- Julie Coker Graham, Philadelphia (PA) Chapter, President and CEO, Philadelphia Convention & Visitors Bureau; first African American woman to lead a major convention center.

- Denise Paige Hood, Greater Wayne (MI) Chapter, Chief Judge of the United States District Court for the Eastern District of Michigan.

- Eddie Bernice Johnson, Dallas (TX) Chapter, first African American and first woman to chair the House Science, Space, and Technology Committee after being elected to the position in January 2019.

- Suzanne Shank, Great Lakes (MI) Chapter, CEO of two billion-dollar financial service institutions and the first African American woman to head a publicly traded financial institution.

- Ruth Simmons, president of Prairie View A&M University (TX); also served as the first African American president of an Ivy League institution (Brown University, Providence, RI).

- Doris Carson Williams, Pittsburgh (PA) Chapter, Chairman of the Federal Reserve Bank of Cleveland-Pittsburgh Branch.

Lybra Clemons Gloria Boyland Cheri Beasley Alicia Boler-Davis Paula Coates

Julie Coker Graham Denise Page Hood Eddie Bernice Johnson Suzanne Shank Doris Carson Williams

Missing Links, 5th (1953) Assembly, Buffalo (NY)

Connecting Links at 41st (2018) Assembly, Indianapolis (IN)

RIGHT: Heir-O-Link Kimberly Jeffries Leonard with her mom, Dr. Mary Jeffries

BELOW: Heir-O-Links visiting Conner Prairie, Indiana's first Smithsonian affiliate

Mattiwilda Dobbs (third from the left)

The most prominent grouping of Links is honorary members, who are elected in recognition of note-worthy achievements at the National level. Since the 28th (1992) Assembly, elections have been limited to one per Assembly in intervals of four years. Honorary members cannot vote, chair committees, or hold office unless they relinquish their honorary status. Eleven women have been inducted as honorary members.

Inducted June 26, 1970, at the 17th National Assembly in Cincinnati, Etta Moten Barnett was the first honorary member. Best known for her signature Broadway performance in the title role of George Gershwin's *Porgy and Bess* in 1942, Barnett was the first person to break the stereotypical portrayal of African Americans in the movies, appearing as a widowed housewife in *Golddiggers* (1933), and she was also the first Black woman to sing at the White House (1934 at FDR's birthday celebration).

Barnett expressed humility for the honor:

> *I am grateful that you deemed my feeble efforts at helping build bridges of Cultural and Racial Understanding at Home and Abroad worthy of this type of signal recognition .... I am proud to become a Link in a chain of Women Doers manifested in*

your three-pronged program—Extending Services to Youth, Fostering Freedom in the Fine Arts, and International Trends and Services.

Impressed with the work of Linkdom and not content to sit on the sidelines, however, Barnett opted to become an active member and subsequently chaired the ad hoc committee on International Trends and Services (1974–1978) and the International Women's Decade (1978–1986); from 1986 to 1990, she also served as the non-governmental organization (NGO) representative.

Ten other women were also elected:

- 1972 – Marian Anderson, internationally acclaimed soprano who made history when she sang at the Lincoln Memorial on Easter Sunday in 1939 after being barred from performing to an integrated audience in Constitution Hall and at a local high school because Anderson was Black.

- 1976 – Mattiwilda Dobbs was the first black singer to be offered a major international career in opera and the first to sign a long-term contract with the Metropolitan Opera Company.

Patricia Roberts Harris

Constance Baker Motley (left)

Leoyntyne Price (right)

- 1978 – Patricia Roberts Harris, Esq., was the first African American woman to hold a US Cabinet post (Secretary of Housing and Urban Development in 1977).

- 1980 – Constance Baker Motley was the first African American woman to serve as a federal judge. Longtime counsel for the NAACP, Motley was part of "nearly every important civil rights case for two decades."

- 1984 – Elizabeth Duncan Koontz was the first African American woman to serve as president of the National Education Association.

- 1989 – Leontyne Price was the Metropolitan Opera's first Negro superstar and widely recorded artist.

Condoleeza Rice

Ellen Johnson Sirleaf (center)

Kamala Harris (second from the left)

- 2003 – Rosa Louise McCauley Parks was the "first lady of civil rights" and "mother of the freedom movement." Parks is best known for refusing to give up her seat on a bus in Montgomery, Alabama.

- 2013 – Ellen Johnson Sirleaf, president of Liberia and the first female elected head of state in Africa (2005).

- 2013 – Condoleeza Rice, the first African American woman to serve as Secretary of State for the United States.

- 2018 – Kamala Harris, US Senator (D–CA), first African American attorney general, State of California, and 2020 Democratic presidential candidate.

CHAPTER 17
THE LINKS BRAND

Many had called for an official Links pin ad nauseum, but the pleas were commonly met with rebukes that included a not-so-friendly admonition, "Links is not a sorority." However, the Links pin emerged in 2018 as the latest identifier in the Links collection of names, emblems, marks, and other definers. "Created exclusively for the membership of The Links, Incorporated," the Official Links Pin was introduced by 16th National President Glenda Newell-Harris in May of 2018.

Resistance to the pin was a testament to the sanctity Links have placed on symbolic embodiments. The name "Links," the green and white color scheme, and the white rose are iconic representations of the values, ideals, customs. and personality of The Links. Consequently, a new depiction was not welcomed.

Cognizant of the power of branding, the founding group gave careful thought to what would define and distinguish the organization. They even used the generic "club" as a temporary identifier. Consequently, while the club was organized November 9, 1946, two months passed before the group selected its most important brand—the name. Other elements, including the official piece of jewelry (The Links bracelet), were carefully added; but for more than 72 years, the pin had not been deemed essential until it was installed as a legitimate brand alongside the vintage elements created by the founding group.

The pin debuted in May 2018 in concert with the opening of The Official Links Boutique. Touting the value of The Links brand, Links officials promoted the boutique as "part of the comprehensive initiative to control, protect and monetize The Links brand, which … had amassed enormous value and have achieved under intellectual property law 'acquired distinctiveness' in the marketplace."

THE NAME, PLEDGE, SONG, AND BRACELET

Lillian Hudson Wall suggested "Links" as the group's moniker at the January 1947 meeting. "It best expressed the meaning of the club," charter member Dorothy Wright wrote in a 1951 sketch on the founding and development of The Links. The pledge, song, and bracelet also originated with the Philadelphia Links. Co-Founder Sarah Strickland Scott penned the pledge, Frances Atkinson wrote the lyrics for the song, and Co-Founder Margaret Hawkins designed the bracelet.

When National Links was formed in 1947, the existing 13 clubs endorsed the retention of the symbols of the Philadelphia Links. Building on the club's brands, 1st National President Sarah Scott sought other identifiers she deemed fundamental to operations. By the January 20, 1951, meeting of the Executive Council, Scott had a Links insignia, music for the song, and the promise of a journal. She also noted, "Margaret Hawkins has designed a more artistic, smaller bracelet for those who prefer it."

Introduced by Ethel Lowry, Greater (NY) Chapter and financial secretary, the emblem was designed by Lowry's daughter-in-law Susan Lowry. Scott called it "an outstanding piece of work and one which symbolized The Links perfectly as a chain of friendship around the world."

In 2010, the Communications/Public Relations Committee held a contest to secure a tagline to be added to the insignia. "Linked in Friendship, Connected in Service" was chosen from those submitted. Bunnie R. Ransom, chair, announced the selection at the 37th (2010) National Assembly and presented Bobbie R. Verrett, Gulf Coast Apollo (TX) Chapter, who received the $500 prize for coining the phrase.

The official emblems were outlined in the 1951 *Bylaws of The Links*:

- Flower – White Rose
- Colors – Green and white
- Jewelry– The official jewelry is a bracelet, the purchase of which is optional.
- Incorporation Seal – The official seal shall be used by the Recording Secretary only to validate documents and official papers issued by her office. Under no circumstances can it be used by a Chapter or a member.
- There shall be a Link insignia which may be used on all official stationery and publications.

Scott also expressed pleasure that there was a tune to go with Atkinson's lyrics. Word of mouth about Sallie Armstrong, Wilson-Rocky Mount-Tarboro (NC) Chapter, having composed music for the Links song had initially surfaced at the 2nd (1950) Assembly, and the delegation eagerly approved it based on the review by Ethel Hines, also a member of the Wilson-Rocky Mount-Tarboro group.

The group asked Armstrong to send copies, and at the Executive Council meeting, Scott gratefully proclaimed, "We now have original music to our Links song, thanks to the creative ability of Sallie Armstrong." The admiration was short-lived. In 1959, Armstrong's melody was replaced with the Links Song in use today, which was arranged by Marietta Hall Cephas, Petersburg (VA) Chapter.

Other traditions and staples also emerged. A signet ring became the signature gift for a retiring National President at the 23rd (1982) Assembly, and the 28th (1992) Assembly that met in Dallas approved a design by Carolyn Jennings Tate, Plano North Metroplex (TX) Chapter, as the official flag.

A Links Medal has also been added to the Links collection. Through the years, National Presidents and committees had recognized exceptional performances and outstanding achievement with assorted laurels. Alpha

Links Medal sculptor Ed Dwight with Alpha Blackburn, creator

Blackburn, Indianapolis (IN) Chapter and The Arts facet director (2010–2014), felt that The Links, Incorporated should create an award that was distinctively Linkdom, one that was inextricably linked to the organization— The Links needed its own Spingarn Medal, its Medal of Honor, its Presidential Medal of Freedom. Sitting National President Margot James Copeland enthusiastically embraced the idea, and following unanimous endorsement by the Executive Council, Copeland entrusted the execution of the medal to Blackburn.

Designed by renowned artist Ed Dwight, the Links Medal "depicts figures, representing, in resolute stature and dignity, the diversity of accomplishments of our esteemed sisterhood." The award honors an organization or entity that has made a significant and positive impact on African American culture for more than 25 years. Conferral is by the National President, who may bestow only one during her tenure. Copeland presented the inaugural award to *Ebony* magazine as part of Links' 65th anniversary celebration in 2011, and 16th National President Glenda Newell-Harris made the second conferral to the NAACP during the 40th Assembly in 2018.

PUBLICATIONS, CEREMONIES, AND TERMINOLOGY

The Journal

The Executive Council authorized publication of the first *Journal* as a gift to each chapter at the 3rd (1951) Assembly and further specified that it should be kept in the chapter's file.

The release of the May 1966 issue of *The Links Journal* under 4th National President Vivian Jones Beamon was also considered a first. "At long last a dream has finally come true—our first National Journal is off the press," exclaimed editor Will Florence Robbins. Subsequently, the 17th (1970) Assembly approved a public relations position and authorized two issues (Fall and Spring) per year. The Assembly also mandated that the publication "become solely an internal organ carrying the news of the chapters."

Link to Link

The 17th (1970) Assembly also mandated that The Links move to individual communication to members, rather than one notification to chapter presidents. Fifth National President Helen Gray Edmonds's Executive

Publications

Council, meeting on August 1, 1971, approved a president's newsletter to be issued four times a year (March 1, June 1, September 1, and December 1) and mailed directly to members. Subsequently, budgetary constraints have determined the number of issues.

The Official History

Marjorie H. Parker, Washington (DC) Chapter, penned the first published history in 1981 under the direction of 7th National President Julia Brogdon Purnell. Parker also released a subsequent edition in 1992. Fifth National President Helen Gray Edmonds had set the stage for the history, telling the Executive Council in 1971, "There is nothing so needed at this time as the history of the beginning, growth and development of this organization." She immediately created an ad hoc Archives and History Committee, which was accorded standing status by the 18th (1972) Assembly.

Fourteenth National President Gwendolyn B. Lee tapped Earnestine Green McNealey, Tuscaloosa (AL) Chapter, to take the lead on the third edition. McNealey, chair of the Archives and History Committee, was assisted by committee members and designated Links. *Linked for Friendship and Service* was released in 2010 at the 37th Assembly.

Early manuscripts tracing the history were written by charter members Lillian Stanford and Dorothy Wright. Stanford, the first National historian, also compiled an unpublished volume for the 3rd (1951) Assembly.

Friendship Service

National Vice President and Program Chairman Lottie Lee Dinkins wrote the "Ceremonial of Friendship" in 1953 for use at the closings of Area and National meetings.

White Rose Banquet

The name was coined in the Southern Area in 1976 during Southern Area Director Julia Brogdon Purnell's administration.

Leaders across Linkdom gather at 2019 Governance Meeting

Connecting Link

Called "Missing Links" as late as the 5th (1953) Assembly, husbands were later dubbed "Connecting Links."

Heir-O-Link

The current moniker for children of Links; at the 5th (1953) Assembly, they were called Bob-o-Links.

A Code of Ethics that encapsulates the core values at the heart of the organization was approved by the 35th (2006) Assembly. Heralding the code, 13th National President Gladys Gary Vaughn said, "By embracing and adhering to the Code of Ethics … we guarantee that we will pass on to the next generation of Links a legacy of excellence." So it is with the marks of distinction by which The Links shall continue to be known.

~ *Earnestine Green McNealey, PhD*

Heir-O-Link Rozalynn Frazier with her mom, 9th National President Regina Jollivette Frazier

Appendices

Executive Council 2018–2020

Kimberly Jeffries Leonard, PhD
Arlington (VA) Chapter

National President

Ethel Isaacs Williams, JD
West Palm Beach (FL) Chapter

National Vice President
Chair, Membership Committee

Crystal L. Kendrick
Queen City (OH) Chapter

National Recording Secretary
Chair, Committee of Secretaries

Ethelyn S. Bowers
Essex County (NJ) Chapter

National Treasurer
Chair, Finance Committee

Tyna D. Davis, EdD
Montgomery (AL) Chapter

National Parliamentarian
Chair, Constitution & Bylaws Committee

Shuana Tucker-Sims, PhD
Fairfield County (CT) Chapter

Eastern Area Director

Sylvia Perry
Bold City (FL) Chapter

Southern Area Director

Glenda Masingale Manson
Central Illinois (IL) Chapter

Central Area Director

Lorna C. Hankins
Gulf Coast Apollo (TX) Chapter

Western Area Director

Glenda Newell-Harris, MD
Alameda Contra Costa (CA) Chapter

Immediate Past National President

Evelyn Rose Coker
Las Vegas (NV) Chapter

National Financial Secretary

1988–2000 Executive Council (Frazier)

2004–2006 Executive Council (Vaughn)

Gwendolyn E. Boyd, DMin
Capital City (DC) Chapter

Interim Executive Director

Margaret Elaine Flake, DMin
Greater New York (NY) Chapter

Interim Chaplain
Chair, Spiritual Enrichment & Wholeness Committee

Earnestine Green McNealey, PhD
Columbia (SC) Chapter

Chair, Archives and History Committee

F. Denise Gibson Bailey
Arlington (VA) Chapter

Chair, Awards/Recognition Committee

Michele V. Hagans, DMin
Capital City (DC) Chapter

Chair, Building Operations Committee

Anne T. Herriott
Greater Miami (FL) Chapter

Chair, Chapter Establishment

Rozalynn S. Frazier
Metro-Manhattan (NY) Chapter

Chair, Communications Committee

2008–2010 Executive Council (Lee)

2016–2018 Executive Council (Newell-Harris)

Vivian R. Pickard Renaissance (MI) Chapter	Chair, Corporate Relations Committee
Gwendolyn B. Lee, PhD South Suburban Chicago (IL) Chapter	Chair, Council of Presidents 14th National President
Bridget W. Chisholm Greensboro (NC) Chapter	Chair, Economic Empowerment Committee
Jarnell Burks-Craig Indianapolis (IN) Chapter	Chair, Elections Committee
Alice Strong Simmons Oklahoma City (OK) Chapter	Chair, Ethics and Standards Committee
Caroline R. Lang, PhD Prince George's County (MD) Chapter	Chair, Evaluations Committee
Valerie Wardlaw, PsyD Southern Area Affiliate	Chair, Events, Conferences and Assembly Planning Committee
Rosalind L. Hudnell Sacramento (CA) Chapter	Director of Philanthropy/Chair, Fund Development Committee
Marnese Barksdale Elder Mid-Cities (TX) Chapter	Chair, Human Resources Committee
Karen Jefferson Morrison, JD Columbus (OH) Chapter	Chair, Legislative Issues, Public Affairs and Resolutions Committee
Carol H. Williams Oakland Bay Area (CA) Chapter	Chair, Marketing and Brand Management Committee
Raynetta C. Waters Asheville (NC) Chapter	Chair, National Nominating Committee
Larnell Burks-Bagley Indianapolis (IN) Chapter	Chair, Protocol Committee
Cynthia Hightower-Jenkins Shreveport (LA) Chapter	Chair, Rituals Committee

Stephanie Mays Boyd Philadelphia (PA) Chapter	Chair, Strategic Partnerships Committee
Patricia Bush Washington (DC) Chapter	Chair, Strategic Planning Committee
Sharon Dixon Gentry Music City (TN) Chapter	Chair, Technology Committee
Kristie Patton Foster Mid-Cities (TX) Chapter	Chief of Staff to the National President
Karen M. Dyer, EdD Greensboro (NC) Chapter	Co-Chair, Organizational Effectiveness/Leadership Development
Jan T. Collins-Eaglin, PhD Claremont Area (CA) Chapter	Co-Chair, Organizational Effectiveness/Leadership Development
Mildred A. Edwards, PhD Topeka (KS) Chapter	Dean, Scott Hawkins Leadership Institute
Pamela Freeman Fobbs, JD Fresno (CA) Chapter	Director, National Programs
Tammy King Bergen County (NJ) Chapter	Director, Services to Youth Facet
Joyce M. Jackson, PhD Baton Rouge (LA) Chapter	Director, The Arts Facet
Sonya Simril Alameda Contra Costa (CA) Chapter	Director, National Trends and Services Facet
Barbara Nance McKee Patuxent River (MD) Chapter	Director, International Trends and Services Facet
Nicholette M. Martin, MD Arlington (VA) Chapter	Director, Health and Human Services Facet

Elected and Appointed Officials 1949–2019

1949–1950
President – Sarah Strickland Scott
Vice President – Letitia Rose
Recording Secretary – Beatrice Butler
Corresponding Secretary – Myrtle Manigault Stratton
Financial Secretary – Ethel Lowry
Treasurer – Dorothy Reed
Legal Officer – Julia Delany

1950–1951
President – Sarah Strickland Scott
Vice President – Letitia Rose
Recording Secretary – Beatrice Butler
Corresponding Secretary – Myrtle Manigault Stratton
Financial Secretary – Ethel Lowry
Treasurer – Dorothy Reed
Legal Officer – Julia Delany

1951–1952
President – Sarah Strickland Scott
Vice President – Lottie Dinkins
Recording Secretary – Beatrice Butler
Corresponding Secretary – Myrtle Manigault Stratton
Financial Secretary – Ethel Lowry
Treasurer – Dorothy Reed
Legal Officer – Sarah Speaks

1952–1953
President – Sarah Strickland Scott
Vice President – Lottie Dinkins
Recording Secretary – Beatrice Butler
Corresponding Secretary – Myrtle Manigault Stratton
Financial Secretary – Ethel Lowry
Treasurer – Dorothy Reed
Legal Officer – Sarah Speaks

1953–1954
President – Margaret Rosell Hawkins
Vice President – Lottie Dinkins
Recording Secretary – Beatrice Butler
Corresponding Secretary – Norvleate Downing
Financial Secretary – Hazel Reid
Treasurer – Fairfax Holmes
Legal Officer – Thelma Austin

1954–1955
President – Margaret Rosell Hawkins
Vice President – Lottie Dinkins
Recording Secretary – Alice Jones
Corresponding Secretary – Norvleate Downing
Financial Secretary – Hazel Reid
Treasurer – Fairfax Holmes
Legal Officer – Thelma Austin

1955–1956
President – Margaret Rosell Hawkins
Vice President – Lottie Dinkins
Recording Secretary – Alice Jones
Corresponding Secretary – Norvleate Downing
Financial Secretary – Hazel Reid
Treasurer – Fairfax Holmes
Legal Officer – Thelma Austin

1956–1957
President – Margaret Rosell Hawkins
Vice President –Bernice Martin
Recording Secretary – Bernice McAllister
Corresponding Secretary – Norvleate Downing
Financial Secretary – Hazel Reid
Treasurer – Fairfax Holmes
Legal Officer – Sarah Speaks

1957–1958

President – Pauline Weeden (Maloney)

Vice President – Bernice McLendon

Recording Secretary – Bernice McAllister

Corresponding Secretary – Norvleate Downing

Financial Secretary – Hazel Reid

Treasurer – Fairfax Holmes

Legal Officer – Sarah Speaks

1958–1959

President – Pauline Weeden (Maloney)

Vice President – Bernice McLendon

Recording Secretary – Bernice McAllister

Corresponding Secretary – Georgia Schanck

Financial Secretary – Gertrude Thomas

Treasurer – Anna Julian

Legal Officer – Elreta Alexander

1959–1960

President – Pauline Weeden (Maloney)

Vice President – Bernice McLendon

Recording Secretary – Bernice McAllister

Corresponding Secretary – Nannie Inborden

Financial Secretary – Gertrude Thomas

Treasurer – Anna Julian

Legal Officer – Elreta Alexander

1960–1962

President – Pauline Weeden (Maloney)

Vice President – Vivian Jones Beamon

Recording Secretary – Josephine Smith

Corresponding Secretary – Norvleate Downing (Acting)

Financial Secretary – Gertrude Thomas

Treasurer – Anna Julian

Legal Officer – Elreta Alexander

1962–1964

President – Vivian Jones Beamon

Vice President – Anna Julian

Recording Secretary – Josephine Smith

Corresponding Secretary – Norvleate Downing

Financial Secretary – Gertrude Thomas

Treasurer – Minnie Gaston

Legal Officer – Elreta Alexander

1964–1966

President – Vivian Jones Beamon

Vice President – Anna Julian

Recording Secretary – Josephine Smith

Corresponding Secretary – Norvleate Downing

Financial Secretary – Ruth McCants

Treasurer – Minnie Gaston

Legal Officer – Elreta Alexander

1966–1968

President – Vivian Jones Beamon

Vice President – Anna Julian

Recording Secretary – Josephine Smith

Financial Secretary – Ruth McCants

Treasurer – Minnie Gaston

Legal Advisor – Elreta Alexander

1968–1970

President – Vivian Jones Beamon

Vice President – Bessie Hill

Recording Secretary – Madeline Haskins

Financial Secretary – Ruth McCants

Treasurer – Minnie Gaston

Member-at-Large – Edwina Higgins

Legal Advisor – Elreta Alexander

1970–1972

President – Helen Gray Edmonds

Vice President – Bessie Hill

Recording Secretary – Madeline Haskins

Financial Secretary – Ruth McCants

Treasurer – Minnie Gaston

Member-at-Large – Edwina Higgins

Legal Advisor – Allie L. Weeden

1972–1974

President – Helen Gray Edmonds

Vice President – Vera Codwell

Recording Secretary – Madeline Haskins

Financial Secretary – Ruth McCants

Treasurer – Beatrice Butler

Member-at-Large – Vivian Pinn

General Counsel – Allie L. Weeden

1974–1976

President – Pauline Allen Ellison

Vice President – Vera Codwell

Recording Secretary – Laura Banks

Financial Secretary – Celestine Cook

Treasurer – Beatrice Butler

Member-at-Large – Vivian Pinn

General Counsel – Allie L. Weeden

1976–1978

President – Pauline Allen Ellison

Vice President – Allie L. Weeden

Recording Secretary – Laura Banks

Financial Secretary – Celestine Cook

Treasurer – Louise Quarles Lawson

Member-at-Large – Regina Frazier

Parliamentarian – Millicent Smith

1978–1980

President – Julia Brogdon Purnell

Vice President – Allie L. Weeden

Recording Secretary – Laura Banks

Treasurer – Louise Quarles Lawson

Member-at-Large – Regina Frazier

Parliamentarian – Patricia Russell-McCloud/
    Janet Ballard

1980–1982

President – Julia Brogdon Purnell

Vice President – Thelma Hardiman

Recording Secretary – Ruth Williams

Treasurer – Leatrice Pride

Member-at-Large – Vel Phillips

Parliamentarian – Janet Jones Ballard

1982–1984

President – Dolly Desselle Adams

Vice President – Thelma Hardiman

Recording Secretary – Ruth Williams

Treasurer – Leatrice Pride

Member-at-Large – Mose Yvonne Hooks

Parliamentarian – Faye Price

1984–1986

President – Dolly Desselle Adams

Vice President – Regina Jollivette Frazier

Recording Secretary – Dolores Albury

Treasurer – Sara Butler

Members-at-Large – Mose Yvonne Hooks/
    Patricia Russell-McCloud

Parliamentarian – Faye Price

1986–1988

President – Regina Jollivette Frazier

Vice President – Marion Schultz Sutherland

Recording Secretary – Dolores Albury

Treasurer – Sara Butler

Member-at-Large – Gwendolyn B. Lee

Parliamentarian – Ernestine S. Sapp

1988–1990

President – Regina Jollivette Frazier

Vice President – Marion Schultz Sutherland

Recording Secretary – Jacqueline F. Bontemps

Treasurer – Clinita A. Ford

Member-at-Large – Gwendolyn B. Lee

Parliamentarian – Ernestine S. Sapp

1990–1992

President – Marion Schultz Sutherland

Vice President – Patricia Russell-McCloud

Recording Secretary – Jacqueline F. Bontemps

Treasurer – Clinita A. Ford

Member-at-Large – June Skinner Banks

Chair, Nominating Committee – Gwendolyn B. Lee

Parliamentarian – Barbara Oliver-Hall

1992–1994

President – Marion Schultz Sutherland

Vice President – Patricia Russell-McCloud

Recording Secretary – Leola Travis

Treasurer – Frances Flippen

Member at Large – June Skinner Banks

Chair, Nominating Committee – Gwendolyn B. Lee

Parliamentarian – Barbara Oliver-Hall

1994–1996 National Officers
(Russell-McCloud)

1994–1996

President – Patricia Russell-McCloud
Vice President – JoAhn Brown-Nash/
    Barbara Dixon Simpkins
Recording Secretary – Jacquelyn C. Shropshire
Treasurer – Frances Morton Flippen
Member-at-Large – Michele Ayers Minnix
Chair, Nominating Committee – JoAnne Loftin Bates
Parliamentarian – Algenita Scott Davis

1996–1998

President – Patricia Russell-McCloud
Vice President – Barbara Dixon Simpkins
Recording Secretary – Jacquelyn C. Shropshire
Treasurer – Erma Chansler Johnson
Member-at-Large – Michele Ayers Minnix
Chair, Nominating Committee – Bishetta D. Merritt
Parliamentarian – Arthenia Joyner

1998–2000

President – Barbara Dixon Simpkins
Vice President – Gladys Gary Vaughn
Recording Secretary – Gwendolyn B. Lee
Treasurer – Erma Chansler Johnson
Chair, Nominating Committee – Bishetta D. Merritt
Parliamentarian – Arthenia Joyner

2000–2002

President – Barbara Dixon Simpkins
Vice President – Gladys Gary Vaughn
Recording Secretary – Gwendolyn B. Lee
Treasurer – Erma Chansler Johnson
Chair, Nominating Committee – Barbara Lord Watkins
Parliamentarian – Mattie Peterson Compton

2002–2004

President – Gladys Gary Vaughn
Vice President – Gwendolyn B. Lee
Recording Secretary – Cecelia B. Henderson
Treasurer – Evelyn Rose Coker
Chair, Nominating Committee – Joyce Elizabeth Glaise
Parliamentarian – Johnetta Randolph Haley

2004–2006

President – Gladys Gary Vaughn
Vice President – Gwendolyn B. Lee
Recording Secretary – Cecelia B. Henderson
Treasurer – Evelyn Rose Coker
Chair, Nominating Committee – Joyce Elizabeth Glaise
Parliamentarian – Johnetta Randolph Haley

2006–2008

President – Gwendolyn B. Lee

Vice President – Margot James Copeland

Recording Secretary – Josephine D. Davis

Treasurer – Lula Lang-Jeter

Chair, Nominating Committee – Glenda Newell-Harris

Parliamentarian – Jacqueline Spriggs Revis

2008–2010

President – Gwendolyn B. Lee

Vice President – Margot James Copeland

Recording Secretary – Josephine D. Davis

Treasurer – Lula Lang-Jeter

Chair, Nominating Committee – Glenda Newell-Harris

Parliamentarian – Jacqueline Spriggs Revis

2010–2012

President – Margot James Copeland

Vice President – Glenda Newell-Harris

Recording Secretary – Kimberly Jeffries Leonard

Treasurer – Katherine E. Wilson

Chair, Nominating Committee – Pamela Gentry

Parliamentarian – Margaret Winn

2012–2014

President – Margot James Copeland

Vice President – Glenda Newell-Harris

Recording Secretary – Kimberly Jeffries Leonard

Treasurer – Katherine E. Wilson

Chair, Nominating Committee – Joyce Lanier

Parliamentarian – Margaret Winn

2014–2016

President – Glenda Newell-Harris

Vice President – Kimberly Jeffries Leonard

Recording Secretary – Josephine Davis

Treasurer – E. Rose Corker (Acting)

Chair, Nominating Committee – Pamela J. Gentry

Parliamentarian – Margaret Winn

2016–2018

President – Glenda Newell-Harris

Vice President – Kimberly Jeffries Leonard

Recording Secretary – Crystal L. Kendrick

Treasurer – Carolyn E. Lewis

Chair, Nominating Committee – Jeannine Quick Frasier

Parliamentarian – Tyna Davis

2018–2020

President – Kimberly Jeffries Leonard

Vice President – Ethel Isaac Williams

Recording Secretary – Crystal L. Kendrick

Treasurer – Carolyn E. Lewis

Chair, Nominating Committee – Jeannine Quick Frasier

Parliamentarian – Tyna Davis

Notes

The office of Corresponding Secretary was discontinued in 1966.

Member-at-Large became an office in 1968 and was discontinued in 1998.

Legal advisor, legal counsel, and general counsel have been used interchangeably. Additionally, in 1980, the term "general counsel" was shelved, and the parliamentarian assumed those duties.

Chapters by Chartering Dates

Area	Chapter Name	Charter Date	Area	Chapter Name	Charter Date
EA	Philadelphia (PA)	11/9/46	CA	Louisville (KY)	10/13/51
EA	Atlantic City (NJ)	2/28/48	EA	Newport News (VA)	2/15/52
EA	Wilmington (DE)	4/10/48	EA	Norfolk (VA)	2/24/52
CA	St. Louis (MO)	4/15/48	EA	Richmond (VA)	3/1/52
EA	Washington (DC)	4/17/48	EA	Hampton (VA)	3/2/52
EA	Petersburg (VA)	5/7/48	EA	Albany District (NY)	3/8/52
EA	Baltimore (MD)	9/24/48	WA	Sacramento (CA)	3/15/52
EA	Pittsburgh (PA)	12/5/48	WA	Phoenix (AZ)	3/22/52
SA	Raleigh (NC)	4/18/49	SA	Orlando (FL)	4/5/52
SA	Wilson-Rocky Mount-Tarboro (NC)	4/18/49	SA	Columbia (SC)	4/15/52
			WA	Denver (CO)	5/5/52
EA	Greater New York (NY)	5/12/49	EA	Brooklyn (NY)	11/15/52
EA	Central New Jersey (NJ)	5/28/49	CA	Memphis (TN)	11/15/52
CA	Dayton (OH)	5/28/49	CA	Nashville (TN)	11/17/52
EA	North Jersey (NJ)	6/1/49	SA	Greenville (SC)	2/7/53
SA	Winston-Salem (NC)	3/23/50	SA	Atlanta (GA)	2/14/53
CA	Columbus (OH)	3/26/50	EA	Danville (VA)	11/11/53
CA	Cincinnati (OH)	3/30/50	SA	Greensboro (NC)	10/22/55
EA	Lynchburg (VA)	4/1/50	SA	Greater Miami (FL)	11/5/55
CA	Chicago (IL)	5/21/50	CA	Huntington (WV)	11/12/55
EA	Buffalo (NY)	5/24/50	SA	Charlotte (NC)	12/3/55
EA	Niagara Falls (NY)	5/24/50	CA	Youngstown (OH)	12/3/55
EA	Westchester (NY)	6/10/50	WA	Greater Seattle (WA)	12/9/55
WA	Los Angeles (CA)	9/16/50	CA	Little Rock (AK)	1/13/56
WA	Oakland Bay Area (CA)	9/23/50	SA	Birmingham (AL)	2/4/56
WA	San Francisco (CA)	9/23/50	CA	Springfield (OH)	10/26/56
CA	Omaha (NE)	9/30/50	SA	Savannah (GA)	11/3/56
EA	Roanoke (VA)	10/7/50	WA	San Diego (CA)	9/28/57
CA	Cleveland (OH)	10/28/50	WA	Portland (OR)	11/5/57
CA	Wilberforce (OH)	11/11/50	WA	Dallas (TX)	11/9/57
EA	Portsmouth (VA)	12/30/50	CA	Des Moines (IA)	11/9/57
CA	Southern West Virginia (WV)★	1/7/51	SA	New Orleans (LA)	11/20/57
EA	Boston (MA)	2/24/51	SA	Augusta (GA)	11/23/57
WA	Houston (TX)	3/3/51	CA	Oklahoma City (OK)	11/30/57
CA	Detroit (MI)	3/10/51	SA	Durham (NC)	10/11/58
CA	Indianapolis (IN)	3/17/51	CA	Northern Indiana (IN)	11/1/58
SA	Charleston (SC)	3/29/51	SA	Daytona Beach (FL)	11/15/58
SA	Wilmington (NC)	4/7/51	CA	Topeka (KS)	11/29/58
EA	South Jersey (NJ)	5/11/51	SA	Montgomery (AL)	12/8/58
CA	Charleston-Institute (WV)	5/12/51	EA	Syracuse (NY)	11/7/59
SA	Tallahassee (FL)	5/19/51	SA	Jackson (MS)	11/21/59
CA	Greater Kansas City (MO)	6/1/51	WA	Fort Worth (TX)	12/5/59

Area	Chapter Name	Charter Date	Area	Chapter Name	Charter Date
WA	Peninsula Bay (CA)	11/5/60	SA	Shreveport (LA)	4/15/73
WA	Austin (TX)	12/9/60	WA	San Fernando Valley (CA)	5/5/73
WA	San Antonio (TX)	12/10/60	WA	Orange County (CA)	6/2/73
EA	Annapolis (MD)	8/20/62	EA	Bergen County (NJ)	3/2/74
EA	Long Island (NY)	10/27/62	WA	Waco (TX)	5/25/74
WA	Tucson (AZ)	11/23/62	SA	Fort Lauderdale (FL)	9/21/74
SA	Tuskegee (AL)	12/1/62	EA	Rancocas Valley (NJ)	10/26/74
WA	East Texas (TX)	12/2/62	WA	Monterey Bay (CA)	11/16/74
CA	Milwaukee (WI)	12/8/62	EA	Waterbury (CT)	5/24/75
WA	Pasadena-Altadena (CA)	2/9/63	EA	Columbia (MD)	6/28/75
WA	Angel City (CA)	2/10/63	EA	Penn Towne (PA)	9/6/75
CA	Jackson (TN)	11/7/64	SA	Spartanburg (SC)	9/27/75
EA	Delaware Valley (PA)	11/21/64	EA	Reston (VA)	9/29/75
SA	Baton Rouge (LA)	11/28/64	CA	Central Illinois (IL)	11/3/75
SA	Orangeburg (SC)	12/4/64	EA	Chesapeake/Virginia Beach (VA)	4/24/76
CA	Tulsa (AZ)	12/5/64	EA	Fairfield County (CT)	5/15/76
SA	Columbus (GA)	12/19/64	WA	Las Vegas (NV)	5/27/76
WA	Tacoma (WA)	10/13/66	CA	Quad Cities (IL)	6/2/76
WA	Stockton (CA)	10/15/66	EA	Middlesex County (MA)	6/5/76
EA	Bucks County (PA)	10/29/66	CA	South Suburban Chicago (IL)	6/6/76
WA	Harbor Area (CA)	11/6/66	CA	West Towns (IL)	6/13/76
SA	Jacksonville (FL)	11/12/66	CA	Kent Area (OH)	6/19/76
EA	Arlington (VA)	11/19/66	EA	Harrisburg (PA)	6/20/76
SA	Brunswick (GA)	12/10/66	EA	Montgomery County (PA)	6/20/76
CA	Wichita (KS)	12/7/68	SA	Vicksburg (MS)★	6/26/76
CA	Frankfort-Lexington (KY)	12/14/68	CA	Hendersonville Area (TN)	8/14/76
SA	West Palm Beach (FL)	2/8/69	SA	Treasure Coast (FL)	10/30/76
SA	Fort Valley (GA)	3/1/69	WA	Bakersfield (CA)	6/11/77
EA	Princess Anne (MD)	3/15/69	WA	Fresno (CA)	6/12/77
CA	Pine Bluff (AK)	5/17/69	EA	Eastern Shore (NY)	9/17/77
CA	Knoxville (TN)	11/14/70	WA	El Paso (TX)	9/17/77
WA	Golden Triangle (TX)	5/8/71	WA	Spokane (WA)	5/27/78
SA	Macon (GA)	10/8/72	CA	Ann Arbor (MI)	3/10/79
CA	Toledo (OH)	10/21/72	CA	Chattanooga (TN)	3/24/79
CA	Lansing/East Lansing (MI)	10/28/72	CA	Fort Wayne (IN)	3/24/79
EA	Silver Spring (MD)	11/18/72	EA	Prince Georges County (MD)	3/24/79
CA	North Shore (IL)	11/19/72	SA	Fayetteville (NC)	3/31/79
SA	Pensacola (FL)	11/25/72	CA	Flint Area (MI)	3/31/79
CA	Minneapolis/St. Paul (MN)	12/10/72	EA	Farmington Valley (CT)	4/28/79
EA	New Haven (CT)	12/18/72	WA	San Bernardino Valley (CA)	5/4/79
SA	Alexandria (LA)	4/14/73	WA	Inglewood Pacific (CA)	5/6/79
SA	Monroe-Grambling (LA)	4/14/73	WA	Missouri City (TX)	5/12/79

Area	Chapter Name	Charter Date	Area	Chapter Name	Charter Date
SA	Brevard County (FL)	6/23/79	EA	Greater Hartford (CT)	5/31/86
SA	LaGrange (GA)	6/30/79	EA	Greater Springfield (MA)	5/31/86
EA	Capital City (DC)	8/9/79	SA	Dade County (FL)	6/1/86
EA	Metropolitan (DC)	8/11/79	CA	Windy City (IL)	5/2/87
CA	Tri-City (MI)	8/16/80	WA	Port City (TX)	5/16/87
WA	Tri-Cities (WA)	5/9/81	CA	Western Reserve (OH)	6/20/87
CA	Oakland County (MI)	5/21/81	CA	Renaissance (MI)	6/26/87
WA	San Jose (CA)	6/6/81	SA	St. Petersburg (FL)	6/26/87
CA	Music City (TN)	6/27/81	SA	Tampa (FL)	6/26/87
CA	Jackson County (MO)	7/25/81	EA	Erie County (NY)	10/3/87
CA	Greater Wayne County (MI)	8/1/81	CA	Twin Rivers (OH)	2/20/88
SA	Piedmont (NC)	5/1/82	SA	LeFleur's Bluff (MS)	3/5/88
EA	Southern Maryland Chain (MD)	5/15/82	EA	Metro-Manhattan (NY)	4/23/88
SA	Lake Gaston Area (NC)	5/22/82	WA	Town Lake (TX)	4/30/88
EA	Morris County (NJ)	5/22/82	CA	Parthenon (TN)	6/18/88
SA	Dogwood City (GA)	6/5/82	EA	Southside (VA)★	10/22/88
WA	Channel Islands (CA)	6/26/82	SA	Asheville (NC)	12/10/88
WA	Palos Verdes (CA)	6/27/82	WA	Plano North Metroplex (TX)	4/1/89
EA	James River Valley (VA)	5/14/83	SA	Aiken (SC)	4/22/89
SA	Albany (GA)	5/21/83	SA	Nassau (Bahamas)	5/19/89
EA	Rochester (NY)	5/5/84	WA	Alburquerque (NM)	6/10/89
CA	Hoffman Estates (IL)	5/12/84	CA	Greater Racine (WI)★★★	10/14/89
SA	Crescent City (LA)	6/2/84	CA	Cream City (WI)	3/24/90
SA	Triangle Park (NC)	6/9/84	EA	Patapsco River (MD)	3/31/90
EA	Potomac (VA)	6/16/84	CA	South Bend Area (IN)	4/21/90
SA	Elizabeth City (NC)	6/23/84	EA	Greater Hudson Valley (NY)	4/28/90
CA	Shelby County (TN)	2/23/85	EA	Frankfurt (Germany)★★	5/25/90
WA	Mid-Cities (TX)	4/20/85	SA	Magnolia (GA)	3/2/91
SA	Gainesville (FL)	5/18/85	SA	Greater Mobile (AL)	3/22/91
WA	Beverly Hills West (CA)	5/25/85	CA	Great Lakes (MI)	1/30/93
WA	Claremont (CA)	5/26/85	SA	Tuscaloosa (AL)	4/17/93
CA	Paducah (KY)	6/15/85	CA	River City (TN)	5/15/93
CA	Madison Metropolitan (WI)	8/31/85	SA	Bold City (FL)	5/29/93
EA	Harbor City (MD)	10/5/85	SA	Crown Jewels (NC)	6/19/93
EA	Suffolk (VA)	10/12/85	EA	Jamestown (NY)★★★	7/31/93
WA	Hawaii (HI)	1/11/86	CA	Archway (MO)	8/14/93
SA	Natchez (MS)	4/10/86	SA	Magic City (AL)	8/21/93
SA	LaCapitale (LA)	4/12/86	EA	Old Dominion (VA)	9/18/93
EA	Dover (DE)	4/19/86	WA	Solano County (CA)	1/29/94
EA	Essex County (NJ)	4/26/86	CA	Harbor Lites (IL)	4/23/94
EA	Raritan Valley (NJ)	4/26/86	WA	Trinity (TX)	5/14/94
CA	Gateway (MO)	5/5/86	SA	Pontchartrain (LA)	5/29/94
EA	Milford (CT)	5/17/86	WA	Alameda Contra Costa (CA)	2/9/95
SA	Altamonte Springs (FL)	5/31/86	SA	Columbus-Lowndes (MS)★★★	3/4/95

Area	Chapter Name	Charter Date	Area	Chapter Name	Charter Date
WA	Texas Spring Cypress (TX)	3/11/95	WA	South Bay Area (CA)	2/6/10
EA	Greater Providence (RI)	4/8/95	SA	Tri-County (AL)	6/12/10
SA	Selma (AL)	4/29/95	SA	Miami Biscayne-Bay (FL)	6/30/10
SA	North Broward County (FL)	5/27/95	WA	Greater Denton County (TX)	6/9/12
SA	Azalea City (GA)	6/24/95	SA	Mississippi Delta (MS)	8/25/12
SA	Buckhead-Cascade City (GA)	6/27/95	EA	Greater Rappahannock (VA)	3/22/14
WA	Gulf Coast Apollo (TX)	10/7/95	WA	Lone Star (TX)	4/26/14
CA	Circle City (IN)	11/18/95	EA	Greater Bronx (NY)	5/31/14
CA	Lake Shore (IL)	1/20/96	WA	Greater Pearland Area (TX)	6/14/14
SA	Bradenton/Sarasota (FL)	2/9/96	EA	Patuxent River (MD)	6/27/14
WA	Fort Bend County (TX)	3/3/96	WA	Colorado Springs (CO)	5/2/15
EA	Greater Queens (NY)	3/9/96	SA	Mississippi Roses (MS)	10/31/15
SA	Greater Huntsville (AL)	9/20/97	CA	Central Missouri (MO)	4/4/16
EA	Charlottesville (VA)	3/28/98	EA	Mount Rose (MD)	6/4/16
EA	Commonwealth (VA)	6/6/98	SA	Gulf Coast (MS)	11/18/17
CA	Kalamazoo (MI)	4/26/01	SA	Hilton Head (SC)	11/4/17
WA	Anchorage (AK)	5/3/01	SA	Katy-Richmond (TX)	4/14/18
CA	Macomb (IL)★	6/7/01	CA	Northwest Arkansas (AR)	4/28/18
SA	Athens (GA)	5/1/04	EA	London (UK)	5/26/18
CA	Queen City (OH)	5/28/05	EA	Central Massachusetts (MA)	6/9/18
SA	Camellia Rose (GA)	11/7/09			

★ Charter revoked
★★ Inactive
★★★ Name changed

The Links, Incorporated
Schools in Africa and Liberia
Total Number of Schools Adopted (64)

SOUTH AFRICA SCHOOLS (60)

ADOPTER	SCHOOL AND GRADE LEVEL
National (1 School)	
In Memory of Co-Founders	
Margaret Rosell Hawkins and Sarah Strickland Scott	Daki-Biyu LEA Primary School
Eastern Area (18 Schools)	
Connecticut Cluster	Mabibi School (Grades 1–7)
Essex County (NJ) Chapter	Mvuzemvuze School (Grades 1–7)
Baltimore (MD) Area Cluster	Dr. Made School (Grades 5–7)
Bergen County (NJ) Chapter	Nansindlela School (Grades R–7)
Berns-J Cluster, New York	Ndlandlama School (Grades R–4)
Buffalo (NY) Chapter	Ntwela School (Grades R–4)
Central Virginia Cluster	Ekanyisweni School (Grades R–7)
Chesapeake/Virginia Beach (VA) Chapter	Dabulizizwe School (Grades R–7)
Ethel and Gardner LaClede	Khulabebuka Secondary
Greater Hudson Valley (NY) Chapter	Putellos School (Grades R–7)
In memory of Dr. Betty Shabazz	
Keystone (PA) Cluster	Esizibeni School (Grades 8–12)
Long Island (NY) Chapter	Nombizo School (Grades 1–6)
Norfolk and Portsmouth (VA) Chapters	Nthutukoville School (Grades R–7)
North Jersey (NJ) Chapter	Balungise School Grades (R–7)
Raritan Valley (NJ) Chapter	Isinkontshe (Grades R–7)
South Central New Jersey Cluster	Sibuyele School (Grades R–12)
Washington, DC, Virginia, Maryland Cluster	Njuqwana School (Grade 1–5)
Eastern Area	Dondotha School (Grade 8–12)
Southern Area (14 Schools)	
Atlanta (GA) Cluster	Motsoaledi Pre-Primary School
Bold City (FL) Chapter	Makgabutle Pre-Primary School
Bradenton-Sarasota (FL) Chapter	Ekudeyeni School (Grades 5–7)
	Zimlindile School (Grades 1–6)
	Lukhozana School (Grades 10–12)
	Bhekulwandle School (Grades R–4)
Brevard County (FL) Chapter	Masuku School (Grades R–7)
North Broward County (FL) Chapter	Inkanyezi (Grades R–7)
Pensacola (FL) Chapter	Ukuzamakwethu School (Grades 8–12)
In memory of Dr. Barbara Dixon Simpkins,	
12th International President	

Dr. Mary McKinney Edmonds and Daughter Jacquelyn Edmonds, Georgia — Phembisizwe School (Grades 8–12)

Mississippi Magnolia (MS) Cluster — Nqabane School (Grades 10–12)

Tallahassee (FL) Chapter — Zwelixolile School (Grades 1–6)

Tampa (FL) Chapter — Nguberhamba School (Grades R–5)

Southern Area — Boredi School (Grades 1–7)

Western Area (10 Schools)

Austin & Town Lake (TX) Chapter — Umgijimi School (Grades R–4)

Beverly Hills West (CA) Chapter — Ziphembeleni School (Grades 8–12)

Denver (CO) Chapter — Sandakahle School (Grades 1–7)

Harbor Area (CA) Chapter — Cetywayo School (Grades R–9)

Houston (TX) Chapter — Sawpits School (Grades R–7)

Emma Taylor, California — Lingelethu School (Grades R–9)
Funded by Dr. Thad Taylor, Jr.

North Texas Cluster — Zwelesithebiso School (Grades 4–7)

Port City (TX) Chapter — Masobuza School (Grades 1–6)

San Fernando Valley (TX) Chapter — Tetelegu School (Grades R–7)

Dweshula Inkomba School (Grades R–7)

Central Area (17 Schools)

Arkansas-Tennessee Cluster — Valentine School (Grades 1–7)

Chicago (IL) Metropolitan Cluster — Mofu School (Grades R–7)

Etta Moten Barnett/W.K. Kellogg Foundation — Manzamnyama School (Grades R–7)

Flint Area (MI) Chapter — Mbambangwe School (Grades 8–12)

Greater Wayne (MI) County Chapter — Phangisa (Grades R–7)

Heartland (IA) Cluster — Gabangenkosi School (Grades R–7)

Hoffman Estates (IL) Chapter — Nsukumbili School (Grades R–7)

Kalamazoo (MI) Chapter — Edendale School (Grades 5–7)

Lake Erie (OH) Cluster — Dumehlezi School (Grades 8–12)

Louisville (KY) Chapter — Henryville School (Grades 1–7)

Minneapolis-St. Paul (MN) Chapter — Lungisile School (Grades R–7)

Northshore (IL) Chapter — Halalisa School (Grades R–4)

Oklahoma City (OK) Chapter — Ngilosi School (Grades R–4)

Renaissance (MI) Chapter — Thuthukani Mabheleni School (Grade R–3)

Rosalind E. Griffith, MD, Michigan — Igugulabanguni School (Grade R–7)

South Suburban Chicago (IL) Chapter — Mndunduzeli School (Grade R–7)

Volunteer State Cluster, Tennessee — Ingugulabasha School (Grade 8–12)

SCHOOLS IN LIBERIA (4)

Todee Presbyterian Mission School

African Methodist Episcopal University

Ann Sandell School

School for the Blind

Source: National Headquarters

Bibliography

INTRODUCTION

"Assembly and Executive Council Minutes." 18th General Assembly, New Orleans, LA, June 26–July 1, 1972.

Constitution of the Links. Philadelphia, PA. Philadelphia Links, 1947.

Dedication of the National Headquarters. Washington, DC: The Links, Incorporated, 1985.

"Minutes." 29th National Assembly. Louisville, KY, June 25–July 2, 1994.

"Minutes of the Executive Council." The Links, Incorporated, Fairfax, VA, November 10–12, 2006.

"Our Life Members." The Crisis (August–September 1954).

"New Orleans Health Clinic." Link to Link VI (Fall 2007).

Beamon, V. J. "The Call to the Sixteenth National Assembly." The Links Journal II (June 1968).

———. President's Report 1962–1970. The Links, Incorporated, 1970.

Copeland, M. J. Report to the Executive Council. Washington, DC: The Links, Incorporated, 2006.

———. Membership Committee Report to the Executive Council. Seattle, WA: The Links Incorporated, 2007.

———. Biennium Report of the National Vice President. Seattle, WA: The Links, Incorporated, 2008.

Edmonds, H. G. Chapter Establishment: The Lamp of Experience. Nashville, TN, 1986.

Ellison, P. President's Biennial Report: The High Cost of Transition. 21st National Assembly, Chicago, IL, July 2–9, 1978.

Frazier, R. J. Guidelines on Public Policy Report. Executive Council, Chicago, IL, November 12–14, 1976.

Frazier, R. J. "Enhancing the Legacy—Fulfilling the Dream." Link to Link 3 (January 1987).

Jackson-Ransom, B. "Links Build Schools in South Africa." Link to Link VI (Fall 2007).

Jarrett, V. "There Are Other Important Blacks." Chicago Tribune, October 5, 1975.

Lee, G. B. Report of the National President. Seattle, WA: The Links, Incorporated, Executive Council Meeting, 2007.

Lee, Gwendolyn B. "State of the Organization Address." Link to Link (Fall 2007).

Parker, M. H. A History of The Links, Incorporated. 2nd ed. Washington, DC: The Links, Incorporated, 1992.

Purnell, J. B. Seventh National President's Report. Washington, DC: The Links, Incorporated, 1987.

Robbins, W. F. "Our Movement in an Era of Dynamic Dimensions." The Links Journal III (June 1970).

Russell-McCloud, P. "Letter to Link Sisters." Washington, DC: The Links, Incorporated, 1996.

Simpkins, B. D. "Programs." Public Relations Portfolio. Washington, DC: The Links Incorporated, 1998.

———. "Message from the President." Window of Opportunity: 2000–2002 Program Planning Guide. July 2000.

Vaughn, G. G. "Links Membership: A Safe Place for Sister, Soul, and Spirit." Link to Link (Fall–Winter 1999).

Warren, V. L. "National Links Organization." The Oregonian, April 25, 1973.

Wright, D. B. Reminiscences. Unpublished manuscript. Philadelphia, PA, 1969.

CHAPTER 3

"A Leader of Vision." Bluefield, WV: National Links, Inc., 1954.

"African-American Population, Statistical Abstract of the United States: 2003," and "We, The American Blacks, U. S. Census Bureau, 1993." Society and Culture > Race and Ethnicity > Population/Demographics (Vol. 2008): Infoplease.

"After 163 Years, African-American Legal Scholar and Abolitionist George B. Vashon to Be Admitted to Pennsylvania Bar." In Duane Morris, October 13. Pittsburgh, PA: Dune Morris, 2010.

"Anna Nicholson in the Pennsylvania and New Jersey, Church and Town Records, 1669-2013." In Historic Pennsylvania Church and Town Records. Philadelphia, PA: Historical Society of Pennsylvania, 2011.

"The Art of Inspiring Careers." In Moore College of Art and Design: Mission and History, April 20, 2019. moore.edu.

"Atkinson, Frances Vashon" in The Philadelphia Inquirer (Philadelphia, PA), May 18, 2009.

"Board of Trustees/Council of Trustees." West Chester University Catalog 1871–1989. West Chester, PA: West Chester University, 2008.

"Citizens and Southern Bank" Explore PA History. 1991. Retrieved March 20, 2008, from http://www. explorepahistory.com

"City Dentist Gets NAACP Post." The Philadelphia Inquirer, May 18, 2019.

"Co-Founders: Tribute to the Founders." The Journal, 1962.

"Dorothy Bell Wright, 85, Black Leader." The Philadelphia Inquirer, May 18, 1996.

"Educational Attainment by Race and Hispanic Origin, 1940–2006." Washington, DC: U.S. Census Bureau, 2006. "Educational Attainment by Sex, 1940–2006." Washington, DC: U. S. Census Bureau, 2006.

"Employment Status by Industry, 1929–1998." Infoplease.com, 2007. 1946 [electronic version]. Retrieved April 20, 2008, from www.infoplease.com/year/1946html.

"Executive Council Meeting Minutes." The Links Incorporated, Washington, DC, April 4–6, 1975.

"Frederick Campbell Hawkins Sr in the U.S., Social Security Applications and Claims Index, 1936–2007" [database on-line]. In "U.S., Social Security Applications and Claims Index, 1936–2007." Provo, UT: Ancestry.com Operations, Inc., 2015.

"Frederick Hawkins in the 1940 United States Federal Census." In "Census Place: Philadelphia." Philadelphia, PA: Ancestry.com, 2015.

"Historical National Population Estimates: July 1, 1900 to July 1, 1999." 2000.

"Katie Murphy Greene." In Hold High the Torch: Alpha Kappa Alpha, Omega Omega Chapter 1926–2014. Philadelphia, PA: Omega Omega Chapter, Alpha Kappa Alpha, 2014.

"History and National Program Manual." 6th ed. Savannah, GA: Jack and Jill of America, 1996.

"In Memoriam: Link Sarah Strickland Scott." Philadelphia, PA: The Links, Incorporated, July 15, 1988.

"In Memory of our Departed Co-Founder Link Margaret Hawkins." 14th National Assembly. The Links, Incorporated, June 25–28, 1964.

"Katie Greene in the U.S., Social Security Death Index, 1935–2014." Ancestry.com, 2014. Provo, UT: Ancestry.com Operations Inc, 1973.

"Notes of Remembrance." Link to Link 5 (January 1996).

"The Philadelphia Links Present a Coronation Carnival." Philadelphia, PA: The Links, 1948.

"Population Distribution by Age, Race, Nativity, and Sex Ratio, 1860–2005." United States > U. S. Statistics > Population (Vol. 2008): Infoplease.

"Social Security Board." Employment Security Review IX, no. 7 (July 1942).

Anderson, S. "Black Leadership Gap: Eyes on the Prizes, Not the People." The Nation 249 (October 16, 1989).

Dagbovie, P. G. "Black Women, Carter G. Woodson, and the Association for the Study of Negro Life and History, 1915–1950." The Journal of African American History 88, vol. 1 (2003).

Edmonds, H. G. Chapter Establishment: The Lamp of Experience. Unpublished manuscript. Nashville, TN, 1986.

Hawkins, Bruce. "Interview with Bruce Hawkins: Youngest Son of Margaret Rosell Hawkins." The Links, Incorporated, June 13, 2013.

Hawkins, Dr. Frederick C., Jr., and Bruce R. Hawkins. "Margaret R. Hawkins: Sole Founder of the Links." Philly.com (The Inquirer), October 4, 2013.

Herron, Vanessa. "A Milestone for a Social Force." Philadelphia Inquirer, 1986.

John-Hall, Annette. "Links: A 60-Year Success." The Philadelphia Inquirer, June 25, 2006.

Jones-Wilson, F. C., ed. Encyclopedia of African-American Education. Westport, CT: Greenwood Press, 1996.

Lewis, J. J. "History Quotes." Wisdom Quotes, 1995. Retrieved June 20, 2007, from http://www.wisdomquotes.com/cat_history.html

Murray, Philip. War Manpower Commission, Utilization of Reserve Workers: Recently Reported Placements of Negroes in Skilled Occupations, 1942.

Parker, M. H. A History of The Links, Incorporated. 2nd ed. Washington, DC: The Links, Incorporated, 1992.

Schlesinger, A. "Biography of a Nation of Joiners." The American Historical Review 50, vol. 1 (1944): 25.

Scott, S. S. "Greetings from the Co-Founder." The Journal IV (1976).

Stanford, L. History of the National Links, Inc. 1946–1951. Unpublished manuscript. Philadelphia, PA, 1951.

Thomas, K. K. "Dr. Jim Crow: The University of North Carolina, the Regional Medical School for Negroes, and the Desegregation of Southern Medical Education 1945–1960." The Journal of African-American History 88, vol. 3 (2003).

Watson, D. L. (2005). "Memorandum on Visit of Los Angeles Complainant in Post Office Cases." In Papers of Clarence Mitchell, Jr. (Vol. II). Athens, OH: Ohio University Press, 2005.

"Women in the Labor Force, 1906–2006." Business and Finance > Economy > Labor and Employment (Vol. 2008): Infoplease.

Wright, D. B. Reminiscences. Unpublished manuscript. Philadelphia, PA, 1969.

Wright, D. The Philadelphia Links. Unpublished manuscript. Philadelphia, PA, 1951.

Wynn, N. A. The Afro-American and the Second World War. New York: Holmes & Meier, 1993.

CHAPTER 6

"Agreement of Merger." Link to Link 1 (1980, May).

"Assembly and Executive Council Minutes." 19th General Assembly, Washington, DC, June 25–29, 1974.

"Business Conference." Philadelphia, PA: The Philadelphia Links, 1949.

"Chartering Date Index." The Journal 10 (July 1996).

Constitution of The Links. Philadelphia, PA: The Philadelphia Links, 1947.

Constitution & Bylaws. The Links, Incorporated (2008): 39.

Constitution & Bylaws 2018–2020. Washington, DC: The Links, Incorporated, July 2018.

"Interview with 16th National President Glenda Newell-Harris." From Through Their Eyes: The Links, Oral History Collection, January 2019.

"Interview with 13th National President Gladys Gary Vaughn." From Through Their Eyes: The Links, Oral History Collection, January 2019.

"Pa. Medic Cut by Wife in Bridge Dispute." Jet, September 22, 1955.[Field]

"President's Report." Pittsburgh, PA: National Links, 1951.

Brown, JoAnn. "Chapter Establishment." Link to Link (Spring/Summer, 1999).

Butler, B. T. "Executive Council Minutes." Paper presented at The Links, Incorporated, Baltimore, MD, January 20, 1951.

Codwell, Vera A. Membership Report to the Executive Council. Washington, DC: The Links Incorporated, April 4–6 1975.

Davis, Josephine D. "Minutes, Executive Council Meeting." Fairfax, VA: The Links, Incorporated, November 10–11, 2006.

Edmonds, Helen G. Biennial Address of the National President to the 18th General Assembly. New Orleans, LA: The Links, Incorporated, June 26–July 1, 1972.

———. Some Reflections and Perspectives on the Links, Incorporated. Washington, DC: The Links, Incorporated, June 25–29, 1974.

Hardiman, Thelma. "Sarah Strickland Scott, My Beautiful Friends." From Through Their Eyes: The Links Oral History Collection. The Links, Incorporated, 2013. History and National Program Manual. 6th ed. Savannah, GA: Jack and Jill of America, 1996.

Johnson, Toki Schalk. "Toki Types." Pittsburgh Courier, May 9, 1953.

Julian, Anna J. Report of the Chapter Establishment Officer. Washington, DC: The Links, Incorporated, June 25–29, 1974. Kendrick, Crystal. "Minutes of the Meeting of the 41st National Assembly." Indianapolis, IN: The Links, Incorporated, June 28–June 30, 2018.

Leonard, Kimberly Jeffries. National Membership Committee Report. The Links, Incorporated, June 2018.

———. "State of the Organization Address to the Southern Area Conference." Orlando, FL: The Links, Incorporated, May 4, 2019.

Parker, M. H. A History of The Links, Incorporated. 1st ed. Washington, DC: The Links, Incorporated, 1981.

———. History of The Links, Incorporated. 2nd ed. Washington, DC: The Links, Incorporated, 1992.

Perdue, W., and Hogan & Hartson. "Compliance with New Jersey Corporation Laws." In N. D. Johnson, ed. Washington, DC: The Links, Inc., 1980.

Purnell, J. "Our Incorporated Status—A Matter of Importance." Link to Link 1 (May 1980).

———. Report of the Seventh National President of The Links, Incorporated to the 23rd National Assembly. Las Vegas, NV. The Links, Incorporated, 1982.

Robinson, Jacqueline. "Report of the Chapter Establishment Officer." 25th National Assembly. Nashville, TN, June 28–July 4, 1986.

Scott, Sarah S. "Greetings from the Co-Founder." The Journal, 1976.

Shropshire, Jacquelyn C. "Minutes, 31st National Assembly." Paper presented at The Links, Incorporated. Boston, MA, 1998.

Stanford, L. History of the National Links, Inc. 1946–1951. National Links, Incorporated, 1951.

Sutherland, Marion Schultz. "The State of the Links, Incorporated." Dallas, TX: The Links, Incorporated, June 30–July 3, 1992.

Warren, Virginia Lee. "National Links Organization." The Oregonian, April 25, 1973.

Wright, D. B. Reminiscences. Unpublished manuscript. Philadelphia, PA, 1969.

CHAPTER 7

Annual Meeting and Executive Council Minutes." The Links, Incorporated, Washington, DC, May 21–23, 1981.

"Assembly and Executive Council Minutes." 18th General Assembly. New Orleans, LA, June 26–July 1, 1972.

"Assembly and Executive Council Minutes." 19th General Assembly. Washington, DC, June 25-29, 1974.

Constitution & Bylaws. The Links, Incorporated (2008): 39.

Constitution & Bylaws (2018–2020). The Links, Incorporated (July 2018): 1, 27.

"Interview with 13th National President Gladys Gary Vaughn." From Through Their Eyes: The Links, Oral History Collection, January 2019.

"Executive Council Meeting Minutes." The Links, Incorporated, Washington, DC, April 4–6, 1975.

"Minutes." Paper presented at the 21st National Assembly. Chicago, IL, July 2–9, 1978.

"Minutes." General Meeting. The Links Foundation, Las Vegas, NV, July 9, 1982.

"Minutes." 21st National Assembly. Chicago, IL, July 2–9, 1978.

"Minutes." 23rd National Assembly. Las Vegas, NV, July 5–10, 1982.

"Minutes." 24th National Assembly. Philadelphia, PA, 1984.

"Minutes of the Executive Council." The Links, Incorporated, Fairfax, VA, November 13–15, 1998.

"Minutes of the Executive Council." The Links, Incorporated, Fairfax, VA, February 23–24, 2002.

"Minutes of the Executive Council." The Links, Incorporated, Fairfax, VA, November 10–12, 2006.

"Minutes of the First Business Conference." The Links, Philadelphia, PA, June 4, 1949.

Copeland, Margot James. "Vision • Voice • Impact: Call to Assembly." Washington, DC: The Links, Incorporated, April 2014.

Beamon, V. J. "The Call to the Sixteenth National Assembly." The Links Journal III (June 1968).

———. "The Call to the Seventeenth National Assembly." The Links Journal III (June 1970): 3.

Butler, B. T. "Minutes." Executive Council. Baltimore, MD, January 20, 1951.

Coldwell, V. A. Membership Report. The Links, Incorporated, 1975.

Davis, J. D. "Minutes." Executive Council Meeting. The Links, Incorporated, Fairfax, VA, November 10–11, 2006. Edmonds, H. G. "Biennial Address of the National President to the 18th General Assembly." New Orleans, LA: The Links, Inc., 1972.

Henderson, C. "Minutes." 35th National Assembly. June 26–July 2, 2006.

Lee, G. B. "Letter from the President." Seattle, WA: The Links, Incorporated, 2008.

Nixon, L. Excerpts, from the History of National Links, Inc. Unpublished manuscript. Orlando, FL, 1979.

Parker, M. H. A History of The Links, Incorporated. 1st ed. Washington, DC: The Links, Incorporated, 1981.

———. History of The Links, Incorporated. 2nd ed. Washington, DC: The Links, Incorporated, 1992.

Revis, J. S., PRP. "Strategic Planning Motions Adopted." Link to Link VI (2007).

Shropshire, J. C. "Minutes." 31st National Assembly. The Links, Incorporated, Boston, MA, 1998.

Smith, J. "Minutes." 14th National Assembly. Nassau, Bahamas, June 25–28, 1964.

Travis, L. M. "Minutes." 29th National Assembly. Louisville, KY, June 25–July 2, 1994.

CHAPTER 8

"About the Office of Centralization." The Links Journal I (May 1966).

"A Leader of Vision." Bluefield, WV: National Links, Inc. 1954

"Annual Meeting and Executive Council Minutes." The Links, Incorporated, Washington, DC, May 21–23, 1981.

Articles of Incorporation of The Links Foundation. Washington, DC: The Links Foundation, Incorporated (1979): 6.

"Assembly and Executive Council Minutes." 19th General Assembly, Washington, DC, June 25–29, 1974.

"Certificate of Death: Vivian J. Beamon" (#3101, File #067919, Registrar #5340): Division of Vital Statistics, The Ohio Department of Health.

"Co-Founders: Tribute to the Founders." The Journal, 1962.

"Co-Founders Unveiling Ceremony." The Links, Incorporated 37th Eastern Area Conference Newsletter, 2003.

"Central Area Conference." The Journal VI (Spring–Summer 1984): 152.

"Dedication of the National Headquarters." Washington, DC: The Links, Incorporated, 1985.

"Executive Council Adopts New Journal Format." Link to Link 3 (January 1987).

"Executive Council Meeting Minutes." Washington, DC: The Links Incorporated, April 4–6, 1975.

"Interview with 8th National President Dolly Desselle Adams." From Through Their Eyes: The Links, Oral History Collection, January 2019.

"In Memory of our Departed Co-Founder Link Margaret Hawkins." The Fourteenth National Assembly of Links, Incorporated, June 25–28, 1964.

"Interview with 9th National President Regina Jollivette Frazier." From Through Their Eyes: The Links, Oral History Collection, January 2019.

"Interview with 13th National President Gladys Gary Vaughn." From Through Their Eyes: The Links, Oral History Collection, January 2019.

"Interview with 14th National President Gwendolyn Byrd Lee." From Through Their Eyes: The Links, Oral History Collection, January 2019.

"Interview with 15th National President Margot James Copeland." From Through Their Eyes: The Links, Oral History Collection, January 2019.

"Interview with 16th National President Glenda Newell-Harris." From Through Their Eyes: The Links, Oral History Collection, January 2019.

"LDF Timeline." From http://www.naacpldf.org/timeline.aspx.

"National Links' Policy Position on Public Affairs." The Links Journal III (April 1969).

"Meet our New Executive Secretary." The Links Journal I (May 1966).

"Minutes." Executive Council. The Links, Incorporated, Cincinnati, OH, November 15–17,1968.

"Minutes." General Meeting. The Links Foundation, Chicago, IL, July 2, 1978.

"Minutes." Board of Directors Meeting. The Links Foundation, Washington, DC, May 21, 1981.

"Minutes." General Meeting. The Links Foundation, Incorporated, Las Vega, NV, July 9, 1982.

"Minutes." General Meeting. The Links Foundation, June 30, 1986.

"Minutes of the Executive Council." The Links, Incorporated, Fairfax, VA, February 23–24, 2002.

"Next Steps." Link to Link 3 (October 1988).

"1986 Assembly Mandates and Updates." Link to Link 3 (September 1986).

"Profile of Mrs. Pauline A. Ellison." Washington, DC: The Links, Incorporated, 1974.

"Project LEAD: High Expectations." Link to Link 3 (October 1988).

"Reinstatement Fee Determined." Link to Link 3 (January 1987).

Adams, D. D. The Morning Message. Unpublished Manuscript. Las Vegas, NV, 1982.

———. Report of the National President to the 24th National Assembly. Philadelphia, PA: The Links, Incorporated, 1984.

———. "Tomorrow Can Be Better Than Yesterday." The Journal V (Spring–Summer 1983): 1.

Beamon, Vivian J. "The Call to the Sixteenth National Assembly." The Links Journal III (June 1968).

———. Presidential Proclamation at 16th General Assembly. Oakland, CA: The Links, Incorporated, 1968.

———. "From the Desk of the President." The Links Journal III (April 1969): 2.

———. The Call to the 17th National Assembly. The Links Journal III (June 1970): 3.

———. President's Report 1962–1970. The Links, Incorporated, 1970.

Boulware, H. "Juvenile Justice Project." Link to Link 1(1981): 9.

Bowens, N. T. Southern Area History: The Links, Incorporated 1949–1989 (Vol. I). Durham, NC, 1989.

Carlis, Lydia. "Success Profile: Margot Copeland, chair and CEO, KeyBank Foundation on Career and Giving Back." Walker's Legacy, January 30, 2018. www.walkerslegacy.com/success-profile-margot-copeland-chairand-ceo-keybank-foundation-on-career-and-giving-back/. Accessed June 10, 2019.

Clark, I. P. D. "Increasing the Capacity of Voluntary Organizations for the Prevention and Treatment of Delinquency Among Girls - A Two Year Assessment from October 1, 1978-September 30, 1980" [electronic version]. NCJRS Abstract. 1981. Retrieved May 1, 2008, from http://www.ncjrs.gov/App/Publications/abstract.aspx?ID=79327.

Davis, J. D. Minutes. Executive Council Meeting, The Links, Incorporated, Fairfax, VA, November 10–11, 2006.

Dixon, J. Southern Area Focus (Vol. 1). Cocoa Beach, FL: The Links Incorporated, 1998.

Edmonds, H. G. Biennial Address of the National President to the 18th General. New Orleans, LA: The Links, Incorporated, 1972.

———. Chapter charters. In Executive Council (Ed.) (pp. Memo), 1972.

———. Memo to Executive Council, 1972

———. "Link Women in Action." The Links Journal III (March 1973).

———. "Links' Commitment to UNCF." In C. Edley (Ed.) (pp. Letter). New York, NY, 1973.

———. "Chapter Establishment: The Lamp of Experience." Unpublished manuscript. Nashville, TN, 1986

———. "Reaction to Draft History." Durham, NC, 1980.

———. "Helen G. Edmonds' Presidential Tenure in The Links, Inc.," 1991.

Ellison, P. President's Biennial Report. Seattle, WA: The Links, Incorporated, 1976.

———. Report on Links' National Headquarters. Seattle, WA: The Links, Incorporated, 1976.

———. Report to the 21st Assembly. Chicago, IL: The Links, Incorporated, 1978.

———. From the Twenty-first National Assembly into the Twenty-first Century—On to Higher Ground. Unpublished manuscript, Chicago, IL, 1978.

Franklin, John Hope and Alfred A. Moss, Jr. From Slavery to Freedom: A History of African Americans. 7th ed. New York, NY: McGraw-Hill, Inc., 1994.Frazier, R. J. "A Tribute to Link Sarah Strickland Scott." Link to Link 3 (October 1988).

Frazier, R. J. Guidelines on Public Policy. Chicago, IL: The Links, Incorporated, 1976.

———. "Acceptance Speech: Enhancing the Legacy—Fulfilling the Dream." Nashville, TN: The Links, Incorporated, 1986.

———. "Enhancing the Legacy—Fulfilling the Dream." Link to Link 3 (January 1987).

———. "A Tribute to Link Sarah Scott." Link to Link 3 (October 1988).

Gilmette, Johnese. National Legislative Issues of the Public Affairs Committee. Washington, DC: The Links, Incorporated, July 3, 2010.

Harris, Hamil R. "Links Inc. gala celebrates Ebony magazine's legacy." The Washington Post, November 11, 2011. https://www.washingtonpost.com/local/therootdc/links-inc-gala-celebrates-ebony-magazines-legacy/2011/11/13/gIQA87rxIN_story.html?utm_term=.e77d04cc1f55. Accessed June 10, 2019.

Henderson, C. "Minutes." 35th National Assembly. June 26–July 2, 2006.

Johnson, N. Research on The Links Fund/Foundation. Washington, DC, 1981.

———. "Spotlighting the Links Foundation." The Journal IV (Spring–Summer 1980).

Julian, A. J. Report of the Chapter Establishment Officer. Chicago, IL: The Links, Incorporated, 1978.

Lang-Jeter. "Looking for a good return on your investment." Link to Link 5 (January 1996).

Lee, G. B. " National Trends & Services." The Journal X (1996).

Lee, Gwendolyn B. "The Links Foundation—Building." In Links (Ed.) (pp. Letter). Washington DC: The Links, Incorporated, 2007.

———. In Links (Ed.) (pp. Letter). Washington, DC: The Links, Incorporated, 2008.

———. Work Plan, Executive Council Meeting. Fairfax, VA: The Links, Incorporated, 2006.

———. "State of the Organization Address." Link to Link 1 (Fall 2007).

———. "Capital Campaign Plan." In Links (Ed.) (pp. Letter). Washington, DC: The Links, Incorporated, 2008.

———. "Letter from the President." 36th National Assembly. Seattle, WA: The Links, Incorporated, 2008.

———. Report of the National President. Executive Council Meeting. Seattle, WA: The Links, Incorporated, 2008.

———. "State of the Organization Address." Seattle, WA: The Links, Incorporated, 2008.

———. National Vice President Official Report. Philadelphia, PA: The Links, Incorporated, 2006.

———. "Leading with Enthusiasm." Link Up (Spring, 2016).

Leonard, Kimberly Jeffries "Minutes of the Meeting of the 39th National Assembly." The Links, Incorporated, National Harbor, MD, July 3–5 2014.

———. Leonard, Kimberly Jeffries. National Membership Committee Report. The Links, Incorporated (June 2018).

———. State of the Organization Address to the Southern Area Conference. The Links, Incorporated (Orlando, FL: May 4, 2019).

Leonard, Kimberly L. Jeffries and Karen Jefferson Morrison. National Trends and Services Report. The Links, Incorporated (Seattle, WA: July 2–6 2008).

Manning, A. F. National Program Committee Official Report. Philadelphia, PA: The Links, Incorporated, 2006.

Miller, L. R. "First Annual Fund-Raising Campaign." The Journal X (1996).

Newell-Harris, Glenda. Building a Healthy Legacy: Our Prescriptions for the Future. Washington, DC: The Links, Incorporated, 2018.

Parker, M. H. A History of The Links, Incorporated. 2nd ed. Washington, DC: The Links, Incorporated, 1992.

Patterson, L. "The Negro in Music and Art." In The International Library of Negro Life and History. New York, NY: 1968.

Purnell, J. "Our Incorporated Status—A Matter of Importance." Link to Link 1 (May 1980).

———. "The National President Speaks: Women Must Struggle in Order to Progress." The Links Journal IV (Spring–Summer 1980).

———. "The National President Speaks." The Links Journal IV (Fall–Winter 1979).

———. "Report of the National President—'The First Year'." Link to Link 1 (September 1979).

———. "Inspire—Inform—Ignite." Link to Link 1 (May 1980).

———. Report of the Seventh National President of The Links, Incorporated to the 23rd National Assembly. Las Vegas, NV: The Links, Incorporated, 1982.

Robbins, W. F. "Our National Presidents through Twenty-Five Years." The Links Journal III (March 1973).

Rouson, J. Interview with Patricia Russell-McCloud (telephone interview). Raleigh, NC, 2007.

Russell-McCloud, P. "Linkages … Labor of Love." Link to Link 5 (January 1995).

———. "On Your Mark … New Orleans Here We Come." Link to Link 5 (September 1995).

———. "Going for the Gold." Link to Link 5 (January 1996).

———. 1994–1996 Biennium Report. The Links, incorporated, 1996.

———. Biennium Report. Washington, DC: The Links, Incorporated, 1996.

———. Letter to Link Sisters. Washington, DC: The Links, Incorporated, 1996.

———. Linkages … Toward the Possible Program Initiatives. Washington, DC: The Links, Incorporated, 1996.

———. "Message from the President." The Journal X (1996).

———. "The Reunion." Link to Link 5 (January 1997).

———. "The Cost of Going First Class." Link to Link 5 (May 1997).

———. "The President Speaks." Link to Link (1998).

Scott, S. S. "Greetings from the Co-Founder." The Journal IV (1976).

Shabazz, B. "International Trends & Services." The Journal X (1996).

Smith, J. B. Biennial Program Report, 1982–1984. 24th National Assembly. Philadelphia, PA, July 1984. Strategic Planning Progress Report. 1993.

Salzberg, C. S. "The Ultimate Community Service: Linkages to Life." Link to Link 6 (Spring/Summer 2000).

Shropshire, J. C. "Minutes, 31st National Assembly." The Links, Incorporated, Boston, MA, 1998.

Simpkins, B. D. "Programs." From Public Relations Portfolio. Washington, DC: The Links Incorporated, 1998.

———. "Friend to Friend." Link to Link (Fall/Winter 2000).

———. "Message from the President." From Window of Opportunity: 2000–2002 Program Planning Guide. July 2000.

———. "Friend to Friend." Link to Link 6 (Spring/Summer 2000).

———. Membership Report. San Francisco, CA: The Links, Incorporated, 2000.

———. "Thanks for the Memories." Link to Link (Spring/Summer 2002).Stanford, L. Philadelphia Chapter.

———. Unpublished manuscript. 1951.

Stavrianos, L. S. A Global History: From Prehistory to the Present. Englewood Cliff, NJ: Prentice Hall, 1988.

Stokes, B. Archives and History Committee. Las Vegas, NV: The Links, Incorporated, 1982.

Sutherland, Marion Schultz. "The Call to Assembly." Link to Link, May 1992.

———. *The State of the Links, Incorporated*. The Links, Incorporated (Dallas, TX: June 30-July 3, 1992 1992).

———. "Welcome to the Foundation." *Link to Link*, May 1993.

———. "For Links Only." *Link to Link*, January 1993.

Vaughn, G. G. "Services to Youth." The Journal (1996).

———. "Links Membership: A Safe Place for Sister, Soul and Spirit." Link to Link (1999).

———. "Statement Regarding Candidates' Concept of The Links, Incorporated." Link to Link 6 (Spring/Summer 2002).

———. Final Report to the Executive Council. Atlanta, GA: The Links, Incorporated, 2002.

———. "Letter from the National President." 34th National Assembly. Atlanta, GA: The Links, Incorporated, 2004.

———. "Touching Tomorrow Today: Call to Assembly." Washington, DC: The Links, Incorporated, 2004.—.

Walker, E. C. Report of the Journalist. Chicago, IL: The Links, Incorporated, 1978.

Weeden, P. F. "National Officers." The Journal, 1960.

———. Memorandum in L. E. Board (Ed.). Lynchburg, VA, 1962.

———. Memo: "Establishment of Central Links Office." Lynchburg, VA, 1964.

Williams, J. C. "From the Desk of the National Journalist." The Journal VII (Spring–Summer 1986): 3.

Winlock, Sadie. Partners in the Progress of Black America. Unpublished manuscript. 2014.

Wilson, E. H. Hope and Dignity. Philadelphia, PA: Temple University Press, 1983.

Wright, D. B. Reminiscences. Unpublished manuscript. Philadelphia, PA, 1969

PART V, AREA AND CHAPTER CONDUITS

Constitution & Bylaws. The Links, Incorporated (2008): 39.

Constitution & Bylaws 2018–2020. Washington DC: The Links, Incorporated, July 2018.

Copeland, M. J. Report of the National Membership Committee. Seattle, WA: The Links, Incorporated, 2008.

Currie, M. Report of the Special Committee Re: Amendment # 22. Seattle, WA: The Links, Incorporated, 2008.

McNealey, Earnestine Green, ed. Linked for Friendship and Service: The History of The Links, Incorporated. Washington, DC: The Links, Incorporated, 2010.

Parker, M. H. A History of The Links, Incorporated. 2nd ed. Washington, DC: The Links, Incorporated, 1992.

Revis, J. S., PRP. Disposition of Amendments to the Constitution and Bylaws of The Links, Incorporated at the 36th National Assembly. Seattle, WA: The Links, Incorporated, 2008.

Scott, S. President's Report. Pittsburgh, PA: National Links, 1951.

Wright, D. The Philadelphia Links. Unpublished manuscript. Philadelphia, PA, 1951.

CHAPTER 9

Hardiman, Thelma. "Sarah Strickland Scott, My Beautiful Friend." From Through Their Eyes: The Links Oral History Collection. The Links, Incorporated, July 25, 2013.

McNealey, Earnestine Green, ed. Linked for Friendship and Service: The History of The Links, Incorporated. Washington, DC: The Links, Incorporated, 2010.

Merritt, B. The Eastern Area. Seattle, WA: The Links, Incorporated, 2008.

Parker, M. H. A History of The Links, Incorporated. 2nd ed. Washington, DC: The Links, Incorporated, 1992.

Price, Suzanne D., ed. Eastern Area historical Facts, 1946–1995: Strengthening the Black Family through Friendship, Love and Service. 3rd ed. The Links, Incorporated, 1995.

Spraggins, A. "Living Treasures: 30 Years of Area Stars."

Stokes, B. Eastern Area Historical Facts (Vol. 1): The Links, Incorporated, 2007.

Winlock, Sadie. Partners in the Progress of Black America. Unpublished manuscript. 2014.

CHAPTER 10

Brown-Nash, JoAhn. "Biographical Sketch." June 20, 2001.

Caldwell-Johnson, T. "Central Area Powering the Promise" [electronic version], 2007. Retrieved October 18, 2008, from http://www.centralarealinks.com/.

Central Area History, 1987.

Central Area History, 2007.

Copeland, Margot James. "Minutes of the 38th Central Conference." June 20–24, 2001.

———. Report of the Central Area Director. November 1999.

McNealey, Earnestine Green, ed. Linked for Friendship and Service: The History of The Links, Incorporated. Washington, DC: The Links, Incorporated, 2010.

Parker, Marjorie H. A History of The Links, Incorporated. 2nd ed. Washington, DC: The Links, Incorporated, 1992.

Simmons, Alice Strong. "Spotlight: Central Area History." Link Up (Spring 2016).

St. Louis Chapter History. Spring 2007.

W. E. B. DuBois Honors Day Convocation Program. April 8, 2004.

Waugh, Judy. Central Area History. 2001.

Waugh, Judy. Interview. August 22, 2007.

Winlock, Sadie. Partners in the Progress of Black America. Unpublished manuscript. 2014.

CHAPTER 11

"Southern Area Conference Minutes." 31st, 33rd, 36th, 38th, 42nd, 43rd.

"Southern Area Conference Report Books." 33rd, 36th, 42nd.

Bowens, Nancy Thompson, ed. Southern Area History 1949–1989. 1st ed. Chapel Hill, NC: Colonial Press.

Jones, Jessie M., ed. Southern Area History, The Links, Incorporated, 1948–1998, Volume 1. 2nd ed. Rocky Mount, NC.

McNealey, Earnestine Green, ed. Linked for Friendship and Service: The History of The Links, Incorporated. Washington, DC: The Links, Incorporated, 2010.

Parker, Marjory H. A History of The Links, Incorporated. 2nd ed. Washington, DC: The Links, Incorporated, 1992.

Sweet, Kimberly, ed. The Southern Area of the Links, Incorporated, Embracing Our Legacy. 3rd ed.

———. The Southern Area Journal 2015: Our Chapters and History, Volume 1.

CHAPTER 12

"California Black Pioneers." www.safero.org. 2013.

"Percentage of African Americans in Arizona in 1950–60s." www.en.wikipedia.org.

"Western Area Chapter Presidents." Chapter History Updates and Interviews. 2019.

Aldridge, Winstona. "Minutes." First Western Area Conference. The Links, Incorporated, 1954.

Arroyo, Cuahutemoc. "'Jim Crow' Shipyards: Black Labor and Race Relations in East Bay Shipyards During World War II." 2013.

Cole, Karen, and Lorna Hankins. Western Area Membership Data Base. 2019

Cooper, Ada. "Minutes." Thirty-sixth Western Area Conference. The Links, Incorporated, 2003.

Henry, Kevin. "The Links, Incorporated, Celebrating 50 Years of Good Works in Seattle's African American Community." Seattle Woman (2006): 13–17.

Interviews. Heir-O-Links and descendants. Anne Bradford Luke, Los Angeles Chapter; Deborah Beavers, Watford, Los Angeles Chapter; Vellet Wyatt Finley, San Diego Chapter; Evelyn Codwell, Houston Chapter; Augusta McCarroll Mann and Vivian Hambrick, San Francisco Chapter.

Lin, Joanna. "1940 Census Reveals California Led the Country in Education." California Watch, 2012.

Lowe, Clarice. The Links, Incorporated. The Journal (1991).

McNealey, Earnestine Green, ed. Linked for Friendship and Service: The History of The Links, Incorporated. Washington, DC: The Links, Incorporated, 2010.

Metze. Brenda. Fiftieth Anniversary Journal 1946–1996. The Links, Incorporated, 1996.

Mitchel, Rose. Researcher, A. C. Bilbrew Library. Sentinel.

Myers, Lois. "Western Area Historical Facts, 1954–1995." 1995.

———. "Western Area Archives Brief, 1995–97." 1997.

Parker, Marjorie H. A History of The Links, Incorporated. 2nd ed. Washington, DC: The Links, Incorporated, 1992.

Pinckney, Eloise. 60 Years of Chapters' Accomplishments, Commitments, Interests and Ideas,1950–2010. 2010

Ruffin-Boston, Barbra. "Minutes." Thirty-seventh Western Area Conference. The Links, Incorporated, 2005.

Smith, Constance F., and Eloise Pinckney. Western Area History. Unpublished Links history. 2013.

———. Western Area History Update. 2014.

CHAPTER 13

"About the Office of Centralization." The Links Journal I (May 1966).

"Assembly and Executive Council Minutes." 19th General Assembly. Washington, DC, June 25–29, 1974.

"Dedication of the National Headquarters." Washington, DC: The Links, Incorporated, 1985.

"Interview with 8th National President Dolly Desselle Adams." From Interviews with Former National Presidents of The Links, Incorporated. The Links, Incorporated, January 2019.

"Interview with 11th National President Patricia Russell-McCloud." From Through Their Eyes: The Links, Oral History Collection, January 2019.

"Interview with 13th National President Gladys Gary Vaughn." From Through Their Eyes: The Links, Oral History Collection, January 2019.

"Interview with 14th National President Gwendolyn Byrd Lee." From Through Their Eyes: The Links, Oral History Collection, January 2019.

"Interview with 15th National President Margot James Copeland." From Through Their Eyes: The Links, Oral History Collection, January 2019.

"Interview with 16th National President Glenda Newell-Harris." From Through Their Eyes: The Links, Oral History Collection, January 2019.

"Meet our New Executive Secretary." The Journal I (May 1966).

"Minutes." 21st National Assembly. Chicago, IL, July 2–9, 1978.

"Minutes." 23rd National Assembly. Las Vegas, NV, July 5–10, 1982.

Adams, Dolly Desselle. "President's Message." Washington, DC: The Links, Incorporated, 1985.

Beamon, V. J. President's Report 1962–1970. The Links, Incorporated, 1970.

Copeland, Margot James. "Interviews with Former National Presidents of the Links, Incorporated." The Links, Incorporated, January 2019.

Edmonds, H. G. Biennial Address of the National President to the 18th General Assembly. New Orleans, LA: The Links, Incorporated, 1972.

Ellison, Pauline A. "President's Biennial Report: The High Cost of Transition." 21st National Assembly. Chicago, IL, July 2–9, 1978.

———. From the Twenty-first National Assembly into the Twenty-first Century—On to Higher Ground. Unpublished manuscript, Chicago, IL, 1978.

———. Report on Links' National Headquarters. Seattle, WA: The Links, Incorporated, 1976.

Gladden, Q. "Building and Properties Committee." 36th National Assembly. Seattle, WA, 2008.

Harris, Hamil. "Links Inc. Gala Celebrates Ebony Magazine's Legacy." The Washington Post, November 13, 2011. Kendrick, Crystal. "Minutes of the Meeting of the 41st National Assembly." Paper presented at The Links, Incorporated, Indianapolis, IN, June 28–June 30, 2018.

Lee, Ciara. "Minutes of the Meeting of the 40th National Assembly." The Links, Incorporated, Las Vegas, NV, June 30–July 2, 2016.

Lee, Gwendolyn B. "The Links Foundation—Building." In Links (Ed.) (pp. Letter). Washington DC: The Links, Incorporated, 2007.

———. "State of the Organization Address." Link to Link 1 (Fall 2007).

Leonard, Kimberly Jeffries. "State of the Organization Address to the Southern Area Conference." The Links, Incorporated, Orlando, FL, May 4, 2019.

McNealey, Earnestine Green, ed. Linked for Friendship and Service: The History of The Links, Incorporated. Washington, DC: The Links, Incorporated, 2010.

Newell-Harris, Glenda. Building a Healthy Legacy: Our Prescription for the Future. Washington DC: The Links, Incorporated, 2018.

Parker, M. H. A History of The Links, Incorporated. 2nd ed. Washington, DC: The Links, Incorporated, 1992.

Purnell, J. B. Report of the Seventh National President of The Links, Incorporated to the 23rd National Assembly. Las Vegas, NV: The Links, Incorporated, 1982.

CHAPTER 14

Power Channels

Beamon, Vivian J. "The Call to the Seventeenth National Assembly." The Links Journal (June 1970): 3.

McNealey, Earnestine Green. Linked for Friendship and Service: The History of The Links, Incorporated. Washington, DC: The Links, Incorporated, 2010.

Nixon, Leola. Excerpts, from the History of National Links, Inc. Orlando, FL.

Robbins Will Florence. "Our Movement in an Era of Dynamic Dimensions." The Links Journal IV, no. 5 (June 1970).

Services to Youth

"A Leader of Vision." Bluefield, WV: National Links, Incorporated, 1954.

"Minutes." 16th General Assembly. Oakland-Berkeley, CA, June 25–30, 1968.

"1994–1996 Biennium Report." Washington, DC: The Links, Incorporated, 1996.

"Why our National Project." The Links, Incorporated, 1960.

"Window of Opportunity: 2000–2002 Program Planning Guide." Washington, DC: The Links, Incorporated, 2000.

Beamon, Vivian J. President's Report 1962–1970. The Links, Incorporated, 1970.

Campbell, L. P. "National Services to Youth—The New Millennium!" Link to Link VI (2007).

———. Services to Youth. Seattle, WA: The Links, Incorporated, 2008.

McNealey, Earnestine Green, ed. Linked for Friendship and Service: The History of The Links, Incorporated. Washington, DC: The Links, Incorporated, 2010.

Parker, M. H. A History of The Links, Incorporated. 2nd ed. Washington, DC: The Links, Incorporated, 1992.
    Shropshire, J. C. "Minutes." 31st National Assembly. The Links, Incorporated, Boston, MA, 1998.

Smith, J. B. Report to the Twenty-Fifth National Assembly. Nashville, TN: The Links, Incorporated, 1986.

Vaughn, G. G. Services to Youth: Room at the Top. Washington, DC: The Links, Incorporated, 1995.

Walton, F. Project LEAD: High Expectations. Dallas, TX: The Links, Incorporated, 1992.

National Trends and Services

Orientation Manual. Washington, DC: The Links, Incorporated, 1984.

Orientation Manual. Washington, DC: The Links, Incorporated, 1997.

1994–1996 Biennium Report. Washington, DC: The Links, Incorporated, 1996.

"Links Together, Lithograph, and Poster: About the Art and the Artist." Link to Link (Spring 1999).

Strategic Planning/Joint Task Force Comprehensive Summary. Louisville, KY, 1994.

Beamon, V. J. President's Report 1962–1970. The Links, Incorporated, 1970.

Hill, B. Educating for Democracy. 1968.

Hogan, D. J., ed. Civil Rights Chronicle. Lincolnwood, IL: Publications International, Ltd, 2003.

Lee, G. "National Trends and Services." The Journal X (1996).

———. "National Trends and Services: To Revitalize and Nurture." Washington, DC: The Links, Incorporated, 1998.

Leonard, K. J. National Trends and Services Program Report. Seattle, WA: The Links, Incorporated, 2008.

Parker, M. H. A History of The Links, Incorporated. 2nd ed. Washington, DC: The Links, Incorporated, 1992.

Smith, J. "Minutes." 14th National Assembly. Nassau, Bahamas, June 25–28, 1964.

The Arts

Blackmon, J. M. The Arts Official Report to the 35th Assembly. Philadelphia, PA: The Links, Incorporated, 2006. Fontenot, L. J. "The Arts in the New Millennium: Destination Global." Link to Link (Spring 1999).

McNealey, Earnestine Green. Linked for Friendship and Service: The History of The Links, Incorporated. Washington, DC: The Links, Incorporated, 2010.

Parker, M. H. A History of The Links, Incorporated. 2nd ed. Washington, DC: The Links, Incorporated, 1992.

Pierce, A. "The Arts: A Living Legacy." The Journal X (Spring 1996).

Vaughn, G. G. "Services to Youth." The Journal (1996).

White, M. D. Interview with Aaronetta Pierce. Roslyn, NY, 2007.

———. Interview with Joyce Blackmon. Roslyn, NY, 2007.

———. The National Arts Committee Report. Seattle, WA: The Links, Incorporated, 2008.

International Trends and Services

"Minutes of the Executive Council." The Links, Incorporated, Fairfax, VA, November 13–15, 1998.

"Minutes of the Executive Council." The Links, Incorporated, Fairfax, VA, February 23–24, 2002.

"Minutes of the Executive Council." The Links, Incorporated, Fairfax, VA, November 10–12, 2006.

Orientation Manual of The Links, Incorporated. Washington, DC, 1993.

Buckner, J. K. International Trends and Services Report. Seattle, WA: The Links, Incorporated, 2008.

Metze, B. R. "Linkages … Toward the Possible." The Journal II (1998): 16–19.

Parker, M. H. "International Trends." In A History of The Links, Incorporated. 2nd ed. (pp. 99–100; 125–131; 179–182). Washington, DC: The Links, Incorporated, 1992.

Prophet, F. A. "International Trends and Services." Link to Link 4 (September 1991): 11–12.

———. "International Trends and Services." Link to Link 4 (September 1992): 7.

———. "International Trends and Services." Link to Link 4 (September 1993): 11.

———. "International Trends and Services." Link to Link (May 3, 1994): 3–5.

Russell-McCloud, Patricia. "The President Speaks." Link to Link (1998).

Shabazz, B. "International Trends and Services." The Links Journal 10 (1996).

Simpkins, B. D. "Thanks for the Memories." Link to Link (Spring/Summer 2002).

Smith, J. S. "International Trends and Services." Link to Link 5 (September 1996): 9–10.

———. "Dedicated to Internationalism and Education across the Miles." Link to Link 6 (Spring/Summer 2002).

Health and Human Services

Beamon, Vivian J. "The Call to the Seventeenth National Assembly." The Links Journal (June 1970): 3.

Newell-Harris, Glenda. Building a Healthy Legacy: Our Prescription for the Future. Washington, DC: The Links, Incorporated, 2018.

Winlock, Sadie. Partners in the Progress of Black America. Unpublished manuscript. 2014.

CHAPTER 15

"Articles of Incorporation." The Links, Incorporated, 1979.

"Board of Directors Meeting." The Links Foundation, Washington, DC, May 21, 1981.

"General Meeting." The Links Foundation, July 2, 1978.

"General Meeting." The Links Foundation, June 30, 1986.

"Guidelines for Tax Exempt Organizations." 2007.

"Minutes of the Executive Council." The Links, Incorporated, Cincinnati, OH, November 15–17, 1968.

"Minutes." Twenty-first National Assembly. The Links, Incorporated, Chicago, IL, July 2–9, 1978.

"Minutes." General Meeting. The Links Foundation, Incorporated, Las Vega, NV, July 9, 1982.

"Strategic Planning Progress Report." The Links, Incorporated, 1993.

Adams, Dolly D. Report of the National President to the Twenty-fifth National Assembly. The Links, Incorporated, July 1986.

Davis, Josephine D. "Executive Council Meeting Minutes." The Links, Incorporated, Fairfax, VA, November 10–11, 2006.

Henderson, C. B. "Minutes." Thirty-fifth National Assembly. June 26–July 2, 2006.

———. "Executive Council Minutes." The Links, Incorporated, Philadelphia, PA, June 25, 2006.

Johnson, N. D. Research on The Links Fund/Foundation. Washington, DC, 1981.

———. "Spotlighting the Links Foundation." The Journal IV (Spring/Summer 1980).

Parker, Marjorie H. A History of the Links, Incorporated. 2nd ed. Washington, DC: The Links, Incorporated, 1992. Preparation Workbook for the 28th Assembly. 1992.

Sutherland, M. S. "Welcome to the Foundation." Link to Link 4 (May 1993).

CHAPTER 16

"Constitution & Bylaws." The Links, Incorporated, 2008 (p. 39).

"Honorary Members." In Public Relations Portfolio. Washington, DC: The Links, Incorporated, 2000.

Bontemps, J. F. "Minutes." 28th National Assembly. Dallas, TX, June 30–July 3, 1992.

Julian, A. J. Profile Study – Progress Report. Nassau, BH: The Links Incorporated, 1964.

Malone, S. D. Code of Ethics and Standards Quality Control Document. Washington, DC: The Links, Incorporated, 2008.

Mosby, C. L. Commission on Ethics and Standards Official Report. Philadelphia, PA: The Links, Incorporated, 2006.

Parker, M. H. A History of The Links, Incorporated. 2nd ed. Washington, DC: The Links, Incorporated, 1992.

Taylor, A. Woman Power Commission Report. 31st National Assembly. Boston, MA, 1998.

CHAPTER 17

The Code of Ethics. Philadelphia, PA: The Links, Inc, 2006.

Butler, B. T. "Minutes." Executive Council. Baltimore, MD, January 20, 1951.

Dinkins, L. L. A Ceremony of Friendship. 1953.

Dixon, J., ed. Did You Know? In 1999 Calendar. Southern Area, The Links Incorporated, 1998.

Frazier, R. J. Memorandum #3. In Southern Area Chapters (Ed.). Miami, FL, 1981.

Parker, M. H. A History of The Links, Incorporated. 1st ed. Washington, DC: The Links, Incorporated, 1981.

Scott, S. President's Report. Pittsburgh, PA: National Links, 1951.

Stanford, L. History of the National Links, Inc. 1946–1951. National Links, Incorporated, 1951.

Wright, D. The Philadelphia Links. Unpublished manuscript. Philadelphia, PA, 1951.

Index

Linked in Friendship, Connected in Service